Ethan

33

Sara J was probably here

Sara J was probably here
2015-2016

Sam.M
2017

Malachi
2013-2014
BOSS

LoL nope

Amelie 2016-2017

Amir

Saley

Marcus

or here

1978

Their Stories, Our History

Canada's Early Years

Bob Aitken • Jan Haskings-Winner • Robert Mewhinney • Bernie Rubinstein

THOMSON
DUVAL™

Australia Canada Mexico Singapore Spain United Kingdom United States

Their Stories, Our History: Canada's Early Years

Bob Aitken • Jan Haskings-Winner • Robert Mewhinney • Bernie Rubinstein

Thomson Duval Project Team

Project Managers: Karen Iversen, Lauri Seidlitz

Editors: Lauri Seidlitz, Lynn Hamilton

Cover and Text Design: Claudia Pompei, Obsidian Multimedia

Photo Research: Joanne Meredith, David Strand

Production: Claudia Pompei, Obsidian Multimedia, Priscilla Cheung

Maps: Johnson Cartographics Inc., Wendy Johnson

Illustrations: Mitch Fortier, Carol Powers

Index: Elizabeth Bell, Pinpoint Indexing

Photographer: Darren Wolf, Wolf Photography

Photo Shoot Coordinator: Roberta Wildgoose

Photographic Models: Shivani Chotalia, Maureen Kruhlak, Ron Kruhlak, Claudia Pompei, Sean Sonego, Joshua Tang, Tamam Tarrabain, Stephanie Warden, Kashtin White, Brandon Zon

Student Project Examples: Erika Haskings

ISBN 1-55446-057-3

Printed and bound in Canada by Transcontinental Interglobe

2 3 4 08 07 06

Author Acknowledgements
Thank you to our families for their encouragement and patience. Projects like this one require the support of those closest to us, for it is the time we take away from our families that allows us to complete our task. Our heartfelt thanks go to Roberta, Ray, Virginia, and Ferne.

A special thank you to Lauri Seidlitz, who took our words and ideas and made them read as one voice. She became our caring friend. Karen Iversen and the staff at Duval fully encouraged us to try something new, and added ideas based on years of success in the publishing world. Thank you also to our reviewers, who saw what we were attempting to accomplish and gave us suggestions on how to make our project work even better for students and teachers.

Review Team

Educational
Mary Cairo
Language Resource Teacher
Toronto Catholic District School Board

Elizabeth Freeman-Shaw
Curriculum Consultant
Social Studies, History, Social Sciences
District School Board of Niagara

Doug Gordon
Education Consultant
London, Ontario

David J. Padley
Intermediate Teacher
Simcoe County District School Board

Wendy Ramirez
Elementary Teacher, Ascension School
Halton Catholic District School Board

Elaine Reynolds
Grade 7 Teacher
Halton District School Board

Pina Sacco
Program Resource Teacher, Literacy 7–12
York Catholic District School Board

Luci Soncin
Principal, St. Fidelis Catholic School
Toronto Catholic District School Board

Jennifer Watt
Instructional Leader
Toronto District School Board

Content
Neil Andersen *(Literacy Content)*
Literacy and Media Education Consultant
Toronto, Ontario

Brenda Davis *(Aboriginal Content)*
Cayuga, Six Nations of the Grand River Territory

Kathryn McPherson *(Historical Content)*
Department of History
York University

Ken Ramphal *(Bias Review)*
Scarborough Centre for Alternative Studies
Toronto District School Board

Pronunciation Guide
Billy Joe Laboucan (*First Nations Languages*)
Little Buffalo Lake, Alberta

André Bléoo (*French Language*)
Retired High School Teacher
Gatineau, Québec

Image and Text Credits

Every effort has been made to trace ownership of all copyrighted material and to secure permission from copyright holders. In the event of any question arising as to the use of any material, we will be pleased to make the necessary corrections in future printings.

Legend: b = bottom; bd = background; c = centre; l = left; m = middle; p = page; r = right; t = top
AO = Archives of Ontario; BMP = Barrett and Mackay Photography; GA = Glenbow Archives; GOAC = Government of Ontario Art Collection; LAC = Library and Archives Canada; LC = Library of Congress; MCSQ = Musée de la civilisation, collection du Séminaire de Québec; MMM = McCord Museum, Montreal; TPL = Toronto Public Library

Front cover (clockwise from tl)
Henry Sandham, LAC Acc. No. 1996-282-7; LAC C-146340; *Radisson & Groseilliers Established the Fur Trade in the Great North West*, 20th century, M993.154.313, McCord Museum, Montreal; M.A. Hayes, LAC Acc. No. 1991-116-4; Toronto Public Library, J.Ross Robertson Collection, T16600; C.W. Jefferys, LAC Acc. No. 1990-568-1; (bd) www.istockphoto.com/Oleg Prikhodko

Back cover (clockwise from tl)
Fergus Kyle; George Craig, Musée acadien, Université de Moncton; (soldier) Alan Daniel, Originally published in *The Story of Canada*, Key Porter 1992; LAC Acc. No. 1972-118-2; C.W. Jefferys; Soeurs de la charité de Montréal "les Soeurs Grises"; JRR 2422 Toronto Public Library, Watercolour by William Armstrong 1908 (*Numbering the Indians, Wikwemikong, Manitoulin Island (Ontario), 16 August 1856*). Slide # MTL 2213

title page (bd) www.istockphoto.com/Oleg Prikhodko **piv, pv** (bd) www.istockphoto.com/Hans Doddema **pv** Fred Cattroll **pxi** ©Ron Karten/Omni-Photo Communications **p2** (t) **p4** (t) *The Discovery of Canada*, J.D. Kelly, CLG, Courtesy of Rogers Communications Inc. **p2** (b) **p38** (t) LAC Acc. No. 1990-568-1 **p2** (bd) www.istockphoto.com/Martin de Wit **p3, p74** (t) LAC Acc. No. 1997-214-1 **p4** (b) © Alan Daniel, Originally published in *Heritage of Canada* by Reader's Digest, 1978 **p4, p38, p74** (bd) www.istockphoto.com/tanya c **p6** Sidebar adapted from "The Days of Wabakinine" by Donald B. Smith. Published in *Horizon Canada*, vol 4, page 1139 **p15** C.W. Simpson/LAC Acc. No. 1991-35-3 **p17** LAC C-006680 **p21** LAC Acc. No. 1996-282-3 **p22** LAC C-016952 **p23** LAC Acc. No. 1936-239-1 **p25** LAC C-017338 **p27** LAC C-002336 **p29** (pot) www.istockphoto.com/Laura Neal (kettle) www.istockphoto.com/Mats Tooming (rifle) © Stockbyte Silver/Alamy **p30** LAC C-028332 **p31** C.W. Jefferys, *The Picture Gallery of Canadian History*, Toronto: Ryerson. 1:103 **p32** LAC **p33** (l) Martyrs' Shrine, Midland, Ontario (r) LAC Acc. No. 1989-479-9:B **p34** *Harvest Festival*, William Bent Berczy, #16648, National Gallery of Canada, Ottawa **p35** LAC C-139973 (text in tinted box) Courtesy of Canadian Museum of Civilization, http://www.civilisations.ca/vmnf/boucher/3.5/3.5.1.htm **p36** (l) Image from *The Kids Book of Canadian History* by Carlotta Hacker and illustrated by John Mantha is used by permission of Kids Can Press Ltd., Toronto, Canada. Illustration © 2002 John Mantha. (r) Troy Davidson **p37** (l) Bryan & Cherry Alexander Photography/Alamy (r) www.istockphoto.com/Anna Bryukhanova **p38** (l) **p68** LAC C-007183 **p41** (t) Réunion des Musées Nationaux/Art Resource, NY (b) Art Media/Heritage-Images **p42** Mark Tomalty/IPNstock **p44** MCSQ, *Portrait de l'intendant Talon*, Théophile Hamel, Pierre Soulard, photographe N° 1991.51 **p45** Adapted from: *Cross-curricular Literacy: Key Strategies for Improving Secondary Students' Reading and Writing Skills*, reproduced with permission, © 2006, Toronto District School Board **p48** LAC Acc. No. 1983-45-3 **p49** (l) *Le Regiment de Carignan-Salières* (1665), 1966, M993.154.272, MMM (r) E.F. Brickdale/LAC Acc. No. 1996-371-1 **p50** *Radisson & Groseilliers Established the Fur Trade in the Great North West*, 20th century, M993.154.313, MMM **p52** © Parks Canada/St. Jacques, P./H.05.52.05.06(75) (text) Adapted from "Habitant Days" by Marie-Aimée Cliché, *Horizon Canada*, Vol. 1, pp.140-144. Reproduced with author's permission. **p53** *A View of the Château Richer, Cape Torment*, Thomas Davies, #6275, National Gallery of Canada, Ottawa **p55** (b) *Habitant Room, Chateau de Ramezay*, 1904, VIEW-3730.A, MMM (t) *Bake Oven*, 1898 VIEW-3235.A, MMM **p56** Henri Beau/LAC C-017059 **p57** LAC Acc. No. 1989-524-2 (detail) **p59** LAC Acc. No. 1990-553 **p60** LAC Acc. No. 1989-283-3 **p61** LAC C-016734 **p62** *Canada's First Shipyard*, Rex Woods, CLG, Courtesy of Rogers Communications Inc. **p64** (l) MCSQ, *Portrait de Mgr François de Laval*, Inconnu, Pierre Soulard, photographe. N° 1995.3480 (r) Archives départmentales de la Gironde, H Jésuites, fol.16; with the permission of the Conseil Général de la Gironde **p65** (t) Jules-Ernest Livernois/LAC PA-023411 (b) LAC Acc. No. 1996-23-5 **p67** Réunion des Musées Nationaux/Giraudon/Art Resource, NY **p70** Clarence Gagnon (1881-1942) *Fetching Water* 1928-1933; oil pastel over graphite on paper, 23.5 x 23.1 cm, Gift of Col. R.S. McLaughlin, McMichael Canadian Art Collection 1969.4.44 **p71** GA NA-1406-55 **p72** Copyright © Lazare and Parker **p73** LAC C-011224 **p74** (b) **p97** LAC C-146340 **p77, p78, p79** History Collection, Nova Scotia Museum, Halifax, paintings by Azor Vienneau **p80** LAC FC3058.2 O54 1880 **p84** *View from a Warship, 1745*, Lewis Parker, Courtesy of Fortress of Louisbourg, © Parks Canada **p86** LAC Acc. No. 1972-26-768 **p87** Musée acadien, Université de Moncton, George Craig **p90** © Peter Horree/Alamy **p91** BMP **p93** (l) Bridgeman-Giraudon/Art Resource, NY (r) Artwork from MAA 23 Montcalm's Army, artwork by Michael Roffe, © Osprey Publishing Ltd, www.ospreypublishing.com **p95** New Brunswick Museum, Saint John, N.B., W907 **p96** *The Death of General Wolfe* 1770, Benjamin West, #8007, National Gallery of Canada, Ottawa **p98** LAC Acc. No. 1989-283-11 **p99** Adam Sherriff Scott/LAC Acc. No. 1996-292-2 **p100** LAC Acc. No. 1997-227-1 **p102** Courtesy of Simon DeJocas **p103** (tl) Soeurs de la charité de Montréal "les Soeurs Grises" (bl) National Portrait Gallery, London (r) Archives Nationales du Québec, Quebec/P600-6/N-1076-254 **p104** CP PHOTO/Jacques Boissinot (Interpretation #2 text) Excerpt from *New France: The Last Phase, 1744-1760* by George F.G. Stanley. Used by permission of McClelland & Stewart Ltd. **p105** www.istockphoto.com/FredS **p106** (r) **p108** LC-USZ62-9487 **p106** (l) **p132** (r) LAC C-061557 **p106** (bd) www.istockphoto.com/Brian Palmer **p107, p164** (t) *The Death of Brock at Queenston Heights*, c. 1908 by C. W. Jefferys, GOAC, AO, 619871 **p108, p132, p164** (bd) www.istockphoto.com/William Walsh **p111** Alfred Bobbet/LAC C-11250 **p114** Mabel B. Messer/LAC Acc. No. 1997-8-1 **p116** LC-USZC4-2568 **p118** *Tory Refugees on Their Way to Canada* by Howard Pyle **p119** (l) LAC Acc. No. 1996-282-7 (r) LAC C-020587 **p120** LAC Acc. No. 1990-553-1235 **p121** Alan Daniel, Originally published in *The Story of Canada*, Key Porter 1992 **p122** LAC FC3058.2 O54 1880 **p123** LC-USZ62-16969 **pp124-125** (text) From *Dear Canada, With Nothing But Our Courage: The Loyalist Diary of Mary Macdonald*, text copyright © 2002 by Karleen Bradford. All rights reserved. Reprinted by permission of Scholastic Canada Ltd. **p128** Robert Judd, Waterford, Ontario **p130** Courtesy AO **p132** (b) **p133** Courtesy of Kimberly Hurst U.E., United Empire Loyalists Association of Canada. Thanks to Kingsville Historical Park's Charlie Campbell Museum in Kingsville, Ontario for hosting the Loyalist program **p134** LAC Acc. No. 1989-218-1 **p135** LAC Acc. No. 1983-47-21 **p136** (t) LAC Acc. No. 1970-188-1090 (b) Photo courtesy of Cathy Holmes, The Coast Guard **p138** LAC Acc. 1970-188-2367 Purchased with a grant from the Secretary of State **p139** (sidebar) Adapted from Smith, Patricia L. and Tompkins, Gail E. (1988, October). "Structured notetaking: A new strategy for content area readers." *Journal of Reading*, 32 (1), 46-53. Copyright ©2006 by the International Reading Association **pp141-143** Text: *Thayendanegea*, Dictionary of Canadian Biography Online © Library and Archives Canada. Reproduced with the permission of the Minister of Public Works and Government Services Canada (2006). Source: LAC's website (www.collectionscanada.ca). Also © Université Laval and University of Toronto **p144** LAC C-20006 **p148** *Colonel John Graves Simcoe* c. 1881 by George Theodore Berthon, GOAC, AO, 694156 **p149** LAC Acc. No. 1970-188-2092 **p150** (t) TPL, TRL, T1793/4Mlrg **p152** LAC Acc. No. 1972-118-2 **p153** *Castle Frank*, 1796. Simcoe family fonds, AO, F 47-11-1-0-230 **p154** LAC Acc. No. 1957-101 **p157** (l) C.W. Jefferys (r) LAC Acc. No. 1997-91-5 **p158** (l) New Brunswick Museum, Saint John, N.B., 1966.8.5 (r) Provincial Archives of New Brunswick "PANB P4-3-3" **p159** (l) New Brunswick Museum, Saint John, N.B., W6531 (r) *Mill on the Gananocoui*, ca. 1792, by Elizabeth Simcoe, GOAC, AO,F 47-11-1-0-63 **p160** (tl, bl) BMP (tr) © Canada Post Corporation. Reproduced with permission/© Société canadienne des postes. Reproduit avec permission (c) Courtesy of the City of Brantford **p162** Historica Fairs Program **p164** (b) LAC Acc. No. 1997-229-2 **p166** (l) Bridgeman-Giraudon/Art Resource, NY (r) U.S. Naval Historical Center **p169** Major-General Sir Isaac Brock, c. 1883 George Theodore Berthon, GOAC, AO, 694158 **p170** C.W. Jefferys, *The Picture Gallery of Canadian History*, Toronto: Ryerson. 3:116 **p172** LAC Acc. No. 1972-26-1360 **p173** TPL, Benjamin Lossing, J.Ross Robertson Collection, T16600 **p174** *Laura Secord on Her Journey to Warn the British*, c. 1921, C.W. Jefferys, GOAC, AO, 621223 **p175** (t) Right Rev. John Strachan, 1860, AO, F983-a (b) With permission of the Royal Ontario Museum © ROM **p178** LAC C-000276 **p179** LC-USZC2-6326 **p180** LAC C-003297 **p181** *The Battle of Lundy's Lane*, c. 1921 by C. W. Jefferys, GOAC, AO, 621234 **p183** *Newcastle District Clerk of the Peace High Treason in War of 1812*. AO, RG 22-3782 **p184** Frances Roberts/Alamy **p185** AO **p186** LAC Acc. No. 1972-26-795 **p188** (bd) www.istockphoto.com/g2710 **p188** (l) **p222** (l) LAC Acc. No. 1970-189-19 **p188** (r) **p190** LAC Acc. No. 1992-566-6 **p189, p250** (t) LAC Acc. No. 1955-128-11 **p190, p222, p250** (bd) www.istockphoto.com/Bernd Klumpp **p192** C.W. Jefferys, *The Picture Gallery of Canadian History*, Toronto: Ryerson. 3:17 **p196** TPL, Canadian Historical Picture Collection, J. Ross Robertson Collection, JRR 826 **p198** (l) J.W.L. Forster/LAC Acc. No. 1996-115-1 (r) Mackenzie Printery & Newspaper Museum **p200** LAC Acc. No. 1972-26-1384 **p201** LAC Acc. No. R9266-3154 **p202** Fergus Kyle **p203** Penny Tweedie/Stone/Getty (Conflict sidebar) Adapted from *Reducing School Violence Through Conflict Resolution* by R. Johnson et al 1995. Reproduced with permission, Association for Supervision and Curriculum Development, MD. **p204** *The First St. Lawrence Canal*, by Rex Woods, 1955, CLG, Courtesy of Rogers Communications Inc. **p205** LAC Acc. No. 1932-266 **p208** (t) LAC Acc. No. 1932-266 (m) LAC Acc. No. 1992-566-3 (b) C.W. Jefferys, *The Picture Gallery of Canadian History*, Toronto: Ryerson. 3:16 **p209** (t) C.W. Jefferys/TPL/T13350(1086) (m) LAC Acc. No. 1973-9-9 (b) www.canadianheritage.ca ID #20021 **p210** LAC Acc. No. 1992-566-2 **p211** (l) LAC C-001242 (r) LAC Acc. No. 1991-116-4 **p214** C.W. Jefferys, *The Picture Gallery of Canadian History*, Toronto: Ryerson. 3:18 **p215** LAC Acc. No. 1972-26-1385 **p218** LAC Acc. No. 1991-90-32 **p220** (t) AO, I0003075[1] (bl) *Sir Louis Hippolyte Lafontaine*, c. 1880, M981.207.4, MMM (br) *Sir Francis Hincks*, 1869, M981.207.4, MMM **p222** (r) C.W. Jefferys, *The Picture Gallery of Canadian History*, Toronto: Ryerson. 3:10 **p224** *The Embarkation, Waterloo Docks, Liverpool, 1850*, M993X.5.1530.1, MMM **p226** (t) LAC C-001669 (b) Photograph courtesy of the City of Ottawa Archives; CA 0219 **p227** (SEARCH strategy) Silver Strong and Associates. (2001). *Words' Work!: Reading Styles and Strategies for Thoughtful Education*. [Workshop Materials]. Ho-Ho-Kus, NJ: Strong, R.W. & Silver, H.F. **p230** Parks Canada/Morin, B./H.06.69.06.09(08) **p231** City of London/Heritage-Images **p232** Chest, M21681.1-2, MMM **p233** (l) LAC 0515010416 (r) *Cholera Plague, Québec*, Joseph Légaré, c. 1832, Acc. # 7157, National Gallery of Canada, Ottawa **p234** (l) LAC Acc. No. 1983-121-1 (r) Parks Canada/Simmons, L./H.05.46.07.03(04) **p236** LAC Acc. No. 1981-42-42 Source: Dr. Nigel Davies, Gelati, Mexico **p239** LAC Acc. No. 1990-554-260 **p241** (l) © Canada Post Corporation. Reproduced with permission/© Société canadienne des postes. Reproduit avec permission (r) LAC **p242** (t) *John H. Alexander and Pupils of King Street School, Amherstburg ca. 1890*, Alvin D. McCurdy fonds, AO, F 2076-16-5-2-25 (b) Nova Scotia Archives and Records Management **p243** TPL **p244** (l) LAC e000755352 (r) *Plan of Elgin Settlement in the Township of Raleigh, County of Kent, Canada West [1866]*, AO, C 279-0-0-0-3, J.S. Wilson, Lith. **p245** (l) LAC C-029977 (r) Courtesy of Abraham Lincoln Historical Digitization Project, Northern Illinois University Libraries **p247** LAC Acc. 1966-094 **p248** Stones Mica Mine, Buck Lake [ca 1900], AO, C 130-1-0-6-2 **p249** CP PHOTO/Sarnia Observer/Nora Penhale **p250** (b) TPL, Canada farmer v. 1 1847 22 May [p. 61] **p253** LAC C-127216 **p254** James Bruce, Earl of Elgin, about 1855, M22464, MMM **p257** (l) *Lord Elgin and Staff Leaving Government House for Parliament*, April 1849, M2001.30.3, MMM (r) Robert Julian Agnel **p258** LAC Acc. No. 1971-64-112 **p259** LAC Acc. No. 1972-26-764 **p265** LAC C-002726 **p267** (t) LAC Acc. No. 1989-279-7 (b) LAC Acc. No. 1934-402 **p268** (t) LAC Acc. No. 1972-26-536 (b) *Bilking the Toll*, Cornelius Krieghoff (1815-1872), M967.100.14, MMM **p269** LAC Acc. No. 1989-201-32 **p271** (t) LAC Acc. No. 1970-188-2121 (b) © Robert Estall photo agency/Alamy **p273** *The Quebec Railway Policy: "ALL ABOARD FOR THE WEST!"* M994X.5.260, MMM **p274** With permission of the Royal Ontario Museum © ROM **p276** I.N. Phelps Stokes Collection, Miriam and Ira D. Wallach Division of Art, Prints and Photographs, The New York Public Library, Lenox and Tilden Foundations. 54577: Hill, John William. *View on the Erie Canal*. 1829. Watercolor **p277** LAC Acc. No. 1970-188-1478 **p282** (tl) TPL, TRL, J. Ross Robertson Collection, T16581/slide MTL 1232 (tr) *The Underground Railroad*, by Charles T. Webber, Accession # 1927.26. Cincinnati Art Museum, Subscription Fund Purchase (bl) *Blondin's Tightrope Feat, Crossing the Niagara River*, ON, 1859, M982.530.129, MMM (bm) *Mrs. Major Garrett*, Montreal, QC, 1861, 1-2228.1, MMM (br) *George Firmin*, Montreal, QC, 1863, I-6379, MMM **p283** (tl) Légaré, Joseph. Canadian 1795-1855. *L'Incendie du Quartier Saint-Jean Vue Vers L'Ouest, 1845*. Oil on Canvas. 151.1 x 2230 cm. © Art Gallery of Ontario, Toronto. Purchased with assistance from Wintario, 1976. Photo Credit: Larry Ostrom (tr) JRR 2422 TPL, Watercolour by William Armstrong 1908 (Numbering the Indians, Wikwemikong, Manitoulin Island (Ontario), 16 August 1856). Slide # MTL 2213 (bl) LAC Acc. No. 1970-188-2096 (br) LAC C-059227 **p287** (tr) *Mrs. Major Garrett*, Montreal, Qc, 1861, 1-2228.1, MMM *p289* Saskatchewan Archives Board R-A11995-3 **p290** (t) LAC (b) Hunter & Co./LAC C-009553 **p291** *View of the Special Court*, 1854, M5524, MMM **p292** *St. Lawrence & Atlantic R.R. Longueuil Station*, 1855, M982.530.129, MMM (b) LAC **p293** (l) GA NA-293-2 (r) Notman/LAC PA-74102 **p294** TPL **p295** LAC C-010383 **p296** (l) LAC Acc. No. 1991-35-14 (r) LAC

Contents

To the Student

Countries are like people. Each has a unique identity. A country's identity is influenced by its environment and the experiences of the people who live there.

In *Their Stories, Our History: Canada's Early Years*, you will learn about some of the first groups of people to live in Canada. These peoples' stories are part of Canada's cultural, economic, political, and social roots. As you read, you will follow the changing relationships between First Nations and early explorers and immigrants from France and Britain. You will also learn about the relationships between the French and British in North America.

Throughout history, these groups—First Nations, French, and British—have each made contributions to Canada's story. People from other countries around the world have joined them. Each person and group has had a unique experience in this country. Their stories have become our history.

Canada's Early Years covers three main topics:

- the foundation and early history of New France
- the battle for North America between Britain and France
- Canada's history as a British colony until the mid-nineteenth century

Much of Canada's identity as a country stems from events and decisions made during this period. Many of the issues that people faced then are still issues today. Managing economic growth, the effects of new technology, and changing roles are issues of the past and present. How people deal with these issues becomes part of Canada's history.

- What does this stop sign tell you about Canada's history?

Historical Literacy

Just as various sports and types of music each have a language, so does history. People who are historically literate understand the language of history. Three features of this book will help you to become historically literate:

- You will often act as a historian, examining historical documents to understand the thinking and actions of real people from the past. You will be asked to evaluate and question decisions made by these people. In the end, you will form your own opinions about historical events and learn to support your opinions with evidence.
- You will learn many skills needed to understand history, such as identifying cause and effect and asking questions. However, you will also improve your literacy skills: reading, writing, and oral communication. These literacy skills will help your study of history, as well as your study of other subjects.
- You will often learn about the tensions and conflicts of the past through historical fiction. These stories come from an author's imagination, but they are based on real events. The stories can help you understand and empathize with people's actions. You may even make connections between your life and their experiences.

How to Use This Book

Pages vi to xvii will guide you through the features of *Their Stories, Our History: Canada's Early Years*.

Textbook Organization

This textbook has three units. Each unit has three chapters.

Their Stories, Our History: Canada's Early Years

UNIT 1
New France

Chapter 1:
The Early History of New France

Chapter 2:
New France under Royal Government

Chapter 3:
The Fall of New France

UNIT 2
British North America

Chapter 4:
British North America after the Fall of New France

Chapter 5:
Loyalists in British North America

Chapter 6:
The War of 1812

UNIT 3
Conflict and Change

Chapter 7:
Roots of Conflict

Chapter 8:
Social Change

Chapter 9:
Economic and Political Change to 1856

Unit Overview

Begin and end your study of each unit by reading the Unit Overview.

Illustrations and paintings representing key events or issues in each chapter give you a general sense of what to expect in the unit.

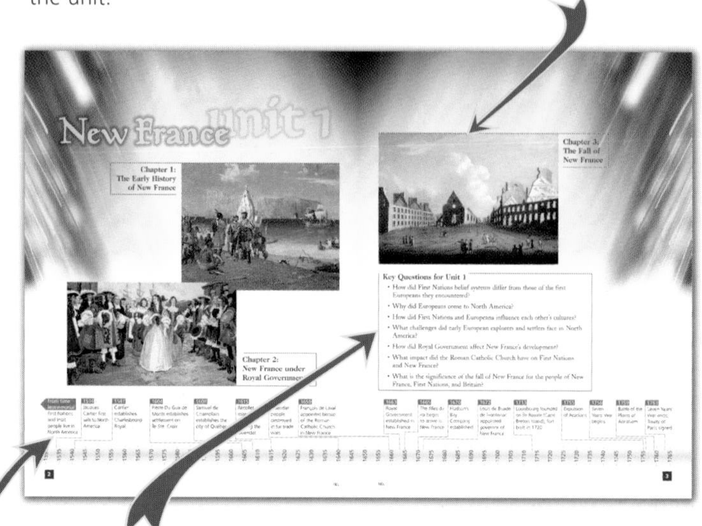

Key Questions help you consider important historical issues. Read them quickly before beginning the unit and more carefully after you have finished. By the end of the unit, you should be able to answer all the questions.

The **Unit Timeline** shows a series of key events from the unit. At the end of a unit, review the timeline and ask yourself why these events were chosen. Would you take some events off the timeline? What events would you add? Why? This is a good way to check to see if you are prepared for a test or to move on to the next unit.

Chapter Overview

Begin and end your study of each chapter by reading the Chapter Overview. The information in the Chapter Overview summarizes the knowledge and skills featured in the chapter.

Chapter Review

The Chapter Review is the last page of each chapter. It reviews some of the most important knowledge and skills covered in the chapter. Your teacher will indicate which activities should be completed. You may wish to review the others in preparation for tests and quizzes.

Questions guide you to "walk" into the illustration or painting. When you first look at the Chapter Overview, you may know very little or nothing at all about the events and people you are about to study. You do, however, know a great deal about how you might feel about being placed in the middle of a battle, for example. Analyze the illustration or painting from your perspective. Use your own experiences to guide you.

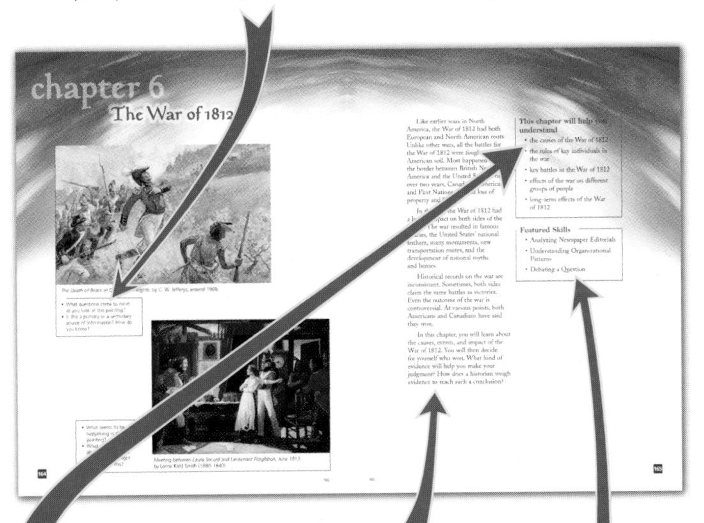
chapter 6
The War of 1812

This chapter will help you understand

Featured Skills
- Analyzing Newspaper Editorials
- Understanding Organizational Patterns
- Debating a Question

A **summary of the main ideas** in the chapter helps set the context for your learning. Read it for a general introduction and overview.

A **list of events and ideas** highlights what you will know by the end of the chapter.

Featured Skills include some of the most important skills you will use in the chapter.

Compress activities ask you to summarize the chapter's main ideas.

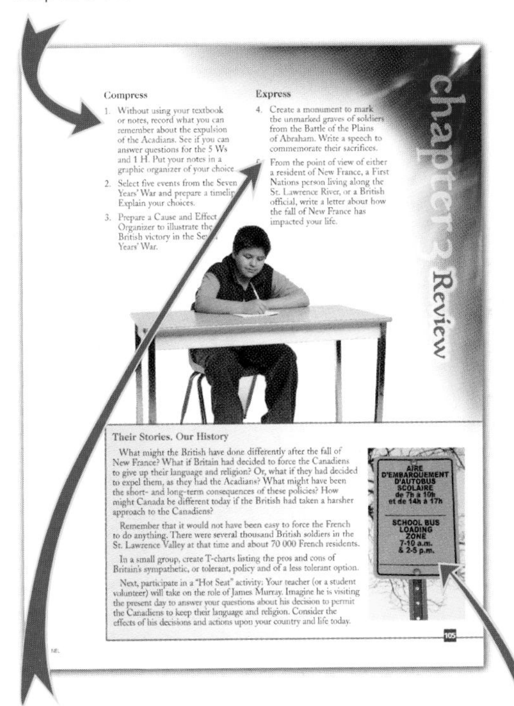
chapter 3 Review

Compress
1. Without using your textbook or notes, record what you can remember about the expulsion of the Acadians. See if you can answer questions for the 5 Ws and 1 H. Put your notes in a graphic organizer of your choice.
2. Select five events from the Seven Years' War and prepare a timeli Explain your choices.
3. Prepare a Cause and Effect Organizer to illustrate the British victory in the Se Years' War.

Express
4. Create a monument to mark the unmarked graves of soldiers from the Battle of the Plains of Abraham. Write a speech to commemorate their sacrifices.
5. From the point of view of either a resident of New France, a First Nations person living along the St. Lawrence River, or a British official, write a letter about how the fall of New France has impacted your life.

Their Stories, Our History

What might the British have done differently after the fall of New France? What if Britain had decided to force the Canadiens to give up their language and religion? Or, what if they had decided to expel them, as they had the Acadians? What might have been the short- and long-term consequences of these policies? How might Canada be different today if the British had taken a harsher approach to the Canadiens?

Remember that it would not have been easy to force the French to do anything. There were several thousand British soldiers in the St. Lawrence Valley at that time and about 70 000 French residents.

In a small group, create T-charts listing the pros and cons of Britain's sympathetic, or tolerant, policy and of a less tolerant option.

Next, participate in a "Hot Seat" activity: Your teacher (or a student volunteer) will take on the role of James Murray. Imagine he is visiting the present day to answer your questions about his decision to permit the Canadiens to keep their language and religion. Consider the effects of his decisions and actions upon your country and life today.

Express activities ask you to apply what you have learned to communicate your ideas.

Their Stories, Our History activities help you think about the place of history in our world. The activities make connections between the stories of the past and current issues and events.

Topics

Each chapter is divided into several topics. Each topic includes three sets of questions and activities: Before Reading, During Reading, and After Reading.

Before Reading sections begin each new topic. These questions help you think about what you already know about the topic you are about to study. Your own experiences can give you many insights into historical events. Most of the questions ask you to share your ideas with a partner, a group, or your class. Participating in this discussion can help you improve your ability to express your ideas and communicate with other people.

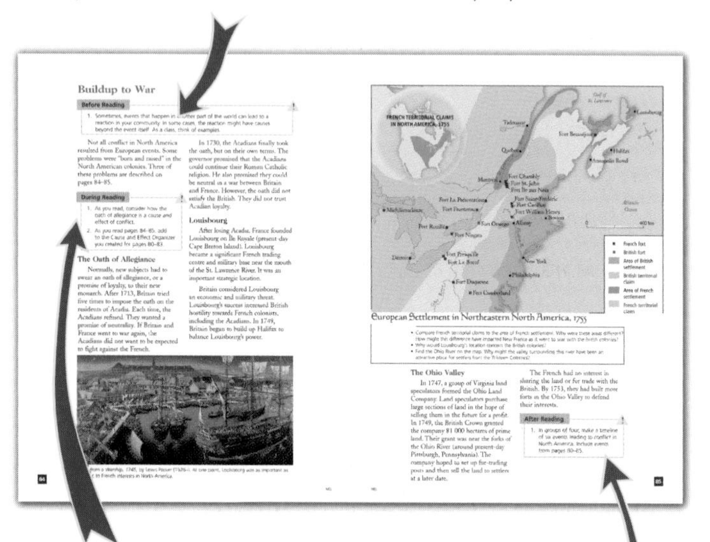

During Reading sections help you understand key points. They can help you stay focused and check that you understand what you are reading.

After Reading activities ask you to summarize main ideas, draw conclusions, or apply what you have learned to new situations.

Think It Through Features

Some topics include an additional feature. Think It Through pages give examples of how good readers might approach the activity or question. This feature allows you to follow the ideas of another student to see how he or she is thinking.

Pages labelled **Think It Through** will help you better understand the thinking process involved in a particular skill.

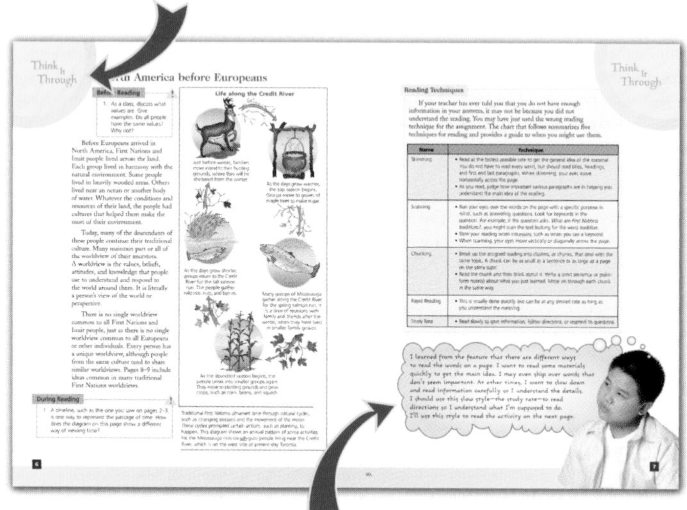

Think It Through examples are not the only answers or approaches possible. However, if you are not sure how to handle a new skill, the examples may guide you.

Response Journal Activities

Response Journal activities are a chance for you to write personal responses to what you read—*what* you are learning. You might also be asked to think about your learning and thinking process—*how* you are learning. Your journal is the place to jot down unanswered questions, new ideas, and conclusions. Be creative with your entries; some of your responses may be in the form of sketches or poems.

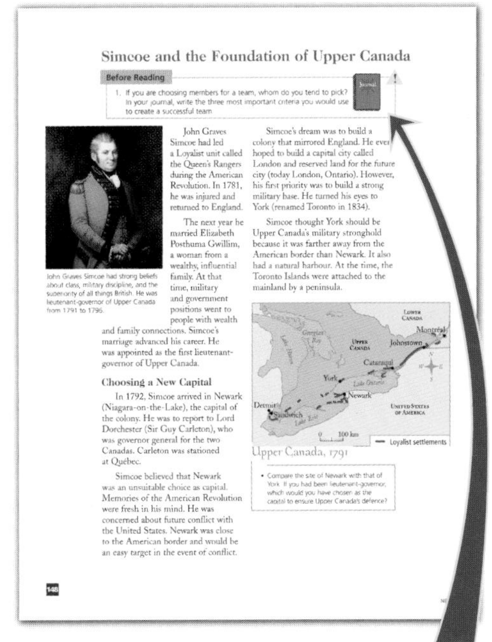

Simcoe and the Foundation of Upper Canada

Before Reading

1. If you are choosing members for a team, whom do you tend to pick? In your journal, write the three most important criteria you would use to create a successful team.

John Graves Simcoe had strong beliefs about class, military discipline, and the superiority of all things British. He was lieutenant-governor of Upper Canada from 1791 to 1796.

John Graves Simcoe had led a Loyalist unit called the Queen's Rangers during the American Revolution. In 1781, he was injured and returned to England.

The next year he married Elizabeth Posthuma Gwillim, a woman from a wealthy, influential family. At that time, military and government positions went to people with wealth and family connections. Simcoe's marriage advanced his career. He was appointed as the first lieutenant-governor of Upper Canada.

Choosing a New Capital

In 1792, Simcoe arrived in Newark (Niagara-on-the-Lake), the capital of the colony. He was to report to Lord Dorchester (Sir Guy Carleton), who was governor general for the two Canadas. Carleton was stationed at Québec.

Simcoe believed that Newark was an unsuitable choice as capital. Memories of the American Revolution were fresh in his mind. He was concerned about future conflict with the United States. Newark was close to the American border and would be an easy target in the event of conflict.

Simcoe's dream was to build a colony that mirrored England. He even hoped to build a capital city called London and reserved land for the future city (today London, Ontario). However, his first priority was to build a strong military base. He turned his eyes to York (renamed Toronto in 1834).

Simcoe thought York should be Upper Canada's military stronghold because it was farther away from the American border than Newark. It also had a natural harbour. At the time, the Toronto Islands were attached to the mainland by a peninsula.

Upper Canada, 1791

- Compare the site of Newark with that of York. If you had been lieutenant-governor, which would you have chosen as the capital to ensure Upper Canada's defence?

148

A **Response Journal** is a place for your thoughts, observations, and reactions to the things you read, see, do, or hear in your History class. This is not a diary, so there is no need to make daily entries. A booklet stored in your binder, separate from your history notes, makes a good journal.

How does a Response Journal help you?

1. Your journal is a place to record your experiences and your feelings about what you are reading, doing, and learning. These are then shared with the teacher who can respond. The journal becomes a written dialogue with your teacher. Consider the prompts that follow to help you get started:
   - I wonder...
   - I'm surprised that...
   - I didn't know...
2. Your journal is a place where you can evaluate your contributions to class activities.
   - If I had to do a similar task again, I would...because...
   - I used...as a strategy to do this work because...
   - The most important thing I learned was...
   - I worked best when I was able to...
3. Your journal is a place to let your teacher know when you are having trouble with the class material. Tell your teacher through your journal what you have tried and where you see the problem:
   - ...confuses me.
   - I need to clarify...

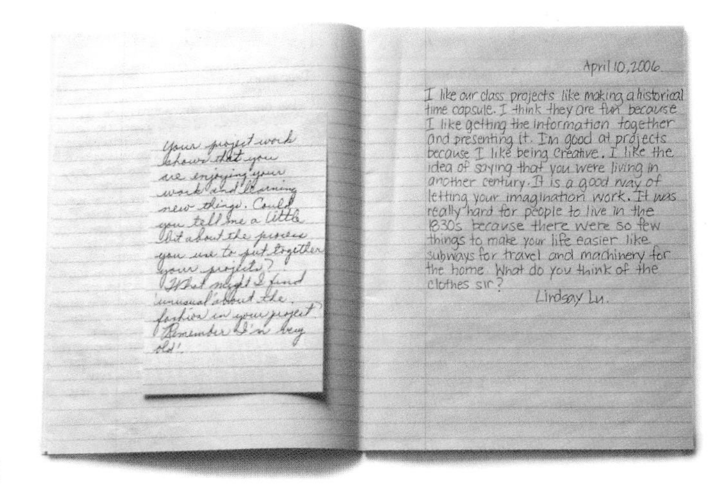

Learning from Different Types of Information

This textbook is full of information. Much information is in the form of words arranged in sentences and paragraphs. Other information is contained in photographs, illustrations, maps, and graphic organizers.

No matter how it is presented, all the information was chosen carefully to help you learn something about history. Nothing is there by accident or chance. Like a jigsaw, each piece adds something to your picture of the history being discussed. Ask yourself, *Why am I reading this or looking at this visual clue? What is its purpose on the page?* Asking these questions can help you become a better reader.

This style of heading tells you a new topic is beginning. You will see a Before Reading section immediately following it.

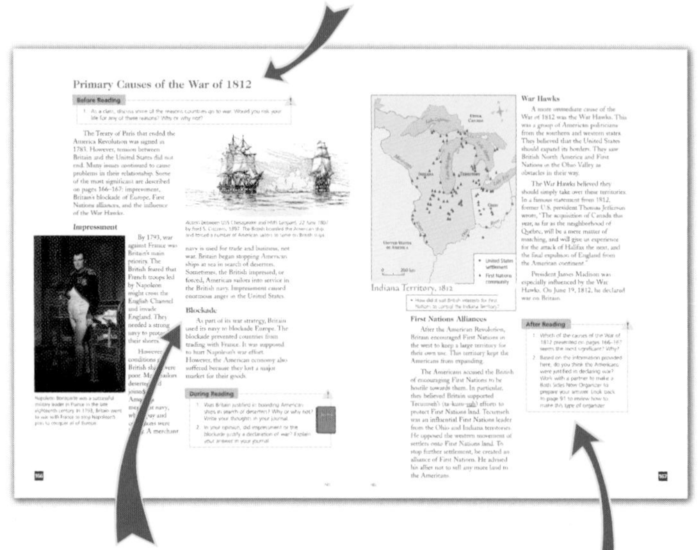

Primary Causes of the War of 1812

Before Reading

Impressment

Blockade

During Reading

Indiana Territory, 1812

First Nations Alliances

War Hawks

After Reading

This style of heading indicates a subsection of the main topic. Subsections break up longer topics and can help you organize your notes.

The After Reading activity concludes the topic.

Before you begin reading any new topic, find the Before Reading and After Reading sections so you know how long the topic is. Think of the Before Reading and After Reading sections as bookends on the topic.

Also read headings and captions that catch your interest. Take a look at the kind of information you are going to be reading. Are there paragraphs? Photographs? Illustrations? Maps? Charts? Many subheadings or just a few? A timeline? Each of these forms of information will add to your knowledge in specific ways. The pages that follow will explain how.

Primary and Secondary Sources

Imagine there has been an accident on the school soccer field, but the principal did not see it. She needs the help of eyewitnesses to write an accident report.

Historians and students of history work in much the same way. They use eyewitnesses to help them understand events from the past.

Obviously, there are no living eyewitnesses to historical events like the Rebellions of 1837, so what do historians do? They turn to eyewitness testimony in the form of diaries, drawings, maps, statistics, letters, newspapers, and other records of the period. Sometimes, historical evidence comes in the form of an **artifact**, such as a piece of ancient pottery, a tool, or a drawing on a cave wall.

Accounts by eyewitnesses are called **primary sources**. They can open a window to the past, allowing historians to peek at an event through someone else's eyes.

Think back to the example of the accident on the soccer field. Many students give the principal their accounts of the event. However, the principal finds the stories are not all the same. She sorts through the various versions and tries to find the ones that are most consistent. The principal is evaluating the eyewitness reports.

Her accident report will likely combine parts of several stories about the accident. Another way to see the report is to view it as history—a story about an event that happened in the past.

During Reading

1. As a class, discuss the difference between the past and history.

A historian's work is like the principal's work in this example. Historians analyze and interpret the evidence they find in primary sources. They may then write books or essays that communicate their ideas. The books and essays become new sources of information called **secondary sources**. Articles in magazines, textbooks, and encyclopedias are examples of secondary sources.

Comparing Primary and Secondary Sources of Information

Primary Sources	Secondary Sources
• First-hand evidence or eyewitness accounts of an event, circumstance, or person	• Second-hand accounts of an event, circumstance, or person made after the time period being recorded
• Has a fairly narrow view, telling about the event from the point of view of the participant/recorder	• Attempts to take a broad point of view by analyzing or explaining an event • Combines a variety of primary sources and may select and interpret evidence from the past
• Reflects the attitudes of the time period in which it was written or produced	• Reflects the attitudes of the time period in which it was written or produced
• Reflects the values, attitudes, beliefs, and purpose of the person writing	• Reflects the values, attitudes, beliefs, and purpose of the person writing

Because primary sources reflect the values and attitudes of the time they were created, they sometimes use names for certain groups of people that are now often considered offensive. Out of respect for these groups today, some terms have been changed in the primary sources in this textbook to reflect language that is preferred today. Such changes are shown in grey type.

During Reading

1. Paraphrase the four points of view that follow.
2. Which points of view seem to agree? Which conflict? Group them accordingly.

PRIMARY SOURCE 3-4

Letter by Mother Marguerite d'Youville (dee-yoo-vil)

We had flattered ourselves that France would not abandon us, but we were wrong in our expectation.... What is even more distressing for us is that this poor country is more and more forsaken [bleak]. All the good citizens are leaving it.

Mother Marguerite d'Youville

PRIMARY SOURCE 3-5

Orders from Charles Wyndham, British Secretary of State, to Jeffery Amherst, 1761

You should earnestly *enforce* [insist] to the several Governors... the conciliating [calming] part of the Instructions, which you have been given, and that you Recommend... the most vigilant [careful] attention, and take the most effectual [effective] care that the French Inhabitants... be humanely and kindly treated.

Charles Wyndham

PRIMARY SOURCE 3-7

Speech by Jean-Olivier Briand (zhawn-olee-vay bree-an), Vicar General of the District of Québec, 1763

The surrender of Québec left you at the mercy of a victorious army. At first, you were undoubtedly alarmed, frightened, and dismayed. Your feelings were justified... but you were ignoring that a kind and watchful Providence [God] had reserved for you a Governor who, by his moderation, his stern justice, his generous and humane sentiments [feelings], his tender compassion for the poor and wretched, and his rigid discipline towards his troops, would remove all the horrors of war. Show me the vexations [aggravation], the distortions [lies], the plunders [theft], that ordinarily follow in the wake of a victory. Did not those noble victors, once they became our masters, appear to forget that they had been our enemies, in order to concern themselves solely with our needs and with ways of satisfying them? Surely, you have not forgotten the good actions of his Excellency, the illustrious and charitable General Murray.

Jean-Olivier Briand

PRIMARY SOURCE 3-6

Letter from Some Can[illegible] the Consul of the French Republic in New [illegible] 1792

Accept the best wishes of the greater [illegible] of the Canadiens. They all love France, detest t[illegible]lish, and passionately desire to be re-united to t[illegible] motherland from which they have been sepa[illegible] too long.... Day by day the British tyrants [u[illegible] rulers], under whose yoke [heavy burden] they [illegible] want to make their chains heavier. The Canadi[illegible] wish to break them, and all they require to do s[illegible] favourable word and a little help from the Rep[illegible]

During Reading

1. Compare your paraphrases with those of a partner. Even though you likely used different words, do your paraphrases capture the same main ideas? Discuss any differences.
2. The quotation from 1792 was written thirty-two years after the conquest. What does it say about the attitude of the French in Québec towards the British in the years following the conquest? In your journal, predict how you think this attitude would affect Canada's development.

NEL 103

In this textbook, most primary text sources are labelled. Some short quotations are in the main text. These are surrounded by quotation marks. All other texts are secondary sources.

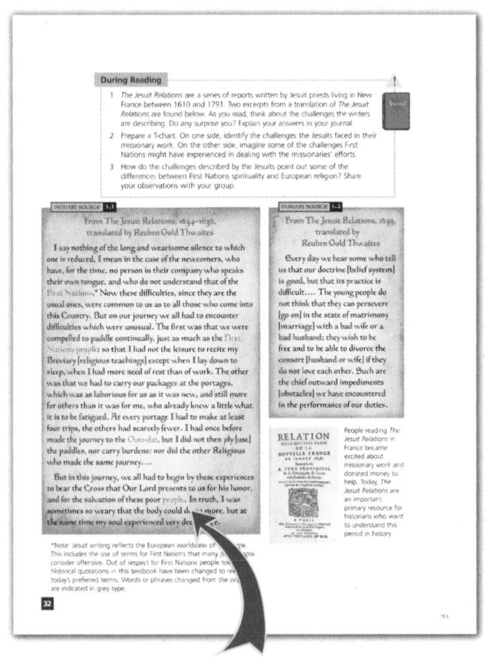

During Reading

1. *The Jesuit Relations* are a series of reports written by Jesuit priests living in New France between 1610 and 1791. Two excerpts from a translation of *The Jesuit Relations* are found below. As you read, think about the challenges the writers are describing. Do any surprise you? Explain your answers in your journal.
2. Prepare a T-chart. On one side, identify the challenges the Jesuits faced in their missionary work. On the other side, imagine some of the challenges First Nations might have experienced in dealing with the missionaries' efforts.
3. How do the challenges described by the Jesuits point out some of the differences between First Nations spirituality and European religion? Share your observations with your group.

PRIMARY SOURCE 1-1

From The Jesuit Relations, 1634–1636, translated by Reuben Gold Thwaites

I say nothing of the long and wearisome silence to which one is reduced, I mean in the case of the newcomers, who have, for the time, no person in their company who speaks their own tongue, and who do not understand that of the First Nations.* Now these difficulties, since they are the usual ones, were common to us as to all those who come into this Country. But on our journey we all had to encounter difficulties which were unusual. The first was that we were compelled to paddle continually, just as much as the First Nations people; so that I had not the leisure to recite my Breviary [religious teachings] except when I lay down to sleep, when I had more need of rest than of work. The other was that we had to carry our packages at the portages, which was as laborious for us as it was new, and still more for others than it was for me, who already knew a little what it is to be fatigued. At every portage I had to make at least four trips, the others had scarcely fewer. I had once before made the journey to the Ouendat, but I did not then ply [use] the paddles, nor carry burdens: nor did the other Religious who made the same journey....

But in this journey, we all had to begin by these experiences to bear the Cross that Our Lord presents to us for his honor, and for the salvation of these poor people. In truth, I was sometimes so weary that the body could d[illegible] more, but at the same time my soul experienced very dee[illegible]

*Note: Jesuit writing reflects the European worldview of [illegible]me. This includes the use of terms for First Nations that many p[illegible] now consider offensive. Out of respect for First Nations people to[illegible] historical quotations in this textbook have been changed to re[illegible] today's preferred terms. Words or phrases changed from the or[illegible] are indicated in grey type.

PRIMARY SOURCE 1-2

From The Jesuit Relations, 1639, translated by Reuben Gold Thwaites

Every day we hear some who tell us that our doctrine [belief system] is good, but that its practice is difficult.... The young people do not think that they can persevere [go on] in the state of matrimony [marriage] with a bad wife or a bad husband; they wish to be free and to be able to divorce the consort [husband or wife] if they do not love each other. Such are the chief outward impediments [obstacles] we have encountered in the performance of our duties.

RELATION

People reading *The Jesuit Relations* in France became excited about missionary work and donated money to help. Today, *The Jesuit Relations* are an important primary resource for historians who want to understand this period in history.

32 NEL

Changes to primary source documents are indicated in square brackets or grey type. Otherwise, the spellings, grammar, and punctuation are as they were in the original.

During Reading

1. With a partner, review the chart comparing primary and secondary sources. Make a list of words, ideas, or points you do not understand. Clarify them in a class discussion.

Historical Fiction

Historical fiction is fictional stories based on real people or events from the past. Historical fiction can make history come alive. The author can use dramatic literary techniques, write conversations, develop people's personalities, and describe an atmosphere surrounding historical events. These fictional additions breathe life into stories about the past. Historical fiction can often help you make connections between your own life and the people and events of the past.

However, not all historical fiction can help you learn history. The story's quality as a source of information depends on the accuracy of the author's research. Check any information you learn from historical fiction against other sources of information.

During Reading

1. With a partner, flip through the textbook to find at least three examples of historical fiction.
2. Is historical fiction a primary or secondary source of information? How do you know?

In this textbook, **historical fiction** takes many forms.

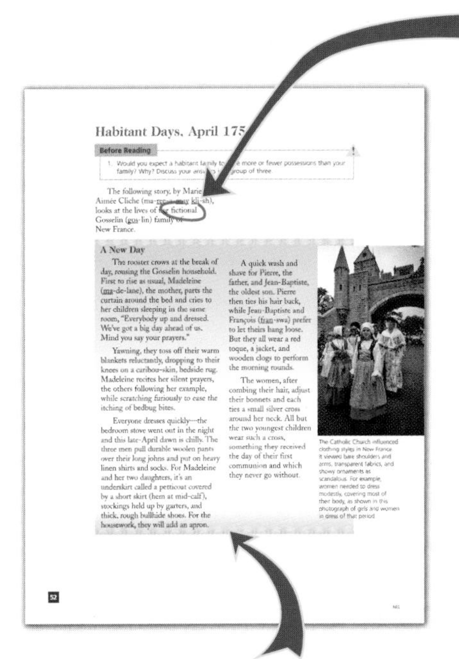

Some fiction is in the form of stories that last several pages.

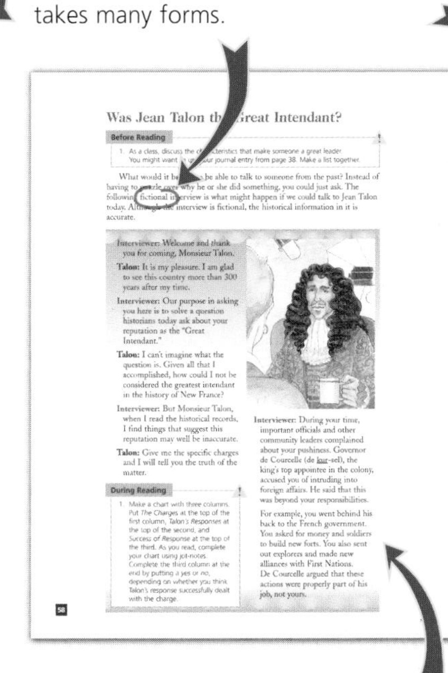

Some historical fiction takes the form of modern-day interviews with people from the past.

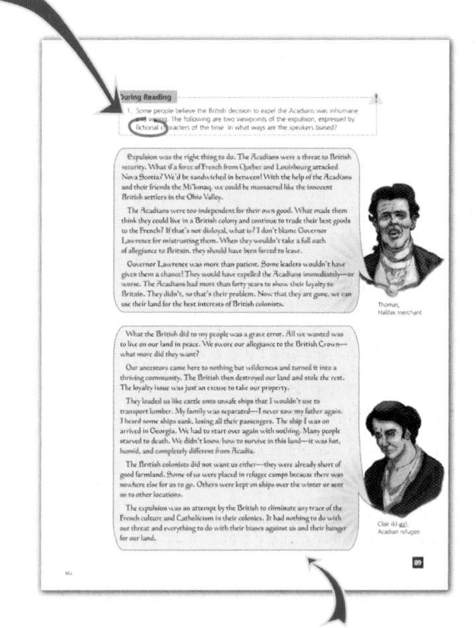

Some historical fiction is presented as though written or spoken by real historical figures. Other viewpoints are presented by fictional individuals. In either case, they are meant to express a selection of common or realistic ideas and emotions of that time.

Images

Have you heard the saying *A picture speaks a thousand words*? The saying captures the power of visual images. Drawings, paintings, illustrations, and photographs are significant sources of information for historians. A single historical image can reveal values, attitudes, and other information at a glance.

To "read" an image, use your imagination to "enter" it. Imagine you can walk around and interact with the people and events surrounding you. Ask questions. A list of sample questions follow, but it is not necessary to answer them all. Just select two or three that will help give you ideas about the image.

- What is happening in this picture?
- What would I ask a character from the picture?
- Who are the people in the picture?
- What is the setting?
- What puzzles me about the picture?
- On what occasion might this picture have been made?
- What is the story that leads up to this picture? What may have happened before or after the events shown in this image?
- How can I use this picture to understand the topic?
- What action is emphasized?
- What do the picture's details contribute to my understanding of the picture?
- Why was the picture created and when?
- What background details give me clues about the setting?
- What is not in the picture? What do omissions tell me about the artist's purpose, values, and attitudes?

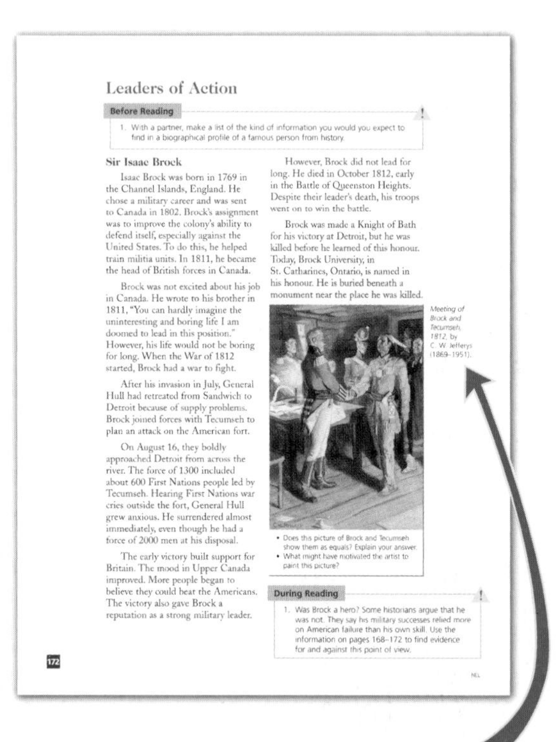

Leaders of Action

Before Reading

1. With a partner, make a list of the kind of information you would you expect to find in a biographical profile of a famous person from history.

Sir Isaac Brock

Isaac Brock was born in 1769 in the Channel Islands, England. He chose a military career and was sent to Canada in 1802. Brock's assignment was to improve the colony's ability to defend itself, especially against the United States. To do this, he helped train militia units. In 1811, he became the head of British forces in Canada.

Brock was not excited about his job in Canada. He wrote to his brother in 1811, "You can hardly imagine the uninteresting and boring life I am doomed to lead in this position." However, his life would not be boring for long. When the War of 1812 started, Brock had a war to fight.

After his invasion in July, General Hull had retreated from Sandwich to Detroit because of supply problems. Brock joined forces with Tecumseh to plan an attack on the American fort.

On August 16, they boldly approached Detroit from across the river. The force of 1300 included about 600 First Nations people led by Tecumseh. Hearing First Nations war cries outside the fort, General Hull grew anxious. He surrendered almost immediately, even though he had a force of 2000 men at his disposal.

The early victory built support for Britain. The mood in Upper Canada improved. More people began to believe they could beat the Americans. The victory also gave Brock a reputation as a strong military leader.

However, Brock did not lead for long. He died in October 1812, early in the Battle of Queenston Heights. Despite their leader's death, his troops went on to win the battle.

Brock was made a Knight of Bath for his victory at Detroit, but he was killed before he learned of this honour. Today, Brock University, in St. Catharines, Ontario, is named in his honour. He is buried beneath a monument near the place he was killed.

Meeting of Brock and Tecumseh, 1812, by C. W. Jefferys (1869–1951).

- Does this picture of Brock and Tecumseh show them as equals? Explain your answer.
- What might have motivated the artist to paint this picture?

During Reading

1. Was Brock a hero? Some historians argue that he was not. They say his military successes relied more on American failure than his own skill. Use the information on pages 168–172 to find evidence for and against this point of view.

172

NEL

Many captions provide a date the artwork was created. This information can help you decide whether an image is a primary or secondary source of information.

During Reading

1. Flip through the textbook to find a picture that interests you. Take a walk through the picture. Ask questions to see what you can learn or what you want to learn.

New Vocabulary

If you see a sentence with a red boldface word or phrase, read the sentences before and after the bold type. Often, these sentences will explain the term. You can also find a definition in the glossary beginning on page 299.

This textbook has another way of helping you with words that are new to you. Primary sources often contain language and grammar that sound unfamiliar to people in the twenty-first century. To help you read and understand these sources, challenging vocabulary is explained in square brackets. For example, in the quotation "While these meetings were in continuance [going on] Mr. M'Kenzie," the words in the square brackets explain the phrase "in continuance."

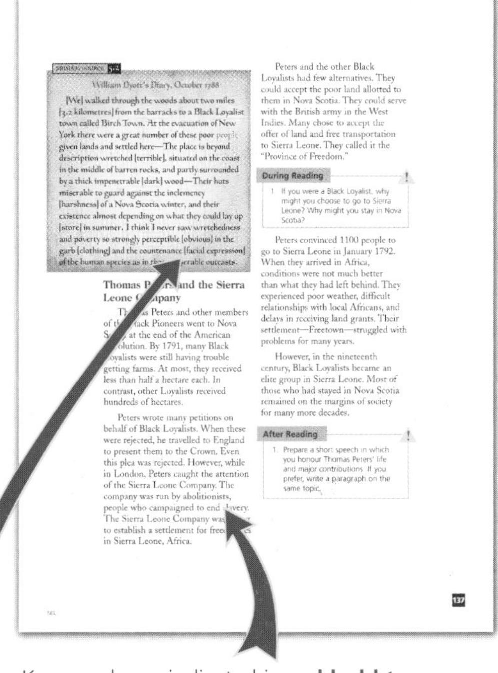

PRIMARY SOURCE 5.2

William Dyott's Diary, October 1788

[We] walked through the woods about two miles [3.2 kilometres] from the barracks to a Black Loyalist town called Birch Town. At the evacuation of New York there were a great number of these poor people given lands and settled here—The place is beyond description wretched [terrible], situated on the coast in the middle of barren rocks, and partly surrounded by a thick impenetrable [dark] wood—Their huts miserable to guard against the inclemency [harshness] of a Nova Scotia winter, and their existence almost depending on what they could lay up [store] in summer. I think I never saw wretchedness and poverty so strongly perceptible [obvious] in the garb [clothing] and the countenance [facial expression] of the human species as in [illegible] outcasts.

Thomas P[illegible] and the Sierra Leone [illegible]

Th[illegible] Peters and other members of [illegible] Pioneers went to Nova S[illegible] at the end of the American [illegible]olution. By 1791, many Black [illegible]oyalists were still having trouble getting farms. At most, they received less than half a hectare each. In contrast, other Loyalists received hundreds of hectares.

Peters wrote many petitions on behalf of Black Loyalists. When these were rejected, he travelled to England to present them to the Crown. Even this plea was rejected. However, while in London, Peters caught the attention of the Sierra Leone Company. The company was run by abolitionists, people who campaigned to end [illegible]very. The Sierra Leone Company was [illegible] to establish a settlement for free[illegible] in Sierra Leone, Africa.

Peters and the other Black Loyalists had few alternatives. They could accept the poor land allotted to them in Nova Scotia. They could serve with the British army in the West Indies. Many chose to accept the offer of land and free transportation to Sierra Leone. They called it the "Province of Freedom."

During Reading

1. If you were a Black Loyalist, why might you choose to go to Sierra Leone? Why might you stay in Nova Scotia?

Peters convinced 1100 people to go to Sierra Leone in January 1792. When they arrived in Africa, conditions were not much better than what they had left behind. They experienced poor weather, difficult relationships with local Africans, and delays in receiving land grants. Their settlement—Freetown—struggled with problems for many years.

However, in the nineteenth century, Black Loyalists became an elite group in Sierra Leone. Most of those who had stayed in Nova Scotia remained on the margins of society for many more decades.

After Reading

1. Prepare a short speech in which you honour Thomas Peters' life and major contributions. If you prefer, write a paragraph on the same topic.

NEL 137

Key words are indicated in **red bold type** the first time they appear.

Challenging vocabulary in primary sources is explained inside the **square brackets**.

Pronunciation Guide

A pronunciation guide has been provided for some French and First Nations words in the textbook. The first time the name of a French or First Nations person or organization appears, it is followed by a phonetic pronunciation guide in parenthesis. If you encounter the name later in the book and do not remember how to say it, turn to the pronunciation guide on page 298 for help.

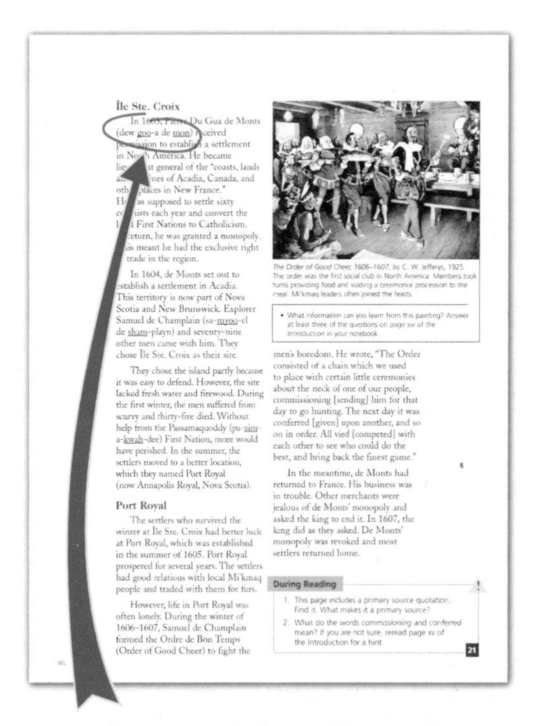

Île Ste. Croix

In 16[illegible] Du Gua de Monts (dew goo-a de mon) [illegible]ceived [illegible] to establi[illegible] a settlement in No[illegible] America. He became lie[illegible] general of the "coasts, lands a[illegible]ines of Acadia, Canada, and oth[illegible] places in New France." H[illegible] as supposed to settle sixty c[illegible]ists each year and convert the [illegible] First Nations to Catholicism. [illegible]eturn, he was granted a monopoly. [illegible]is meant he had the exclusive right [illegible] trade in the region.

In 1604, de Monts set out to [illegible]stablish a settlement in Acadia. This territory is now part of Nova Scotia and New Brunswick. Explorer Samuel de Champlain (sa-myoo-el de sham-playn) and seventy-nine other men came with him. They chose Île Ste. Croix as their site.

They chose the island partly because it was easy to defend. However, the site lacked fresh water and firewood. During the first winter, the men suffered from scurvy and thirty-five died. Without help from the Passamaquoddy (pa-zim-a-kwah-dee) First Nation, more would have perished. In the summer, the settlers moved to a better location, which they named Port Royal (now Annapolis Royal, Nova Scotia).

Port Royal

The settlers who survived the winter at Île Ste. Croix had better luck at Port Royal, which was established in the summer of 1605. Port Royal prospered for several years. The settlers had good relations with local Mi'kmaq people and traded with them for furs.

However, life in Port Royal was often lonely. During the winter of 1606–1607, Samuel de Champlain formed the Ordre de Bon Temps (Order of Good Cheer) to fight the men's boredom. He wrote, "The Order consisted of a chain which we used to place with certain little ceremonies about the neck of one of our people, commissioning [sending] him for that day to go hunting. The next day it was conferred [given] upon another, and so on in order. All vied [competed] with each other to see who could do the best, and bring back the finest game."

The Order of Good Cheer, 1606–1607, by C. W. Jefferys, 1925. The order was the first social club in North America. Members took turns providing food and leading a ceremonial procession to the meal. Mi'kmaq leaders often joined the feasts.

- What information can you learn from this painting? Answer at least three of the questions on page xiv of the Introduction in your notebook.

In the meantime, de Monts had returned to France. His business was in trouble. Other merchants were jealous of de Monts' monopoly and asked the king to end it. In 1607, the king did as they asked. De Monts' monopoly was revoked and most settlers returned home.

During Reading

1. This page includes a primary source quotation. Find it. What makes it a primary source?
2. What do the words *commissioning* and *conferred* mean? If you are not sure, reread page xv of the Introduction for a hint.

21

To use the **pronunciation guide**, sound out the syllables in the parenthesis. Repeat the word several times, until you can say it smoothly.

During Reading

1. Turn to the pronunciation guide on page 298. With a partner, take turns practising some of the names.
2. Find three boldface words in the textbook. Use the clues in the sentences surrounding the word to write a definition. Turn to the glossary on page 299 to check your work.

Maps

When you see a map, you know the events or circumstances you are going to read about take place in a particular area or are affected by the environment or setting.

Ask yourself how the map relates to the topic you are studying. You will learn more about reading maps later in the textbook.

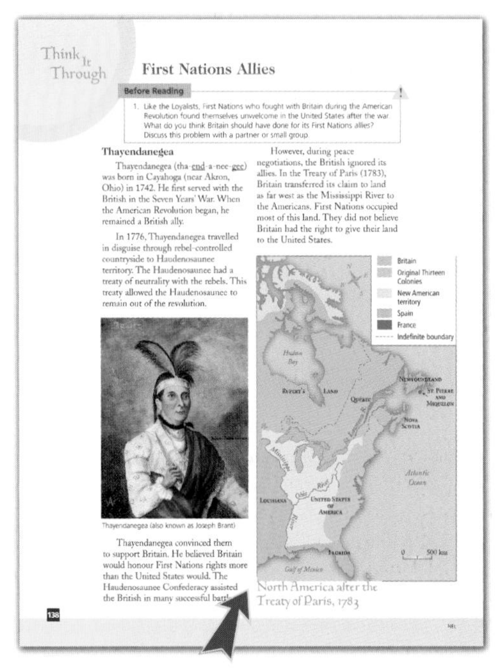
Think It Through

First Nations Allies

Before Reading

1. Like the Loyalists, First Nations who fought with Britain during the American Revolution found themselves unwelcome in the United States after the war. What do you think Britain should have done for its First Nations allies? Discuss this problem with a partner or small group.

Thayendanegea

Thayendanegea (tha-end-a-nee-gee) was born in Cayahoga (near Akron, Ohio) in 1742. He first served with the British in the Seven Years' War. When the American Revolution began, he remained a British ally.

In 1776, Thayendanegea travelled in disguise through rebel-controlled countryside to Haudenosaunee territory. The Haudenosaunee had a treaty of neutrality with the rebels. This treaty allowed the Haudenosaunee to remain out of the revolution.

Thayendanegea (also known as Joseph Brant)

Thayendanegea convinced them to support Britain. He believed Britain would honour First Nations rights more than the United States would. The Haudenosaunee Confederacy assisted the British in many successful batt

However, during peace negotiations, the British ignored its allies. In the Treaty of Paris (1783), Britain transferred its claim to land as far west as the Mississippi River to the Americans. First Nations occupied most of this land. They did not believe Britain had the right to give their land to the United States.

North America after the Treaty of Paris, 1783

138

Maps help show how geography and the environment influence historical events.

Timelines

A timeline shows selected events in **chronological** order. This means events are placed in the order in which they occurred. Understanding the order of events can help you see relationships between them. The key to learning from a timeline is to understand these relationships. Did one event have an impact on something that followed? Did events occur close together or over a long period of time? What is the purpose of the timeline? How does it add to the discussion of the topic?

Think It Through

Battle of Lake Erie, by Percy Moran, around 1911 Many battles in the War of 1812 were fought on the Great Lakes. The Americans were confident they could defeat British forces by land. The British were just as confident they could conquer the Americans at sea. As the war went on, both were proved wrong. The Battle of Lake Erie (or Battle of Put-in-Bay), shown here, gave the Americans dominance on the Great Lakes.

The Battle of Put-in-Bay

In September 1813, the British at Amherstburg (near Detroit) were facing a winter with supply problems. The Americans had an advantage on the Great Lakes because the British navy was busy blockading the American coast. They could not send many ships to the Great Lakes.

Forces at Amherstburg could not depend on supplies getting past the Americans. On September 10, six British ships fought nine American ships. The sea battle raged from early in the morning until late afternoon. The Americans finally captured the British ships and control of Lake Erie.

179

Timelines can help you make connections between events, determine crisis points, and make predictions about the future.

During Reading

1. Find a map in the textbook. Without reading everything on the page, predict how the map will help you understand the topic. What clues did you use?

Graphs

Graphs give statistical or numerical information in a clear, brief form. When you see a graph on the page, begin as you do with maps and other types of information. Ask yourself, *How does the information relate to the topic being discussed?*

Once you know why the information is important, you can apply skills you have learned in mathematics, science, or geography to analyze it. You will learn more about reading graphs later in the textbook.

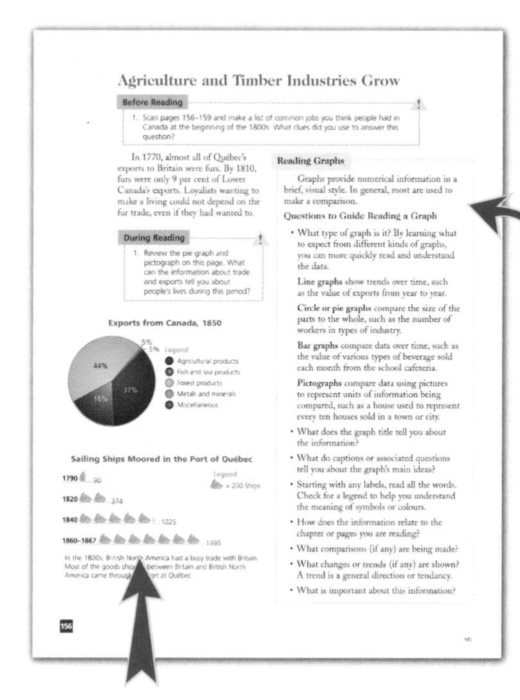

Agriculture and Timber Industries Grow

Before Reading

1. Scan pages 156–159 and make a list of common jobs you think people had in Canada at the beginning of the 1800s. What clues did you use to answer this question?

In 1770, almost all of Québec's exports to Britain were furs. By 1810, furs were only 9 per cent of Lower Canada's exports. Loyalists wanting to make a living could not depend on the fur trade, even if they had wanted to.

During Reading

1. Review the pie graph and pictograph on this page. What can the information about trade and exports tell you about people's lives during this period?

Exports from Canada, 1850

44%
37%
15%
5%
5%
Legend
Agricultural products
Fish and sea products
Forest products
Metals and minerals
Miscellaneous

Sailing Ships Moored in the Port of Québec

Legend
= 200 Ships
1790 90
1820 374
1840 1025
1860–1867 1395

In the 1800s, British North America had a busy trade with Britain. Most of the goods ship[illegible] between Britain and British North America came throug[illegible] ort at Québec.

Reading Graphs

Graphs provide numerical information in a brief, visual style. In general, most are used to make a comparison.

Questions to Guide Reading a Graph

- What type of graph is it? By learning what to expect from different kinds of graphs, you can more quickly read and understand the data.

  Line graphs show trends over time, such as the value of exports from year to year.

  Circle or pie graphs compare the size of the parts to the whole, such as the number of workers in types of industry.

  Bar graphs compare data over time, such as the value of various types of beverage sold each month from the school cafeteria.

  Pictographs compare data using pictures to represent units of information being compared, such as a house used to represent every ten houses sold in a town or city.
- What does the graph title tell you about the information?
- What do captions or associated questions tell you about the graph's main ideas?
- Starting with any labels, read all the words. Check for a legend to help you understand the meaning of symbols or colours.
- How does the information relate to the chapter or pages you are reading?
- What comparisons (if any) are being made?
- What changes or trends (if any) are shown? A trend is a general direction or tendancy.
- What is important about this information?

156

Many **graphs** help make comparisons easier to see. Graphs are especially useful for seeing changes that take place over time. You can often use graphs to make predictions about the future.

Skill Features

Skill features help you complete questions and activities. They will also help you develop your reading, writing, and oral communication skills.

Being historically literate is not about memorizing dates and events. Historical literacy requires many other skills. To understand this, think about the job of a historian. First, historians select, analyze, and evaluate primary sources. They then develop their own ideas about the historical event. Finally, they communicate their ideas effectively for their specific purpose and audience. These are the steps you will take as you work through this textbook.

Skill features are all presented on a light purple background. They will help you develop the reading, thinking, and communication skills of a historian.

During Reading

1. Find a graph in the textbook that allows you to see changes over time. Explain the changes you see.
2. Flip through the textbook to find one example of a skill feature for reading, one for writing, and one for oral communication. Each chapter opener includes a list of skills featured in the chapter.

Unit 1
New France

Chapter 1: The Early History of New France

Chapter 2: New France under Royal Government

- **from time immemorial** First Nations and Inuit people live in North America
- **1534** Jacques Cartier first sails to North America
- **1541** Cartier establishes Charlesbourg-Royal
- **1604** Pierre Du Gua de Monts establishes settlement on Île Ste. Croix
- **1608** Samuel de Champlain establishes the city of Québec
- **1615** Récollet missionaries go to live among the Ouendat
- **1640** Ouendat people destroyed in fur trade wars
- **1659** François de Laval appointed bishop of the Roman Catholic Church in New France

1530 1535 1540 1545 1550 1555 1560 1565 1570 1575 1580 1585 1590 1595 1600 1605 1610 1615 1620 1625 1630 1635 1640

Chapter 3: The Fall of New France

Key Questions for Unit 1

- How did First Nations belief systems differ from those of the first Europeans they encountered?
- Why did Europeans come to North America?
- How did First Nations and Europeans influence each other's cultures?
- What challenges did early European explorers and settlers face in North America?
- How did Royal Government affect New France's development?
- What impact did the Roman Catholic Church have on First Nations and New France?
- What is the significance of the fall of New France for the people of New France, First Nations, and Britain?

1663 Royal Government established in New France

1665 The filles du roi begin to arrive in New France

1670 Hudson's Bay Company established

1672 Louis de Buade de Frontenac appointed governor of New France

1713 Louisbourg founded on Île Royale (Cape Breton Island); fort built in 1720

1755 Expulsion of Acadians

1756 Seven Years' War begins

1759 Battle of the Plains of Abraham

1763 Seven Years' War ends; Treaty of Paris signed

1655 1660 1665 1670 1675 1680 1685 1690 1695 1700 1705 1710 1715 1720 1725 1730 1735 1740 1745 1750 1755 1760 1765

chapter 1
The Early History of New France

- What do you think is happening in this painting?
- What questions do you have?
- What does this painting tell you about the early history of New France (the subject of this chapter)?
- How is the title of the painting inaccurate?

The Discovery of Canada, painted by John David Kelly in 1932, shows explorer Jacques Cartier (zhawk kar-tee-ay) meeting First Nations people in North America.

Habitation at Québec, 1608, by Alan Daniel (1939–).

- What questions do you have about this painting?
- What questions about life in New France does this painting not answer?

The first people to live in North America were the **First Nations** and **Inuit** (in-oo-weet). They lived on the land long before Europeans began to explore and settle the continent. Inuit people had communities in the North and many First Nations lived across the rest of North America.

Each First Nation group had a unique way of life. Their traditions were very different from those of the Europeans. It did not take long for the Europeans and the First Nations people to recognize one another's differences. They also found similarities and mutual needs. They learned from one another and developed relationships that were sometimes cooperative and sometimes conflicting. The effects of these relationships are still felt today in North America.

New France's early history began when French people first decided to stay in North America. They had many reasons for this decision. Some wanted to spread their religious beliefs. Others hoped to have a better life than they could have in France.

However, before they could succeed at meeting either goal, they had to learn how to survive. North America's environment was unfamiliar and many Europeans were unprepared for its challenges. First Nations people often shared their knowledge and experience to help early settlers.

This chapter will help you understand

- how First Nations and European beliefs and values in the sixteenth century compared with each other
- why Europeans first explored and decided to stay in North America
- how First Nations and Europeans interacted
- problems faced by the first French settlements in North America
- how the fur trade led to cooperation and conflict
- the role of religion in New France

Featured Skills

- Reading Techniques
- Compare and Contrast
- Note-Making Skills
- Writing in Role and Role-Play
- Split-Page Note-Making

Think It Through

North America before Europeans

Before Reading

1. As a class, discuss what *values* are. Give examples. Do all people have the same values? Why not?

Before Europeans arrived in North America, First Nations and Inuit people lived across the land. Each group lived in harmony with the natural environment. Some people lived in heavily wooded areas. Others lived near an ocean or another body of water. Whatever the conditions and resources of their land, the people had cultures that helped them make the most of their environment.

Today, many of the descendants of these people continue their traditional culture. Many maintain part or all of the **worldview** of their ancestors. A worldview is the values, beliefs, attitudes, and knowledge that people use to understand and respond to the world around them. It is literally a person's view of the world or perspective.

There is no single worldview common to all First Nations and Inuit people, just as there is no single worldview common to all Europeans or other individuals. Every person has a unique worldview, although people from the same culture tend to share similar worldviews. Pages 8–9 include ideas common in many traditional First Nations worldviews.

During Reading

1. A timeline, such as the one you saw on pages 2–3, is one way to represent the passage of time. How does the diagram on this page show a different way of viewing time?

Life along the Credit River

Traditional First Nations observed time through natural cycles, such as changing seasons and the movement of the moon. These cycles prompted certain actions, such as planting, to happen. This diagram shows an annual pattern of some activities for the Mississauga (mis-sis-sah-guh) people living near the Credit River, which is on the west side of present-day Toronto.

Reading Techniques

If your teacher has ever told you that you do not have enough information in your answers, it may not be because you did not understand the reading. You may have just used the wrong reading technique for the assignment. The chart that follows summarizes five techniques for reading and provides a guide to when you might use them.

Name	Technique
Skimming	• Read at the fastest possible rate to get the general idea of the material. You do not have to read every word, but should read titles, headings, and first and last paragraphs. When skimming, your eyes move horizontally across the page. • As you read, judge how important various paragraphs are in helping you understand the main idea of the reading.
Scanning	• Run your eyes over the words on the page with a specific purpose in mind, such as answering questions. Look for keywords in the question. For example, if the question asks, *What are First Nations traditions?*, you might scan the text looking for the word *tradition*. • Slow your reading when necessary, such as when you see a keyword. • When scanning, your eyes move vertically or diagonally across the page.
Chunking	• Break up the assigned reading into clusters, or chunks, that deal with the same topic. A chunk can be as small as a sentence or as large as a page on the same topic. • Read the chunk and then think about it. Write a short sentence or point-form note(s) about what you just learned. Move on through each chunk in the same way.
Rapid Reading	• This is usually done quickly, but can be at any desired rate as long as you understand the meaning.
Study Rate	• Read slowly to gain information, follow directions, or respond to questions.

I learned from the feature that there are different ways to read the words on a page. I want to read some materials quickly to get the main idea. I may even skip over words that don't seem important. At other times, I want to slow down and read information carefully so I understand the details. I should use this slow style—the study rate—to read directions so I understand what I'm supposed to do. I'll use this style to read the activity on the next page.

Think It Through

During Reading

1. As you read, summarize the characteristics of traditional First Nations worldviews. Traditional worldviews are those that existed before contact with Europeans. Some contemporary First Nations people continue to hold some or all of these beliefs.

This activity asks me to summarize, so I'll use chunking. As I learned on page 7, this technique results in a summary statement. The directions don't ask for sentences, so I think I'll use point form.

When I chunk, I divide the material I'm reading into sections. How can I figure out what to use as a chunk? When I scan pages 8 and 9, I see there are four subheadings: *Spirituality, Individual Choice, Natural World*, and *Community*. Each of these subheadings seems to be a separate topic, so each will be one of my chunks.

Spirituality

In traditional First Nations cultures, worldviews were rooted in **spirituality**. Spirituality is a person's sense of his or her place in the universe. This place includes a relationship to a higher power, such as God or the Creator.

Traditional First Nations spirituality often included a belief that everything in the world has two connected parts: physical and spiritual. To live well, humans must live in harmony with both parts. All actions and decisions must keep the physical and spiritual parts in balance.

For example, most First Nations cultures had a tradition of thanking the spirit of anything they used from the earth. This included animals that were killed for food and land that provided a crop or useful plant.

Therefore, even though a person might take from the physical world by killing an animal or picking a plant, they gave to the spiritual world through their thanks. The give and take maintained balance.

The section about spirituality includes several ideas, but my activity directions ask me to summarize. This means I'll have to leave out the details. I'll try to write one idea that seems the best.

- Spirituality: belief that everything in world has spiritual AND physical parts that need to be kept in balance

I think this note is the best I can do. When I read it, I'll remember the interesting details, such as the idea that First Nations people help keep balance through traditions that give thanks.

Individual Choice

Many traditional First Nations worldviews included the belief that the Creator has a purpose for everyone. This belief meant traditional communities respected all their members. Each person was seen as part of the Creator's plan. Groups encouraged individuals to fit in with the community and its goals. However, they accepted each person's right to disagree. Even children could make their own choices and live with the consequences.

Natural World

Many traditional worldviews included the idea that the natural world's relationship with humans is like a mother and her children. Nature is not to be conquered or controlled. Instead, Mother Earth should be respected and honoured.

One way humans can show respect is by taking only as much from the natural world as they need. This maintains a balance between human needs and the needs of other parts of existence. For example, although the traditions of most First Nations include trapping and hunting animals, traditional worldviews ensure that people do so with respect.

Many First Nations people believed their prey willingly gave its life so the hunter's family and community could survive. No one hunted for sport or extra possessions. To do so would show disrespect for the animal's gift of life.

Community

In traditional worldviews, most First Nations stressed the importance of the community. People relied on one another to take care of their day-to-day needs. Communities shared the work and the results of that work. Sharing ensured that everyone survived. Each person in a community had something to contribute and all contributions were valued.

After Reading

1. Arrange your notes in a graphic organizer.

The directions don't tell me what kind of organizer to use, so I'll make my own. I want to remember that each of these chunks describes one part of First Nations worldviews, so I should put worldview at the centre. To help me remember that worldview means how a person sees the world, I'm going to make the circle a person's head.

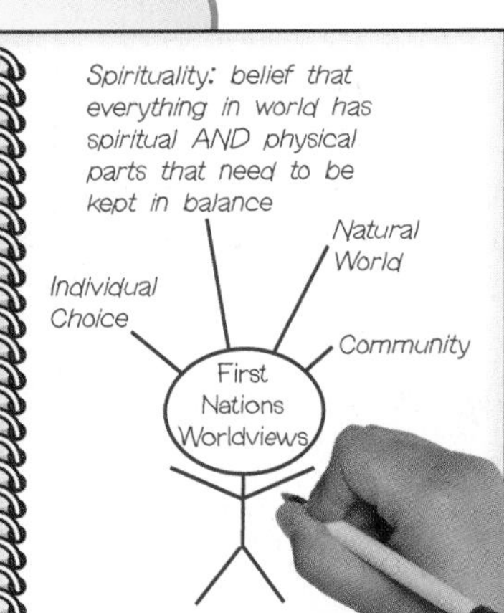

First Nations worldviews are traditionally taught through the group's oral tradition. An oral tradition is the collection of a people's knowledge, history, and culture. This information passes from older generations to younger generations through the spoken word.

Comparing First Nations and European Worldviews

Before Reading

1. With a partner, discuss how you would feel if strangers told you they now owned your home and you would have to live under a new set of rules.

The sixteenth and seventeenth centuries (1500s and 1600s) in European history are referred to as the Age of Discovery. During that time, new knowledge and technology allowed more Europeans to travel greater distances. They began to make regular contact with people from other continents. In particular, monarchs in Europe wanted more regular trade with China. It was the source of valuable spices, silk, and other treasures. However, the overland route to China was dangerous and expensive.

European monarchs paid explorers to find a better route to Asia. Some went south and east. Those who went north or west, across the Atlantic Ocean, reached a land that was previously unknown to them. There they met people who had ways of life that differed significantly from that of the Europeans.

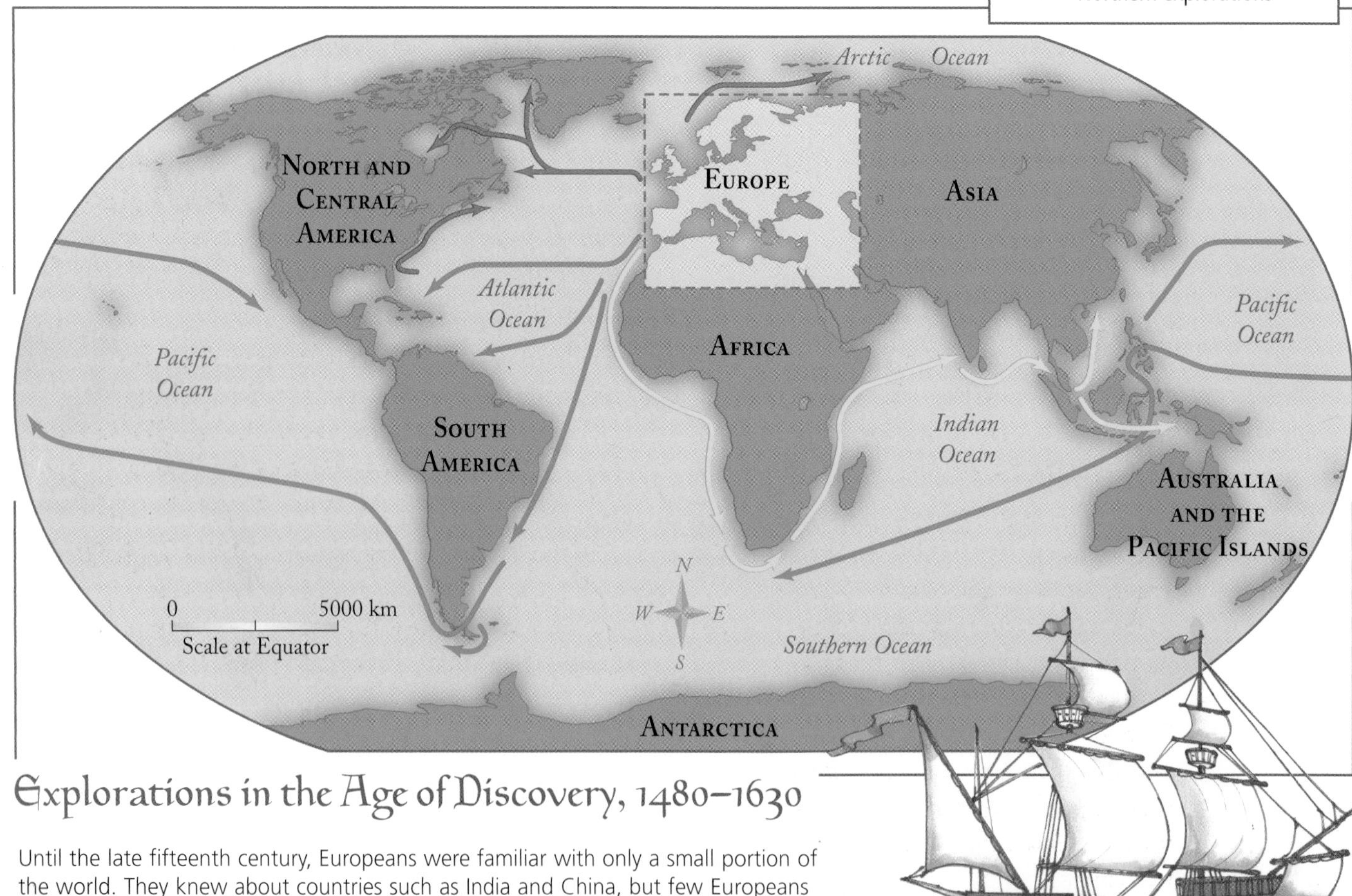

Explorations in the Age of Discovery, 1480–1630

Until the late fifteenth century, Europeans were familiar with only a small portion of the world. They knew about countries such as India and China, but few Europeans had visited them. Europeans did not know Australia and the Americas even existed.

During the Age of Discovery, European knowledge and territory expanded rapidly. Many Europeans saw this expansion as proof that their ways of life were superior. Some concluded that it was their right to conquer and rule other lands and people. Pages 10–13 compare key aspects of European worldviews during this time with those of First Nations of the time.

During Reading

1. As you read each comparison on pages 11–13, write a sentence describing your own point of view, or perspective, on the topic. For example, *Religion (or spirituality) plays...role in my life because...*

Religion

Religious beliefs played a prominent role in the lives of Europeans in the sixteenth century. France's dominant religion, the Roman Catholic Church, was particularly influential. It played a role in all of the country's major institutions.

The Church placed high value on **converting** people to the Catholic Church. This meant convincing people to adopt Roman Catholicism as their own faith. From the Church's perspective, converting people was one of the best ways of serving God.

Religion is different from the spiritual beliefs that were central to First Nations worldviews. Spirituality is learned and explored over the course of people's lives. Each person is challenged to find his or her own path. In contrast, religions tend to follow sets of written principles. The challenge for individuals is to learn and live according to their religion's teachings.

Land

In Europe, land was a measure of wealth and power. The goal of countries and individuals was to claim and control as much territory as possible. When European explorers reached new areas, they typically planted their nation's flag in the ground and claimed all they saw for their home country.

This concept of land ownership was not part of First Nations' worldviews. For First Nations people, Mother Earth could not be owned or given away. Even a **treaty**, which could seal nations' agreement to share the *use* of the land, could never give *ownership* of the land.

Compare and Contrast

In studying history, you will often be asked to compare and contrast.

To compare is to assess the points of similarity and the points of difference between two or more topics or ideas. Words and phrases indicating a comparison is being made include *on the other hand, similarly, either...or*, and *however.*

To contrast is to make a special kind of comparison. A contrast highlights points of difference between whatever is being compared. Key words indicating a contrast include *as opposed to, neither...nor*, and *unlike.*

Many graphic organizers, such as T-charts and Venn Diagrams, can help you make comparisons. You will learn to use these and many other types of organizers in this textbook.

Social Structure

Europe had a **hierarchical** class structure, which means some people in society were seen as more important than other people. In a hierarchy, more important groups are viewed as higher in status than others in the society. Individuals from higher-status groups can often control the actions of those from lower-status groups.

According to European worldviews at that time, it was natural for some people to be superior to others. The purpose of life for the lower classes was to serve those above them. This gave the higher classes more time to advance their country's wealth, art, scientific knowledge, and territory.

At the top of the hierarchy were **absolute monarchs**. These were kings or queens who did not have to consult with others. They could, and often did, make laws without considering the laws' effects on major parts of the population. They had absolute, or total, control over their subjects.

In contrast, in First Nations groups, many people played a role in the decisions that affected their communities. Leaders often negotiated a **consensus** as a way of making decisions. A consensus is an agreement that best addresses all points of view. People reach a consensus through discussion.

Feudal European Social Structure

Absolute Monarch
- rules the country
- receives support from the nobles

Nobles and Church Leaders
- control most of the land
- serve the monarchy

Freemen and Freewomen
- work for wages as farmers and skilled craftspeople
- have the freedom to move to find work

Serfs
- farm the nobles' land
- have little freedom to move or change their lives

- What is the relationship between the number of people in a social class and that class's power in society?
- How does this diagram show the most powerful and least powerful classes?

Traditional First Nations Decision Making

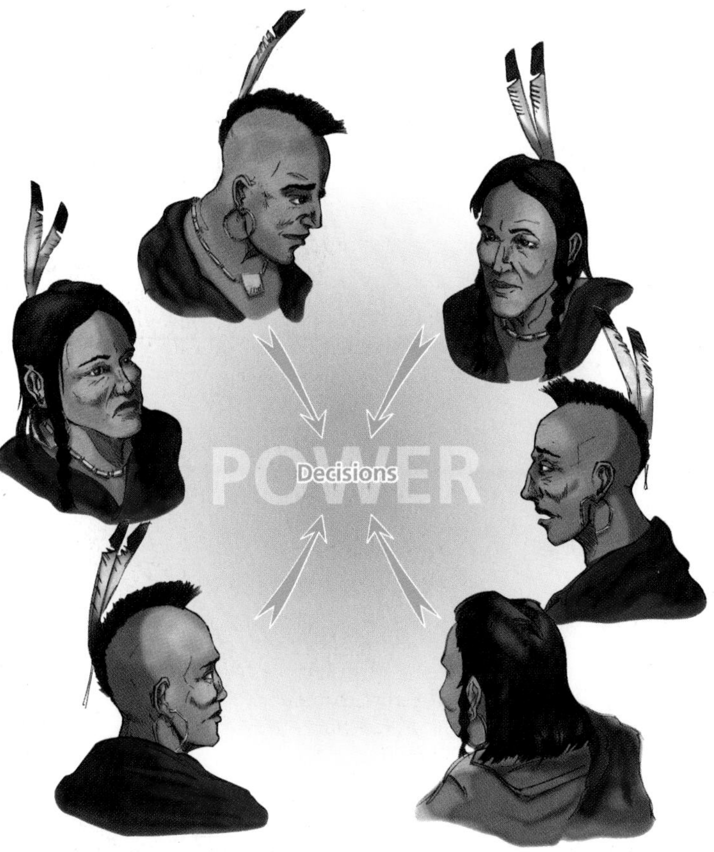

- How does this diagram show who has the power to make decisions in traditional First Nations communities? How does this system compare to the one shown in the diagram on page 12?

Economic Differences

In traditional First Nations communities, people lived as others in their community. When times were good, everyone thrived. When times were hard, all suffered.

In contrast, some Europeans lived in great luxury, while the vast majority barely survived. Those lower in the social hierarchy had few supports. For example, people who got sick or lost their jobs had to depend on family or their church to help them. Those high in the social hierarchy sometimes saw the suffering of those below them as proof of their inferiority. They did not feel a responsibility to share their own wealth to ensure everyone around them survived.

Note-Making Skills

As you may have experienced, people tend to quickly forget what they have heard or read. Good note-making skills will help you understand and remember important information. Most of the best note-making techniques use a combination of headings and questions. In this textbook, you will learn several ways to take notes. After trying and practising these approaches, you might create your own technique.

Tips for Note-Making

- Read for a purpose. Be clear about what information you need.
- Use chapter and section headings to organize your notes.
- Use jot-notes, or point form, not complete sentences. Set off each point with a dash or a dot.
- Use keywords and phrases from what you read, but make notes in your own words. Put any direct quotations in quotation marks and include the page number for future reference.
- Use your own shorthand and symbols such as arrows.

After Reading

1. A T-chart can help you organize your notes. It is especially useful when you want to contrast two ideas. In your notebook, draw a T-chart like the one below. Use the information on pages 6–9 and 10–13 to fill in points on each side.

First Nations Worldviews	European Worldviews

2. Why is a T-chart useful when you want to contrast ideas? How else might you organize contrasting ideas? Share your thoughts with a partner.

Early European Contact with First Nations People

Before Reading

1. What are some potential problems when people with different worldviews come into contact? Consider how First Nations and European attitudes towards land ownership differed in the sixteenth century. Discuss as a class.

In the late fifteenth century, explorers Christopher Columbus and Giovanni Caboto (or John Cabot, as he was known in England) made voyages across the Atlantic Ocean. Monarchs from Spain and England sponsored their trips. Both explorers set out to find a route to Asia. Instead, they found a new source of wealth.

Spanish ships returned with gold and silver treasure from Central and South America. Farther north, Cabot told England about the rich cod fisheries in the Grand Banks just off the shores of Newfoundland. Fish was in high demand in Europe and was another source of wealth. With Spain and England reporting these riches, it did not take long before the king of France decided he had to sponsor a voyage as well.

A Meeting at Stadacona

In 1534, Jacques Cartier made his first of three voyages to North America. He became the first European known to have sailed into the St. Lawrence River. There he made contact with Mi'kmaq (mig-mah) and Haudenosaunee (hoh-den-oh-shoh-nee) people. (In other resources, you may sometimes see the Mi'kmaq people called Micmac and the Haudenosaunee people called the Iroquois.)

In the Gulf of St. Lawrence and Gaspé Peninsula region, he met a group of Haudenosaunee from a village called Stadacona, close to the present site of Québec. After a brief visit, Cartier returned to France. Without consent, he took the two sons of Chief Donnacona (do-na-koo-nuh), Stadacona's leader.

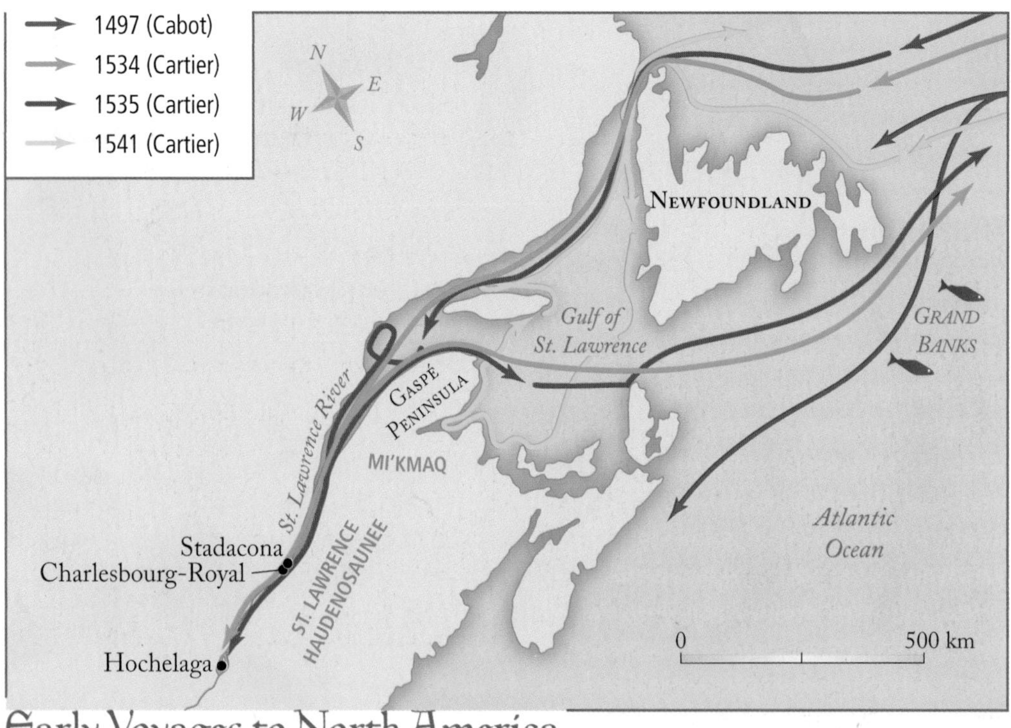

Early Voyages to North America

During Reading

1. People sometimes look at the actions of people of the past and suggest that what they did does not make sense. They might wonder, *How could they do that?* or think, *I wouldn't have let them do that to me!* Take a moment to recall what worldview means and how First Nations and European worldviews differed at this time. The fictional passages that follow represent what might have been going through the minds of Jacques Cartier and Chief Donnacona during their early encounters. Are these primary or secondary sources of information? If you are not sure, review pages xi–xii of the Introduction.
2. Working with a partner, read each passage aloud. Each partner should read one role and then discuss how these passages represent the worldview of each person. Use your notes from pages 6–13 to help you.

I look around me and see nothing but wilderness waiting to be tamed! I claim this land for my country and am pleased I got here before our rivals, England and Spain. As I raise this cross with the fleur-de-lys, symbol of France and my king, I hope these new lands will bring wealth to my country. The people of this land tell us of riches in the distance.

These people are eager to trade for our metal goods and give excellent furs in return. Yet, they are clearly not Christians. I can only improve their lives by introducing them to the only true faith and the benefits of European civilization. It is God's will that I found them.

Jacques Cartier

Jacques Cartier at Gaspé, by Charles Walter Simpson, 1927. On July 24, 1534, Jacques Cartier claimed the Gaspé Peninsula in the name of King François I of France, even though First Nations had lived there for generations.

Who is this man who raises a wooden pole on the land of our ancestors? I don't see him giving proper thanks to the spirit of this place.

His behaviour is offensive, but then his people have many strange ways. They seem harsh, even among each other. Their leader speaks sharply to the men who are with him and they seem to just follow his orders. Can none of them think for themselves?

However, they have interesting goods to trade and seem content with the furs we give in return. Their leader is pleased and excited by stories of gold and jewels, so we tell him many.

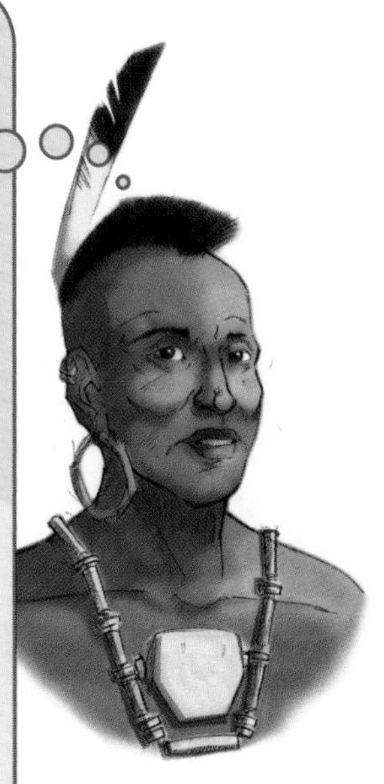

Chief Donnacona

Cartier's Second Voyage

Cartier returned to Canada in 1535. He was guided to Stadacona by Domagaya (doo-mag-u-yuh) and Taignoagny (tag-nog-nee), Donnacona's sons. While in France, the boys had learned to speak French and could now be interpreters for Donnacona and Cartier.

Donnacona tried to prevent the French from sailing farther up the St. Lawrence, but Cartier disregarded his wishes. He was sure that a route to China could be found upriver. Cartier reached the village of Hochelaga, which is the site of present-day Montréal, and then returned to Stadacona.

The Europeans built a small fort and experienced their first Canadian winter. Most of Cartier's men were too weak to work because of **scurvy**, a disease caused by a lack of fruits and vegetables. The Haudenosaunee had a cure for this disease, called *annedda*. It was made by boiling the bark and needles of certain trees. This produced a bad-tasting but nutritious drink that was high in vitamin C.

In the spring, Cartier returned to France. This time he kidnapped Donnacona and nine other people from the First Nation, including four children.

I have returned to Stadacona with the two boys. They have proved to be good interpreters and guides and I feel they must have benefited from their time in France. Chief Donnacona seems hostile about our plans for exploration. He probably wants to keep the riches for himself.

I must return to France with evidence of wealth. Otherwise, my king might not give funds for another voyage. I will probably have to bring the chief himself to convince the king. We all must make sacrifices for the greater glory of France.

Jacques Cartier

I am pleased my sons have returned to our land, but I can no longer trust that man from across the sea. He has no regard for our customs. Why didn't he leave two of his men with our people when he took my sons? I would have then been assured of his good intentions.

Instead, it seems his intention is only to offend. We discouraged him from travelling farther up the river, but he ignored our wishes. He seems to have no regard for the spirits and yet he expects our help. Despite my misgivings, we shared our medicine with the Europeans to cure their sickness. We could not watch them suffer when Mother Earth provides a cure for the disease.

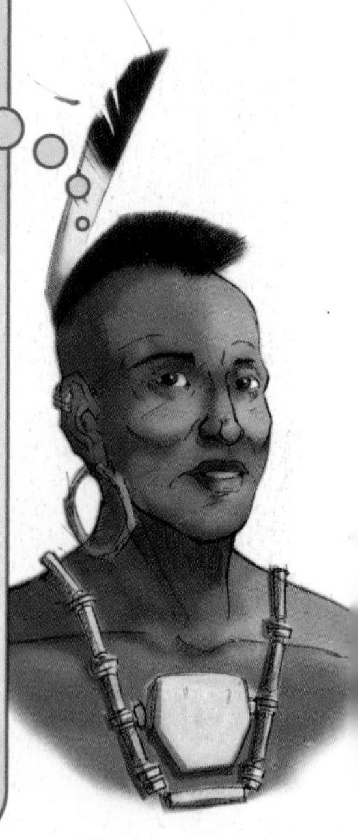

Chief Donnacona

Cartier's Third Voyage

Cartier did not make his third voyage to North America until 1541. All but one of those he had kidnapped five years earlier had died in France. This time, Cartier wanted to establish a settlement. He built Charlesbourg-Royal at the mouth of the Rivière du Cap-Rouge, 14 kilometres from Stadacona. It was the first French settlement in North America.

Stadacona had a new chief, named Agona (a-goh-nuh), who was not pleased about the return of the Europeans. To the Haudenosaunee, the European visits had caused enough trouble. When the French showed signs of staying, the Haudenosaunee launched a number of raids to convince them they were not welcome.

The First Prescription in Canada, 1536, by C. W. Jefferys, around 1942. First Nations people often shared their knowledge of local plants to help European explorers and settlers when they became ill. In this painting, Cartier is being shown the cure for scurvy.

In the spring of 1542, Cartier returned to France with what he thought was a load of diamonds and gold. However, the cargo was only quartz and iron pyrite, also known as fool's gold. France lost interest in further voyages to Canada. By 1543, Charlesbourg-Royal was abandoned.

Writing in Role and Role-Play

An interesting way of showing you understand history is to play the role of a person who took part in or observed a historical event. To do this, you pretend to be a person of the time, showing the thoughts and feelings of that person about what he or she sees or experiences.

Writing in role means you write something from the perspective of the person whose identity you have adopted. Common forms of writing in role include letters to another person or a newspaper, newspaper editorials, and journal entries.

A role-play allows you to represent this person through action and word. Common forms of role-play include debates and dramatic presentations.

Writing or acting in a play both depend on similar preparation:

- accurate historical research
- thoughtful analysis of the motives and viewpoints of the character you have been assigned

The key is to capture the person's situation and feelings, while remaining historically accurate.

After Reading

1. Write a passage that shows Cartier or Agona's thoughts after Cartier's third voyage. Look at the examples on pages 15–16 to guide your work.

Reasons for European Contact with North America

Before Reading

1. What reasons might people have for leaving their home country for another?
2. What challenges would you predict people faced when they decided to leave France for another continent in the 1600s? (At that time, there were few books and no telephones or Internet to provide information.) Share your thoughts with a partner.
3. Why did Europeans come to North America? To answer this question quickly, scan the subheadings on pages 18–19. Do any of the reasons surprise you? Explain.

Pages 18 and 19 discuss four of the most common reasons for travelling to New France in the sixteenth century.

Fishing

In 1497 and 1498, John Cabot became the first European to explore Newfoundland's rich cod fisheries. By 1550, more than 400 ships and 12 000 people came every year to fish the Grand Banks. The ships were from Britain, Portugal, Spain, and France. While some Europeans rarely landed while fishing, the French had cod fishing operations in the Gaspé Peninsula area, as well as in the areas now known as New Brunswick, Nova Scotia, and Newfoundland.

Furs

The driving motivation for many Europeans to come to New France was fur, especially beaver pelts. Before the arrival of the Europeans, it is estimated that there were over 10 million beaver in North America. Between 1600 and 1900, the animal was hunted almost to extinction. Today, there are healthy beaver populations across Canada.

I have followed the path of my father and his father before him. We have always lived by the sea and harvested the fish. This time, I've travelled farther than ever before. I have never spent such a long time at sea. I've heard stories of this place where fish leap right into your ship! While those stories were an exaggeration, the fish here are certainly plentiful. My arms hurt from the effort of pulling in the catch. This is tiring work. Risky, too. There are many accidents on the ship, so I have to be careful. When the ship is full, we pull ashore, clean the cod, place them on a drying rack in a building, then we set out for more. I think this is better than the way of my father—he had to gut and salt the cod on the ship. Just imagine the smell!

Pierre (pee-yair)

I decided to leave my home for a chance to travel and have some adventure. I had heard of an opportunity to make a fortune catching beaver. Sounds good to me! I wonder how you catch a beaver. Do they bite? Luckily, I have a new gun. I'll shoot them if they try to get me. I was talking to a man who has been to New France before and he laughed at me when I told him about my gun. I wonder why?

George (zhor-zhe)

During Reading

1. Which person would you have rather been, Pierre or George? Why?
2. On pages 18–19, some paragraphs are background information on the topic and others are fictional journal entries from the perspective of someone at the time. How can you tell them apart? How does the information in the journal entries compare to the other information on the page? Check your ideas with those of a partner.

Religion

A major reason for Europeans to come to North America was **missionary** work. Missionaries want to convert people to their own faith. Many missionaries from the Roman Catholic Church came to New France in order to convert First Nations people to Christianity.

Employment

By the middle of the seventeenth century, France had decided to settle more people in North America. The growing **colony** needed labourers, carpenters, masons, and domestic servants. This prompted a new group of arrivals: the **engagés**, or hired men. Most engagés were about twenty years old and looking for a chance to get a better life than they had in France.

Indentured servants were the largest group of these immigrants. Indentured servants had their passage to North America paid by someone for whom they were to work in the new land. Indentured servants were free once they had worked for their employer long enough to repay the fee.

I pray every day for these people's souls and for the success of our mission. The people are friendly enough, but I don't think they are prepared to change their ways. They say, "We have our way of doing things and you have yours." Our task could take time. I believe God sent us here for this purpose, but we are tested every day. Even the mosquitoes seem designed to test our faith.

André (on-dray)

I am looking forward to my new life. They call people like me a "trente-six-mois" because I have signed a contract for thirty-six months. I received some of my wages before I left, which I gave to my father for safekeeping. In my new home, I will get food, clothing, and a place to live. This means I will not be a burden to my family. I'm not sure if I will stay longer than thirty-six months. If I decide not to, the man who signed me up has to pay my way back to France. But maybe I'll find some land of my own and decide to stay. I'm excited. It seems like my life has more potential now than it had when I was in France.

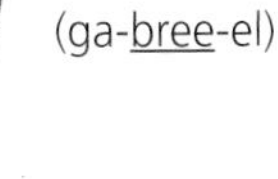
Gabriel (ga-bree-el)

After Reading

1. Write a journal entry from the perspective of a parent or friend of one of the people on pages 18–19. Include your concerns and hopes for your son/friend.

The First French Settlements in North America

Before Reading

1. With a partner, discuss your typical day, starting with waking up and ending with going to bed. What aspects would you expect to be different from and similar to those of a person your age living in the seventeenth century?

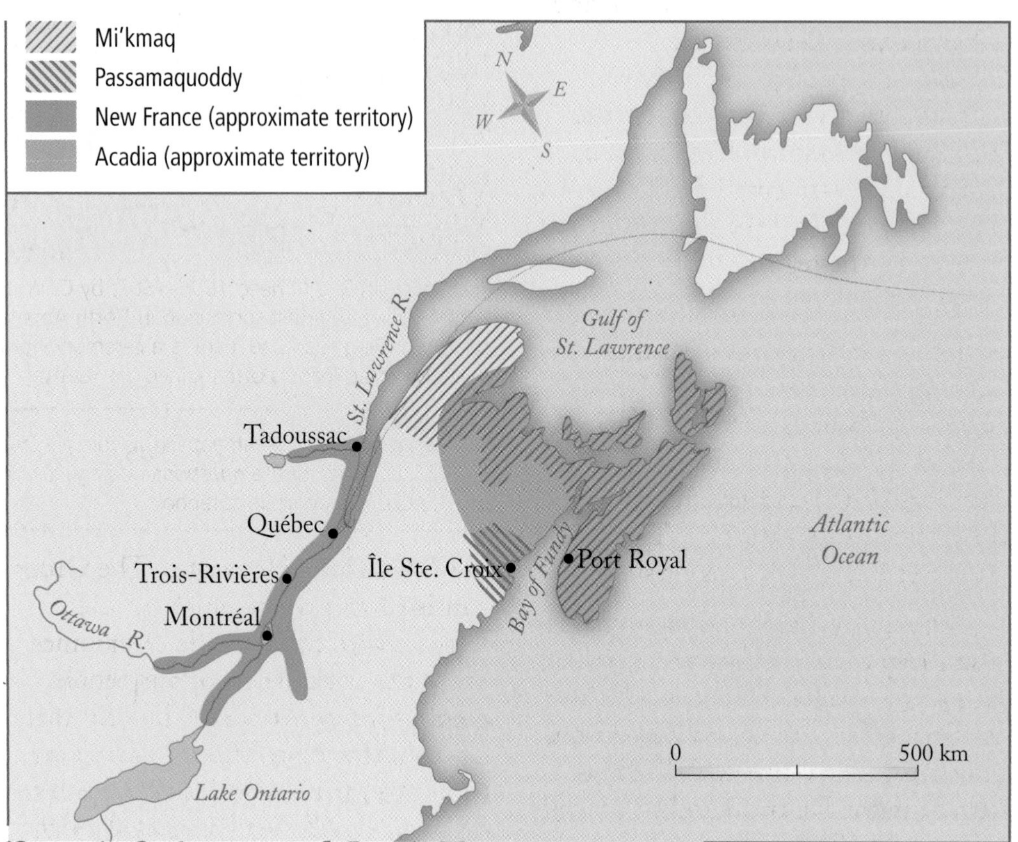

French Colonies in North America, 1649

After the failure of Charlesbourg-Royal, France did not try to establish a colony in North America until the early seventeenth century. Even then, building settlements in New France was slow and difficult. The French government wanted the settlements to maintain its claim to the land. However, settlers sometimes had different ideas. Many pursued their own economic goals, rather than the king's political plans.

During Reading

1. Prepare a T-chart as follows in your notebook. You will use it to take notes for pages 20–23.

Important	Interesting

   a) Before you begin taking notes, think about which reading techniques you will use for this activity. Review page 7 if you would like ideas. Discuss your plan with a partner.
   b) For each of the settlements under discussion, note at least one point you consider important and one point you consider an interesting detail.

Île Ste. Croix

In 1603, Pierre Du Gua de Monts (dew goo-a de mon) received permission to establish a settlement in North America. He became lieutenant general of the "coasts, lands and confines of Acadia, Canada, and other places in New France." He was supposed to settle sixty colonists each year and convert the local First Nations to Catholicism. In return, he was granted a **monopoly**. This meant he had the exclusive right to trade in the region.

In 1604, de Monts set out to establish a settlement in Acadia. This territory is now part of Nova Scotia and New Brunswick. Explorer Samuel de Champlain (sa-myoo-el de sham-playn) and seventy-nine other men came with him. They chose Île Ste. Croix as their site.

They chose the island partly because it was easy to defend. However, the site lacked fresh water and firewood. During the first winter, the men suffered from scurvy and thirty-five died. Without help from the Passamaquoddy (pa-zim-a-kwah-dee) First Nation, more would have perished. In the summer, the settlers moved to a better location, which they named Port Royal (now Annapolis Royal, Nova Scotia).

Port Royal

The settlers who survived the winter at Île Ste. Croix had better luck at Port Royal, which was established in the summer of 1605. Port Royal prospered for several years. The settlers had good relations with local Mi'kmaq people and traded with them for furs.

However, life in Port Royal was often lonely. During the winter of 1606–1607, Samuel de Champlain formed the Ordre de Bon Temps (Order of Good Cheer) to fight the men's boredom. He wrote, "The Order consisted of a chain which we used to place with certain little ceremonies about the neck of one of our people, commissioning [sending] him for that day to go hunting. The next day it was conferred [given] upon another, and so on in order. All vied [competed] with each other to see who could do the best, and bring back the finest game."

The Order of Good Cheer, 1606–1607, by C. W. Jefferys, 1925. The order was the first social club in North America. Members took turns providing food and leading a ceremonial procession to the meal. Mi'kmaq leaders often joined the feasts.

- What information can you learn from this painting? Answer at least three of the questions on page xiv of the Introduction in your notebook.

In the meantime, de Monts had returned to France. His business was in trouble. Other merchants were jealous of de Monts' monopoly and asked the king to end it. In 1607, the king did as they asked. De Monts' monopoly was revoked and most settlers returned home.

During Reading

1. This page includes a primary source quotation. Find it. What makes it a primary source?
2. What do the words *commissioning* and *conferred* mean? If you are not sure, reread page xv of the Introduction for a hint.

Québec

In 1608, Samuel de Champlain founded the settlement that became the city of Québec. The site had once been Stadacona, the Haudenosaunee village visited by Jacques Cartier. Now it lay abandoned. No one is sure why the Haudenosaunee left. Climate change, warfare, or illnesses brought during Cartier's visit may be to blame.

Champlain believed it would be an excellent location for the fur trade. The site gave easy access to the interior down the St. Lawrence River. He also hoped to continue to search for a route to China.

The site was also good for settlers. Acadia could be reached by travelling down the Chaudière River. Québec settlers could keep in touch with those in Acadia. In addition, the surrounding land was fairly level. Champlain believed it would make good farmland.

As with other early settlements, the first winter was difficult. Settlers had a hard time establishing themselves. Many did not make it to spring.

Louis Hébert (loo-wee ay-bear) was one of the first successful European colonists in North America. He was born in Paris around 1575 and trained in medical arts and science. In 1604, he was the ship's doctor on one of Samuel de Champlain's voyages. He travelled to North America two more times and finally decided to settle in Québec. In 1617, Hébert's wife, Marie Rollet (ma-ree roh-lay), joined him and became the first French woman to live in New France.

By 1627, there were eighty French people living in Québec. Of these, only five were women and six were girls.

Louis Hébert Sowing, by A. C. Hébert, 1918. Louis Hébert was the first person to plant wheat in North America. In addition to providing most of Québec's food from his farm, Hébert was the colony's doctor, chief magistrate, and the first French judicial officer. He died in 1627, after a fall.

- Based on what you see in this illustration, what challenges did farmers in New France face?

Champlain tried to attract more settlers, but fur-trading merchants resisted his efforts. They were afraid clearing the land for farming would make it harder to find beaver to trap.

Cardinal Richelieu (ree-sha-lee-uh) was especially concerned about slow settlement growth. Richelieu was a powerful official in King Louis XIII's court. He wanted large numbers of settlers in New France to protect France's claim to the land.

Richelieu founded the Company of 100 Associates in 1627 and gave them a monopoly over the fur trade in New France. In return, Richelieu hoped the company would bring settlers to New France.

Ville-Marie (Montréal)

Paul de Chomedey de Maisonneuve (pol de shum-day de may-zoh-nuh-ve) and Jeanne Mance (zhawn-ne mon-se) founded Ville-Marie (soon known as Montréal) in 1642. It was located at the abandoned site of Hochelaga, a Haudenosaunee settlement that had also been visited by Cartier. Wealthy people in France donated money to build a mission and hospital at the site. Although Montréal began as a mission, the fur trade soon became a significant focus of the settlement.

Located where the St. Lawrence and Ottawa Rivers meet, Montréal was an ideal trading centre. Montréal eventually dominated the profitable western fur trade.

However, in its early years, the settlement's population grew slowly. By 1653, it had 100 settlers. By the end of the seventeenth century, it had barely 1000.

Ville-Marie in 1642, by J. Armstrong, around 1886.

- Notice the tipis surrounding the log building. How do you explain their presence? Note that the First Nations in the Montréal region did not live in tipis and Europeans had not yet made contact with western First Nations in 1642.

I haven't had much success in this new land. We barely made it through the winter last year. Was I ever glad when spring finally arrived. Local First Nations people showed us which berries and plants can be eaten safely. Without their help, I think we might have died.

The winters are unbelievably cold. I wouldn't have thought that people could even survive such weather. The snow is almost a metre deep in some places! We have to strap on these things called snowshoes to walk around without sinking to our hips. Even in the spring, sometimes everything was frozen when I went out in the morning to start my chores.

We're pretty isolated at the farm where I work. Our nearest neighbour is a long way away and it takes days to get any news. Our last news wasn't good. We heard that one of our neighbours was attacked by a group of Haudenosaunee. His farm is near a fur trade route. The British think our farms help the French government take over their trade, so they encourage their partners, the Haudenosaunee, to attack us. How ridiculous! As if we have time to worry about what the French government wants! I'm scared that we might be attacked, too.

I did not imagine this kind of life when I left my family last year. I wonder if they miss me.

Gabriel

After Reading

1. Write a journal entry in the role of a French settler at Île Ste. Croix, Port Royal, Québec, or Montréal. Consider writing as a farmer, engagé, member of the Order of Good Cheer, missionary, or as one of the few women in New France.

Cooperation in the Fur Trade

Before Reading

1. Make a list of objects you value. Examine your list closely, placing an F beside those items that are part of current trends or are considered fashionable.
2. Explain to a partner how having these goods improves some aspect of your life.

For thousands of years, First Nations had encountered one another as they followed seasonal patterns. These encounters often included an exchange of news, ideas, and goods. Trade provided useful items and built relationships between different nations. It was natural for First Nations to extend these traditions to European newcomers.

Europeans who came to North America to fish found people eager to trade. Trade gradually became a more significant part of fishing trips. In the early 1600s, when the French decided to establish a colony in North America, it was the fur trade, not fish, that was their main goal.

Sharing Knowledge and Trade Goods

In the early stages of the fur trade, both French and First Nations benefited.

Early settlers relied on First Nations for basic survival. They needed to learn what to eat, what to plant and when, what medicines could be obtained from plants, what to wear, and how to get around.

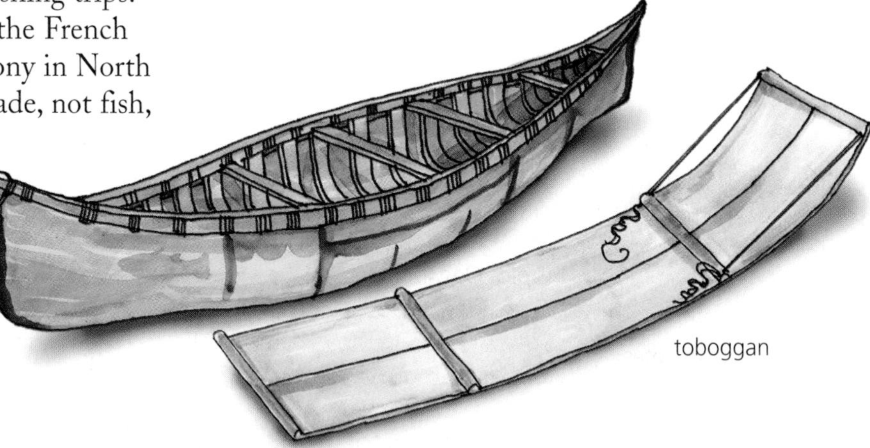

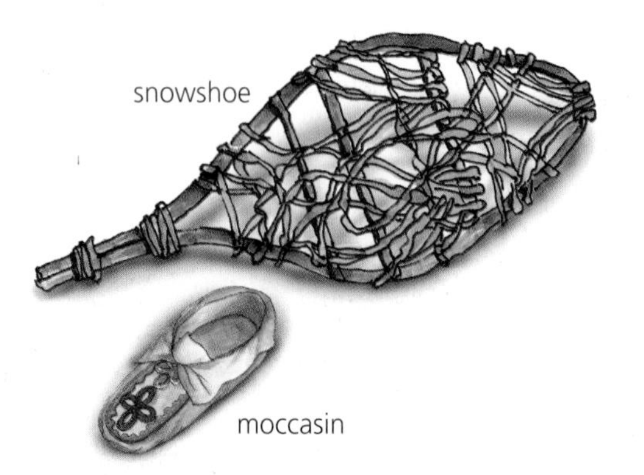

These illustrations show some of the plants and technology First Nations shared with Europeans.

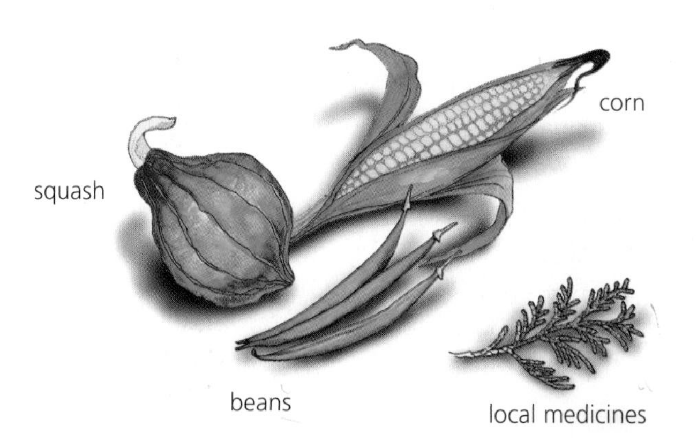

The fur trade depended on the cooperation of First Nations. Only First Nations had the skills and technology to trap, prepare, and transport the large number of furs wanted by Europeans.

For First Nations people, metal goods, such as pots and knives, were the most prized trade items. Their technology did not include the smelting of iron ore, so they valued the European tools, which made many tasks easier. Other European goods, such as beads, added variety to traditional decorative work.

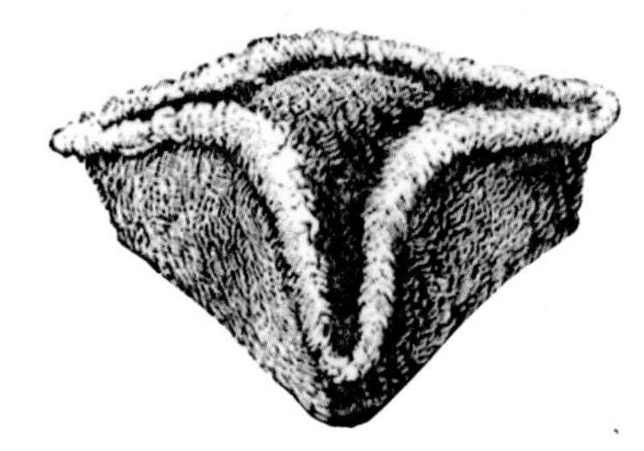

The most prized fur was the beaver pelt. It was used in Europe to make fashionable hats. The two styles shown here are the Continental (on the left) and the D'Orsay (on the right). The best pelts were those that had the long outer hairs removed. First Nations people wore the fur next to their skin to rub the long hairs off over time.

Split-Page Note-Making

Split-page notes are one of the most common and useful systems for taking notes. To make these notes, set up a page in your notebook according to the model that follows.

Your teacher might give you the topic. If not, you might use the heading from the pages you read.

Date of your work

Page references help you look back if you need clarification.

Topic: *Cooperation in the Fur Trade* **Date:** *September 21, 2006*

Page References: pages 24–27

Organize your notes with the headings and subheadings from the reading. If you prefer, create questions to guide your reading. Place these headings/questions on the left side of the page, leaving space between each heading for a response.

Main Ideas	Details
Sharing Knowledge	- *medicines (e.g., cure for scurvy)* - *new foods (e.g., squash, beans, corn)* - *clothing (e.g., moccasins)* - *transportation methods (e.g., canoe, toboggan, snowshoes)*
Trade Goods	- *French received furs* - *First Nations received European trade goods, such as metal pots and beads*

Write point-form notes for each heading or question on the right-hand side of the page.

Split the page of your notebook with a vertical line.

Questions

- *What did French emigrants to New France bring with them to survive?*

List new words and questions at the bottom of the page. These questions can be raised in a class discussion or you might seek help from a classmate or your teacher.

During Reading

1. Use the split-page note-making technique described on page 25 to take notes on pages 26–27. Your topic is *Cooperation in the Fur Trade*.

Middlemen

As the fur trade became increasingly profitable, more First Nations became involved. It became hard to find beaver around European settlements. First Nations had to travel farther to find animals to trap. The Europeans had discovered that the best furs came from farther north, since colder temperatures produce a thicker, richer pelt. They encouraged their trading partners to get furs from other First Nations to the north.

First Nations who had once traded furs with the Europeans became **middlemen**. Middlemen did not trap to obtain the furs for trade. Instead, middlemen traded with other First Nations for their furs and then negotiated with the Europeans.

Coureurs de Bois

The French recognized the importance of First Nations in the fur trade and made efforts to adopt First Nations trading traditions. In order to learn of these traditions and build relationships, the French sent some of their people to live with First Nations.

In 1610, Champlain exchanged Étienne Brûlé (ay-tee-n broo-lay) for a young Ouendat (owen-dah) man, who Champlain called Savignon (sa-vee-nyon). (The Ouendat people are sometimes called the Huron in other books.) Each man learned the ways of the other's people. Their knowledge helped make the trading process easier.

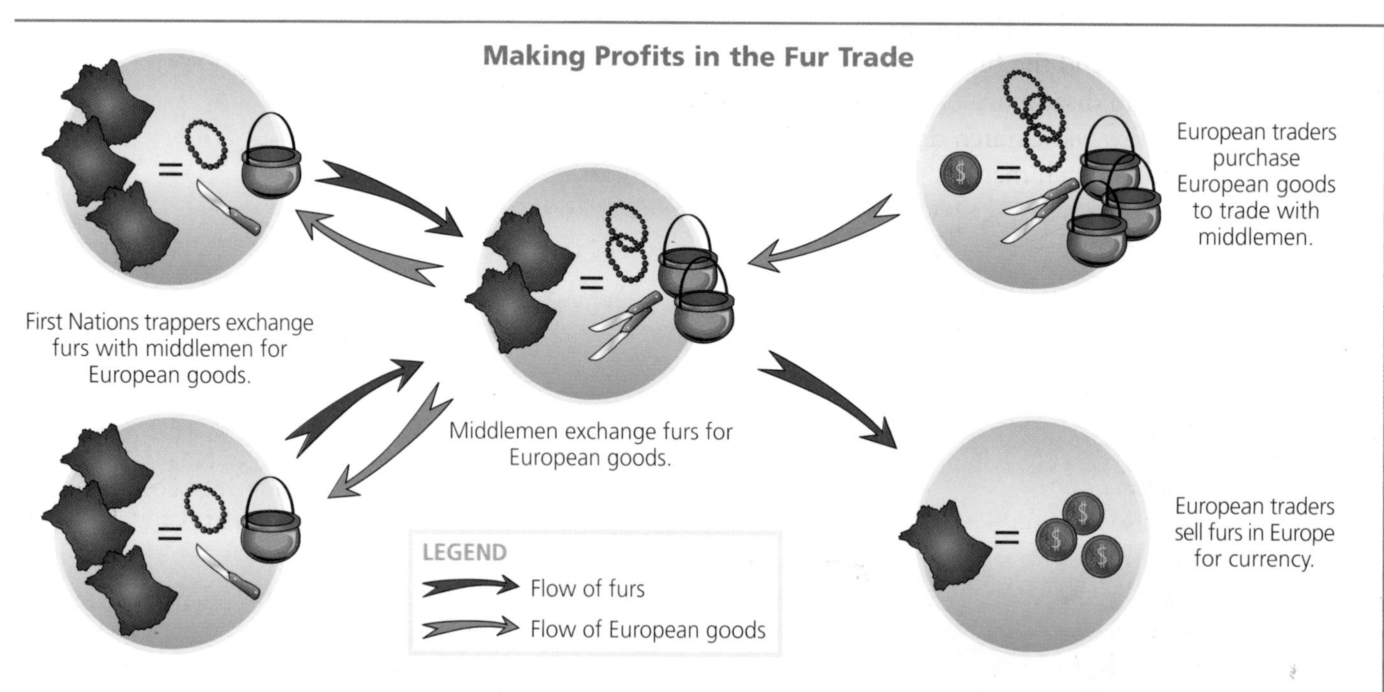

The middleman role was profitable. A **profit** is made in an exchange of goods or money if a person receives more than they gave in the exchange.

- Based on this diagram, who makes the most profits in the fur trade? Who makes the least profits?

Coureurs de bois were known for their strength and endurance. They often paddled for more than twelve hours a day for many months at a time. When they reached rapids or had to travel by land to reach the next water route, they carried their canoes and trade goods on their backs. This was called a **portage**, shown here in an engraving done by S. Bradshaw in 1841.

As time passed, more young men from the French settlements went to live among and trade with the First Nations. They became known as **coureurs de bois**, a term that literally means "runners of the woods."

Many coureurs de bois left New France in search of profit and adventure. The Roman Catholic Church and the fur-trading companies came to disapprove of the coureurs de bois. The Church did not like seeing young French men leaving the watchful eye of the priest. Fur-trading companies objected because the coureurs de bois tended to be highly independent. The companies could not always be sure the coureurs de bois worked in the companies' best interests.

Despite these objections, the coureurs de bois helped build relationships between the French and First Nations trading partners. They learned and adopted First Nations ways of life. They often lived and travelled with First Nations groups for months or years at a time.

Many coureurs de bois married First Nations women. The children of these partnerships were at first raised as either Europeans or First Nations people. By the eighteenth century, many were raised with a combination of both cultures and worldviews. It was these children who became the **Métis** (may-tee), a nation of people with a distinct culture of their own.

The coureurs de bois were also responsible for much European exploration beyond New France. For example, Étienne Brûlé was the first European to explore what is now southern Ontario and the Great Lakes region.

After Reading

1. Reread your split-page notes. Clarify anything that is unclear by rereading the text, or asking a partner or your teacher. If you have questions or find vocabulary you do not understand, find the answers before moving on.
2. What do you like best about split-page notes? What do you dislike?
3. Using your notes, identify four examples of how First Nations and Europeans cooperated in the fur trade.

The Impact of the Fur Trade on First Nations

Before Reading

1. From what you have read so far, how did the fur trade cause Europeans and First Nations to interact in positive ways? Discuss your ideas with a partner.

Competition and Conflict

The fur trade was a valuable industry. All groups involved wanted to protect or expand their share of it. Therefore, while France was trying to establish a colony along the St. Lawrence River, Britain and Holland were establishing their own colonies to the south.

Although most First Nations had peaceful relationships with one another, sometimes conflict occurred. Across the continent, certain groups had long-standing rivalries. This was the case with the Ouendat and the Algonquian-speaking (al-gong-kwin) First Nations, who lived north of the St. Lawrence and the Great Lakes. They had a traditional rivalry with the Haudenosaunee who lived to the south.

The Europeans also had traditional rivalries. Competition with one another was one of the reasons why countries wanted to establish colonies in North America.

During Reading

1. How did the fur trade start to cause problems for First Nations? Make this question the topic for a set of split-page notes. Use the subheadings on pages 28–29 as topics down the left-hand side of the page.

Each European colony formed alliances with First Nations. The French formed a partnership with the Ouendat and the Algonquian-speaking First Nations, while the Dutch and the British made alliances with the Haudenosaunee. The French had the early advantage in the fur trade because they had closer access to the high-quality northern furs.

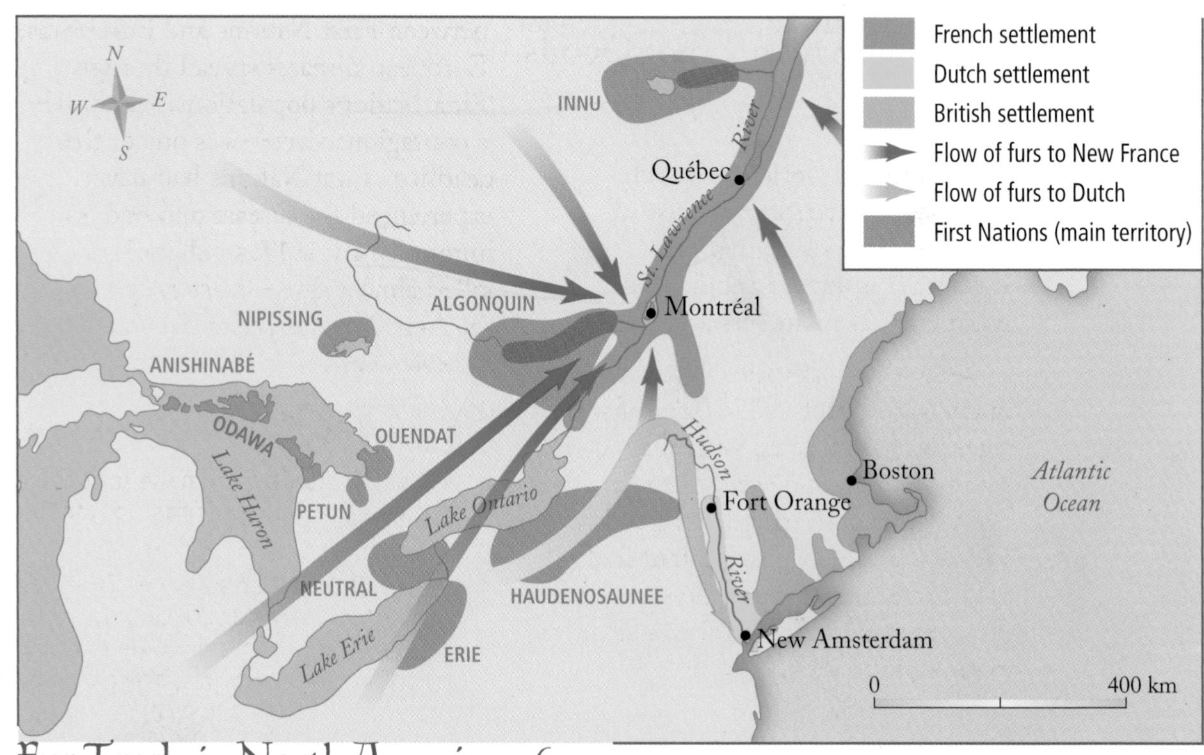

Fur Trade in North America, 1649

Dependence on Trade Goods

At first, First Nations just added European trade goods to their traditional ways of life. The goods were extras that made many day-to-day tasks easier.

However, as the fur trade grew, European goods became more common. In some groups, people began to see them as necessities. Fewer people took the time to make their own weapons and tools. More First Nations depended on European technology. Trapping for trade became a main occupation, instead of a small part of a group's activities.

European trade goods, such as metal pots, kettles, and guns, were highly valued trade items.

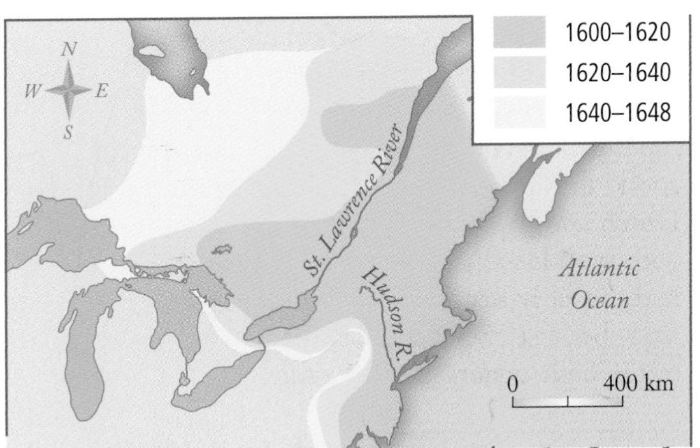

Territory Where European Trade Goods Were Common

Traditional worldviews, such as those that valued careful use of resources, were changing. The Europeans rewarded people who could trade as many furs as possible.

Some First Nations acquired many trade goods. This form of wealth sometimes conflicted with their traditional worldviews. For most First Nations, sharing extra goods had always been an important part of community support. However, the fur trade encouraged individuals to work for themselves.

Some European trade goods had especially destructive effects. Firearms made conflict between groups more deadly. Alcohol disrupted the families, cultures, and health of many of the people who received it in trade. Few people at the time considered the long-term consequences of such trade goods.

Deadly Epidemics

Soon after the first contact between First Nations and Europeans, European diseases spread through First Nations populations. **Smallpox**—a contagious virus—was one of the deadliest. First Nations had never experienced the disease and had no immunity. By 1617, smallpox had killed almost three-quarters of the First Nations population on the east coast.

After Reading

1. Which problems from the fur trade do you think were the most significant for the First Nations? Share your ideas with the class.
2. Use your notes from pages 26–27 and 28–29 to create a story map, or pictorial summary, of the progression of the fur trade from cooperation to conflict. Include one drawing for each main topic.

Missionaries among the Ouendat

Before Reading

1. In a small group, discuss how religion or spirituality can influence a person's worldview.

Ouendake (owen-du-gee) was located in present-day Ontario, near Lake Huron. Called Huronia by the French, the land was home to the Ouendat First Nations. They lived in villages, fished, and grew corn, beans, and squash. They were also skilled traders who exchanged goods with nations to the north and south.

In 1615, the first missionaries arrived in Ouendake. They were of the Franciscan Récollet (ray-koh-lay) order. The Récollets wanted First Nations people to give up their traditional ways of life, move to Québec, and convert to Catholicism. They assumed the Ouendat would welcome the opportunity.

However, few people accepted the offer and the Récollets made little progress in their mission. In 1625, the Récollets invited some Jesuit (zhe-zuit) priests to build missions in New France. By 1629, the Jesuits had taken over the Récollets' work in Ouendake.

During Reading

1. Why do you think the Ouendat resisted the Récollets' efforts to convert them? Discuss this question in a group.

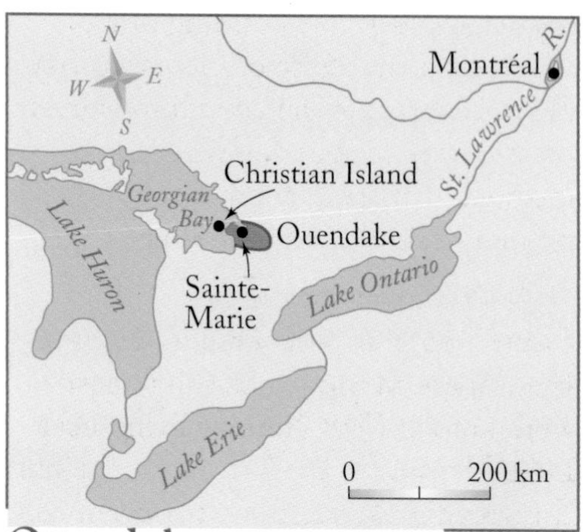

Ouendake, 1639–1649

The Jesuits Welcomed by the Récollets, 1625, by C. W. Jefferys, 1916. Because of the colour of the priests' long cassocks, First Nations called the missionaries "Black Robes." In this illustration, a group of Jesuit priests disembark in North America.

Sainte-Marie among the Hurons (Ouendat)

In 1639, Father Jérôme Lalemant (zhay-rohm la-le-mawn), leader of the Jesuits, oversaw the building of a mission on the shore of Georgian Bay. Sainte-Marie among the Hurons (near present-day Midland, Ontario) included a chapel, storehouses, residences, and other buildings.

The missionaries used Sainte-Marie as their base in the area. From there they pursued missionary work among First Nations living near Lake Huron. Sainte-Marie was the first European settlement in what eventually became Ontario. Lalemant hoped it would be the centre of a thriving Ouendat Christian community.

The main purpose of the mission was to convert First Nations people to Catholicism. However, many missionaries also did some trading. Profits from the fur trade helped the priests support their missionary work. The fur trade also helped the priests build relationships with the Ouendat people.

Like the Récollets, the Jesuits were sometimes disappointed in the results of their efforts. Some Ouendat only converted in order to increase their trade with the French. Some people converted, but continued their spiritual traditions. This frustrated the Jesuits. They wanted the Ouendat to give up their traditional beliefs completely. Instead, many Ouendat adopted only the Catholic traditions that fit within their worldview. They rejected anything that conflicted with traditional beliefs.

Like most Europeans at the time, the missionaries did not understand First Nations spirituality. Spiritual traditions are part of every aspect of life. Traditional spirituality involves how people hunt, cook, harvest food, govern communities, and pray. People could not abandon their spiritual traditions without abandoning their whole way of life. Few Ouendat and other First Nations wanted to do this.

The differences between the Jesuit and the First Nations worldviews meant the Jesuit goal of conversion was difficult to achieve. Priests and First Nations people struggled to understand one another.

Sainte-Marie on the Wye, by C. W. Jefferys (1869–1951). At its peak in 1648, Sainte-Marie was home to nineteen priests working in the surrounding region.

During Reading

1. *The Jesuit Relations* are a series of reports written by Jesuit priests living in New France between 1610 and 1791. Two excerpts from a translation of *The Jesuit Relations* are found below. As you read, think about the challenges the writers are describing. Do any surprise you? Explain your answers in your journal.
2. Prepare a T-chart. On one side, identify the challenges the Jesuits faced in their missionary work. On the other side, imagine some of the challenges First Nations might have experienced in dealing with the missionaries' efforts.
3. How do the challenges described by the Jesuits point out some of the differences between First Nations spirituality and European religion? Share your observations with your group.

PRIMARY SOURCE 1.1

From The Jesuit Relations, 1634–1636, translated by Reuben Gold Thwaites

I say nothing of the long and wearisome silence to which one is reduced, I mean in the case of the newcomers, who have, for the time, no person in their company who speaks their own tongue, and who do not understand that of the First Nations.* Now these difficulties, since they are the usual ones, were common to us as to all those who come into this Country. But on our journey we all had to encounter difficulties which were unusual. The first was that we were compelled to paddle continually, just as much as the First Nations people; so that I had not the leisure to recite my Breviary [religious teachings] except when I lay down to sleep, when I had more need of rest than of work. The other was that we had to carry our packages at the portages, which was as laborious for us as it was new, and still more for others than it was for me, who already knew a little what it is to be fatigued. At every portage I had to make at least four trips, the others had scarcely fewer. I had once before made the journey to the Ouendat, but I did not then ply [use] the paddles, nor carry burdens; nor did the other Religious who made the same journey....

But in this journey, we all had to begin by these experiences to bear the Cross that Our Lord presents to us for his honor, and for the salvation of these poor people. In truth, I was sometimes so weary that the body could do no more, but at the same time my soul experienced very deep peace.

*Note: Jesuit writing reflects the European worldview of their time. This includes the use of terms for First Nations that many people now consider offensive. Out of respect for First Nations people today, historical quotations in this textbook have been changed to reflect today's preferred terms. Words or phrases changed from the original are indicated in grey type.

PRIMARY SOURCE 1.2

From The Jesuit Relations, 1639, translated by Reuben Gold Thwaites

Every day we hear some who tell us that our doctrine [belief system] is good, but that its practice is difficult.... The young people do not think that they can persevere [go on] in the state of matrimony [marriage] with a bad wife or a bad husband; they wish to be free and to be able to divorce the consort [husband or wife] if they do not love each other. Such are the chief outward impediments [obstacles] we have encountered in the performance of our duties.

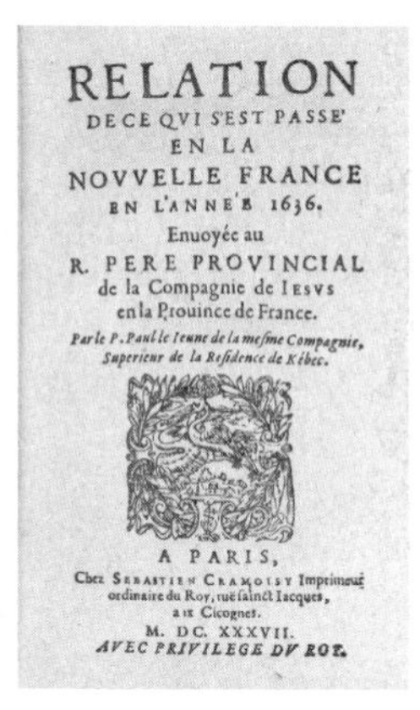
RELATION
DE CE QVI S'EST PASSE'
EN LA
NOVVELLE FRANCE
EN L'ANNE'E 1636.
Enuoyée au
R. PERE PROVINCIAL
de la Compagnie de IESVS
en la Prouince de France.
Par le P. Paul le Ieune de la mesme Compagnie, Superieur de la Residence de Kébec.
A PARIS,
Chez SEBASTIEN CRAMOISY Imprimeur ordinaire du Roy, ruë sainct Iacques, aux Cicognes.
M. DC. XXXVII.
AVEC PRIVILEGE DV ROY.

People reading *The Jesuit Relations* in France became excited about missionary work and donated money to help. Today, *The Jesuit Relations* are an important primary resource for historians who want to understand this period in history.

Destruction of the Ouendat People

By the late 1640s, conflict in the fur trade had reached a crisis. The Ouendat and Jesuits struggled against constant Haudenosaunee raids. The Haudenosaunee were well armed. Their Dutch and British allies readily traded guns for furs. In contrast, few Ouendat had firearms because the French only traded guns to people who converted. The French policy had unintended but deadly consequences.

In addition, disease had weakened the Ouendat. Between 1634 and 1640, about half of the Ouendat population died of European diseases such as smallpox.

Six priests and two other Europeans died during their service at the Jesuit mission in Ouendake. Today, they are collectively known as the Canadian Martyrs. This banner honours their sacrifice.

In 1649, the Jesuits were forced to flee Sainte-Marie from a Haudenosaunee attack. As they left the mission, they burnt it to the ground behind them. They did not want the Haudenosaunee to damage any sacred objects or buildings. Many of the mission's residents escaped to Christian Island in Georgian Bay. They were joined by Ouendat refugees. They formed a new mission called Sainte-Marie II. All struggled through the difficult winter that followed.

In the spring of 1650, the Jesuits moved their missionary work to Québec. Around 300 Ouendat people settled near Québec, at Loretteville. The rest joined the Haudenosaunee or other First Nations groups. The war was over, but the once-powerful Ouendat people had been destroyed.

View of Jeune Lorette, the Village of the Hurons, Nine Miles North of Québec, by Frederick Christian Lewis (1779–1856). The area is still home to many of the descendants of the Ouendat who settled there in 1650.

After Reading

1. Based on what you have read, work with a group to draw a conclusion about the relationship between the missionaries and First Nations. You could use the following sentence starters:
   a) I now realize...
   b) The evidence that supports my thinking is...

The Role of Religion in New France

Before Reading

1. Your provincial government determines what you will learn in school. What other groups have had this role in the past? As a class, discuss why you think the government has this role today.

Along with their missionary work, the Roman Catholic Church had many other roles in New France. These responsibilities included education, building hospitals, and caring for orphans or other people in need of help.

National Gallery of Canada, Ottawa/#16648

Harvest Festival, by William Bent Berczy, around 1840–1850. Throughout New France, the Church was the heart of communities.

- How does this painting show the importance of the Church in the lives of people in New France?

Education

After the collapse of Ouendake, the Jesuits focused on educating the children of colonists. They taught Latin, mathematics, and basic reading skills. The Jesuits opened the first school for the sons of colonists in 1635. By 1653, they had sixteen students.

What were schools like at that time? There were no desks. Students sat on long benches without a back. Religious symbols covered the walls. A lecture stand at the front of the class held the one book used for reading. Only the teacher could turn the pages. A few pens, ink, and paper were imported from France to enable students to practise the alphabet.

The Church also recruited **lay teachers**. Lay teachers were people who knew a little more than others. They were not clergy members and were not formally trained as teachers, but were asked to travel through the country, teaching students along the way. Some took a few students into their home. Teachers needed the local priest's promise that he would be responsible for their conduct. Teachers also had to promise to instruct only children of their own gender.

Girls had few opportunities to attend school. The little education that was offered was primarily for boys. In 1639, at the request of the Jesuits, Marie de l'Incarnation (de lin-car-na-see-on) and a group of Ursuline (ur-siew-lin) nuns founded a Québec school for girls, which was first located in an empty stable. Both French and First Nations girls were welcome.

Marie de l'Incarnation devoted her life to the task of educating young French and First Nations girls in New France. She also wrote about religious matters and put together Algonquian and Haudenosaunee dictionaries.

In 1653, Marguerite Bourgeoys (mar-gu-rit boor-zwa) opened a school for First Nations girls in Montréal. She opened another for the colonists' children. The schools taught mainly domestic skills and religion.

The Venerable Mother Marie de l'Incarnation, First Superior of the Ursulines of New France, by Jean Edelinck, 1677. After reading about the Jesuits' work in North America, Marie de l'Incarnation joined the Ursuline nuns.

During Reading

1. Why might the nuns welcome First Nations girls to their school?
2. Why do you think nuns became attracted to work in New France? Why do you think many spent the rest of their lives in New France, even in the face of the dangers and hard work they found there?
3. The following fictional journal entry captures the experiences of a young colonist. Compare the educational opportunities he describes to your own opportunities.

Since our arrival in New France nearly two years ago, I have not had a single moment of freedom to write in my diary. I can hardly find the time to write because there are trees to cut down, bush to clear, and land to be cultivated; I must also help my mother, who has to take care of my sisters and brother. Today, I am returning to my travel diary so I don't forget these past years. We are living on the farm of the Jesuits, at Notre-Dame-des-Anges. We are happy, although we have lost our good Monsieur de Champlain, who died two years ago on Christmas Day in 1635.

The contract my father signed stated that I would have to work with him to build a house for the workers and the missionaries. The Jesuits preferred educating me. I am still not working. I am going to the Collège de Québec, where the first lessons were given in the fall of 1635. I am part of a group of fewer than ten boys, French and Ouendat, who follow classes there. We are taught mainly religion, but arithmetic and Latin should soon be part of our curriculum.

I am lucky to have been chosen by the missionaries to go to the college. It is the only school in the country. As in France, most boys and girls here do not go to school and don't know how to read and write. They are only taught how to sign their own name. However, they learn a trade, such as woodworking or carpentry. Some of them become apprentices at seven years of age. There is still no school for the girls, but one should open soon.

Françis
(fran-sis)

Hospitals

In 1639, a group of Augustine nuns from the Hospitallers of the Miséricorde de Jésus (mi-zay-ri-kord de zhay-zoo) established Hôtel-Dieu de Québec (hoh-tel dyew de kay-bek). Hôtel-Dieu, meaning "hotel of God," was the name given to all hospitals established by religious groups. Most were funded by wealthy people in France. Two later arrivals furthered the nuns' work at the hospital: Catherine de St.-Augustin (kat-rin de sayn o-gus-tin), a missionary, and Michel Sarrazin (mee-shel sa-ra-zin), a doctor. They helped the hospital achieve a remarkable success rate: nine out of ten patients survived.

The purpose of the Hôtel-Dieu de Québec was to care for the sick, especially among the First Nations. At the time, a smallpox epidemic was killing thousands of First Nations people.

The nuns had many medical skills. They were both nurses and apothecaries, which are like pharmacists. They made medicines, gave anaesthetics, and used scalpels and dental instruments.

Jeanne Mance helped establish the Hôtel-Dieu de Montréal in the 1640s. Although she began treating patients as early as 1642, a proper hospital was not built until 1645. Many patients were those wounded during fur trade conflicts with the Haudenosaunee.

Hôtel-Dieu de Montréal was moved in 1861 from old Montréal to its present site in Mount Royal. Jeanne Mance is honoured with this statue outside the current site.

After Reading

1. Prepare an Important/Interesting T-chart to show how the Roman Catholic Church affected the lives of people in New France. Turn to page 20 to see how to set up your chart.

Compress

1. Prepare a chart comparing how the following factors influenced First Nations people and early French settlers in New France:
   a) environment
   b) religion
   c) fur trade
   d) interaction with people who have a different culture and worldview
2. Draw a picture of early New France that represents the major European goals in coming to North America and the major challenges experienced by settlers. If you prefer, write a detailed description of what your drawing would look like or use a graphic organizer to present your information.
3. Review the timeline on pages 2–3. In your notebook, copy the events from the timeline that were covered in this chapter. Next, review the chapter to add other events and dates that you think are significant. Review page xvi if you need more information about the purpose of a timeline.

Express

4. Assume you are one of the few young people who can read and write in seventeenth-century New France. Write a journal entry focusing on one of the factors listed in question 1.
5. Make up a story about one of the events in this chapter. Include details that transport your listener or reader to the place and time you are describing. Consider using a real person, such as Marie de l'Incarnation or Samuel de Champlain, in your tale. How do you think the person would have felt about the events in your story? Help your listener or reader see the events from this person's eyes.

Their Stories, Our History

What are your personal feelings about furs and the fur industry today? What do your ideas say about your own worldview? What has influenced your point of view?

Compare your ideas about trapping animals with those of First Nations people and Europeans in the sixteenth and seventeenth centuries.

To do this, consider your options for clothing and making a living compared to those of a person in the sixteenth and seventeenth centuries. How do your options influence your point of view? How might your family's ancestry and cultural traditions influence your ideas? Write your answers in your journal.

Journal

chapter 2
New France under Royal Government

- What is happening in the painting?
- What questions do you have as you look at this painting?

The Arrival of the French Girls at Québec, 1667, by C. W. Jefferys (1869–1951).

- What do you assume about a person who is the subject of a statue?
- What characteristics make a person a hero or great leader?
- Do you think your criteria for a hero or great leader are the same as your parents' criteria? Why or why not? Write your ideas in your journal and keep them for a class discussion later in the chapter.

Louis de Buade, Compte de Frontenac (de boo-ad, kon-te de front-nak), Governor of New France. Statue by Louis-Philippe Hébert (1850–1917), on the National Assembly, Québec.

By 1663, the French government decided that New France could no longer remain under the control of fur-trading monopolies. Under France's policy of **mercantilism**, French colonies were to increase France's wealth and power. To do this, New France was supposed to supply a steady stream of raw materials to French industry. Its population was also supposed to purchase goods manufactured in France. At the beginning of the 1660s, New France was doing neither. The colony continued to be more of a burden than a benefit.

France had given the Company of 100 Associates control of New France in 1627, but the company was not especially interested in settling the land. There were no profits in bringing more people to New France and setting them up as farmers. Agriculture sometimes even interfered with the fur trade by keeping people near their farms instead of travelling to trade for furs.

The French monarch, Louis XIV, decided that if New France was to benefit its mother country, he and his ministers would have to take charge. In 1663, the king brought New France under **Royal Government**. Royal Government is one in which a monarch has control.

Royal Government changed three main aspects of life in New France: the structure of government, the system for granting land, and the way the colony was to be settled. These changes had long-lasting effects. Over the next century, the foundations of contemporary Québec would be set.

This chapter will help you understand

- the way the structure of government changed in New France after 1663
- how Royal Government affected New France
- how the seigneurial system worked
- the influence of the seigneurial system on New France
- how Jean Talon (zhawn ta-lun) encouraged colonization in New France
- how the Roman Catholic Church influenced life in New France

Featured Skills

- Reading Maps
- Identifying Main Ideas
- Learning from Historical Fiction
- Holding a Mock Trial
- Forming Questions

The Structure of Royal Government

Before Reading

1. Imagine that you are a partner in a fur-trading company in New France. Rank the importance of the goals that follow:
   a) bringing settlers to New France to farm
   b) expanding French territory
   c) being on good terms with First Nations people
2. If you were the king of France, how might you rank the previous items differently? Discuss your answers as a class.

The Company of 100 Associates had controlled New France since 1627. By 1660, the population of New France was less than 3000 French people. The fur-trading company had failed to develop the colony.

In 1663, King Louis XIV decided to take control. He put Royal Government in place, which was modelled after the way provinces in France were run. In this system, government in New France would be firmly controlled by the monarch and his key advisors in France.

During Reading

1. Compare the chart on this page with the diagram on page 41. Imagine you are a settler in New France. Who in the government do you think would be the most important person in your life? Explain your answer.
2. What other information would you need in order to understand who had the most power?

Positions in Royal Government

Position	How Position Obtained	Duties
Minister of the Marine	Appointed by the king	• In charge of finance, colonies, and maritime affairs
Governor *(member of the Sovereign Council)*	Appointed by the king	• In charge of the colony's relations with other European colonies and First Nations in North America, as well as the defence of the colony
Bishop *(member of the Sovereign Council)*	Appointed by the king and the pope	• Responsible for religious affairs in the colony, such as education, hospitals, and missionary work
Intendant *(member of the Sovereign Council)*	Appointed by the king	• Responsible for settlement, justice, and economic development (fisheries, agriculture, taxation, and the construction of government buildings and roads)
Sovereign Council *Note: The Sovereign Council was led by the bishop, intendant, and governor.*	Appointed by the governor and bishop until 1675, when the king decided to make these appointments	• Made laws for the colony and offered a final court of appeal in criminal and civil cases
Captains of **Militia** (local leaders of a civilian military force)	Appointed by the governor	• Communicated orders from the governor and the intendant to the people

The Structure of Royal Government

In France

King
King Louis XIV was known as the "Sun King." He believed so completely in his right to rule that he compared his place in the world to the place of the sun in the universe.

Minister of the Marine
Jean-Baptiste Colbert (zhawn-ba-tees-te kul-bear) became Minister of the Marine in 1669. He pursued France's policy of mercantilism for many years.

In New France

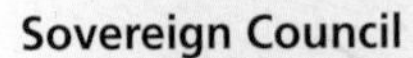

Sovereign Council
The Council included the bishop, intendant, governor and up to twelve other councilors.

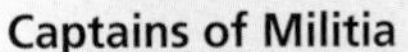

Captains of Militia
In New France, every man between ages sixteen and sixty had to be a member of the militia. Militia captains were not paid, but had high status in the community.

Settlers
Settlers had few ways to influence their government. The Captains of Militia offered a limited way to make their concerns known to those in authority.

- When you look at diagrams like this one, who do you believe is the most powerful person? Why?

After Reading

1. From the perspective of a farmer or another ordinary citizen in New France, create a diagram that ranks the importance of the positions in Royal Government. Compare your diagram to the one on this page and explain any differences.
2. King Louis XIV and most of his closest advisors never visited New France. What problems might have resulted from not being in the country they governed?

The Seigneurial System in New France

Before Reading

1. What can a map represent better than words can? With a partner, discuss the steps you would take to read the maps on page 43.

As in France, the king owned all land in New France. He granted use of large amounts of land to important citizens, such as wealthy merchants and retired military officers. In New France, these landholders were called **seigneurs**. Their land grants were called seigneuries. The seigneurs' main jobs were to promote settlement on their land and increase the amount of food produced by farms.

The seigneurs allowed settlers called **habitants** to farm small plots of land on the seigneuries. In return, the habitants paid their seigneur a number of fees. These included a yearly rental payment and fees to use the seigneur's mill to grind their wheat. Many habitants also worked a few days on the section of land the seigneur kept for his own use. Unlike France, in New France, habitants could eventually own their plot of land.

The long, narrow lots that make up individual farms on the seigneuries had many benefits:

- They ensured that more farms had access to the river or road.
- They permitted settlement that connected each farm to its neighbours.
- They shared land of different types, such as river front, cliffs, valleys, and plateaus.
- They were adaptable to farms of different sizes and irregular river fronts.

Reading Maps

Maps provide information, just as sentences and paragraphs do. As you learned on page xvi of the Introduction, maps show information related to geography and the environment. To read a map, start by locating each of the features listed below.

Features of Maps

- **Title**: often gives the map's main idea
- **Date**: shows the period the map represents
- **Legend**: explains the meaning of the symbols or colours used on the map
- **Map scale**: shows relative distance
- **Compass**: shows direction

Try to connect the information on the map to the topic under discussion.

During Reading

1. Work with a partner to find evidence in the maps on page 43 showing the benefits of the seigneurial system's farm arrangement.

Farms in Québec still reflect the seigneurial system's lot shape.

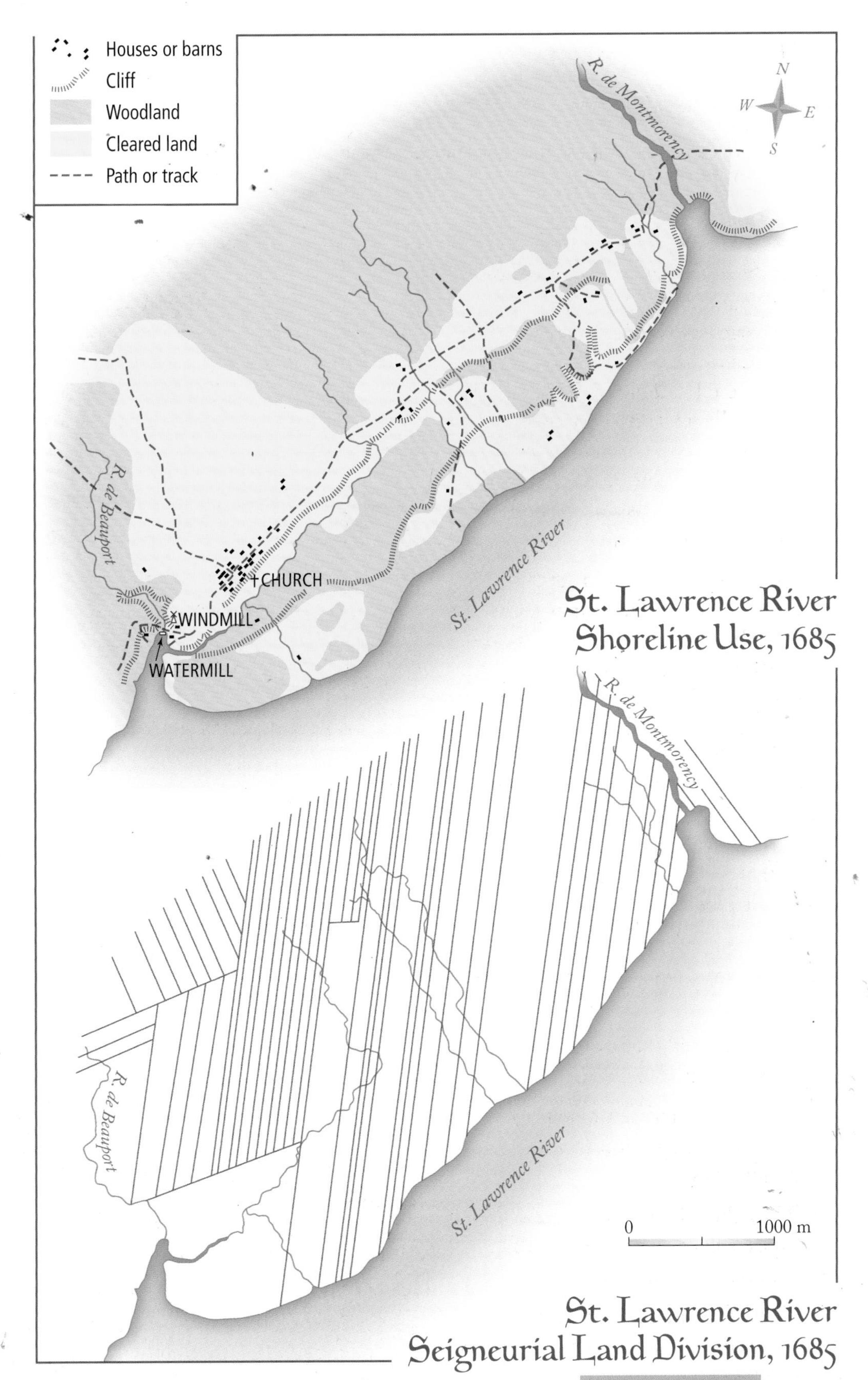

St. Lawrence River Shoreline Use, 1685

St. Lawrence River Seigneurial Land Division, 1685

After Reading

1. How would the seigneurial system's lot shape be helpful if a war suddenly broke out? Explain.

Think It Through

The Problems Facing Jean Talon

Before Reading

1. What problems could New France face with the fur trade as its main economic activity? Discuss as a class.

Jean Talon hoped to make New France a strong and independent colony.

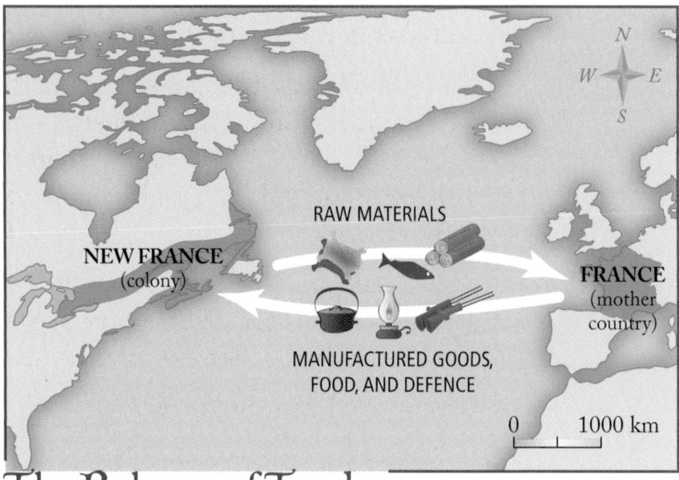

The Balance of Trade under Mercantilism, 1663

Under mercantilism, colonies existed to benefit their mother countries. Colonies were supposed to send inexpensive raw materials, such as lumber, fish, minerals, and fur, to the mother country. The mother country turned the raw materials into manufactured goods. These goods were then sold to the colonies at a great profit. New France had never been profitable because its population grew so slowly and it cost so much to defend.

Jean Talon was appointed as the first intendant of New France. He served from 1665 to 1668 and then again from 1670 to 1672. When he first arrived, he found the colony's economy in trouble. New France's fur trade had been crippled by the destruction of the Ouendat nations in 1660. Without their middlemen allies, the colony could not ship many furs to France. This also meant the colony could not afford to purchase goods from France. Much had to change and Jean Talon was ready to make change happen.

During Reading

1. Identify the main idea of each section on pages 47–49: *Settlement and Land Use, Expand the Economy, Defence*, and *Population*.
2. How did the problem described in each section affect New France's economy?

Identifying Main Ideas

When you are asked to state in your own words what you have read, you are being asked to reduce the information to the most important idea. The ability to do this shows you understand the material. It also makes it easier to remember what you need to know.

To identify the main idea, first skim the text for visual clues. Look at the title, subheadings, illustrations, maps, graphs, and any questions. Quickly read the first and last sentences of a few paragraphs. Look for bolded words. These may be important terms that will help you understand the reading.

Next, read the text again—this time for more detail. It is a good idea to have some questions in mind as you read. You do not have to answer all these questions, but they can guide your reading and give it some focus.

Sample Guiding Questions to Identify Main Ideas

- What or who is this reading about?
- Where and when is something happening?
- Are two or more things being compared?
- Do some paragraphs or sentences give examples or details that support a main idea?
- Does the concluding sentence or paragraph restate an idea? This may be the main idea. Restating information is a common writing practice. Writers often restate ideas to reinforce the most important message.

At this point, state the main idea in your own words. This is sometimes called *paraphrasing*. You will learn more about paraphrasing in Chapter 3.

Once you think you have the main idea, you might find it helpful to check with another student to see if he or she has a similar answer. Do not expect that you will each use the same words, but check to see if your ideas are the same. If you have different ideas, work through the reading together to see if you can help each other.

When I scan pages 44–49, I see the word *economy* many times. I think I'm pretty safe in expecting that the main ideas are going to relate to the economy in New France. I also see Jean Talon's name mentioned in each section. This probably means the main ideas will relate to how he affected New France's economy.

The Problems Facing Jean Talon

Before Reading

The Balance of Trade under Mercantilism, 1663

During Reading

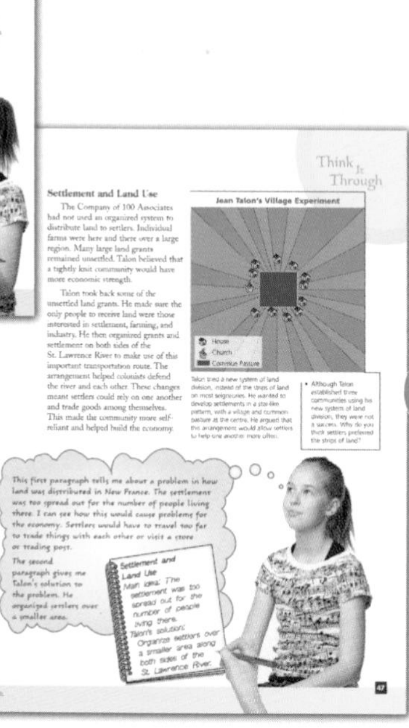

Settlement and Land Use

Jean Talon's Village Experiment

The main heading on page 44 is *The Problems Facing Jean Talon*. Maybe all of the problems described on following pages are economic. I see several subheadings: *Settlement and Land Use*, *Defence*, and *Population*. Each of these headings probably indicates one of the economic problems in New France.

Defence

Population

After Reading

On page 48, I see a section called *Expand the Economy*. It looks different from the other sections of text, so it caught my attention. I'm not sure why it has a different look, but maybe I'll find out as I read more.

Settlement and Land Use

The Company of 100 Associates had not used an organized system to distribute land to settlers. Individual farms were here and there over a large region. Many large **land grants** remained unsettled. Talon believed that a tightly knit community would have more economic strength.

Talon took back some of the unsettled land grants. He made sure the only people to receive land were those interested in settlement, farming, and industry. He then organized grants and settlement on both sides of the St. Lawrence River to make use of this important transportation route. The arrangement helped colonists defend the river and each other. These changes meant settlers could rely on one another and trade goods among themselves. This made the community more self-reliant and helped build the economy.

Jean Talon's Village Experiment

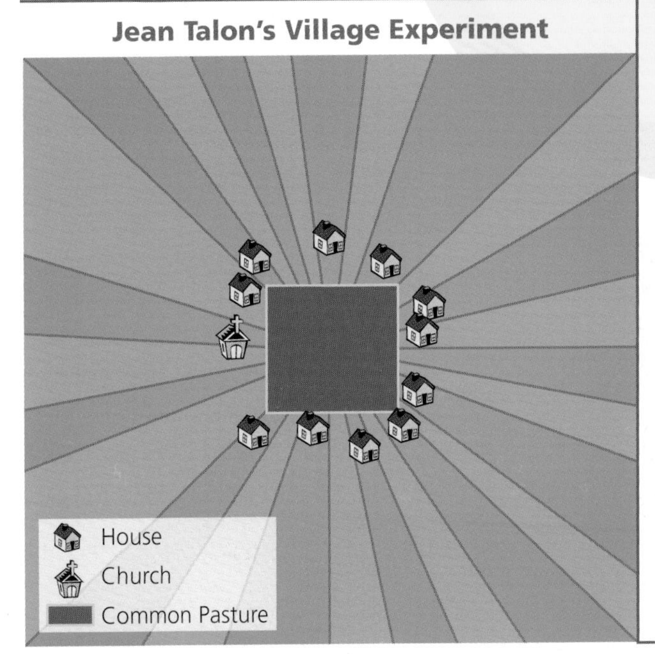

Talon tried a new system of land division, instead of the strips of land on most seigneuries. He wanted to develop settlements in a star-like pattern, with a village and common pasture at the centre. He argued that this arrangement would allow settlers to help one another more often.

- Although Talon established three communities using his new system of land division, they were not a success. Why do you think settlers preferred the strips of land?

This first paragraph tells me about a problem in how land was distributed in New France. The settlement was too spread out for the number of people living there. I can see how this would cause problems for the economy. Settlers would have to travel too far to trade things with each other or visit a store or trading post.

The second paragraph gives me Talon's solution to the problem. He organized settlers over a smaller area.

Think It Through

To Do List

EXPAND the Economy!

- ☑ build sawmills and begin a lumber trade between New France, France, and the West Indies
- ☑ establish a royal shipyard to build ships
- ☑ develop iron and copper mines
- ☑ decrease expensive imports of wine and other alcoholic beverages from France ➡ build breweries
- ☑ establish clothing industry ➡ encourage settlers to raise sheep and grow hemp and flax to weave fabrics
- ☑ open shoe factory ➡ set up tanneries to produce leather

Jean Talon Visiting Settlers, by Lawrence R. Batchelor, around 1931.

- What objects in the painting look like they were produced in France?
- What was likely produced in New France? Explain your reasoning.
- How does this painting relate to the main idea on this page?

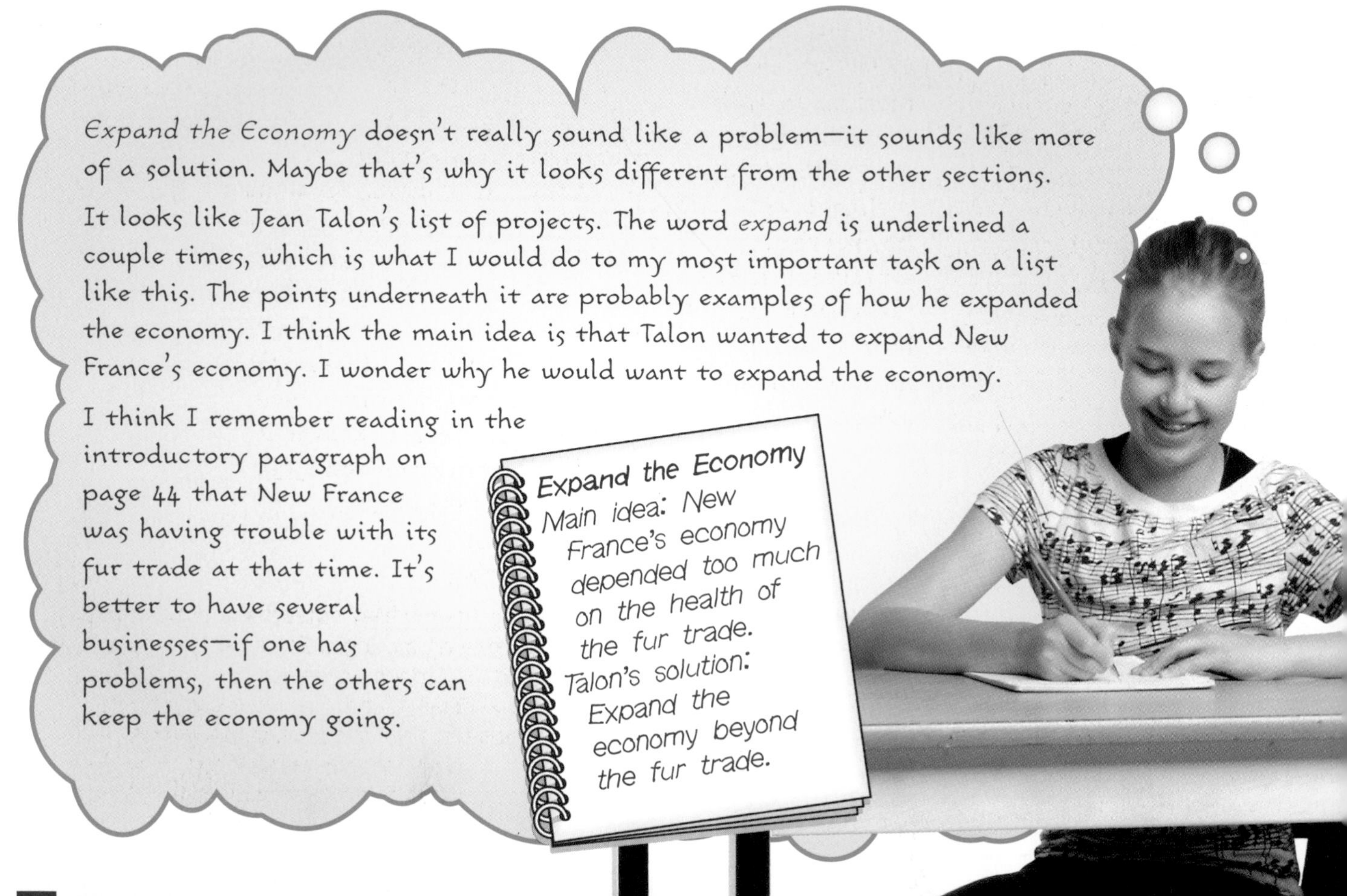

Defence

Talon realized that if the colony was to prosper, it had to be secure. It was difficult to defend a colony that had a small population living in a large region. Talon's changes in land use helped solve this problem.

The king had tried to secure the colony by sending French soldiers from the Carignan-Salières (ka-ree-nyan-sa-lee-air) regiment to New France. In 1665, 1200 soldiers and about 80 officers joined the colony of 3200 settlers.

The Carignan-Salières Regiment (1665) First Regular French Troops to Defend Canada, by Tom McNeely, 1966. The arrival of soldiers and officers from the Carignan-Salières regiment dramatically changed New France. The soldiers established and defended forts throughout the colony. For the first time, New France could defend itself with confidence.

Talon went a step further. He offered land grants to a number of the officers to keep them in the colony after their military service was over. Other settlers felt more secure with the military men around them. In exchange for helping their neighbours defend themselves, the former soldiers received farming advice.

Population

New France's population was growing too slowly. Part of the problem was that the colony's population was mainly young men. As a solution, Talon asked the French government to send single girls to New France. Talon wanted them to marry men in the colony. The girls would help the population grow by having babies. This would save the trouble and expense of importing settlers from France.

Les Filles du Roi, by E. F. Brickdale (1871–1945). Most filles du roi came from humble surroundings. Especially in later years, many were farmers' daughters.

- What impression does this painting give of the filles du roi's social background? Why might the artist have this interpretation?

Jean-Baptiste Colbert, the minister in the French government in charge of colonies, responded by offering young, healthy women free transportation to New France. In addition, the women received a **dowry** of one ox, one cow, two pigs, two chickens, and two barrels of salt pork. A dowry is property a woman brings to her marriage, usually provided by her father. Because the king's treasury was providing their dowry, the girls became known as the *filles du roi* (fee-yuh dew rwa), or daughters of the king.

After Reading

1. You should now have notes that include four main ideas covering the topics *Settlement and Land Use*, *Expand the Economy*, *Defence*, and *Population*. Add one detail to each main idea and arrange your notes in a graphic organizer of your choice. A T-chart, Important/Interesting Chart, or set of split-page notes might be an appropriate choice.

The Fur Trade Expands

Before Reading

1. A K-W-L Organizer can help you plan what you want to learn. It can also be used to make notes on a topic. To practise this technique, prepare a K-W-L Organizer for the Hudson's Bay Company (which you might know as HBC or The Bay).

K What I *know*	W What I *want* to find out	L What I *learned*

The northern and western territory's potential for fur was promoted by two coureurs de bois, Chouart Des Groseilliers (shoo-ar day groh-zay-yay) and Pierre Radisson (ra-dee-son). In the 1650s, fur-trade companies had strict rules to control the fur trade. Radisson and Des Groseilliers were frustrated with the restrictions. They believed they could find the best furs if they travelled west and north of Lake Superior, but the fur-trade companies would not give them a licence to trade in this region.

Radisson & Groseilliers Established the Fur Trade in the Great North West, 1662, by Archibald Bruce Stapleton (1917–1950).

- Pierre Radisson and Chouart Des Groseilliers knew several First Nations languages. How would this skill help a fur trader?

The two men decided to explore the area without permission. In 1660, they returned to Québec after being away for more than a year. They brought more than 100 canoes full of fur. However, rather than a hero's welcome, they were fired upon with cannons from the fort and ships in the harbour. The explorers were fined and their furs were taken from them. Although the men tried to convince France they could find a route to Hudson Bay from the Atlantic Ocean, the French showed no interest.

Rejected by France, the men presented their idea to Prince Rupert, a cousin of the king of England. Through Prince Rupert's influence, King Charles II agreed to finance their first voyage to Hudson Bay in 1669. Only Des Groseilliers's ship made it to the bay, but the expedition was a success. When he returned to England the next year, he had a shipload of furs.

On May 6, 1670, the king of England gave the Hudson's Bay Company a **Royal Charter** to the vast territory draining into the bay and all the furs of that territory. A Royal Charter is an exclusive right to the land and trade of a particular territory. The area covered by the territory was called **Rupert's Land**.

During Reading

1. Add anything you have learned about the HBC to your K-W-L Organizer.

Competition Fuels Exploration

With England in control of the Hudson Bay region, New France suddenly had trouble gaining the rich furs from the North. When Talon began his second term as intendant in 1672, he was more interested in sending out explorers than earlier governments in New France had been. Explorers went west to explore the Great Lakes, south along the Mississippi River, and east to find the best route for a road between Acadia and Québec. Jesuits also went north to found a mission on Hudson Bay.

Rival Trading Systems

In the ninety years following the establishment of the Hudson's Bay Company, the fur trade developed two distinct systems. The Hudson's Bay Company set up trading posts, called **factories**, along Hudson Bay. There the British traders waited for First Nations people to come to them with furs.

French traders used the rivers and Great Lakes to travel out from Montréal to First Nations. The French trade was made of small, competitive partnerships, rather than a large monopoly such as that of the Hudson's Bay Company.

First Nations were good traders who used the rivalry to get the best deals. French traders often tried to meet up with First Nations on their way to HBC posts. They would trade for the best furs and leave the bulkiest, poor-quality furs for their rivals. For many years, the French dominated this system.

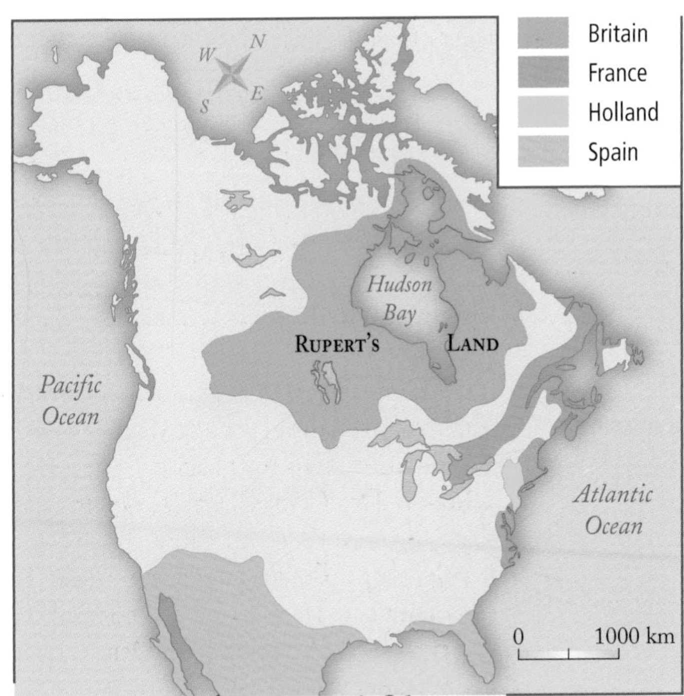

European Territorial Claims in North America, 1670

- How does the legend help you compare the size and location of New France's territory with that of the Hudson Bay region claimed by Britain?
- Using your knowledge that the best furs were coming from the North, how might Britain's claim for this area affect France's fur trade?

After Reading

1. An option in using a K-W-L Organizer is to add two more spaces:

W *What* else would I like to learn about this topic	H *How* would I find this additional information

Fill in these spaces on your chart. Keep this organizer. You will have an opportunity to use it again at the end of the chapter.

Habitant Days, April 1750

Before Reading

1. Would you expect a habitant family to have more or fewer possessions than your family? Why? Discuss your answers in a group of three.

The following story, by Marie-Aimée Cliche (ma-ree-a-may kli-sh), looks at the lives of the fictional Gosselin (gos-lin) family of New France.

A New Day

The rooster crows at the break of day, rousing the Gosselin household. First to rise as usual, Madeleine (ma-de-lane), the mother, parts the curtain around the bed and cries to her children sleeping in the same room, "Everybody up and dressed. We've got a big day ahead of us. Mind you say your prayers."

Yawning, they toss off their warm blankets reluctantly, dropping to their knees on a caribou-skin, bedside rug. Madeleine recites her silent prayers, the others following her example, while scratching furiously to ease the itching of bedbug bites.

Everyone dresses quickly—the bedroom stove went out in the night and this late-April dawn is chilly. The three men pull durable woolen pants over their long johns and put on heavy linen shirts and socks. For Madeleine and her two daughters, it's an underskirt called a petticoat covered by a short skirt (hem at mid-calf), stockings held up by garters, and thick, rough bullhide shoes. For the housework, they will add an apron.

A quick wash and shave for Pierre, the father, and Jean-Baptiste, the oldest son. Pierre then ties his hair back, while Jean-Baptiste and François (fran-swa) prefer to let theirs hang loose. But they all wear a red toque, a jacket, and wooden clogs to perform the morning rounds.

The women, after combing their hair, adjust their bonnets and each ties a small silver cross around her neck. All but the two youngest children wear such a cross, something they received the day of their first communion and which they never go without.

The Catholic Church influenced clothing styles in New France. It viewed bare shoulders and arms, transparent fabrics, and showy ornaments as scandalous. For example, women needed to dress modestly, covering most of their body, as shown in this photograph of girls and women in dress of that period.

Learning from Historical Fiction

National Gallery of Canada, Ottawa/#6275

A View of the Château Richer, Cape Torment, and Lower End of the Îsle of Orleans near Québec, by Thomas Davies, 1787. The painting shows a view of farms and houses along the St. Lawrence River.

Learning history is more than knowing the facts about when events took place or who did what. The events of history become more meaningful if you try to understand the people involved.

As you learned on page xiii, historical fiction can connect readers to the events and personalities of the past. These stories may have real people and events as their "bones," but the writer and reader flesh out the bones with their imaginations. For example, an author's research might lead her or him to the Château Richer painting on this page. This painting might inspire a story about the people seen working or the circumstances behind the creation of the painting.

Historical fiction can help readers feel a personal connection to historical events.

Questions to Analyze Historical Fiction

- At what point did you become interested in the story? Why did this part of the story catch your interest?
- What do you think is the most important idea? Explain why you think so.
- What would you like to find more information about?
- What new ideas or information did you learn?
- Is there a connection between this story and anything else you have read on the same topic?
- Are there any similarities between you and a character in the story? How would you solve the problems that a specific character faced?
- What do you not understand?

During Reading

1. As you read pages 54–55, write in your journal to answer at least one question from the skill feature above on Learning from Historical Fiction.

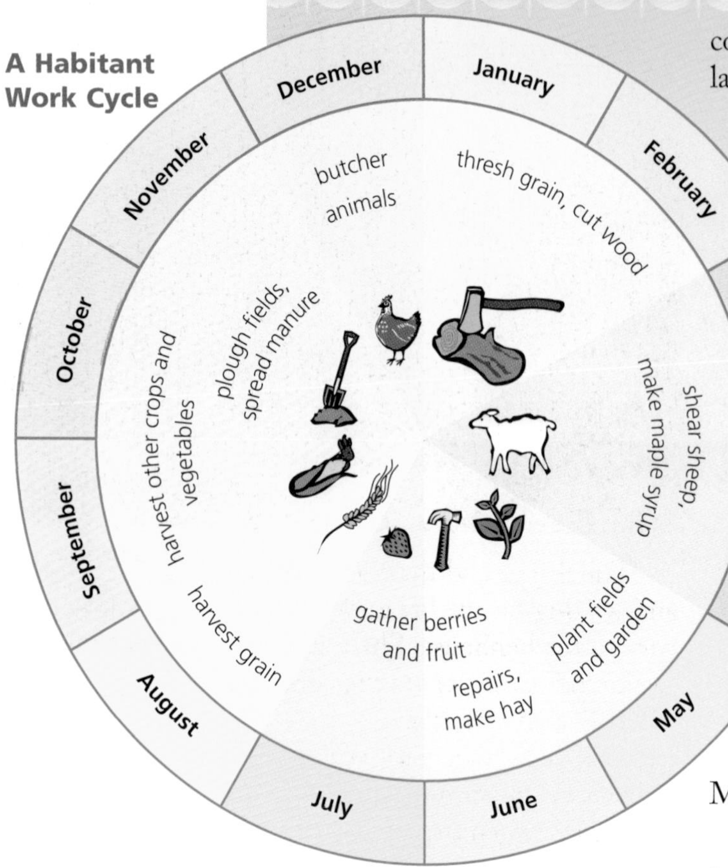

comfortable after having worked this land for two generations, the Gosselins have a good stock of animals: two horses, two bulls, three cows, a sow and her litter, and seven sheep.

Over a simple breakfast—all rattle of tin cups and scraping of earthenware—the day's work is planned. Pierre and Jean-Baptiste are off to the fields to sow the wheat and mend the cedar fence posts. François will haul in the wood for the bread oven. Little Marie-Anne will be off to the school run by the Sisters of the Neuville (noo-vil) Congregation, while Marguerite will help her mother.

Breakfast over, Jean-Baptiste heads to the granary to fetch the sacks of grain for sowing.

"Don't forget to put a handful of blessed grain in each sack," Madeleine advises.

"Don't worry," he replies. "I don't want caterpillars getting into my wheat."

The blessed grain had been given a ritual blessing by the *curé*—the priest. For three days, the whole parish, led by the priest, prayed and fasted and marched in processions, asking God to make the land fruitful. A child then cast the first handful of grain.

The Gosselins are sure God will answer their prayers. If the harvest starts to look bad, they will just ask the priest to organize another procession. Past experience has shown this works.

A Breath of Air

Madeleine opens the windows, hooks the shutters in place, and the spring air sweeps in, cleaning out the night odours. First, make the beds: the reed-filled mattresses must be shaken out and the hemp sheets, red wool blankets, and quilts of homespun linen tidily laid out. Next, something more unpleasant: "Marie-Anne, it's your turn to empty the chamber pots," says Marguerite, "I did it yesterday." Out goes the waste of one night, thrown on the pile of manure behind the stable.

With the women busy inside, the men do the rounds. Even if the cows' milk runs dry in winter, there is plenty of work to be done. Financially

A Small World

Marguerite made her first communion and finished school at the same time last year. She was twelve. Until she marries, she will share the household chores with her mother. Now she cleans up the breakfast dishes, putting them away in the cupboard as her mother prepares the dough for the bread.

After carefully sweeping the bedroom and kitchen, the only rooms in the house, she sprinkles water on the floors to keep the dust down. Washing the floors is only done once or twice a year. Next, Marguerite dusts the few pieces of furniture, all pine: the cupboard, the kitchen table and chairs, the beds, and clothing trunks.

Letting the bread rise, Madeleine goes out to fill the two water buckets.

Ah, this drawing of water—it has to be done twice a day, even more often on washing days. Those who accuse habitants of being dirty have no idea how heavy water buckets can be.

This museum room looks much as the main living area of many habitants would have looked.

Bread was a basic part of habitant diets. Most people made their bread outside in an oven such as the one in this photograph from 1898.

The fire lit and the oven warming and waiting for the bread, Madeleine goes to the henhouse. She raises twenty hens and some other fowl that will be used to pay the seigneurial rent. Fresh eggs are particularly welcome today, Saturday, the day of abstinence, when they go without meat. They can eat an omelet and something from the vegetable cellar, where turnips, cabbage, and onions have kept well through the winter.

The ringing of the church bell, on the stroke of noon, is the signal for dinner. Madeleine serves everyone, starting with her husband, before sitting down herself. Afterwards, while the women clean up the dishes, the men sit on the porch smoking their pipes. Even François enjoys this privilege since he began working like his older brothers.

Work resumes at precisely one o'clock. The seeds sown in the morning must be covered. The women rarely go to the fields—usually only at harvest time to help hay and separate the grain from its husk. Today, the kitchen garden requires all their care.

During Reading

1. In your journal, answer a second question from the feature on page 53.

A Quick Change

With evening coming on, Marguerite has no time to change before going to church, where she wants to go to confession to prepare herself for communion the next day. Her finest clothes she keeps for Sunday. For today, she simply takes off her apron and hides her work clothes under a long, pale grey cape. When she reaches the roadside cross, she will stop as everyone does and say a prayer, then hurry on to church.

The hardworking habitants relaxed in the evenings with games of cards, checkers, or chess. Playing cards such as these were also used in New France as currency. People in the colony had little cash because most was spent on French imports.

Like Marguerite Gosselin, a few parishioners go to confession on Saturday, but most prefer to wait until Sunday morning, just before mass. It saves a trip and, besides, the *curé* is rushed then because he has to say mass, so he has little time to question and scold.

Back home, supper finished, the whole family kneels before a picture of the Holy Family for the rosary. Because it's Saturday evening and there will be little work done tomorrow, everyone stays up a little later than usual. Clustered before the fire, the men puff on their pipes and the women fidget with their needlework, all reviewing the day's activities and thinking of what's to come.

"And when are we going to move into the summer kitchen?" asks Marie-Anne, already excited at the prospect.

"Next month," replies her mother. "After we've done the heavy cleaning. By the way, Marguerite, we're going to start making the soap right away, the day after tomorrow."

Marguerite sighs, "I don't know if we're going to manage to get rid of the bedbugs and crickets this year."

"Get away with you," scoffs Jean-Baptiste. "Every house has these bugs. It's like mosquitoes in the woods. You've become such a fussy little lady since you went to the Sisters' school."

He feels more than a little jealous of his sister, who knows how to read, write, and even recite long Latin prayers, while he remains illiterate, there being no schoolmaster around to teach him.

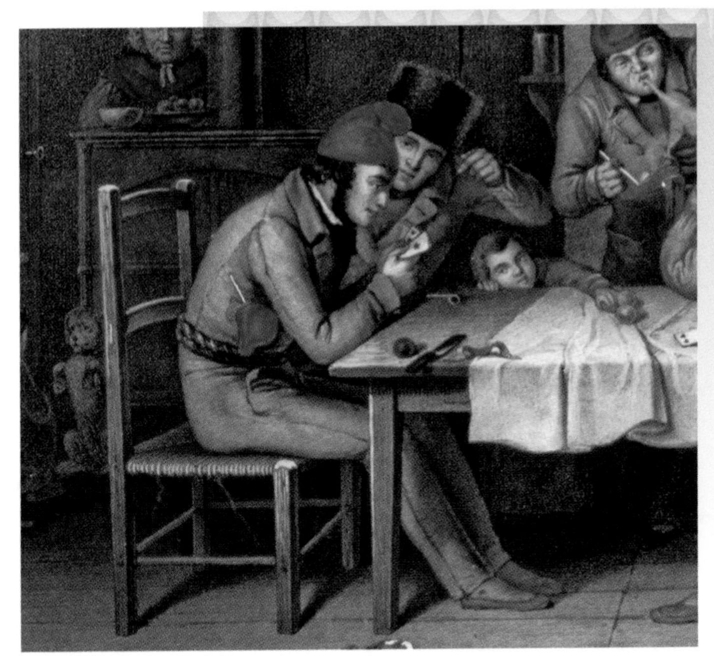

The red knitted cap known as a *toque* was first used by fur traders. They needed a warm hat that would cover their ears. Other people in New France adopted it as a practical solution to winter cold. In the Rebellions of 1837, which you will study in Chapter 7, the red toque was associated with French rebels.

News from Town

A knock at the door cuts off the discussion. All turn their heads towards the door, curious, as Pierre goes to open it. Visitors are always welcome in the country.

"Hey Joseph! Welcome, nephew," Pierre exclaims as Joseph whips off his toque. "Quick, come on in and sit yourself down right by the fire."

The visitor is immediately asked many questions. For two or three years, he has been working in Québec, building ships for the Royal Navy. His country cousins are eager to hear about his way of life, which is so different from their own.

"Do you often get time off?" Joseph is asked.

"Sundays and legal holidays, like everyone else," he offers. Then, warming to his subject, "But wouldn't you know it, the bishop has just gone and taken away seventeen holidays. It's terrible to be changing religion like that."

"He hasn't cancelled the holidays," Madeleine corrects him. "He's simply decided to celebrate them on the closest Sunday."

"It's all the same," Joseph protests. "We have to have all the saints on our side if we're going to beat the British."

The clock strikes nine, parting time. Joseph is going to spend the night with his parents, who live nearby.

Goodbyes over, the women take more pains with their toilette than usual. They make a point of curling their hair for mass the next day. Madeleine takes the Sunday clothes out of the trunk, and the French shoes each will wear.

The stage set for another day, she blows out the candles.

After Reading

1. Create a journal entry that Marguerite or François might have written about their day.

Was Jean Talon the Great Intendant?

Before Reading

1. As a class, discuss the characteristics that make someone a great leader. You might want to use your journal entry from page 38. Make a list together.

What would it be like to be able to talk to someone from the past? Instead of having to puzzle over why he or she did something, you could just ask. The following fictional interview is what might happen if we could talk to Jean Talon today. Although the interview is fictional, the historical information in it is accurate.

Interviewer: Welcome and thank you for coming, Monsieur Talon.

Talon: It is my pleasure. I am glad to see this country more than 300 years after my time.

Interviewer: Our purpose in asking you here is to solve a question historians today ask about your reputation as the "Great Intendant."

Talon: I can't imagine what the question is. Given all that I accomplished, how could I not be considered the greatest intendant in the history of New France?

Interviewer: But Monsieur Talon, when I read the historical records, I find things that suggest this reputation may well be inaccurate.

Talon: Give me the specific charges and I will tell you the truth of the matter.

During Reading

1. Make a chart with three columns. Put *The Charges* at the top of the first column, *Talon's Responses* at the top of the second, and *Success of Response* at the top of the third. As you read, complete your chart using jot-notes. Complete the third column at the end by putting a *yes* or *no*, depending on whether you think Talon's response successfully dealt with the charge.

Interviewer: During your time, important officials and other community leaders complained about your pushiness. Governor de Courcelle (de kur-sel), the king's top appointee in the colony, accused you of intruding into foreign affairs. He said that this was beyond your responsibilities.

For example, you went behind his back to the French government. You asked for money and soldiers to build new forts. You also sent out explorers and made new alliances with First Nations. De Courcelle argued that these actions were properly part of his job, not yours.

Talon: The governor was technically correct. I did expand New France's borders, but my motives were good. Everything I did was to protect the fur trade.

At that time, the Haudenosaunee were taking furs from our allies, the Odawa (o-dah-wuh). They then sold the furs to the British. It was costing the colony a fortune. This *was* my job. The king wanted me to develop New France's economy. I couldn't allow our furs to disappear into British hands!

I wanted forts north and south of Lake Ontario and a ship to make navigation of the lake safe. I was simply defending His Majesty's territories.

As for the explorers and alliances, yes, I sent out people like Louis Jolliet (zho-lee-yet) and Father Jacques Marquette (mar-ket) to find the mouth of the great Mississippi River. After the Radisson and Des Groseilliers disaster, New France couldn't afford not to explore the continent. Britain's claim to Hudson Bay hurt our economy badly. With exploration, I planned to get our fur trade back on track. At the time, I also still hoped we could find a route to China.

De Courcelle was just jealous of me. If he was not doing his job well, someone had to take up the slack. What other choice did I have?

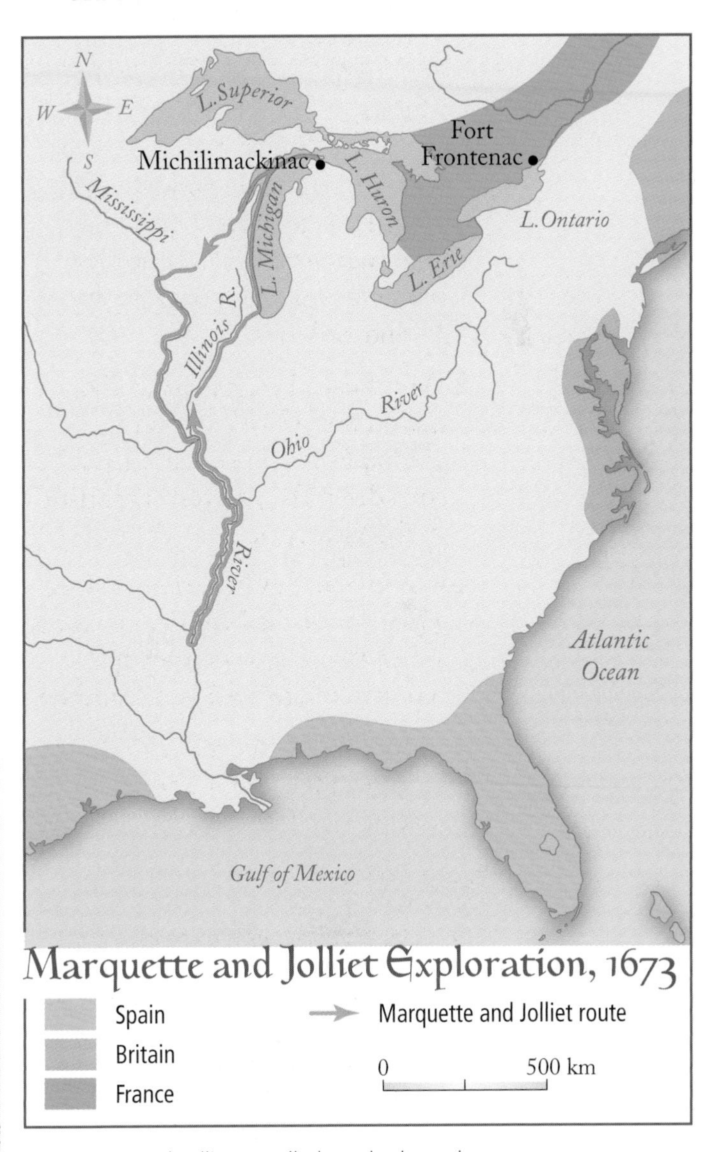

Marquette and Jolliet travelled south along the Mississippi, almost to the mouth of the river. They turned back around the border between present-day Louisiana and Arkansas, fearing they might be taken prisoner in Spanish territory.

Father Marquette and Jolliet Descending the Mississippi, by A. Russell, around 1900.

Interviewer: Bishop François de Laval (de la-val) also complained. He said you challenged the Church's position in the colony.

Talon: The Church's position in the colony was not my decision. I took orders from the king, who definitely wanted to limit the Church's influence among settlers. Bishop Laval and I disagreed many times, but I was only following direction from France.

I recall one situation involving the Dames de la Sainte-Famille (dahm de la sane-t-fa-mee-yuh). When Bishop Laval discovered that these good nuns had taken part in the carnival of 1667, he suspended their group. He was entirely too hard on the poor sisters. They were just having some fun. Laval was well known for his strict views on proper behaviour and dress. This was just one example of the Church interfering in colonists' freedom.

I took the matter to the Sovereign Council. It ruled that gatherings during the carnival could not be banned. The bishop believed I had overstepped my limits, but I believe he overstepped his.

Interviewer: And what do you say about complaints by the merchants? They said you abused your power by bringing products into the colony without an import tax. These cheaper goods flooded the colony's market and hurt their sales.

Talon: Ha! Those merchants were too self-interested. The only thing those goods interfered with was the merchants' ability to charge high prices for poor-quality products. I gave them some healthy competition, which helped the colony as a whole. Keep in mind that I also showed the merchants how they could expand their businesses. My goal was to make their businesses better—not drive them out of business.

- What do you see in this painting?
- How does the palace compare to the Gosselin family's home you learned about on pages 52–57?
- What can you conclude about the intendant's position in New France?
- What questions do you have?

A View of the Intendant's Palace, by William Elliott, 1761.

Interviewer: Regarding these business projects of yours, I have to point out that many of them failed. In agriculture, you introduced crops such as hemp, flax, and hops. After you left the colony, these crops disappeared. The brewery you were so proud of closed three years after you left, as did the lumber industry.

The same thing happened with your ship-building industry, the mining and iron-making industries, and the trading system between New France, France, and the West Indies. It strikes me, Monsieur Talon, that this is a list of failures, not accomplishments.

In the 1600s, many people saw beer as a nutritious drink. Talon built New France's first brewery in Québec in 1668. This house in Longueuil, photographed in the late 1800s, was also a brewery. As Talon built breweries, he restricted imports of other alcohol from France. The Sovereign Council had a monopoly on beer production in the colony, so they profited from Talon's policies.

Talon: Monsieur, all my efforts, even my so-called failures, were tied directly to the king's instructions—to establish New France as a self-sufficient, secure colony that would be a benefit to His Majesty's Kingdom in France.

My fishery and leather-goods industries were successful. As for the others? Well, I did the best I could. I only had time to get them established, which I did. In 1671, I was able to report to the king that I could clothe myself from head to toe in products produced in New France. That these industries didn't succeed after I left was not my fault. They likely failed because later governments didn't invest enough money to keep them going.

You see, under France's policy of mercantilism, New France was not supposed to manufacture goods that would compete with French industries. We could grow hemp and ship it to France, but we weren't allowed to weave the hemp into cloth. We could ship fur, but not make the furs into coats. The system was designed to benefit France at every turn—not to develop New France's industry. Another problem was finding workers. New France lacked the skilled labour these industries needed to thrive.

All of my projects had potential. The proof is in the next century, where each did well. What I did showed others the way.

Canada's First Shipyard, by Rex Woods, 1956. Jean Talon (shown on the left) set up New France's first shipyard. Later intendants pursued this industry with even more energy. New France seemed like an excellent place to build ships because of its ample supply of wood. However, rules designed to benefit France made New France an expensive place to build ships, compared to Europe.

Interviewer: Monsieur Talon, what would you add to support your high reputation?

Talon: Many things. Remember that when I arrived in 1665, the colony was barely surviving. The population was only 3215. By the time I left in 1672, the population had grown to about 7000, a greater increase in seven years than in the previous fifty!

I first conducted a thorough census of the population to determine our needs. I then promoted immigration, brought in the filles du roi, and rewarded retiring soldiers who stayed in New France with land.

There were also rewards for couples to have large families. For example, we gave money each year to families with ten or more children. Unmarried men were strongly encouraged to take wives. If they refused or delayed, we threatened to cancel their hunting licences until they agreed.

I also got the seigneurial system working more smoothly. I ordered seigneurs to live on their seigneuries and work at clearing the land. If they refused, I took away their grant. There was no room in the colony for people who weren't pulling their weight!

I divided up seigneuries that were too large. It was ridiculous for individuals to own vast sections of land they couldn't hope to clear in their grandchildren's lifetime. It was a young country—seigneurs had to accept smaller seigneuries than those in the old country. Breaking up the large seigneuries helped me open new land for settlement.

All of my activities were part of my grand vision for New France:

- a rapidly growing population that would produce raw materials for France and purchase its manufactured goods
- a strong economy based on agriculture, industry, and the fur trade
- solid alliances with First Nations to reduce our need for defence
- an expanded territory to cut the British colonies out of the fur trade

Not only did no one else attempt this much, but no one else had such a clear vision for the potential of New France. I leave the final judgment of my reputation to you.

Interviewer: Thank you for your time today.

Holding a Mock Trial

To hold a mock trial in your class, students should be assigned the following roles:

- 1 or 2 Crown attorneys (prosecutors)
- 1 or 2 defence attorneys
- 1 judge
- jury (several students, usually an odd number)
- witnesses

1. Attorneys should prepare their cases with questions to ask witnesses they believe will help their side. Witnesses should prepare their answers so they can respond to questions in role.
2. The prosecution goes first, and then the defence.
3. Each side's witnesses can be examined by the other side after they have given their original testimony.
4. The judge will run the trial, keeping order and making sure a proper atmosphere of respect is maintained.
5. The jury will listen to the evidence, meet to discuss their opinions, arrive at a common verdict (or a majority one), and present it to the court.
6. At the end, hold a class discussion of the decisions as well as the conduct of the trial.

After Reading

1. In this activity, you and your classmates will participate in a mock trial of Jean Talon. Your premise is that Jean Talon has been charged with fraud. His accusers state that he does not deserve to be called the "Great Intendant."

   a) Appoint students to the positions listed in the feature Holding a Mock Trial. Witnesses will include the real people mentioned in this section (including Talon, Governor de Courcelle, Bishop Laval, and Jean-Baptiste Colbert), and the people affected by Talon's policies:

   - fur traders
   - merchants
   - farmers
   - ship-building industry
   - mining/iron-making industries
   - brewery industry
   - fishing industry
   - leather-goods industry
   - filles du roi
   - seigneurs
   - First Nations

   Each student should prepare to testify at Talon's trial representing their assigned person, group, or industry. Each will be asked questions about how well or poorly various projects or activities went. Reread the interview for clues as to how to answer. Some extra research may be necessary.

   b) Attorneys should prepare their cases based on the positive and negative information in the interview. Cases will be made of questions for witnesses the attorneys believe will help their side. They will call each of their witnesses when it is their turn to present.

Religion under Royal Government

Before Reading

1. What role, if any, does religion or spirituality play in your life? In your school? Write your responses in your journal.

In 1659, the pope made François de Laval the first bishop of Québec. He had been nominated by the Jesuits, who were still at work in New France.

Some church leaders in France opposed the appointment. At this time, the French government controlled the Church in France. The government sometimes felt that the Jesuits were too independent. They did not always follow orders from the French government. The Jesuits preferred to take their priorities from the Catholic Church based in Rome. The government feared that Laval would reinforce this independence.

Bishop Laval resigned his position in 1685, but spent the rest of his life in the Séminaire de Québec.

Laval held his position until 1685, almost thirty years. By the time he resigned, the Catholic Church was well established in the colony. New France had churches, an organized parish system, schools, and many groups of nuns and priests working in the colony. The Church was highly involved in the day-to-day lives and government of people in New France.

Parishes were organized when a community had enough population to build a church and pay the salary of a priest.

Laval also opened the Séminaire de Québec to train young men to become priests. He hoped to help locals become priests so that New France would not have to rely on France to supply its clergy. This would make sure the Church would have strong roots in New France.

Laval University was founded at the Séminaire de Québec in 1852. By the 1890s, when this photograh was taken, Laval was already a major public university.

- How would training local men to become priests help the colony? How would it help the Church in New France?

Bishop Laval was not happy with the arrival of Jean Talon in 1665. In his view, Talon interfered too much with Church affairs. However, Talon's orders came from the king. The French government thought the Church had too much influence in New France. The king directed Talon to limit the Church's authority to **moral** issues alone. In the king's eyes, moral issues were those related to right and wrong behaviour. All other issues, such as finances, were to be Talon's responsibility. In contrast, Laval believed all issues were moral issues.

Reception of the Marquis de Tracy and the Intendant Talon by Mgr. Laval, 1665, by Frank Craig, around 1910. Laval was in New France five years before Jean Talon arrived to establish Royal Government. Until Talon's arrival, the Church was free to organize the social and political rules of the colony without much interference from France.

A Conflict of Views

Since Champlain's time, New France had maintained a policy of not trading alcohol with First Nations people. Anyone who did could be **excommunicated** from the Church. Excommunicated people could not take part in church ceremonies and activities. This was a serious punishment. Most community activities in the colony involved the Church in some way.

Laval strongly supported this policy. At first, Talon agreed, but he later changed his mind. Talon decided that the policy was meddling in business. In 1668, the Sovereign Council permitted the sale of alcohol to First Nations people. Laval fought the change, but could not stop it.

By 1672, the Church could not prevent the spread of alcohol in the fur trade. Bishop Laval's influence on the colonial government had started to decline. As the years passed, he participated less and less, restricting his work to building the strength of the Church in the colony.

During Reading !

1. Why do you think Laval considered the inclusion of alcohol as trade goods as a moral issue? Discuss this as a class.
2. What business decisions today might be considered moral issues?

Forming Questions

At the heart of historical literacy is the ability to ask questions that will guide your research and thinking about significant issues. Questions give a focus to your reading and understanding.

Some questions help gather facts. Factual questions are closed. They have one correct answer. Examples of closed questions include the following:

- When was Talon born?
- During what years was Talon the intendant of New France?

Other questions are open. Open-ended questions require more research, an evaluation of your sources, and sometimes discussion. Generally, the answer to an open-ended question is the best possible answer, not the only answer.

News reporters use a set of questions commonly called the 5 Ws and 1 H to help gather information for their stories. History students can use the same questions to guide their reading and note-making.

- **Who** did it?
- **What** happened?
- **When** did it happen?
- **Where** did it happen?
- **Why** did it happen? or **How** did it happen?

The last two questions help you interpret the facts. They are open-ended, so there may be more than one answer.

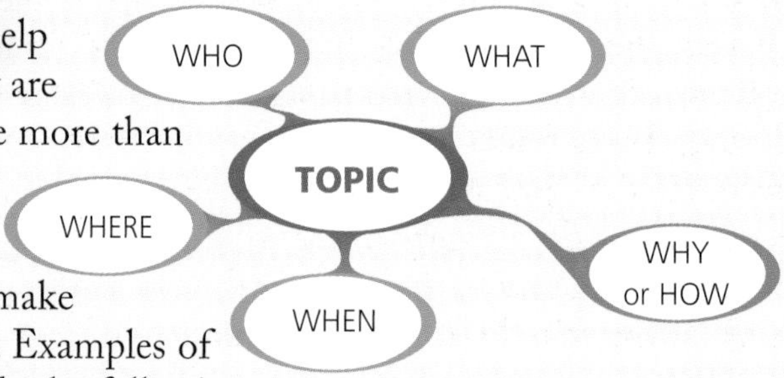

Open-ended questions require you to evaluate and make decisions about information. Examples of open-ended questions include the following:

- Why was Talon a successful intendant?
- Do you find the author's point of view convincing? Explain.

Key words that signal you are being asked an open-ended question include *compare, judge, evaluate, why, analyze,* and *examine.*

Colonists and the Church

Community members paid the salary of a parish priest through a **tithe**, a tax to support the Church.

Laval had asked that the tithe be one thirteenth of each habitant's produce. This was the rate common in France. Ignoring his request, the colony's administration set the rate at one twenty-sixth.

The Church then had to depend on the colony's government for the rest of its income. This situation helped the government influence the Church's actions.

Eventually, income from the Church's seigneuries gave it more independence. By 1759, the Church owned 25 per cent of the land in New France.

Some historians have noted that habitants in New France did not have as much respect for authority as people in France. As evidence, they point to frequent orders from the intendant directing the colonists to show more respect for their priests. Behaviours the intendant found necessary to forbid included arguing and walking out of church in the middle of sermons, and bringing dogs into church.

At the same time, clergy members provided many services to the habitants. Priests conducted religious ceremonies and kept records of baptisms, marriages, and burials. They were usually the most educated members of a community, so they were sometimes asked to read or write for the colonists.

In many ways, they were leaders for communities that lacked the time and resources to organize themselves in other ways.

Nuns Attending the Sick at the Infirmary of the Abbey at Port Royal des Champs, around 1710. The Ursuline nuns did much of the Church's work in the colony. They ran schools, orphanages, hospitals, and organizations to help the poor or others in need.

However, New France's small population was scattered over a large area. Priests had to travel widely to visit parishioners. Making this situation even more difficult, New France had a shortage of priests in the late 1600s. In 1683, the intendant reported that three-quarters of the habitants heard mass only four times a year.

After Reading

1. With a partner, use the 5 Ws and 1 H to write open-ended and closed questions about the Church's role in New France under Royal Government. Consider using a Mind Map like that that on page 66 to format your notes. Exchange questions with another pair of students and use your textbook to try to answer as many of their questions as you can.

Frontenac as Governor

Before Reading

1. In a small group, discuss how a major sports figure or entertainer should be judged. Are the person's character traits as important as his or her success on the field or the stage?

Louis de Buade, Count Frontenac

Count Frontenac was governor of New France from 1672 to 1682 and from 1689 to his death in 1698.

Frontenac's Character

Frontenac was born in France into an upper-class family. He received a good education and entered the military service. However, he tended to spend more than he earned. Creditors—people he owed money—constantly chased him. When he became governor of New France in 1672, he hoped to escape his creditors.

Historians have described Frontenac as vain and difficult. He frequently showed off his possessions and argued with those around him. The French government was often unhappy with his leadership. For example, France ordered that New France should not be expanded too quickly. The French government did not want to leave large areas of its territory undefended. Until the population grew enough to send settlers to new areas, France wanted Frontenac to focus on its current territory. Frontenac ignored this order. He had financial interests in the fur trade and wanted trading to expand.

Less than a year after his arrival in New France, he built Fort Frontenac (now Kingston, Ontario). He also sent explorers, such as Robert LaSalle (roh-bear la-sahl), to push the limits of New France's territory. Other forts followed.

The king recalled Frontenac in 1682 because so many officials in New France complained about him.

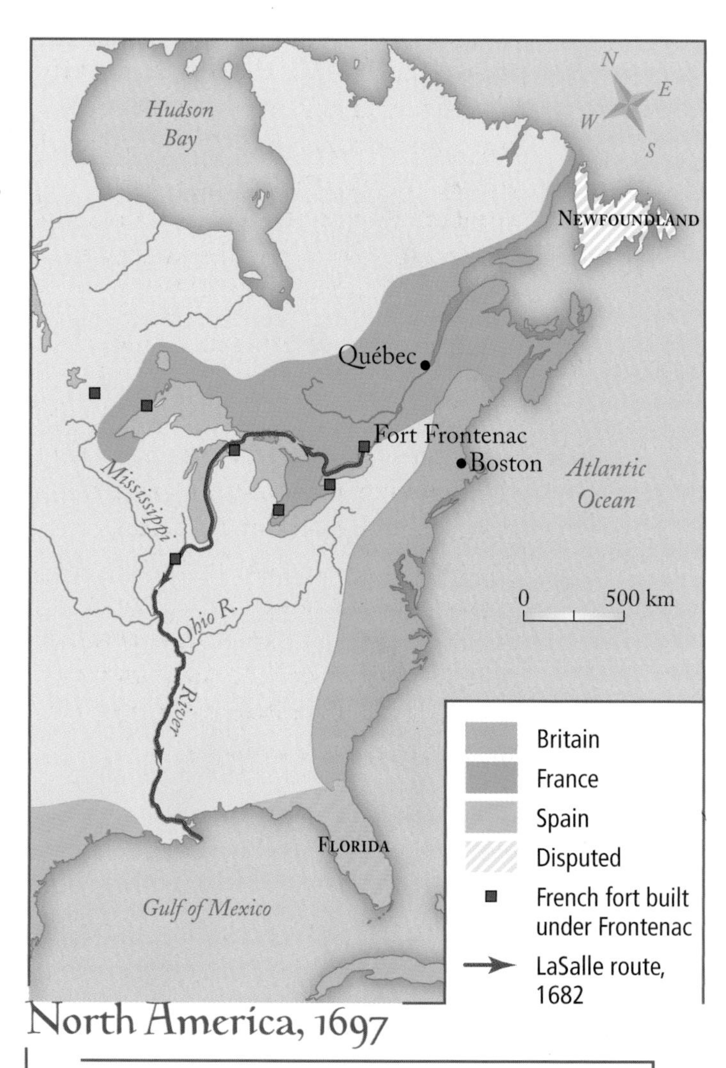

North America, 1697

- Do you think the expansion of French territory in North America was good for New France? Why or why not?
- The light purple colour on this map and others in the textbook is not listed in the legend. Who do you think lives in this region?

During Reading

1. What do you think of Frontenac so far? Why? As you read page 69, jot down any ideas that contrast with your initial opinion.

Frontenac's Second Term

England and France went to war in 1689. Their colonies in North America got involved and launched attacks on each other's settlements. It was at this point that Frontenac returned as governor of New France.

The reason for his return has several interpretations. Some biographers say he was sent by the king to save New France. Others suggest that he was the only man with military experience who France could spare. Some say Frontenac had been asking the king for a new position. When New France's governor no longer wanted the job, the king gave it back to Frontenac.

The image of Frontenac as the saviour of Québec was created in October 1690. That month, a fleet of ships from Boston arrived to sit in the St. Lawrence River outside Québec. A message from the commander, William Phips, demanded that Québec surrender within an hour or be destroyed. In response, Frontenac said, "I have no reply to make to your general other than from the mouths of my cannon and muskets."

My Guns Will Give My Answer—Frontenac, 1690, by Henry Sandham (1842–1910).

- Which man is Frontenac? Which is Phips? What evidence leads you to your answer?
- Which man seems to have the advantage? How does the artist show this?

Phips was dismayed by the show of defiance. Although he landed troops, they never managed to launch an attack on Québec. As the weather grew colder, they finally withdrew to Boston. Frontenac had saved Québec, with almost no casualties.

After Reading

1. Create a T-chart with the title *Frontenac as Hero?* Label one side *Pro* and the other side *Con*. Using the information on Frontenac from pages 68–69, select evidence for each side. Based on your points, discuss with a group whether or not you think Frontenac is a hero.

Picture Yourself as a...

Before Reading

1. Imagine a time machine that allows you to go back to New France. Who would you become? Who would you not want to become? Share your thoughts with a partner.
2. Scan the subheadings in this section. Work with your partner to think of one main idea you recall from earlier readings in this chapter about each of these groups.

Habitant

Habitants had to be highly resourceful. Instead of grocery stores, they had gardens. They also hunted, grew wheat to make bread, and traded for supplies they did not have. Women made candles and most of the family's clothing. All family members had chores and responsibilities—even young children.

Families worked from dawn until dusk. There was always more work to do: land to be cleared, animals to be tended, clothes to make or mend, and countless other tasks.

Fetching Water, by Clarence Gagnon (1881–1942).

- What questions do you have as you look at the picture?

Fille du Roi

Between 1663 and 1673, around 800 filles du roi were shipped to New France. All had to be young enough to bear children. Many were women with few other choices in life. Especially in the beginning, some were beggars or orphans from Paris.

Later on, Talon and other administrators insisted that the girls be healthy and strong. They wanted women who could work hard and live in the harsh climate. In these later years, recruiters in France sent girls from farming families, who were thought better suited to life in New France than "town girls."

When they first arrived, the filles du roi were usually cared for by nuns until they could be married. For most girls, this was no more than a couple of weeks. Men travelled to Québec, Montréal, or Trois-Rivières, chose a wife, and were married by a priest within days.

During Reading

1. Given the information provided so far, what would life in New France be like for women? Give evidence for your conclusions.
2. Predict how life would be different for men. Why was there a difference?

Coureur de Bois

After 1672, two classes of men lived away from the farms and villages of New France, adopting the ways of life of the First Nations. That year, Governor Frontenac ordered that only those with a licence could be runners of the woods. These licenced traders began to call themselves **voyageurs**. The unlicenced traders continued to be called coureurs de bois.

Both voyageurs and coureurs de bois travelled long distances by canoe in search of furs they could bring back to New France to trade. They learned from First Nations how to travel and survive. They lived in portable shelters made of branches and bark and ate deer meat, dried corn and peas, and **pemmican**, a traditional food among some First Nations. Pemmican is dried and pounded meat—usually buffalo—that has been mixed with an equal amount of animal fat and sometimes berries.

Coureur de Bois with Rifle and Axe, by Frederic Remington, 1891. The coureurs de bois, like other people living along New France's rivers, were often plagued by mosquitoes. First Nations taught them to use plants and animal fats or fish oil to fight off the pesky insect.

Clergy Member

Clergy members who made the decision to come to New France chose a difficult path. Jesuits who lived among First Nations had to learn a new way of life. They frequently felt isolated and alone. The Ouendat missions were over 1000 kilometres from the main settlements of New France. This distance meant communication with other Europeans was infrequent.

If their work had been welcomed, it might have made their sacrifices easier. Instead, they were frequently frustrated. Although some First Nations people adopted Catholicism, many did not.

Sometimes the priests even faced hostility. They arrived among the First Nations at the same time as new illnesses such as smallpox. Some First Nations people blamed the priests for the diseases.

Most clergy members, even in New France towns, lived without many comforts. Even Bishop Laval lived much of his time in humble dwellings. Many also faced danger. During conflicts with the British and Haudenosaunee, raids on French villages and settlements were a regular part of life. Along with many other people, missionaries sometimes lost their lives during the raids.

- What evidence can you see in this illustration that shows what the coureurs de bois learned from First Nations?

First Nations Person

The early years of New France were a time of great change for First Nations. They faced many challenges. Some were devastating—European diseases killed thousands of people. Competition in the fur trade and European weapons resulted in deadly conflict between different groups.

Interior of a Longhouse, by Lewis Parker (1926–). Following traditional ways of life became difficult, if not impossible, for many First Nations. Here a group of Ouendat people are shown inside a traditional longhouse.

Increasingly, First Nations found their territories changed by immigrants. Traditional activities, such as hunting, became more difficult as forests were cleared along the rivers to make way for farms. First Nations found themselves pushed farther west, out of their traditional areas.

At the same time, many First Nations enjoyed the conveniences of European trade goods, such as metal knives and cooking pots. These objects made day-to-day tasks easier and were prized possessions.

Seigneur

A seigneur often had a military career before receiving his land grant. As a seigneur, defending the colony continued to be a significant responsibility. Between military activities, each seigneur also tended to the clearing and settlement of his land.

Unlike seigneurs in France, many seigneurs in New France could not rely on income from their habitants alone. Until a seigneur had thirty or forty habitants, his income was not much higher than that of his tenants. To make extra money, seigneurs sometimes got involved in the fur trade or Sovereign Council.

Members of the community usually held seigneurs in high esteem. The front pew in the church was reserved for him and his family. If the seigneur was prosperous and gave money generously to the Church, he was mentioned in the weekly prayers.

After Reading

1. Prepare a graphic organizer to record information about the attractions and drawbacks of life in New France for the groups of people discussed on pages 70–72. Your organizer might look something like the following:

Life in New France	Attractions	Drawbacks
Habitant		

2. Choose one of the following roles: habitant, fille du roi, coureur de bois, clergy member, First Nations person, or seigneur. Select a partner who chose a different role and prepare a dialogue. Discuss your day-to-day life, why you are in New France, and your hopes and dreams. Compare your hopes and dreams to those of others who lived in New France at this time.

Compress

1. Look at the painting below and answer the questions that follow:
   a) Based on what you have read, do you believe this painting is an accurate image of the habitant's life? Why or why not?
   b) What questions do you have about this painting?
   c) How does the life of the habitant compare to that of the intendant? Compare this painting to the one of the intendant's palace on page 60.

Habitants, by Cornelius Krieghoff, 1852.

2. Create a K-W-L Organizer about the role of one of the following groups in New France: women, the Roman Catholic Church, coureurs de bois, habitants, seigneurs, or First Nations. Add the optional W—*What else would I like to learn about this topic?* and H—*How would I find this additional information?* sections. Find the answers to one of your questions. If you prefer, find the answer to one of the questions from the K-W-L Organizer you created on page 51. In your notebook, explain how you found your answer.

Express

3. Select one of the key individuals studied in this chapter, such as Jean Talon, Bishop Laval, or Governor Frontenac. Prepare an argument stating whether you think this person was a great leader or not. Discuss the issue with a partner who has a different point of view.
4. Use an illustration or photograph from this chapter as the inspiration for a short story, journal entry, dialogue, skit, or monologue. Base your work on real people, events, or activities from the past. Be as creative as you can, as well as historically accurate.
5. Reread the maps on pages 51 and 68. State the main idea of each. Using information from the maps, what prediction can you make about the relationship between British and French colonies in North America?

Their Stories, Our History

Create a poster promoting New France as a great destination for the modern time traveller. Include top attractions and activities visitors might see and experience.

If you prefer, work in a small group to write and perform a television or radio advertisement that accomplishes the same purpose.

chapter 3
The Fall of New France

- What do you notice about the buildings in this painting?
- What do you think the people in the painting are discussing? Why?
- Recall the Church's role in New France. How does the artist reflect this role in the painting?
- What do you think happened before the scene shown in this painting? How do you think these events will affect the people in the painting?

A View of the Church of Notre-Dame-de-la-Victoire, Québec City, by Richard Short, 1760.

A View of the Taking of Québec, September 13, 1759, by Laurie & Whittle, 1797. The engraving shows the three stages of the battle: the British disembarking, scaling the cliff, and the fight on the Plains of Abraham.

- Which side in the battle scene appears to have the advantage? Why?
- What techniques has the artist used to make one side look superior to the other? Suggest a reason for these choices.

The fall of New France in 1763 marked the end of a series of wars involving European countries for over seventy years. The conflicts had not been restricted to Europe. They had also fanned the flames of hostilities between British and French colonies in North America.

As in all wars, there were many innocent victims. In particular, the **Acadians** were caught in the struggle between the French and British for control of the continent. The Acadians were descendants of the earliest French inhabitants of Nova Scotia and New Brunswick. Many Acadians still live in this part of Canada.

Other innocent victims included the habitant farmers of New France. For the most part, these farmers had little interest in politics. Most wanted only to make a living from their land. They found themselves caught up in the fighting, with their homes looted and land burned.

First Nations were also caught in the middle and were encouraged to take sides in the European conflict.

The fall of New France also marked the beginning of one of the major themes of Canadian history: French–English relations. After 1763, the British government took over a colony of people who had lived in North America for three generations. They were **Canadiens**. The Canadiens had a distinct language and culture. They were different from the British and even different from people in France. After winning the war, Britain had to decide what to do with the thousands of Canadiens living along the St. Lawrence River.

This chapter will help you understand

- life in Acadia
- causes of the Seven Years' War
- impact of the Battle of the Plains of Abraham
- problems for the British after the fall of New France
- conflicting points of view on the fall of New France

Featured Skills

- Finding Facts, Opinions, and Arguments
- Determining Cause and Effect
- Conflicting Viewpoints and Bias
- Writing a Supported Opinion Paragraph
- Paraphrasing

Life in Acadia

Before Reading

1. What kinds of challenges did Canada's early settlers face?
2. With a partner, discuss things that you wear or use because of your environment. How might these habits be different in a tropical environment or desert? How much does the environment influence what people wear and use?

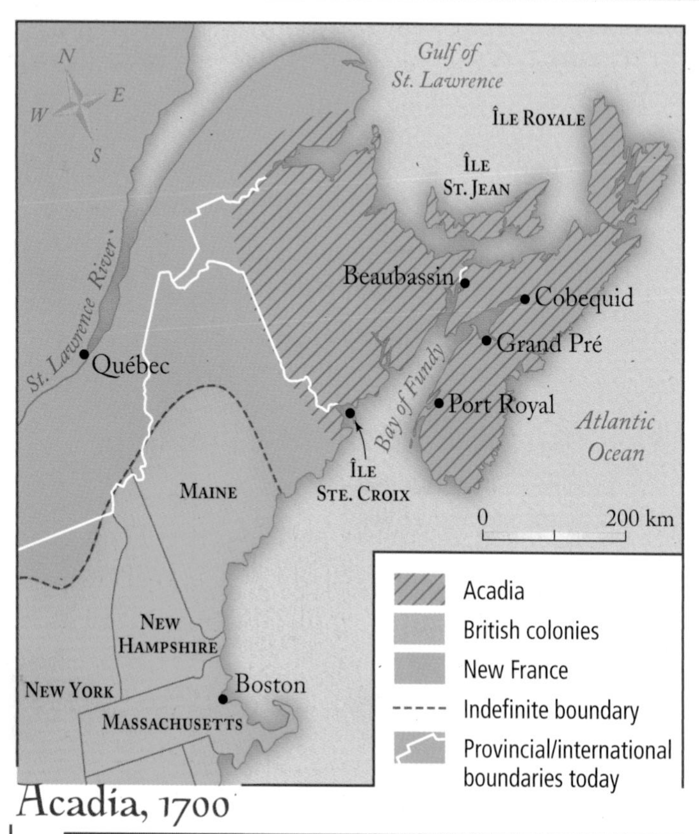

Acadia, 1700

- Do you think it would be easier to travel from Port Royal to Québec or to Boston? How might this situation affect Acadia?

Settlers in Acadia had special farming methods that made them some of the most successful farmers in the colonies. Early Acadians adapted Dutch technology to make a one-way water gate called an **aboiteau**. An aboiteau is a hinged valve in a dyke, which is a type of dam.

The technology helped the Acadians farm areas that were normally covered in ocean water part of the time. Unlike settlers in other parts of New France, farmers did not have to spend many years clearing their land of trees.

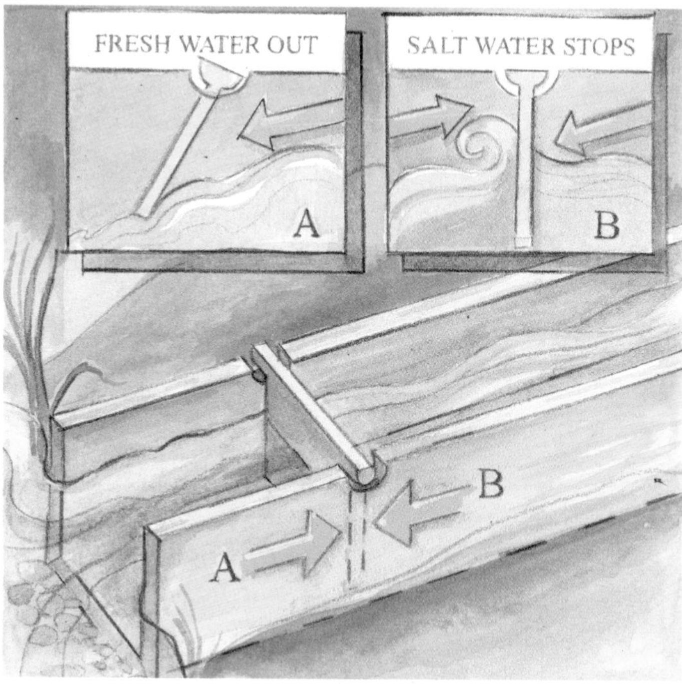

The aboiteaux allowed fresh water to run off the marshes in low tide, but prevented salt water from running onto land in high tide.

The aboiteaux had another benefit. They allowed the Acadians to farm land that had not been traditionally used by local First Nations. This meant the Acadians had few conflicts over the land with Mi'kmaq people near their settlements.

Acadians farmed salt-marsh hay, which also grew naturally in the area. The hay allowed them to keep cattle, sheep, and pigs over the winter. The Acadians also farmed wheat, barley, rye, peas, corn, flax, and hemp. They had gardens of beets, carrots, cabbages, turnips, onions, and chives. Many farms also had fruit trees.

Cutting Salt-marsh Hay, by Azor Vienneau. Using a variety of pitchforks and rakes, the hay was rolled, carried, and piled high on raised platforms called staddles.

- Azor Vienneau created this painting and many others for the Nova Scotia Museum. His work is based on careful historical and archaeological research. How does the audience for Vienneau's paintings affect your impression of his accuracy?

Because they grew such a variety of foods, the Acadians were less dependent on France than other settlers in New France. Settlers in Québec still relied on many imported foods from France. Compared to most French peasants and other settlers in New France, the Acadians had a high standard of living.

Acadia had seigneuries, but seigneurs did not play a significant role in the lives of Acadians. In the rest of New France, the intendant oversaw the seigneurial system. However, Acadia was far from the intendant's watchful eye. For the Acadians, family and church were the most important institutions.

During Reading

1. Read the feature about Finding Facts, Opinions, and Arguments on this page. As you read pages 78 and 79, work with a partner to identify any information that is clearly fact, opinion, or argument. Use a chart to organize your notes.

Finding Facts, Opinions, and Arguments

Writers express a combination of facts, opinions, and arguments. Historical literacy means that you can tell the difference between them. This skill will help you judge whether your information is reliable. You will then be able to draw your own conclusions about historical events and people.

Facts are

- exact, specific
- information that can be investigated and found to have taken place. This means facts can be checked in other sources.

Example: *In 1663, King Louis XIV decided to govern New France with a system of Royal Government.*

Opinions are

- conclusions and viewpoints
- not proven, open to debate
- often expressed with sweeping generalizations, using words such as *always, everyone, never,* and so on
- often introduced with phrases such as *I think* and *I believe*

Example: *Habitants in New France did not respect their priests as much as settlers in Acadia did.*

Arguments are

- reasons someone gives to support his or her opinion
- explanations of why an event has happened or will happen
- attempts to prove something, often by using facts. The more facts used, the stronger the argument.

Example: *The Acadians had access to a wide variety of food and trade goods. This gave them a higher standard of living than other settlers in New France.*

Most couples had ten or eleven children. Close-knit communities worked together to build houses or construct or repair the dykes. They also gathered frequently for evenings of music, with people playing their fiddles and harps.

The Catholic Church was the foundation of Acadian communities. Clergy members were considered community leaders. They often helped resolve disputes or problems among community members.

Raising a Barn, by Azor Vienneau. Acadia tended to have fewer new immigrants than the rest of New France. People in Acadian communities generally knew one another well and had a strong sense of shared identity.

PRIMARY SOURCE 3.1

From the Journal of Robert Hale, New England Medical Doctor Who Travelled to Nova Scotia in 1731

The women here differ as much in their clothing—besides wearing of wooden shoes—from those of New England as they do in features and complexion [skin tone], which is dark enough by living in the smoke in the summer to defend themselves against the mosquitoes, and in the winter against the cold. Their clothes are good enough, but they look as if they were pitched [put] on with pitchforks, and very often their stockings are down about their heels.... They have but one room in their houses,...[a] cellar and sometimes a closet. Their bedrooms are made something after the manner of a sailor's cabin, but boarded all round about the bigness of the bed, except one little hole on the foreside [front], just big enough to crawl into, before which is a curtain drawn and a step to get into it. There stands a chest. They have not above two or three chairs in a house, and those wooden ones, bottom and all. I saw but two mugs among all the French and the lip of one of them was broken down above two inches.

Population Figures from North America

Year	Acadia	New France	British Colonies
1608	10	28	100
1640	200	220	28 000

- What questions do you have about this information?
- What conclusions can be made from this data?

Acadians Trading with New Englanders, by Azor Vienneau.

- What trade goods are visible in the painting?
- Why do you think Acadia had more frequent contact with New England than with Québec? Use the map on page 76 to help you answer this question.

What they could not provide for themselves, the Acadians received in trade. They traded for furs with the Mi'kmaq and used these furs to trade for goods from their other trading partners. They received fabric, lace, firearms, and religious items from the other French settlements.

Unlike other settlers in New France, the Acadians had a lively trade with New England, the British colonies in North America. From these colonies to the south, they obtained molasses, cooking pots, clay pipes, gunpowder, fabric, and rum. Some New England traders even set up warehouses in Acadia.

Despite this active trade, the Acadians were very different from their British neighbours. The Acadians were French, Catholic, and friendly with the First Nations people of their region. Some Acadians even married Mi'kmaq women and raised families. In contrast, settlers in the British colonies were English and Protestant. They were frequently in conflict with the First Nations whose land they wanted.

After Reading

1. First-hand observations are an important primary resource for historians. If you were doing a report about the Acadians and wanted to include some of the information from Robert Hale's journal entry on page 78, how might you do this? How could you show that the information is an individual's observation? Discuss your options as a class.
2. Prepare a Venn Diagram to compare life in New France to life in Acadia. A Venn Diagram includes two overlapping circles:

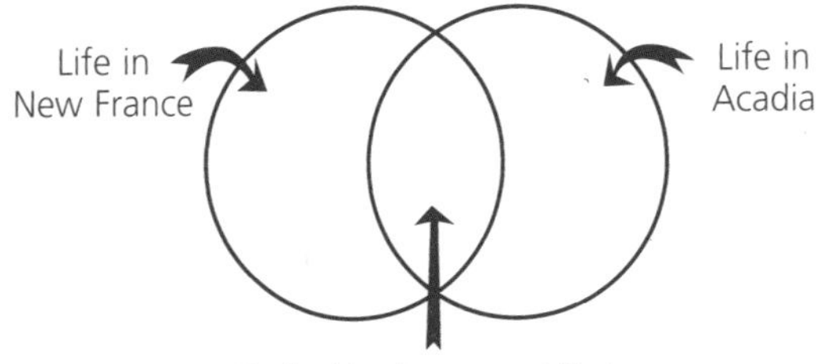

3. Write at least two opinions about life in Acadia or life in New France. Make each opinion into an argument by supporting it with one or more facts.

Think It Through

European Rivalries, North American Conflict

Before Reading

1. Discuss with a partner what is meant by cause and effect. Think of an example where you can identify a cause and effect relationship.

Beginning in 1689, a series of wars began in Europe that would last until 1763. These wars involved most of the nations in Europe. France and Britain were major rivals.

Wars in Europe often sparked conflict in their colonies. This war was no exception. In North America, New France and New England competed for land, furs, and fish. Both countries wanted to dominate the continent.

The British and French colonies in North America were different in a number of ways.

The British colonies were mainly interested in settlement and opening new land for agriculture. The main British region, the Thirteen Colonies, was becoming crowded. Many people wanted to move west into the Ohio Valley, which was controlled by the French and their First Nations fur trade partners.

In contrast, the French were divided between expanding the fur trade and establishing settlements. Because agriculture needed more people than the fur trade, the Thirteen Colonies had ten times more people than New France. The French were mainly settled on farms along the St. Lawrence River and in a few major centres, such as Montréal, Québec, Trois-Rivières, and Louisbourg.

Compared to British goals, French goals were more compatible with First Nations traditions. The fur trade depended on First Nations people maintaining their traditional ways of life, which included hunting and trapping. In contrast, agriculture meant cleared land, fenced farms, roads, and villages. All these aspects of agriculture made traditional First Nations ways of life difficult to maintain.

An Ontario Farm with Partial Improvements, as published in a pamphlet for prospective immigrants to Ontario in 1880. This illustration showed how a farm in the early 1700s might look after about thirty years of work.

- What changes do you see in this illustration that might impact First Nations traditions?

During Reading

1. Pages 81–82 show how to create a graphic organizer summarizing the cause and effect relationships included in the information on page 80. As you read pages 81–82, copy the graphic organizer into your notebook. On your own, complete the organizer using the information on page 83.

Determining Cause and Effect

A *cause* is an action, event, or idea that makes something happen. The *effect* is the result. An event often has more than one cause and more than one effect. In most cases, a series of causes brings on effects that become causes for new actions or events.

For example, you might read a headline in the sports section of your newspaper to find out that the Toronto Raptors fired their head coach. The rest of the news article would probably describe some of the causes of that event. You might also have your own ideas about why this happened.

Graphic organizers, such as the one that follows, can help display the relationship between causes and effects:

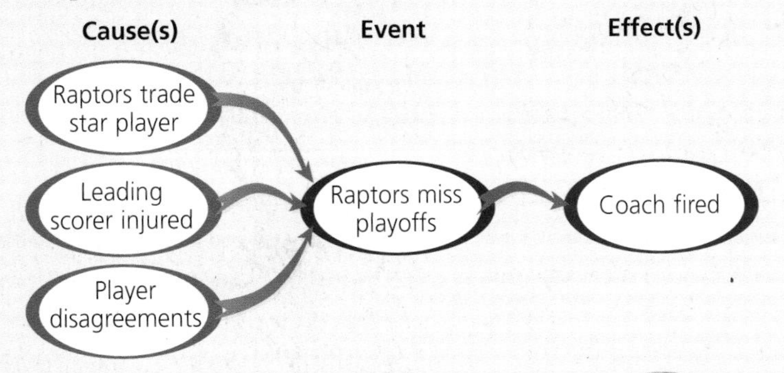

Analyzing cause and effect relationships is not always straightforward. Some causes might be more important than others. For example, the injured player might have made a huge difference in the team's ability to win games. You might underline or star that cause on your organizer to indicate its importance.

Some effects may not be apparent for some time. For example, missing the playoffs may mean fewer people will attend Raptors games the next season. This might result in financial problems for the team.

Key words can signal that you are looking at a cause–effect connection. Cause words and phrases include *because, for this reason, due to*, and *since.* Effect words include *therefore, consequently, thus, so,* and *as a result.*

I'm going to use chunking as a reading technique to do this assignment. I'll consider each paragraph one chunk. After reading a paragraph, I'll record any cause and effect relationships before moving on to the next paragraph.

Think It Through

I don't see any signal words in the first paragraph, so that won't help me. However, the first sentence in the second paragraph provides a general cause and effect pattern: wars in Europe usually started wars in North America. Because war broke out in Europe in 1689, I'm guessing that war broke out in North America around the same time.

The third paragraph gives me another cause of conflict: the British and French colonies had different goals. The other paragraphs explain how they were different. The British wanted land for settlement. The French were more interested in the fur trade. Those are details, so I won't add them to my organizer. I'll just include the main idea.

Cause(s)
Event
Effect(s)
1689: War breaks out in Europe
British and French colonies have different goals
Conflict in North America
Frontenac sent back to New France

I remember from Chapter 2 that some historians think Frontenac was sent back to New France to help protect it. Others believe the king had other reasons for appointing him. Either way, I think the timing of his appointment was connected to war breaking out, so I added it to my list of effects. Now I'll read page 83 to see if I can find other effects of conflict in North America.

Britain Wins Acadia

In Chapter 2, you learned that Frontenac returned to New France in 1689, just as a major European conflict was beginning. Frontenac began his new term in office by launching raids on English settlements and Haudenosaunee villages.

Acadia was often the focus of the British response. New England enjoyed its economic interests in Acadia and wanted more political control. Acadia was invaded by the English in 1689, but was returned to the French with the Treaty of Ryswick in 1697.

In 1701, another major war began in Europe. The French and their First Nations allies took the opportunity to launch raids on British frontier settlements. Stories of British settlers being massacred in the Ohio Valley spread through the Thirteen Colonies. A sense of bitterness towards the French grew.

In response, the British navy launched raids against French fishing fleets and coastal settlements. A combined British and colonial army invaded Port Royal in 1710. The Acadian colony was once again in British hands. This time, it stayed there. The British renamed Acadia as Nova Scotia and Port Royal as Annapolis Royal. In 1713, the Treaty of Utrecht permanently gave Newfoundland and a large part of Acadia to Britain.

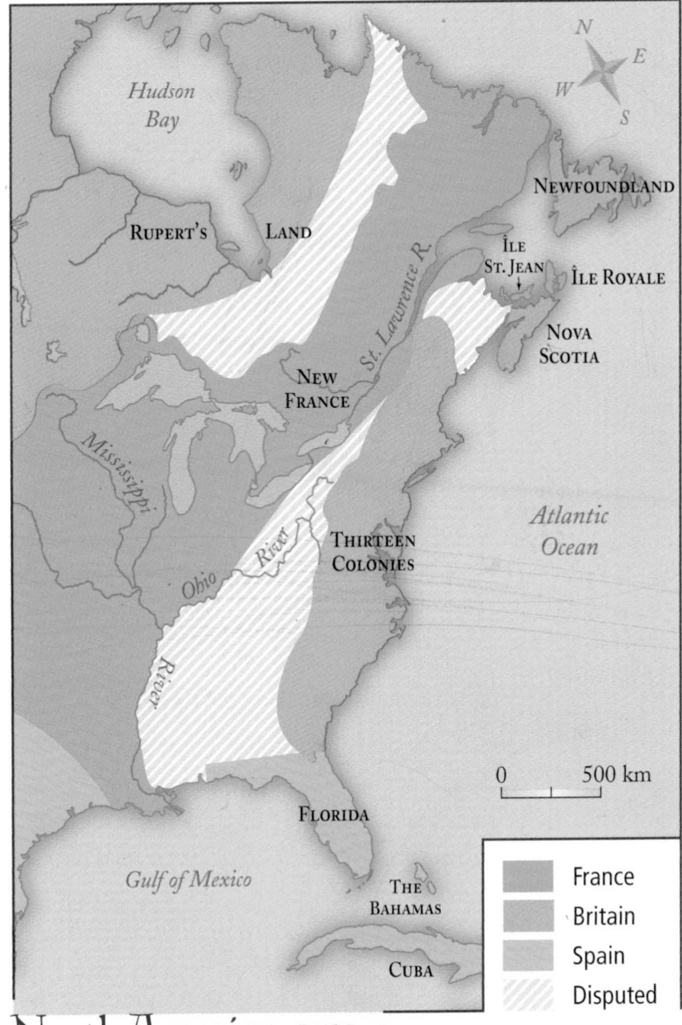

North America, 1713

The Treaty of Utrecht gave Acadia, Newfoundland, and the land around Hudson Bay to Britain, but it did not specify boundaries.

- Why was New France harder to defend after 1713? Compare New France's territory on this map to the territory shown on the map on page 68.
- Why do you think the Treaty of Utrecht did not establish clear boundaries for the territories mentioned?

After Reading

1. Use your Cause and Effect Organizer to summarize the main ideas of this section in no more than three sentences.

Buildup to War

Before Reading

1. Sometimes, events that happen in another part of the world can lead to a reaction in your community. In some cases, the reaction might have causes beyond the event itself. As a class, think of examples.

Not all conflict in North America resulted from European events. Some problems were "born and raised" in the North American colonies. Three of these problems are described on pages 84–85.

During Reading

1. As you read, consider how the oath of allegiance is a cause *and* effect of conflict.
2. As you read pages 84–85, add to the Cause and Effect Organizer you created for pages 80–83.

The Oath of Allegiance

Normally, new subjects had to swear an **oath of allegiance**, or a promise of loyalty, to their new monarch. After 1713, Britain tried five times to impose the oath on the residents of Acadia. Each time, the Acadians refused. They wanted a promise of **neutrality**. If Britain and France went to war again, the Acadians did not want to be expected to fight against the French.

In 1730, the Acadians finally took the oath, but on their own terms. The governor promised that the Acadians could continue their Roman Catholic religion. He also promised they could be neutral in a war between Britain and France. However, the oath did not satisfy the British. They did not trust Acadian loyalty.

Louisbourg

After losing Acadia, France founded Louisbourg on Île Royale (present-day Cape Breton Island). Louisbourg became a significant French trading centre and military base near the mouth of the St. Lawrence River. It was an important strategic location.

Britain considered Louisbourg an economic and military threat. Louisbourg's success increased British hostility towards French colonists, including the Acadians. In 1749, Britain began to build up Halifax to balance Louisbourg's power.

View from a Warship, 1745, by Lewis Parker (1926–). At one point, Louisbourg was as important as Québec to French interests in North America.

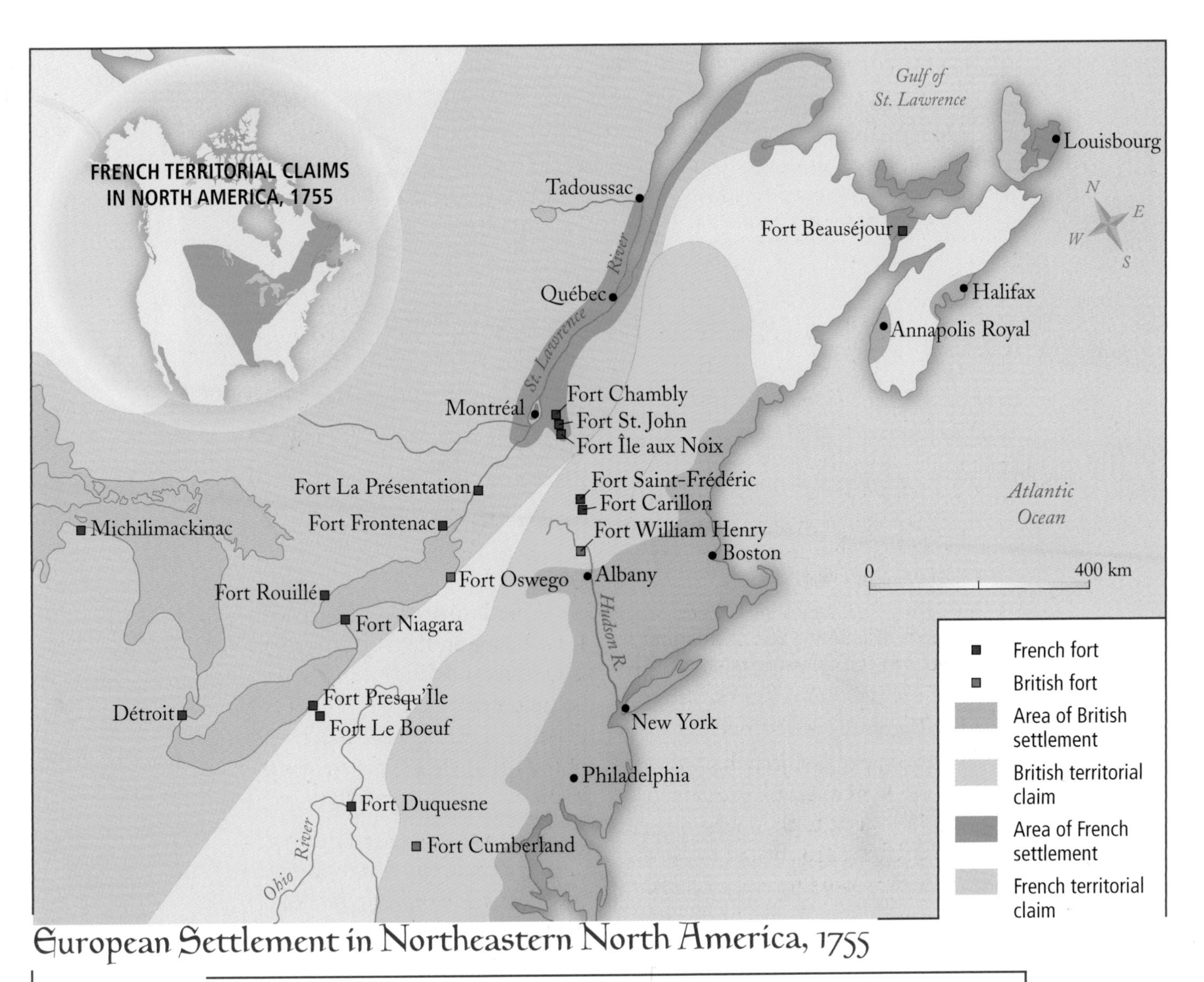

European Settlement in Northeastern North America, 1755

- Compare French territorial claims to the area of French settlement. Why were these areas different? How might this difference have impacted New France as it went to war with the British colonies?
- Why would Louisbourg's location concern the British colonies?
- Find the Ohio River on the map. Why might the valley surrounding this river have been an attractive place for settlers from the Thirteen Colonies?

The Ohio Valley

In 1747, a group of Virginia **land speculators** formed the Ohio Land Company. Land speculators purchase large sections of land in the hope of selling them in the future for a profit. In 1749, the British Crown granted the company 81 000 hectares of prime land. Their grant was near the forks of the Ohio River (around present-day Pittsburgh, Pennsylvania). The company hoped to set up fur-trading posts and then sell the land to settlers at a later date.

The French had no interest in sharing the land or fur trade with the British. By 1753, they had built more forts in the Ohio Valley to defend their interests.

After Reading

1. In groups of four, make a timeline of six events leading to conflict in North America. Include events from pages 80–85.

Expulsion of the Acadians

Before Reading

1. How would you react if you were suddenly expelled from your country? What would you take with you? Record your responses in your journal.

In 1730, the Acadians had sworn an oath of allegiance to Britain. However, they continued to supply French forts with food and firewood. British officials were not happy about it, but let them continue.

By the 1750s, tensions between the British and French were high. Supplying French forts was now seen as outright disloyal. In 1755, British administrators insisted that the Acadians take a new oath of allegiance. This time, the oath would not have the condition of neutrality. Reluctantly, the Acadians agreed.

However, Charles Lawrence, acting governor of Nova Scotia, was still not satisfied. He and his council decided it was time to expel, or remove, the Acadians from Nova Scotia.

On September 5, 1755, 418 Acadian men were brought together in the church at Grand Pré. John Winslow, commissary general of the British forces in Nova Scotia, read them a **resolution**. A resolution is a formal statement of a government's intention. In this case, the resolution told the Acadians "that your lands and tenements [homes], cattle and livestock of all kinds are forfeited [to be given up] to the crown, together with all your other effects, except money and household goods, and that you yourselves are to be removed from this...Province."

The Acadians were not allowed to take more than they could carry. Everything else was to go to the British Crown. The government planned to sell these goods to pay the costs of shipping the Acadians out of the colony. In effect, the Acadians had to pay for their own expulsion.

Reading the Order of Expulsion to the Acadians in the Parish Church at Grand Pré, in 1755, by C. W. Jefferys (1869–1951).

- What clues in this painting suggest that the artist is more sympathetic to one group than the other?

In 1755, over 6000 Acadians were forced to leave Nova Scotia. Families were rounded up, put on ships, and sent to other British colonies. Their homes and barns were often burned to the ground. Aided by the Mi'kmaq, some were able to escape, but then faced a difficult winter trying to survive. Many of the escapees were later caught and deported anyway. Between 1755 and 1762, another 10 000 people were expelled.

The British hoped that sending the French-speaking, Catholic Acadians to English-speaking, Protestant colonies would make the Acadians more like other British colonists.

The expulsion also caused problems for the Mi'kmaq. The Acadians and Mi'kmaq communities had long been friendly. For the most part, they lived side by side in peace. Some Mi'kmaq and Acadian families were related.

The situation under British rule was completely different. Britain immediately increased English-speaking settlement to the area. Settlers came from Britain and the Thirteen Colonies. These settlers were not as open to sharing the land with First Nations. The Mi'kmaq were increasingly pushed out of their traditional territories.

The Expulsion of the Acadians, by George Craig, 1893.

- Based on what you see in this painting, what adjectives would you use to describe the expulsion of the Acadians?
- Why do you think the artist chose to paint the scene from a distance instead of close up? What effect does this have?

Conflicting Viewpoints and Bias

Several people may witness the same event, but have different interpretations of what took place.

How can you decide what really happened? You need to evaluate each viewpoint, looking for similarities and differences. Where there are differences, you need to decide which viewpoint you believe is correct or most valid. Most often, the fairest view is one that considers several viewpoints.

Questions to Examine Conflicting Viewpoints

- What is the viewpoint being presented?
- Does the person use facts or just opinions to make his or her point?
- Who is the writer or speaker? What is his or her background? (This could include where the person was born or raised, or the person's age, gender, or cultural identity.) How might this background affect the person's view of the issue? A person's worldview acts like a lens through which they see the world.
- How would the account or story change if it were told from a different point of view?
- Why is it important to consider this person's point of view?
- What **bias** does this person have toward the issue? A bias is commonly seen as an unfair or unbalanced point of view. A biased view makes no attempt to see the topic from other perspectives.

Sometimes a bias is deliberate. Someone wants to have a convincing argument, so they ignore all opposing evidence. Most often, biases are unconscious. A person's worldview can make their biases invisible to them.

During Reading

1. Some people believe the British decision to expel the Acadians was inhumane and wrong. The following are two viewpoints of the expulsion, expressed by fictional characters of the time. In what ways are the speakers biased?

Expulsion was the right thing to do. The Acadians were a threat to British security. What if a force of French from Québec and Louisbourg attacked Nova Scotia? We'd be sandwiched in between! With the help of the Acadians and their friends the Mi'kmaq, we could be massacred like the innocent British settlers in the Ohio Valley.

The Acadians were too independent for their own good. What made them think they could live in a British colony and continue to trade their best goods to the French? If that's not disloyal, what is? I don't blame Governor Lawrence for mistrusting them. When they wouldn't take a full oath of allegiance to Britain, they should have been forced to leave.

Governor Lawrence was more than patient. Some leaders wouldn't have given them a chance! They would have expelled the Acadians immediately—or worse. The Acadians had more than forty years to show their loyalty to Britain. They didn't, so that's their problem. Now that they are gone, we can use their land for the best interests of British colonists.

Thomas,
Halifax merchant

What the British did to my people was a grave error. All we wanted was to live on our land in peace. We swore our allegiance to the British Crown—what more did they want?

Our ancestors came here to nothing but wilderness and turned it into a thriving community. The British then destroyed our land and stole the rest. The loyalty issue was just an excuse to take our property.

They loaded us like cattle onto unsafe ships that I wouldn't use to transport lumber. My family was separated—I never saw my father again. I heard some ships sank, losing all their passengers. The ship I was on arrived in Georgia. We had to start over again with nothing. Many people starved to death. We didn't know how to survive in this land—it was hot, humid, and completely different from Acadia.

The British colonists did not want us either—they were already short of good farmland. Some of us were placed in refugee camps because there was nowhere else for us to go. Others were kept on ships over the winter or sent on to other locations.

The expulsion was an attempt by the British to eliminate any trace of the French culture and Catholicism in their colonies. It had nothing to do with our threat and everything to do with their biases against us and their hunger for our land.

Clair (kl-air),
Acadian refugee

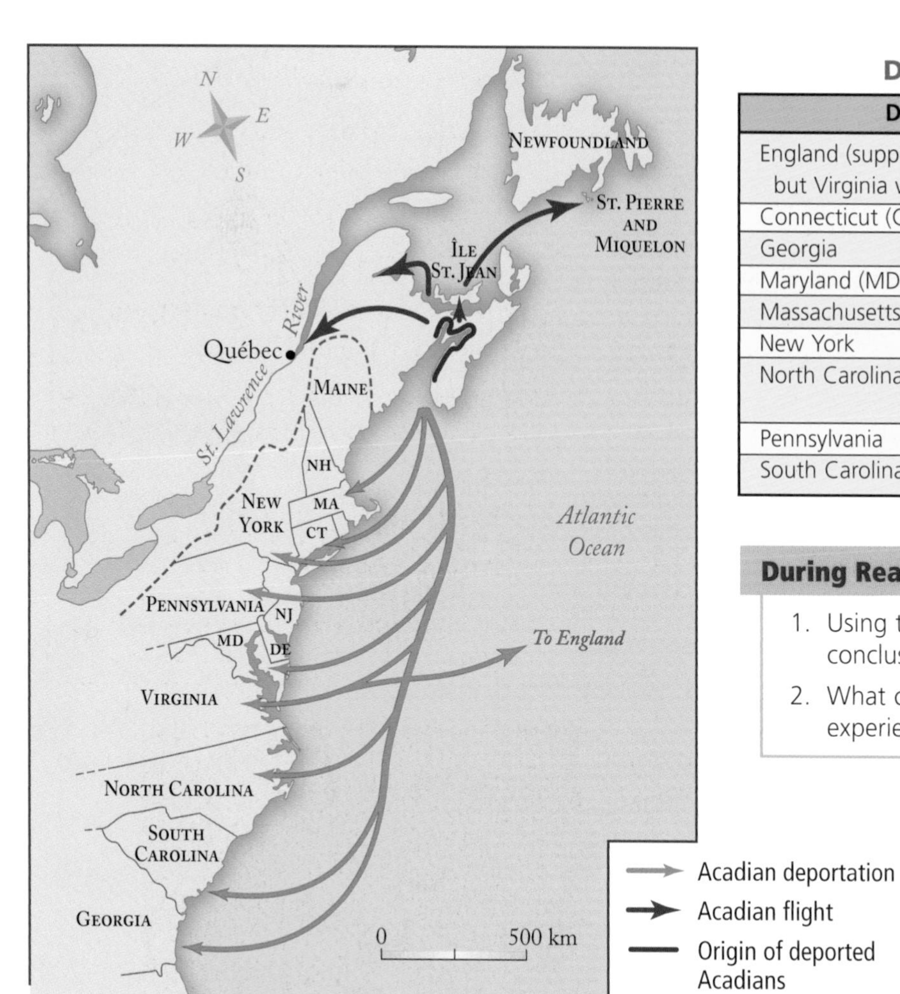

Acadian Deportation, 1755–1757

Deportation Statistics, 1755

Destination	Number Deported
England (supposed to go to Virginia, but Virginia would not accept them)	1500
Connecticut (CT)	731
Georgia	400
Maryland (MD)	913
Massachusetts (MA)	735
New York	344
North Carolina	50 (another 232 escaped)
Pennsylvania	454
South Carolina	942

During Reading

1. Using the information on this page, what conclusions can you make about the expulsion?
2. What challenges do you think the deportees experienced?

Beginning in 1758, many exiled Acadians made their way to New Orleans. Today, New Orleans still has a sizable population with French heritage.

Writing a Supported Opinion Paragraph

Much historical writing involves opinions that are supported by facts. A historian might write, *The British treated the Acadians cruelly in 1755*, but that is only an opinion. What makes that opinion more believable is the quality of the argument that supports it.

A good argument is an opinion backed up by so many facts that the opinion seems to be the most logical conclusion, viewpoint, or interpretation possible. Poor arguments do not offer adequate evidence for the opinion.

A supported opinion paragraph is a well-supported argument.

Steps to Writing a Supported Opinion Paragraph

1. Begin with a sentence that clearly identifies your opinion, such as *The British treated the Acadians cruelly in 1755.*
2. Follow your opinion with two or more sentences that support it. Your next sentences might be, *In that year, over 6000 Acadians were expelled from their homeland. The families were rounded up, and their homes and barns were burned to the ground.*
3. Conclude with a sentence or two that restates your opinion. Your conclusion may also summarize the most important fact that supports your opinion. For example, *The British decision to expel the Acadians resulted in severe hardships for thousands of families that were innocent of any wrongdoing.*

Evangeline: A Tale of Acadie

Waste are those peasant farms, and the farmers forever departed!

Scattered like dust and leaves, when the mighty blasts of October

Seize them, and whirl them aloft, and sprinkle them far o'er the ocean

Naught but tradition remains of the beautiful village of Grand Pré.

The poem *Evangeline*, by Henry Wadsworth Longfellow, was first published in 1847. It tells the story of the expulsion of the Acadians.

- What image in this section of the poem seems to be historically accurate? Explain your answer.

Longfellow's *Evangeline* is the story of an Acadian girl who was separated from her fiancé during the expulsion. This statue of the fictional Evangeline is in Grand Pré, Nova Scotia.

After Reading

1. Copy and complete the following Both Sides Now Organizer to help you decide whether the British decision to exile the Acadians was cruel.

Evidence that Supports • •	**The exile of the Acadians was a cruel and unjustified act by the British.**	Evidence that Opposes • •
Decision		
Reasons		

2. Use your Both Sides Now Organizer to write a supported opinion paragraph about whether you think the expulsion of the Acadians was the right decision.

The Seven Years' War

Before Reading

1. Which country seems to have had the advantage before the war? Scan the rest of this chapter to predict who would win the Seven Years' War.
2. What do you think would happen to the side that lost the war? Share your thoughts with a partner.

Britain declared war on France in 1756. During the war that followed (known as the Seven Years' War), a final conflict took place in North America between the British and French colonies. The results of this conflict changed the course of history in North America.

Britain had a three-pronged plan to defeat the French in North America.

1. In the west, they aimed to capture Fort Niagara, Fort Duquesne, and the French forts in the Ohio Valley.
2. They would capture Louisbourg and Fort Beauséjour in Nova Scotia.
3. The third approach would capture Québec by moving from the south through Fort Saint-Frédéric and Fort Frontenac.

Edward Braddock was sent to oversee the operation.

Different Styles of Fighting

In Europe at this time, the goal of war was to capture territory. Often this was accomplished by laying siege to a fort or castle. A siege involved surrounding the fort, preventing anyone or anything (including food) from leaving or entering. When the fort was surrendered, the territory would be claimed, but the soldiers would be allowed to leave in peace.

- The numbered items above and the map to the right both have information relating to Britain's plan to defeat the French in North America. Which form do you think explains the British strategies best? Why?
- In groups of three, discuss how you would carry out the three-pronged attack planned by the British. Use a blank map to plan the attack. Share your plan with another group.
- Why are maps an important tool of the military?

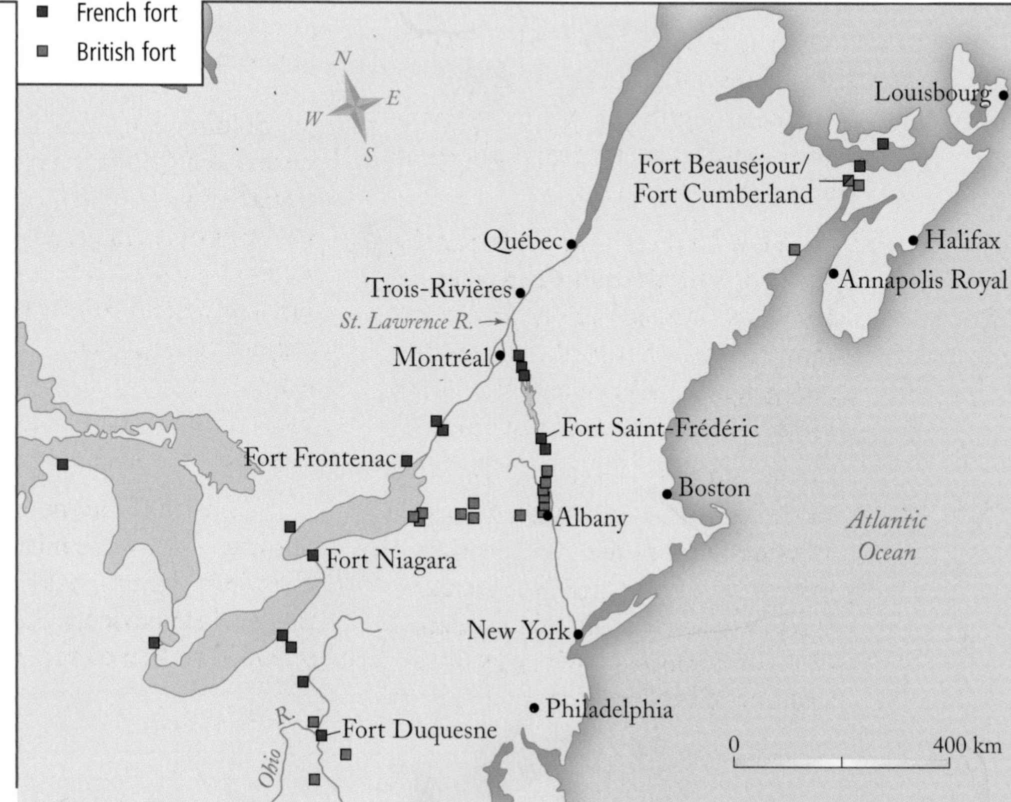

Areas of Conflict in the Seven Years' War, 1756–1763

The Europeans were also accustomed to open-field combat. In this style of fighting, each side lined up its professional soldiers across an open field. The soldiers would then move towards each other as they fired their muskets. As with laying siege, the goal was to gain territory by forcing the other side to retreat or surrender.

Battle of Marengo, June 14, 1800, by Tessier. Traditional European wars were organized events with formal rules and strategies.

In contrast, First Nations warfare was more about demonstrating character and bravery. First Nations men at war would rather fight to the death than surrender.

First Nations weapons technology made open-field combat impractical. Bows and arrows were more accurate than muskets, but could not reach across a long field. They were more useful for close-range fighting.

In addition, North America was more heavily forested than Europe. It made sense to make use of the forests for camouflage. Traditional First Nations warfare relied on an element of surprise, with ambushes and lightning-fast raids.

Supplemented by First Nations allies and some professional soldiers from France, the Canadien militia were the main source of defence for New France.

Soldiers from France and Britain were trained in European warfare. Canadien militia understood the countryside, climate, and First Nations styles of fighting. The Compagnies Franche de la Marine (kum-pa-nyay fran-se de la ma-ree-ne) included many Canadien soldiers. This gave the French a strategic advantage in the early part of the war.

The British had no comparable soldiers. Their force relied on European fighting techniques, without the local expertise the Canadiens provided to French forces.

During Reading

1. As you read about the early stages of the war, place the location of each battle on a copy of the map. Identify French and British successes in your legend.

Early Stages of the War

In the winter of 1755–56, the French sent the Marquis de Montcalm (mar-kee de mon-calm) to command its troops in North America. In August 1756, Montcalm and a force of 3000 left Fort Frontenac to lay siege to Fort Oswego. Montcalm's troops included French soldiers, Canadien militia, and First Nations allies.

When the British commander at Oswego was killed, the fort surrendered. Montcalm allowed the First Nations to take the goods that remained in the fort. The victory strengthened First Nations loyalties towards the French.

In 1757, Montcalm led an attack on Fort William Henry. The French first attacked during the winter. They were equipped with skates, toboggans, and snowshoes. However, without heavy artillery, they could not capture the fort.

Montcalm attacked again in August. This time he brought heavy artillery. On August 17, the French laid siege to the fort.

The British commander surrendered. As was tradition in European wars, Montcalm offered the British the opportunity to leave safely.

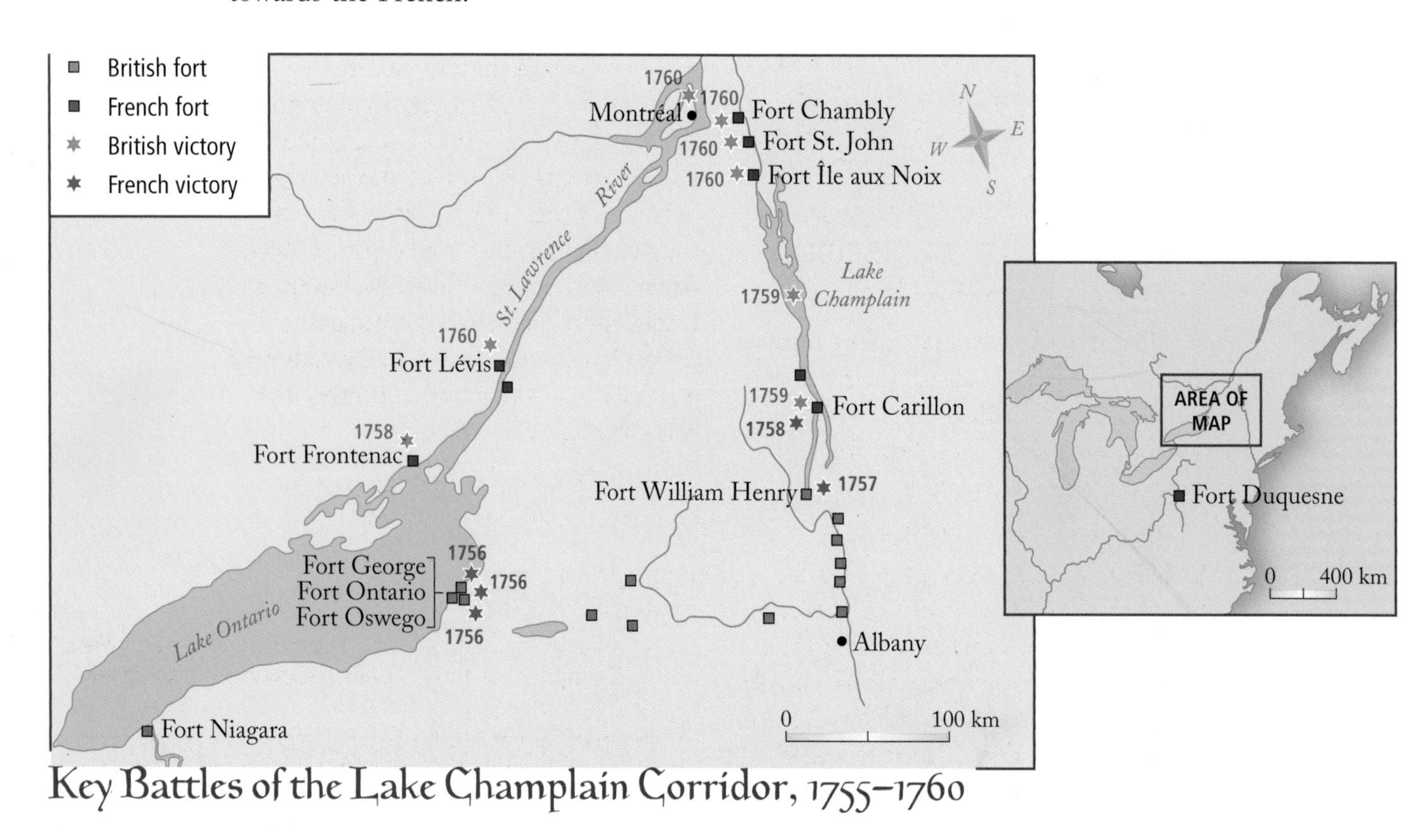

Key Battles of the Lake Champlain Corridor, 1755–1760

Britain's Glory, or the Reduction of Cape Breton by the Gallant Admiral Boscawen & General Amherst, by C. Dicey & Co., around 1758.

- What action do you see taking place in this painting?
- Do you think the creators were French or British? Why?

However, Montcalm's First Nations and Canadien forces did not see honour in this tradition. They considered surrender to be a sign of weakness. As the British soldiers filed out, they were attacked and the fort was looted. Montcalm was shocked at his troops' behaviour. The British vowed revenge.

In the early stages of the war, the French also fended off the British at Fort Duquesne and Fort Niagara.

The British suffered higher losses than the French in all of these military clashes. The French seemed to be holding off the British, but their upper hand was only temporary.

In July 1758, the British sent 15 000 soldiers to defeat the French. It was the largest army ever gathered in North America. The French and their allies were greatly outnumbered. In July 1759, the British captured Fort Carillon and renamed it Fort Ticonderoga. It was a key point on the Lake Champlain route towards Québec.

The British then turned to Louisbourg. In 1758, the British sent thirty-nine ships, 1000 guns, and over 12 000 troops to capture the strategic fort. The French held out as long as they could, but they ran short of food. After seven weeks of bombardment by British guns, the fort's commander surrendered. The people of Louisbourg were deported to France and the fort was destroyed.

The next step would be an attack on the heart of New France.

After Reading

1. Use the model below to prepare a Cause and Effect Organizer for three significant events of the Seven Years' War:

Event	Cause	Effect
1.	Led to	
2.	Led to	
3.	Led to	

Battle of the Plains of Abraham

Before Reading

1. What military strategies seem to have been the most effective so far in the war? Discuss your ideas in a small group.

The Death of Wolfe, by Benjamin West, 1770. General Wolfe, the focus of attention in this painting, had led the capture of Louisbourg and had been given the task of winning Québec.

- What impression of the battle do you get from this painting? Look closely at the landscape, weapons, clothing, and action. How do the artist's colour choices affect your impression?

The Battle of the Plains of Abraham is probably one of the most important battles in Canadian history. Yet it only lasted fifteen minutes and did not end the war.

On September 13, 1759, General James Wolfe decided to invade Québec before the winter, when ships would return his troops to Britain. In the early morning hours, Wolfe's army climbed the cliffs at Anse-aux-Foulons (today called Wolfe's Cove). At the top, they found the Abraham Martin farm, just upstream from Québec. Most of Wolfe's soldiers were professionals trained in open-field combat. The Plains of Abraham were perfect for their combat style.

From Québec, Montcalm heard the sound of musket fire as a small French force met the British. However, he did not believe it was a major attack. He did not think a large force could scale the cliffs at Anse-aux-Foulons. It was many hours before he and his forces advanced towards the British.

When the French militia were less than 40 metres away, the British fired their muskets. They then advanced and fired again. In the smoke and confusion, the militia retreated. Wolfe was killed on the field shortly after the retreat began. Montcalm, while trying to maintain order, was also wounded. He died soon after, in a local doctor's house.

A View of the Taking of Québec, 1759, by Laurie & Whittle, 1797.

- Compare this painting with the map on this page. How does the map help you understand the painting?
- How does the painting help you understand the map?

During Reading

1. What decisions might Montcalm have made differently? Do you think this would have changed the outcome of the battle?

After the battle, the British bombarded Québec with heavy artillery. The city held out as long as it could. After several days, one-third of the houses were destroyed, as were public buildings and the cathedral. Food was scarce and the citizens exhausted.

On September 18, the British moved into Québec and terms of **capitulation**, or surrender, were presented. The French governor, Pierre Vaudreuil (voh-dray), and many of the soldiers and militia fled to Montréal. The costs of the Battle of the Plains of Abraham were enormous. Over 1300 men were killed or wounded. The dead of both sides were buried together, regardless of language, religion, or rank, in a common, unmarked grave on the plains where they died.

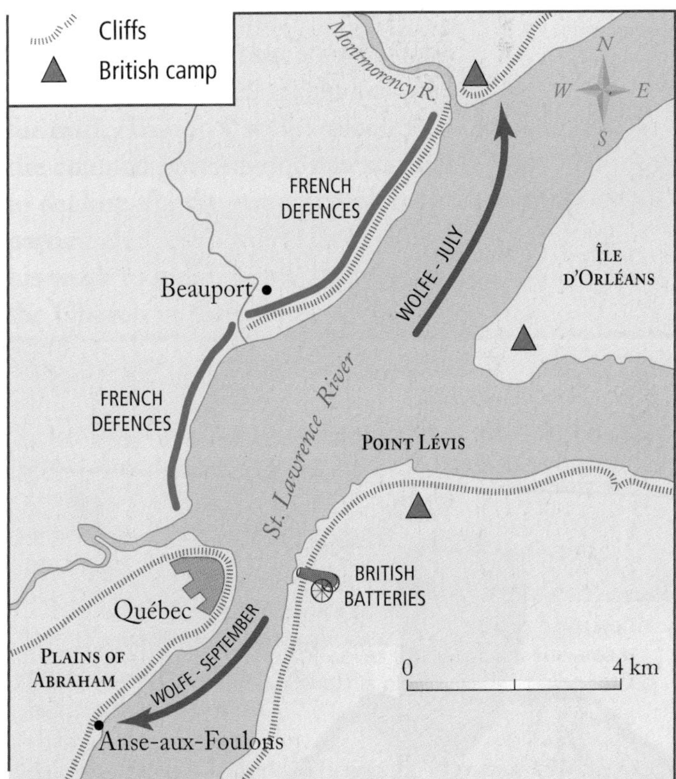

Battle of the Plains of Abraham, 1759

After Reading

1. Who is the greater hero—Wolfe or Montcalm? Write your opinion along with at least one fact to back it up.

The Fall of New France

Before Reading

1. What problems do you think the British had as they took control of Québec? Discuss your answers as a class.

After General Wolfe's death at the Battle of the Plains of Abraham, James Murray took command of the British forces. In Québec, this included the 7000 British soldiers that had survived the Battle of the Plains of Abraham. To prepare for the upcoming winter, Murray knew he would need the cooperation of the soldiers and citizens of Québec. He therefore took a gentle approach in dealing with everyone in his command.

He allowed French soldiers to return to France. The militia could also go home, as long as they swore an oath of allegiance to King George II, the British king. Murray permitted Québec's inhabitants to keep their houses and prevented his army from destroying or looting public buildings.

British soldiers and French civilians worked together to gather crops that had survived the recent battles. Food shortages affected everyone. Civilians had to rely on handouts from army rations, which were also scarce. People were short of firewood and the soldiers were poorly clothed.

During the Battle of the Plains of Abraham, 616 British soldiers had been killed or wounded. In the winter following, 672 died because of the cold and disease. Another 2312 became too sick to stand guard. By spring, only half of Murray's force was considered fit for duty.

In the spring of 1760, the Duke de Lévis (de lay-vee) led a French army of 7000 to regain Québec. However, he did not have the heavy guns needed to break down the city's walls.

De Lévis waited on the Plains of Abraham, hoping more French troops would arrive. Murray led an army of 3800 out to meet him. The Battle of Ste-Foy was bloody for both sides: 833 French and 1088 British were killed or wounded. The British quickly retreated back to Québec and de Lévis returned to Montréal.

During Reading

1. The page you just read describes four significant problems facing Murray: dealing with Québec's civilian population, food shortages, diseases, and counterattacks by the French. In your opinion, which was the most significant problem? Why?

A View of the Bishop's House with the Ruins as They Appear Going Up the Hill from the Lower to the Upper Town (Québec), by Richard Short, 1761. Short was a naval officer who was part of the British fleet that bombarded Québec in 1759.

Entry of the British Troops into Montréal, by Adam Sherriff Scott (1887–1980). On September 7, de Lévis surrendered to the English forces. On September 9th, French soldiers marched out of Montréal and the war was over.

The English responded with an attack on Montréal. General Jeffery Amherst led a force from Oswego, General Haviland from Lake Champlain, and Murray from Québec. On September 8, 1760, de Lévis signed the terms of surrender and the war was over.

The terms of surrender in Montréal were similar to those granted in Québec:

- French soldiers were allowed to return to France. Anyone who stayed had to swear an oath of allegiance to the British king.
- The militia and First Nations allies could return to their homes.
- The Canadiens were allowed to keep their language, property, civil law, and Roman Catholic religion. This term is especially notable because every other part of the British Empire banned Catholicism.
- The Canadiens were promised the same rights in business as British subjects.

First Nations issues were unresolved. With the defeat of the French, First Nations living along the St. Lawrence River had lost their main ally. Although they had not been defeated in the war, they were forced to deal with the conquerors.

In September 1760, Haudenosaunee leaders met with British officers and agreed to an alliance. With the Treaty of Kahnawake, they agreed to "bury the hatchet." The treaty was not one of surrender to British forces. It was a treaty of alliance. One of its clauses guaranteed the right to cross the New York–Canada border. This ensured the Haudenosaunee could freely visit their relatives to the south.

In 1763, the Treaty of Paris ended the war in Europe and North America. It also officially marked the end of French rule in New France.

After Reading

1. What impact do you think the terms of the surrender would have on New France as a British colony? Use a T-chart to help organize your thoughts.

The Treaty of Paris, 1763

Before Reading

1. When offered a choice, how do you make a decision? Discuss with a partner.
2. How do you think leaders of countries make decisions?

On February 10, 1763, Britain, France, Spain, and Portugal signed the Treaty of Paris. The treaty ended the Seven Years' War in Europe and meant that unsettled issues in North America could finally be resolved.

During peace negotiations, Britain had debated whether it should take New France or the Caribbean islands of Guadeloupe and Martinique. The islands produced sugar. At the time, they were far more economically valuable than New France. To the dismay of its business community, Britain decided to keep New France, which it renamed Québec. With Québec, Britain had become the world's largest colonial empire.

James Murray became the first British governor of Québec. With his appointment came instructions from Britain regarding the French inhabitants.

James Murray

During Reading

1. What words or phrases in Murray's instructions might the people of Québec be concerned about? Remember that the people of New France were French and Catholic.

PRIMARY SOURCE 3.2

Communication from Britain to James Murray

You are, as soon as possible, to summon the Inhabitants to meet together... in order to take the Oath of Allegiance... and in case any of the said French Inhabitants shall refuse to take the said Oath,... You are to cause them forthwith [immediately] to depart out of Our said Government....

And to the End that the Church of England may be established both in Principles and Practice, and that the said Inhabitants may by Degrees be induced [forced] to embrace the Protestant Religion, and their Children be brought up in the Principles of it; We do hereby declare it to be Our Intention [that] all possible Encouragement shall be given to the erecting [of] Protestant Schools.

During Reading

1. From a British perspective, consider what Britain's decision to keep New France meant at the time and in the future. Create a Plus/Minus/Interesting (PMI) Chart in your notebook.

Plus	Minus	Interesting

   Organize each of the points listed below in your chart. Add other points from the reading.

   - For many years, the Thirteen Colonies had been wanting the "French threat" removed.
   - First Nations in the Ohio Valley usually allied with the French in any conflicts.
   - Britain now had possession of all land east of the Mississippi River.
   - Britain had to decide what to do with 60 000 French, Catholic residents of New France.
   - The Seven Years' War had been costly. Britain was looking forward to peace.

2. Why do you think Britain decided to keep New France? Use your PMI Chart to help support your answer.
3. As you read the following section from the Treaty of Paris, create another PMI Chart from the point of view of the French in Québec.

PRIMARY SOURCE 3·3

Treaty of Paris, 1763

IV. His Britannick Majesty, on his side, agrees to grant the liberty of the [Catholic] religion to the inhabitants of Canada: he will... give orders that his new Roman Catholic subjects may profess the worship of their religion... as the laws of Great Britain permit.

His Britannick Majesty further agrees, that the French inhabitants, or others who had been subjects of the Most Christian King in Canada [the King of France], may retire [leave Canada] with all safety and freedom wherever they shall think proper, and may sell their estates [land], provided it be to the subjects of his Britannick Majesty [British subjects], and bring away their effects [possessions] as well as their persons, without being restrained [bothered]....

The term limited for this emigration shall be fixed to the space of eighteen months.

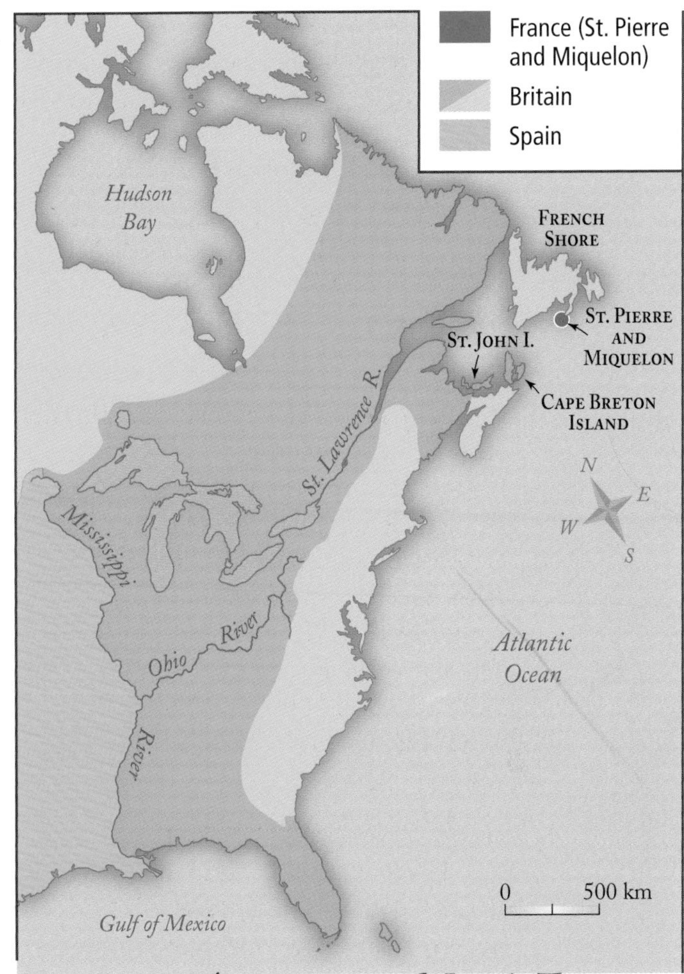

European Territories in North America after the Treaty of Paris, 1763

Under the Treaty of Paris (1763), France kept the islands of St. Pierre and Miquelon, as well as fishing rights on the northern shore of Newfoundland.

- What problems might Britain have experienced in managing its new territory? Look back to the map on page 85 to help you answer this question.

After Reading

1. In groups of three, divide up the topics that follow:
   a) causes of the Seven Years' War
   b) events of the Seven Years' War
   c) results of the Seven Years' War

   Take ten minutes to prepare a summary of your topic. Keep the 5 Ws and 1 H in mind as you work. Share your summaries with one another.

Responses to the Fall of New France

Before Reading

1. What impact do you think the conquest had on the people of New France? Use your journal to record your responses.

As the war ended, French citizens in Québec were anxious about their fate. Some were bitter at the destruction caused by the conflict. Many people's crops had been burned and their property destroyed.

Following the war, most French government and military officials returned to France. Those who stayed, such as the habitants, often lacked economic resources. Rebuilding the colony would take time. The terms of surrender allowed the French to keep many aspects of their way of life, but some people doubted that the British would continue to honour their promises.

Québec's licence plates today read *Je me souviens* (I remember).

- As a class, discuss how this motto might be interpreted as a reaction to the fall of New France. Why might people want to remember this historical event?

Paraphrasing

Paraphrasing is stating something in your own words. As you learned on page 45, it is a way of stating the main idea. Paraphrasing is particularly useful when you are reading something with difficult words or complicated phrases, such as those in some primary sources.

Steps to Paraphrasing

1. First read the text quickly to get a general impression. What is the tone (e.g., angry or positive)? What is the purpose—to persuade, convince, or inform? Who is the audience? Do not worry if you cannot answer these questions right away. Your paraphrase will help you.
2. Next, read the text slowly, jotting down notes that simplify and summarize chunks of the text. Chunks might be as small as words or phrases. Use fewer and simpler words whenever you can. For example, instead of "You should earnestly enforce," you might write "Insist."
3. Use your jot-notes to write a sentence or sentences in your own words. Compare the original text with your paraphrase to be sure you have captured the main idea or ideas. Adjust your paraphrase if necessary.

During Reading

1. Paraphrase the four points of view that follow.
2. Which points of view seem to agree? Which conflict? Group them accordingly.

PRIMARY SOURCE 3.4

Letter by Mother Marguerite d'Youville (dee-yoo-vil)

We had flattered ourselves that France would not abandon us, but we were wrong in our expectation.... What is even more distressing for us is that this poor country is more and more forsaken [bleak]. All the good citizens are leaving it.

Mother Marguerite d'Youville

PRIMARY SOURCE 3.5

Orders from Charles Wyndham, British Secretary of State, to Jeffery Amherst, 1761

You should earnestly enforce [insist] to the several Governors... the conciliating [calming] part of the Instructions, which you have been given, and that you Recommend...the most vigilant [careful] attention, and take the most effectual [effective] care that the French Inhabitants...be humanely and kindly treated.

Charles Wyndham

PRIMARY SOURCE 3.6

Letter from Some Canadiens to the Consul of the French Republic in New York, 1792

Accept the best wishes of the greater part of the Canadiens. They all love France, detest the English, and passionately desire to be re-united to the motherland from which they have been separated for too long.... Day by day the British tyrants [unfair rulers], under whose yoke [heavy burden] they groan, want to make their chains heavier. The Canadiens wish to break them, and all they require to do so is a favourable word and a little help from the Republic.

PRIMARY SOURCE 3.7

Speech by Jean-Olivier Briand (zhawn-oleev-yay bree-an), Vicar General of the District of Québec, 1763

The surrender of Québec left you at the mercy of a victorious army. At first, you were undoubtedly alarmed, frightened, and dismayed. Your feelings were justified...but you were ignoring that a kind and watchful Providence [God] had reserved for you a Governor who, by his moderation, his stern justice, his generous and humane sentiments [feelings], his tender compassion for the poor and wretched, and his rigid discipline towards his troops, would remove all the horrors of war. Show me the vexations [aggravation], the distortions [lies], the plunders [theft], that ordinarily follow in the wake of a victory. Did not those noble victors, once they became our masters, appear to forget that they had been our enemies, in order to concern themselves solely with our needs and with ways of satisfying them? Surely, you have not forgotten the good actions of his Excellency, the illustrious and charitable General Murray.

Jean-Olivier Briand

During Reading

1. Compare your paraphrases with those of a partner. Even though you likely used different words, do your paraphrases capture the same main ideas? Discuss any differences.
2. The quotation from 1792 was written thirty-two years after the conquest. What does it say about the attitude of the French in Québec towards the British in the years following the conquest? In your journal, predict how you think this attitude would affect Canada's development.

Looking Back to the Conquest

Many people argue that the British conquest of New France has had a lasting impact on Québec and Canada. Over the years, historians have interpreted this impact in many ways. This page includes two of the many interpretations. Which do you think best explains current events in Québec today?

During Reading

1. Paraphrase each of the interpretations of the fall of New France on this page.
2. What evidence does each historian offer to support his point of view?
3. Which of the people from page 103 would support each historian's argument? Why?
4. What biases do you think the authors might have? Why?

This photograph was taken at a Fête Nationale celebration on the Plains of Abraham on June 23, 2005. La Fête Nationale is a provincial holiday in Québec to celebrate French-Canadian culture, language, and history.

- In your opinion, how might the location of this particular celebration affect the participants?

Interpretation #1

The English conquest was the grand crisis of Canadian history. It was the beginning of a new life. With England came Protestantism,... Material growth; an increased mental activity; an education, ... a warm and genuine patriotism—all date from the peace of 1763. England imposed by the sword on reluctant Québec the boon [good fortune] of national and ordered liberty. Through centuries of striving she [Britain] had advanced from stage to stage of progress, deliberate and calm.... A happier calamity [disaster] never befell a people than the conquest of Canada by the British arms.

—From The Old Régime in Canada, by Francis Parkman, 1899

Interpretation #2

The terms of the peace of 1763 were no great surprise to the Canadians, and yet they came as a stunning blow. They meant one thing—conquest. And what did conquest imply? Who, in New France, really knew? War had meant empty stomachs, the flames of burning buildings, the blood upon the earth, the smell of death. What did conquest mean? The heavy drum-beat of the army of occupation, the hateful sight of enemy uniforms, the harsh sound of an unfamiliar tongue, the unwelcome triumph of a heretical [unbelieving] religion. War had been the violent expression of something past; conquest opened the terrifying void of something yet to come.

—From New France: The Last Phase, 1744–1760, by George F. G. Stanley, 1968

After Reading

1. As suggested by the photograph on this page, which historian seems to reflect the views of French Canadians today?
2. Do you think all French Canadians hold this view? What is your evidence for your opinion?

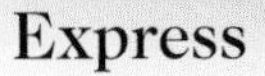

Compress

1. Without using your textbook or notes, record what you can remember about the expulsion of the Acadians. See if you can answer questions for the 5 Ws and 1 H. Put your notes in a graphic organizer of your choice.
2. Select five events from the Seven Years' War and prepare a timeline. Explain your choices.
3. Prepare a Cause and Effect Organizer to illustrate the British victory in the Seven Years' War.

Express

4. Create a monument to mark the unmarked graves of soldiers from the Battle of the Plains of Abraham. Write a speech to honour their sacrifices.
5. From the point of view of either a resident of New France, a First Nations person living along the St. Lawrence River, or a British official, write a letter about how the fall of New France has impacted your life.

Their Stories, Our History

What might the British have done differently after the fall of New France? What if Britain had decided to force the Canadiens to give up their language and religion? Or, what if they had decided to expel them, as they had the Acadians? What might have been the short- and long-term consequences of these policies? How might Canada be different today if the British had taken a harsher approach to the Canadiens?

Remember that it would not have been easy to force the French to do anything. There were several thousand British soldiers in the St. Lawrence Valley at that time and about 70 000 French residents.

In a small group, create T-charts listing the pros and cons of Britain's sympathetic, or tolerant, policy and of a less tolerant option.

Next, participate in a "Hot Seat" activity: Your teacher (or a student volunteer) will take on the role of James Murray. Imagine he is visiting the present day to answer your questions about his decision to permit the Canadiens to keep their language and religion. Consider the effects of his decisions and actions upon your country and life today.

unit 2
British North America

Chapter 4: British North America after the Fall of New France

Chapter 5: Loyalists in British North America

Chapter 6: The War of 1812

Key Questions for Unit 2

- What are the origins of large-scale settlement in British North America?
- Who are the Loyalists?
- How did the arrival of the Loyalists affect British North America?
- What were the causes and impact of the War of 1812?
- How did British North America affect First Nations?
- Who were key individuals in British North America from 1783 to 1815?
- What is the history of your local community?

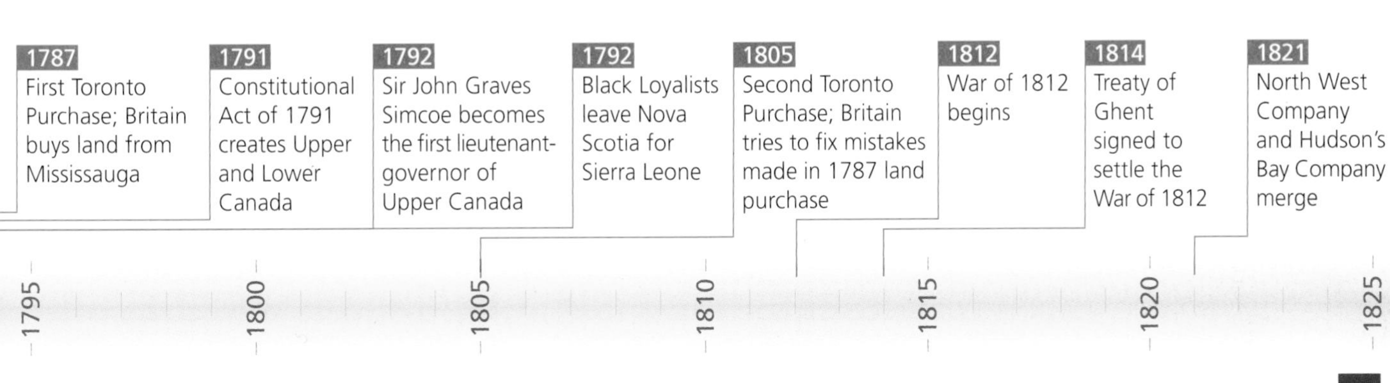

chapter 4
British North America after the Fall of New France

- As shown in this illustration, how are the Bostonians "paying" the excise man (tax collector)?
- Why might people have tarred and feathered someone?
- How would you react if this were done to one of your friends or family members?
- Why would people carry out this punishment in a public place?
- What questions would you like to ask the people in this illustration?

The Bostonians Paying the Excise Man, or Tarring and Feathering, 1774. An excise is a tax and an excise man is a tax collector. Britain's taxes on its North American colonies were one of the main reasons the Thirteen Colonies decided to separate from Britain in the American Revolution.

PRIMARY SOURCE 4.1

From the Charter of Rights and Freedoms,
Part of the Constitution Act, 1982

25. The guarantee in this Charter of certain rights and freedoms shall not be construed [understood] so as to abrogate [cancel] or derogate [take away] from any aboriginal, treaty or other rights or freedoms that pertain to the aboriginal peoples of Canada including

a) any rights or freedoms that have been recognized by the Royal Proclamation of October 7, 1763; and

b) any rights or freedoms that now exist by way of land claims agreements or may be so acquired

Aboriginal peoples is a term defined in the constitution as First Nations, Inuit, and Métis peoples in Canada.

- Many people believe that understanding history helps people understand the present. How does this excerpt from the Charter of Rights and Freedoms support this opinion?
- Based on this excerpt, what questions do you have about the Royal Proclamation of 1763?

Britain defeated New France in 1763. The Seven Years' War was over. The next two decades were highly significant for Canadian history. Three developments were particularly important.

First, it became clear that French people in Québec were not going to become British. New France had fallen, but French language and culture remained strong. Canada would have a French component as part of its future.

Second, the Royal Proclamation of 1763 set out First Nations rights in British North America. It officially recognized that First Nations had a claim to the land. The proclamation is still significant for First Nations rights in Canada.

Third, the Thirteen Colonies separated from Britain. Following the American Revolution, they became the United States. Québec and Nova Scotia stayed loyal to Britain. From this point, Canada and the United States developed along different paths. These differences continue today.

How were ordinary people affected by these major events? Because of the American Revolution, some people left their homes in the United States. They wanted to continue living in British territory. Many came to British North America. These **Loyalists** wanted to make sure Canada kept a strong bond with Britain.

During your lifetime, what events have occurred around you that you think are significant for Canadian or world history?

This chapter will help you understand

- the French response to British rule after 1763
- how Britain handled its new responsibilities in Québec
- the reaction of the Thirteen Colonies to British decisions about Québec
- how ordinary people responded to decisions beyond their control
- how the Loyalist migration affected Québec and Nova Scotia

Featured Skills

- Making Inferences
- Writing a News Report
- Evaluating Sources of Information

Think It Through

The Royal Proclamation of 1763

Before Reading

1. Your parent or guardian says, *Is your favourite TV show on tonight? Your room is a mess.* What message do you think your parent or guardian is really giving you? How did you figure it out? Discuss with a partner.

The Treaty of Paris (1763) ended a war that had lasted seven long years. Britain had devoted much of its resources to fighting France in Europe. The country was worn out militarily and financially. Britain wanted and needed peace to recover. However, it faced many challenges. Both the Thirteen Colonies and Québec posed problems.

During Reading

1. As you read pages 110–113, what inferences can you draw about Britain's priorities after the end of the Seven Years' War? Predict how you think these priorities will affect Québec and the Thirteen Colonies.

In Québec, Britain had to decide how to rule the French Catholic population. The French had lost the war and were not likely going to welcome the British. How could a few British administrators take charge of thousands of Canadiens?

In the Thirteen Colonies, settlers in overcrowded areas were anxious to move into the Ohio Valley. Now that the French were defeated, they saw no reason to wait. However, many First Nations still lived in the Ohio Valley. The First Nations did not see themselves as conquered people. They saw no reason why they should give up their lands.

Making Inferences

Have you ever had trouble answering questions because you cannot find the answers in the textbook? This may be because the answers you need require you to make inferences, or draw conclusions. Making inferences means you go beyond the stated message (written or spoken) to understand implied or suggested meanings.

Many messages have meanings that are not clearly stated. However, the text might have clues about the message. Inferences fill in the unstated message around these clues. Making inferences might be considered reading between the lines. It is as though you are reading messages written in invisible ink.

In the example from the Before Reading question, you can infer that your parent or guardian is telling you: *Clean up your room or you won't get to watch your favourite TV show tonight.* He or she does not have to state this directly. You understand the message based on your experience with his or her expectations. In the same way, good readers use their own knowledge and experiences to better understand what they are reading.

The graphic organizer that follows can be used to help you through this process:

I Read	I Think	Therefore
These are the words you see on the page or hear spoken. They can be paraphrased into your own words.	This is the unstated message those words hint at. Think about what you already know about the information.	These are conclusions you can draw about both stated and unstated messages together. Combine what is stated with what you already know in order to come up with a convincing conclusion.

Key phrases that signal you are being asked to make inferences include *explain how, how might, what do you think, predict,* and *what can be learned from.*

Pontiac's Rebellion

As early as 1763, many First Nations were already unhappy with the new British rulers. Some felt the British were were treating them disrespectfully. When settlers made moves to take their land, it was the final insult.

In 1763, Pontiac (pon-tee-yak), leader of the Odawa First Nation, formed an alliance of First Nations. He and his followers wanted to protect their land from settlers. They took over several British forts close to the Ohio frontier, including Fort Detroit. However, as winter approached, some First Nations left the forts to go to their wintering grounds and Pontiac made peace with the British.

The conflict was over quickly, but Britain wanted to avoid more problems. British leaders decided they needed to slow down settlers' movement west.

I learned in the last chapter that the Seven Years' War was fought in Europe and in North America. On page 110, I read that Britain had spent a lot of money and was tired of fighting wars. I think if there were more challenges after the war, Britain would want to solve them quickly. It certainly wouldn't want a lot of conflict with French residents, especially because there were a lot more French people than British people in Québec.

I also read that the Ohio Valley, which was a major cause of the Seven Years' War in North America, was still a source of conflict after the war. I think that after Pontiac's Rebellion, Britain won't want settlers charging into First Nations land in Ohio. But settlers in the Thirteen Colonies didn't see it that way. They believed they should be allowed to move into the territory immediately. I think I can conclude that no matter what Britain decided, some group would be unhappy. I'll start my chart with these points.

Pontiac in Council, by Alfred Bobbett. Both First Nations and European accounts of Chief Pontiac portray him as a strong and intelligent leader. In this illustration, he is shown speaking to a council of First Nations in the western Great Lakes region.

I Read	I Think	Therefore
• Britain: broke after 7 Years' War • Ohio Valley: still a source of conflict • Britain: wanted to avoid conflict with First Nations and Québec residents	• Britain: wanted to solve problems as quickly and easily as possible	• Britain: in a no win situation

Think It Through

Britain's Proclamation

To prevent more problems in North America, Britain issued a royal proclamation on October 7, 1763. Its stated purpose was to organize the North American territories that had been gained by Britain in the Treaty of Paris (1763). Its unstated goals were to keep peace with First Nations and to **assimilate** the French in Québec to British ways. Assimilation is when people adopt a new culture, usually one that surrounds them.

Key Points from the Royal Proclamation of 1763

- British law was to be established in the colonies.

Unstated message: *After the fall of New France, Britain promised French residents they could keep French property and civil laws. If British law was to be established, then the French were going to have to give up their laws.*

- The governor was to organize a general assembly, which could include French Catholics, to help make laws for the colony.

Unstated message: *Britain was trying to keep the French population content. It was taking away some of their rights, but trying to keep them happy by giving them others. This was a special exception because Catholic people were not allowed to participate in government in the rest of the British Empire.*

- A large area of land in the West was to be reserved for First Nations. Only the British Crown would be allowed to negotiate to obtain these territories. No settlements or posts could be built in this territory. Any non-First Nations people already living there would have to leave.

Unstated message: *Britain wanted to control how and when First Nations territories were settled. It did not want to fight wars with First Nations.*

- Anyone wanting to trade with the First Nations would need a licence from the governor of their colony.

Unstated message: *Britain wanted to control settlers' relationships with First Nations to avoid conflict.*

I Read	I Think	Therefore
• Britain: broke after 7 Years' War • Ohio Valley: still a source of conflict • Britain: wanted to avoid conflict with First Nations and Québec residents • Britain: wanted to assimilate French	• Britain: wanted to solve problems as quickly and easily as possible • Britain didn't want to force assimilation issue right then	• Britain: in a no win situation • Britain: hoped the Royal Proclamation would keep peace • Royal Proclamation: would make First Nations happy, recognized their right to the land • 13 Colonies: unhappy—Ohio Valley reserved for First Nations, 13 C had no new territory • Québec: no strong opinions? assimilation goal unstated and subtle

First Nations and the Royal Proclamation of 1763

The Royal Proclamation of 1763 recognized First Nations rights to the land. To make more land available for European settlement, the proclamation stated that the Crown would have to negotiate with First Nations. Since 1763, the Canadian government has negotiated with First Nations to reach many treaty agreements about land. Treaties usually allowed settlers to live on First Nations land in exchange for certain promises, such as annual payments.

However, in some cases, territory was settled without a treaty agreement. Today, many First Nations have **land claims** with the federal government to resolve this problem. Land claims often ask for compensation for land taken improperly. Many First Nations base their claim on the terms of the Royal Proclamation of 1763.

During Reading

1. Use the questions that follow to help you read between the lines in Primary Source 4.2:
   a) Do you think Britain planned to permanently restrict settlement in the West?
   b) Did the proclamation recognize First Nations claims to the West?
   c) Did the Crown view these claims as ownership?

   Make an I Read/I Think/Therefore Chart for your ideas.

PRIMARY SOURCE 4.2

From the Royal Proclamation of 1763

And we do further declare it to be Our Royal Will and Pleasure, for the present...to reserve under our [the Crown's] Sovereignty, Protection, and Dominion for the use of the said First Nations, all the Lands and Territories [as identified on the map]...but that, if at any Time any of the Said First Nations should be inclined to dispose of the said Lands, the same shall be Purchased only for Us [the Crown] in our Name, at some public Meeting or Assembly of the said First Nations.

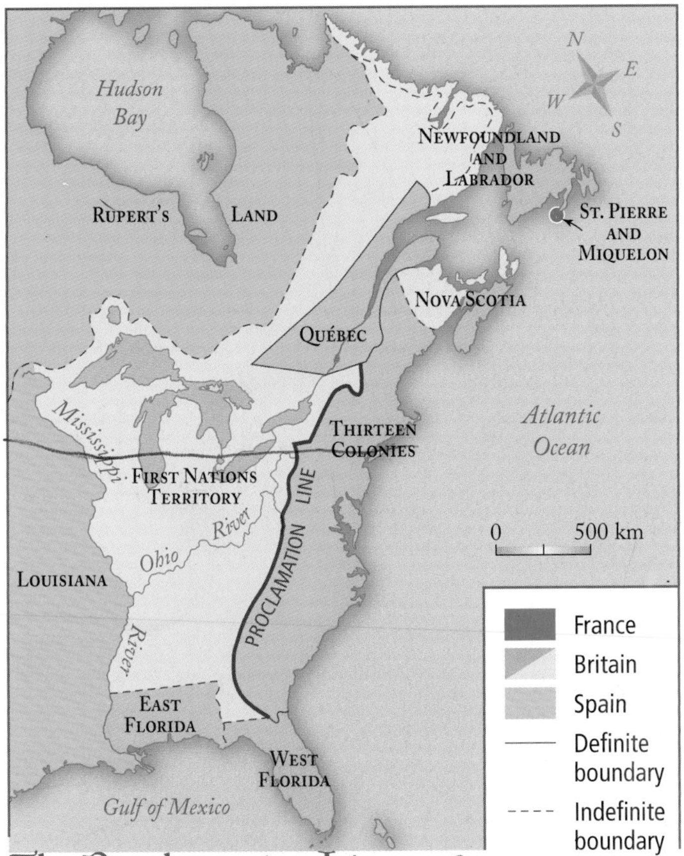

The Proclamation Line, 1763

The territory on the map identified as First Nations Territory did not belong to any colony and colonists were not allowed to purchase these lands.

- What do you think is the British motivation for creating such a large territory reserved for First Nations people?

After Reading

1. Consider the *Key Points from the Royal Proclamation of 1763* on page 112. If the proclamation had clearly stated Britain's intentions, how do you think First Nations, residents of Québec, and residents of the Thirteen Colonies would have responded? Discuss as a class.
2. The Royal Proclamation of 1763 has many unstated messages and goals. Why might Britain have wanted to avoid stating its intentions directly? What are the benefits of such a strategy? What are the drawbacks?

The Québec Act, 1774

Before Reading

1. With a partner, discuss which groups had an interest in the Ohio Valley and why. Refer to page 111, if necessary.

Recall that an unstated goal of the Royal Proclamation of 1763 was to assimilate the French. One way this was going to happen was by closing the Ohio Valley to westward expansion. Britain hoped that settlers in search of land would come to Québec instead. However, the best land in Québec was taken. It was being farmed by 65 000 French-speaking Catholics. People from Virginia or North Carolina could see little advantage to moving north. They became increasingly unhappy with Britain's rules and laws.

Colonists were not much happier in Québec. British merchants complained that Governor James Murray favoured the French. The merchants viewed any rights given to the French population as unfair. These merchants believed they should have more rights than the French. In 1766, Murray was recalled to England. Sir Guy Carleton was appointed to replace him as governor of the colony.

Sir Guy Carleton

Like Murray, Governor Carleton found that the French caused him less trouble than the British merchants in Québec. The merchants continued to complain that their rights were being violated.

During Reading

1. Paraphrase the letters that follow in one sentence each.
2. What opinions did Murray and Carleton share?

PRIMARY SOURCE 4·3

Letter from Governor Murray to the Lords of Trade in England, October 29, 1764

Little, very little, will content [satisfy] the New Subjects [the French] but nothing will satisfy the Licentious [shameless] Fanaticks Trading here [English merchants in Québec], but the expulsion of the Canadians who are perhaps the bravest and best race upon the Globe, a Race, who could they be indulged with a few priveledges which the Laws of England deny to Roman Catholicks at home, would soon get the better of [get over] every National Antipathy [opposition] to their Conquerors [the English] and become the most faithful and most useful set of Men in this American Empire.

PRIMARY SOURCE 4·4

Letter from Governor Carleton to Lord Shelburne, October 25, 1767

The King's Forces in this Province...would amount to sixteen hundred and twenty seven Men, The King's old subjects in this Province [English], supposing them all willing, might furnish about five hundred Men, able to carry Arms....

The new Subjects [Canadiens] could send into the Field about eighteen thousand Men, well able to carry Arms; of which Number, above one half have already served, with as much Valor [bravery], with more Zeal [enthusiasm], and more military Knowledge for America, than the regular Troops of France, that were joined with them.

Carleton's Recommendations

Carleton was concerned about increasing unrest in the Thirteen Colonies. He believed that the French in Québec could be allies if Britain had to fight the Thirteen Colonies. Therefore, he recommended that Britain keep the French as happy as possible. He recommended that they be allowed to maintain their language, religion, and civil laws.

Largely because of Carleton's recommendations, the Québec Act was passed on October 7, 1774. The act cancelled the assimilation goals of the Royal Proclamation of 1763. It also made the Ohio Valley part of Québec.

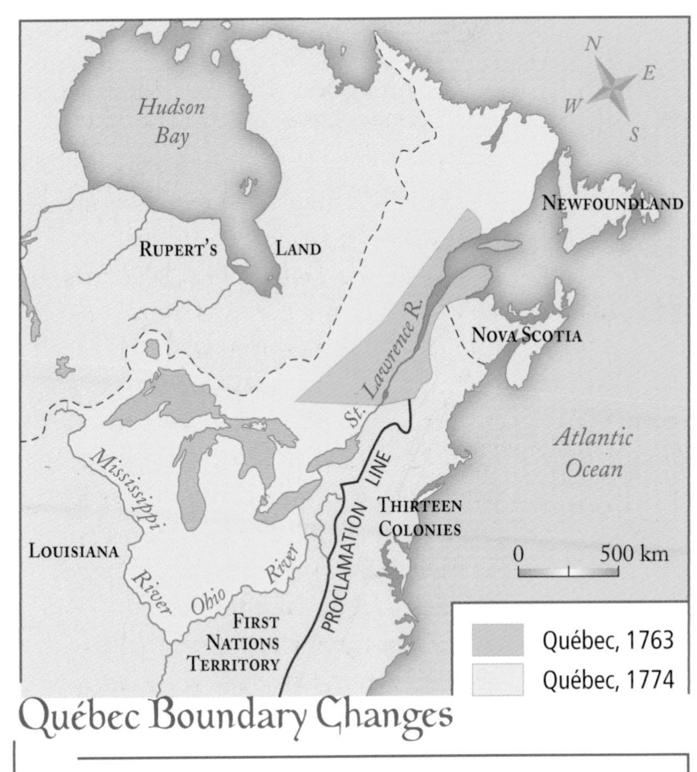

Québec Boundary Changes

- Compare this map to the one on page 113. What group of people seems to have lost the most?

Key Points of the Québec Act

- Québec's boundaries were extended south into the Ohio Valley.
- The French language and Roman Catholic religion were allowed in Québec.
- The seigneurial land-holding system, including the fees tenants paid to seigneurs, would continue.
- The colony was to be governed by British criminal law, but French civil and property laws.
- The Catholic Church in Québec was allowed to continue to collect tithes.

After Reading

1. Imagine yourself as a First Nations person in the Ohio Valley, a priest in Québec, a British Protestant in Virginia, and then a habitant farmer in Québec. How do you feel about the key points of the Québec Act? Write a few jot-notes from each person's perspective in your notes. Consider using a chart or Mind Map to organize your answers.
2. From the perspective of one of these individuals, write a supported opinion paragraph stating your viewpoint and your supporting evidence. Look back to page 91 to review how to write a supported opinion paragraph.

The American Revolution

Before Reading

1. Think of an event that happened in another part of the world that has influenced your life.
2. Why might your point of view about this event be different from another person's point of view? Write your answers in your journal.

Between 1763 and 1776, when the Thirteen Colonies declared their independence, Britain struggled to keep its empire together. The British government passed many laws that affected its colonies.

For example, the Stamp Act, passed by the British parliament in 1765, required colonists to pay a tax for every piece of printed paper they used. The money raised by the tax was to help pay some of the costs of defending the colonies. However, the act caused outrage in the Thirteen Colonies. Colonists organized a **boycott** of British goods, which caused Britain to cancel the act in 1766. A boycott is a form of protest that involves a group of people rejecting a good or service.

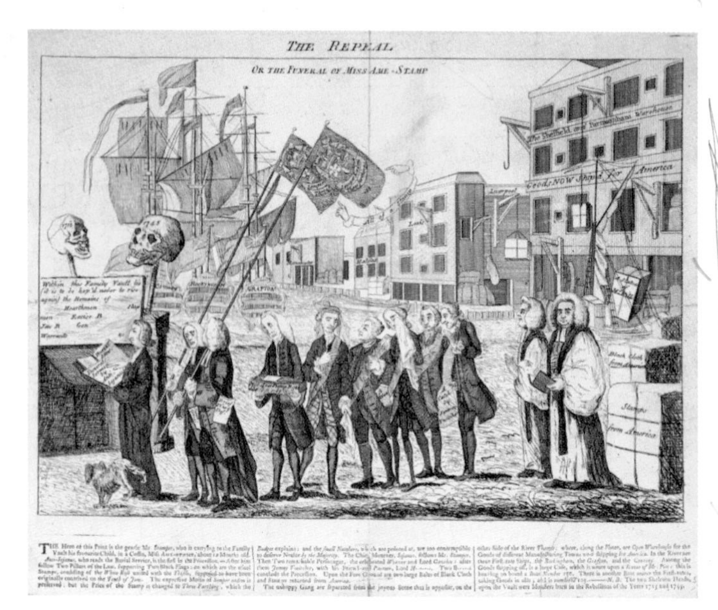

The Repeal of the Stamp Act, 1766. This cartoon shows a mock funeral procession for the "death" of the Stamp Act.

Other British acts caused a similar response. A tax on imported tea caused colonists to board British ships in Boston to dump crates of tea in the harbour. The event became known as the Boston Tea Party.

Most of the legislation dealt with trade and taxation. The Thirteen Colonies felt that Britain was unfairly harming their economy. Many colonists did not believe they should have to pay taxes imposed by Britain. They believed they should only pay taxes from a government they elected themselves. *No taxation without representation!* became their cry for revolution.

The Québec Act of 1774 made many people in the Thirteen Colonies especially angry. They had wanted the Ohio Valley for decades. The Québec Act ignored their need for land and gave it to Québec instead.

By 1775, the Thirteen Colonies were on the verge of revolt. To discuss their plans, they held a meeting called the Continental Congress. They asked Québec and Nova Scotia to join them. Neither colony wanted to attend. Colonists there were not harmed by the British legislation. Some people even benefited from the laws.

The accounts on page 117 present the viewpoints of two fictional colonists from Québec and Nova Scotia reacting to unrest in the Thirteen Colonies.

During Reading

1. List reasons why people in the Thirteen Colonies wanted to rebel against Britain.
2. How many different viewpoints can you identify in the fictional accounts on this page? What reasons are given to support each point of view?

From the Journal of Joseph Habitant (zho-zef ha-bee-tawn), 1775

I heard men talking today about news from the British colonies to the south. Some say that les Anglais (lay zawn-gleh) in these colonies are about to rise up against the British, who rule us all from London. One man even said that we in Québec have been asked to join them in revolt.

I say, let les Anglais fight it out amongst themselves. Their quarrels mean nothing to me. I farm my land as my father and his father did before me. Why should I support one English ruler over another? One is pretty much the same as the other, if you ask me.

In last Sunday's sermon, the priest told us we should support the British because they have allowed us to keep our Catholic faith. He thinks we would not be so lucky under rule by the Protestants to the south. They have always been opposed to us and our religion.

He and Sieur Lannard (see-yur la-nar), my seigneur, think the Québec Act is wonderful, but I don't see what's so great about a law that guarantees my right to pay dues to the seigneur and tithes to the Church.

A Letter from Sarah Brown in Halifax to her Brother in Liverpool, England, 1775

Dear Malcolm,

I hope this letter finds you well. In Nova Scotia we hear that the Thirteen Colonies are about to take up arms against the British government. Fortunately for us, in Halifax there is no such talk. John was asked to be a delegate at the Continental Conference, but he did not want to be involved.

Colonists from Massachusetts and Virginia believe that Britain is taxing them unfairly and limiting their trade and businesses. Here in Halifax, we are doing better all the time. The harbour is busy and John tells me he can hardly keep up. There's really no reason for us to revolt—it would only hurt our economic ties with Britain.

I'm a bit worried about our safety if the Thirteen Colonies go to war, but since Halifax is a major base for the British navy, I think we'll be safe.

Outside of Halifax, the communities include Germans, French, Irish, and Scottish people. They don't seem interested in the appeal from the south either. I will let you know if anything comes of this talk. I think you can rest assured that we will not be involved, so don't worry.

My love to all, Sarah

After Reading

1. List reasons why residents of Nova Scotia and Québec did not want to join the Thirteen Colonies in revolution against Britain.

Who Were the Loyalists?

Before Reading

1. In a conflict situation, how do you decide who to support? Discuss your answer in a small group.

As war between Britain and the Thirteen Colonies broke out, people in the Thirteen Colonies who supported Britain faced a rough time. **Patriots**—those who supported the rebellion against Britain—were on guard against anyone who did not support their cause.

Even people who tried to stay neutral were targets for abuse. For example, in New Jersey in 1775, Thomas Randolph was accused of being an enemy of the country. He was stripped of his clothes, coated with tar and feathers, and paraded around the town on a wagon. He quickly apologized and promised to mend his ways.

During Reading

1. Thomas Randolph decided to stay in the United States after the revolution. Why do you think he made this decision? What questions would you like to have asked him about his decision?

The British lost the American Revolution in 1782. Many people who had sided with the British left their homes in the United States. Some chose to go. Others were forced to leave by their Patriot neighbours. These refugees were called the **United Empire Loyalists**, or Loyalists.

Many of the refugees came north. They were farmers, clergy, lawyers, soldiers, craftspeople, former slaves, and recent immigrants to the Thirteen Colonies. Some were poor; others were wealthy. All they had in common was that they had stronger ties to Britain than they had to the United States.

Approximately 70 000 Loyalists left the United States in 1783 and 1784. Most had European backgrounds: British, Dutch, German, and Scottish. Around 6000 were Black Loyalists. These were former slaves who received freedom by supporting the British during the revolution.

Included in this mass migration were 2000 First Nations people, mainly from the Haudenosaunee Confederacy. They had allied with Britain in the war and had been promised land in exchange for their assistance.

Tory Refugees on Their Way to Canada, by Howard Pyle. Many Loyalists were forced by their neighbours to leave their homes in the United States. Many Americans were not ready to forgive people who had been loyal to Britain in the revolution.

Loyalists had many different reasons for staying loyal to Britain. Some had become involved in the war against their will. They were harassed by their neighbours and Patriot leaders to help the rebel cause. In frustration and anger, some decided to support Britain instead. Others signed up to help Britain as soon as they could.

Each of the Loyalist profiles that follow is based on a real person. Their stories represent the variety of individuals who supported Britain during the revolution.

The Coming of the Loyalists, 1783, by Henry Sandham, 1925.

- Of what economic background do these Loyalists appear to be? What is your evidence?
- How would you describe the environment where they are landing?
- How realistic do you think this painting is? Why?

Munson Jarvis

When the American Revolution began, Munson Jarvis was a silversmith in Connecticut. He was also an enthusiastic Loyalist. **Revolutionary committees** questioned him several times. Revolutionary committees were groups of rebels who were authorized to punish people for being against the revolution. Finally, Jarvis was imprisoned. In Jarvis's own words, he was "condemned and advertised as inimical [harmful] to the Liberty of America."

In 1776, he escaped to Long Island, New York. There he worked for the British for the rest of the war. After the war, he left the United States. He also abandoned about £600 worth of possessions. He received land and about £250 compensation from the British. He and his family settled in Parrtown, Nova Scotia (later Saint John, New Brunswick).

Loyalists on the Way to Canada, by C. W. Jefferys, 1934. Although most Loyalists travelled by ship, many made the journey to British North America by land.

The British Fleet Ready to Leave New York, 1783. After the American Revolution, many ships filled with Loyalists left New York for Nova Scotia.

Sarah Frost

Sarah Frost was born in Connecticut. Her parents had supported the rebels, but she and her husband had not. During the war, rebels drove her and her husband from their home. They spent the rest of the war near a British fort on Long Island, New York. After the war, Frost, her husband, and their two children decided to leave for British territory. Frost was seven months pregnant when she boarded the *Two Sisters* and prepared to set sail.

Her first sight of her new home was of a few tents and log shacks perched on the edge of a rocky shoreline. Behind the landing site was a thick forest.

Primary Source 4.5 describes her trip and first landing in Nova Scotia. Frost and her husband settled in Norton, Nova Scotia (later part of New Brunswick).

PRIMARY SOURCE 4.5

From Sarah Frost's Journal

May 25, 1783—I left Lloyd's neck [Long Island], with my family and went on board the Two Sisters, commanded by Captain Brown, for a voyage to Nova Scotia with the rest of the Loyalist sufferers.... We have very fair accommodation in the cabin, although it contains six families, besides our own. There are two hundred and fifty passengers on board.

Sunday, June 29—This morning it looks very pleasant on the shore. I am just going ashore with my children, to see how I like it. Later—It is now afternoon and I have been ashore. It is, I think, the roughest land I ever saw...but this is to be the city, they say! We are to settle here, but are to have our land sixty miles [96 kilometres] farther up the river. We are all ordered to land tomorrow, and not a shelter to go under.

During Reading

1. How do Sarah Frost's journal entries show a Loyalist bias? Given her experiences, do you think she could avoid this bias? What side of the Loyalist story is not told in her journal?

Thomas Peters

Thomas Peters was born in West Africa in 1738. As a youth, he was kidnapped and taken to the Thirteen Colonies. When the American Revolution began, he was a slave in North Carolina.

In 1775, Governor Lord Dunmore promised freedom to slaves owned by rebels who joined the Loyalists. (Slaves owned by people in Québec and Nova Scotia did not gain their freedom.) Peters escaped from the plantation where he was enslaved and joined the Black Pioneers, an all-Black regiment in the British army.

After the war, Peters ended up in Nova Scotia. He settled with about 200 other Black Loyalists in Brindley Town (near Digby). As with other Loyalists, they were entitled to provisions and land. However, Black Loyalists were treated differently from other Loyalists. In the next chapter, you will learn what happened to them and what Peters decided to do about it.

James Robertson

James Robertson immigrated to the Thirteen Colonies from Scotland in 1766. His brother Alexander joined him in 1768 in Albany, New York. The brothers published a newspaper called the *Royal American Gazette.*

When they refused to support the revolution in 1776, they were forced to leave their homes and newspaper. They had to move four times during the revolution. They continued to publish Loyalist articles each place they went.

After the end of the war, the brothers both went to Shelburne, Nova Scotia. There they continued publishing the *Royal American Gazette.* Like many other Loyalists with enough money, James travelled to England after the revolution to ask the British government to compensate him for the property he lost in the revolution. Most Loyalists could not afford this trip. James received about half of what he claimed.

Alexander died in 1784 and James moved to St. John Island (later Prince Edward Island) in 1787.

This illustration shows the uniform of a Black Loyalist foot soldier in the 60th Royal American Regiment. Many Black people who fought in the revolution were escaped slaves who hoped to gain their freedom at the end of the war.

A Bush Clearing with Log-House, 1880. Although some Loyalists were wealthy, they had to leave the land and most of their belongings behind. Their new life in British North America often meant starting from almost nothing. This included the back-breaking work of clearing new farmland and building a home.

Jacob Waggoner

A German immigrant to the Thirteen Colonies, Jacob Waggoner spoke little English. However, he had great respect for authority. England had helped him immigrate to North America, so he felt more loyalty to the British Crown than anger.

In May 1777, he enlisted to fight for the British. After the war, he decided to move his family to Québec. He left behind his possessions and 40.5 hectares of land in New York's Mohawk Valley. Waggoner later received 80.9 hectares of land at Johnstown (now Cornwall, Ontario).

During Reading

1. Based on what you have read so far, infer how the arrival of thousands of Loyalists could have affected Nova Scotia's and Québec's relationships with Britain. Make an I Read/I Think/Therefore Chart to show your reasoning.
2. Infer how the Loyalists might have affected British North America's relationship with the United States. Add this inference to your chart. Compare your chart with those of classmates in a small group discussion.

Writing a News Report

The purpose of a news report is to provide the reader with the facts and details of something that has happened or will happen in the future.

Characteristics of News Reports

- **Headline:** This catches the eye of readers and interests them to read more. The headline should give the main idea of the report.
- **The 5 Ws and 1 H:** The first paragraph or two capture the essential information about the report. They should answer the questions *who, what, when, where,* and *why* (or *how*). Someone should be able to read just this information and have the basic story without reading further.
- **Supporting Details:** Further paragraphs can expand on the 5 Ws and 1 H with details, statistics, and quotations from experts or people involved in the story. This adds flavour to the report, making it more interesting.

News reports are usually written with an objective point of view. This means the writer does not normally offer his or her own opinion, although he or she might include the opinions of other people through quotations. Ideally, the writer offers a fair and balanced report of the events that allows the reader to form his or her own opinion.

Some people argue that all writing has some kind of bias. Watching for bias in everything you read will help make you a better reader.

During Reading

1. The newspaper article on page 123 is fictional, but based on factual information about a real Loyalist. As you read, watch for examples of each characteristic described in the skill feature on Writing a News Report.

Halifax Chronicle

October 29, 1783

British hero makes Nova Scotia home

Celebrated hero James Moody arrived recently in Sissiboo, Nova Scotia, to begin his life again. He joins thousands of other loyal British citizens who lost their homes and possessions to the rebels.

Moody's many acts of courage earned him much thanks in the loyal colonies. He also earned hostility from the rebels. Rebel force leader George Washington called him "that villain Moody."

Moody's story has much in common with thousands of other people flooding north since the end of the war. Born in New Jersey, he was a farmer who did not plan to take part in the revolution. But when he refused to pledge loyalty to the United States, a band of rebels attacked him at his farm in early 1777.

Moody promptly volunteered with the New Jersey Volunteers, the largest Loyalist regiment in the war. He went on to free dozens of British supporters from American prisons.

His most famous exploit was his own jailbreak. In July 1780, Moody was captured and imprisoned. In September, he broke out of his shackles, grabbed his guard's musket, and ran free. As he left the prison, the alarm was raised. Quick-thinking Moody simply shouldered his musket and joined his pursuers. He then survived on berries and nuts until he could rejoin his regiment.

The New Jersey Volunteers were recently disbanded. Moody will receive half pay as a captain, even though he never reached this rank. His higher pay is reward for his exceptional bravery. As his superior officer reported, "Moody was the bravest man I met and there were many heroes in this war."

During his career, Lieutenant Moody freed many British soldiers held prisoner by the Americans.

After Reading

1. With a small group, discuss how the James Moody article is biased. How might the news report in a Virginia newspaper have been written differently? Consider, for example, the difference between using the word *rebels* instead of *Patriots*. If necessary, review the information about Conflicting Viewpoints and Bias on page 88 to help you answer this question.
2. Using information from one of the Loyalist profiles, write a headline and first paragraph for a fictional news report. Be sure to include the 5 Ws and 1 H.
3. Based on the profiles you have read here, write one or two sentences that answer the question *Who were the Loyalists?* Be sure your answer discusses the diverse kinds of people who stayed loyal to Britain.

The Loyalist Experience

Before Reading

1. Which of the descriptions of Loyalists on pages 118–123 did you find most interesting? Why?
2. When you read about how people lived in the past, what type of information captures your attention? Why?

Most people who left the Thirteen Colonies had to abandon family, friends, and possessions. The experience was often traumatic. Many Loyalists described their experience in letters, journals, and official records.

The following is a fictional journal of a twelve-year-old girl named Mary MacDonald. It is adapted from a book called *With Nothing But Our Courage: The Loyalist Diary of Mary Macdonald*, by Karleen Bradford. The book describes Macdonald's journey with her family from New York to Johnstown, Québec, in 1783. Her account is similar to the stories of many other Loyalists.

From the Loyalist Diary of Mary Macdonald

October 6th, 1783

"Traitor!" they called him. "Coward!" All because he would not sign their Oath of Allegiance to the new United States of America. They seized Father and dragged him out of the school.

October 7th, 1783

They lifted my dear father up and sat him on a mule—backwards! They tied his hands to the handle and whipped the mule forward. They paraded Father through the town that way, shouting vile oaths that I cannot repeat even to this journal. My father! He will die of the shame of this.

October 8th, 1783

(By the light from the campfire)

My hands are shaking so that I can hardly write and I've made so many blots I can hardly read what I have written.

I stopped writing yesterday because I smelled burning. It was our field! They set our cornfield on fire! And that wasn't the worst of it.

When they finally left, Father turned to us. I have never seen his face look like it did at that moment.

"That is it, then," he said. "There is nothing for it but to leave." It seemed as if he had to force the words out through his lips—as if his mouth wouldn't work. I could barely make out what he was saying.

Mother just stood there. She looked as if she had been struck.

We packed the wagon all night with everything that we could fit into it. And the smell of the burned out cornfield was in our noses the whole time.

We each made a bundle of our clothes. I helped Jamie with his, but we still had to leave much behind. Father tied a cage, with as many of our chickens as could fit into it, to the back of the wagon, but we had to leave the geese.

We were just getting ready to leave, after a quick breakfast, when those same men turned up again. What they did was rush into our house and push and shove us out. Out of our own home! Even Grannie! They actually knocked her down and not one of them stopped to help her up. I did that. Father had already harnessed old Blue to the wagon and we fled to it.

And then...I don't want to remember, but the pictures are all in my mind and I don't think I'll ever be able to forget them. Even as we watched, those men ran into the house and began smashing things.

I saw my best friend Lizzie looking out her window as we passed her house. She didn't wave. I didn't wave either. We just sort of stared at each other.

We've left our home behind us. Left everything I've ever known in my life. We're escaping to British Canada, Father says. To the Province of Québec. Father told me that Loyalist families have been promised free land there in compensation for their loyalty to the king, but I can't imagine he ever thought we'd be the ones leaving our homes.

I have no idea at all where Québec is, only that it's a long way from Albany. I am so mixed up and confused and just plain desperate and my head aches so badly. I would give anything for one of Grannie's hot teas right now and I wouldn't even complain about how bitter it was, but I don't dare ask her. Things are bad enough.

Father had tried to explain it to me. Some colonists wanted independence from Britain. Those are rebels, or Patriots, as they call themselves. Some, such as us, wanted to remain British. For that we are called names and thrown out of our homes! Even Lizzie hissed the word traitor at me, but we are not traitors. We are Loyalists! After my brother Angus went off to war to fight for the British, our friends and neighbours began to shun us, but we never imagined things would come to this.

I can write no more tonight, but I will tomorrow. It is important, this writing down of things.

During Reading

1. List the reasons why Mary's family decided to leave New York. Would you have made the same decision? Why or why not?

The Loyalist Diary of Mary Macdonald, continued

May 12th, 1784

Lachine, near Montréal

We have come as far as Lachine and here we sit, waiting for boats to take us upriver to the Johnstown settlement. The river still has some ice in it and the trip so far has been frightening. At one point I thought the small boat we were packed into would tip. One boatman had to fend off huge chunks of ice with a pole while the other rowed with all his might. The current is fierce.

There are thousands of people gathered here, from military settlements as far downriver as Québec, and the confusion, noise, and general disarray is truly alarming.

May 18th, 1784

I am too cold and wet to write much. It has been raining constantly, with the result that we have had no fire and have had to make do with cold johnnycake (cornmeal cake) and salt pork to eat. The mud all around our camp is so deep that we cannot move around very much. Just going over to Hannah's tent today, I got the remains of my boots so muddy that Grannie made me take them off before I came into the tent.

May 20th 1784

Some First Nations men came into the camp today and brought fresh fish. They wanted to trade for flour but of course none of us had any to spare. They left the fish anyway, which I think was very kind of them. The rain has stopped.

June 7th, 1784

Johnstown!

Well, we are here. I can hardly believe it. Johnstown is no more than a collection of tents strewn along the riverside....

About twenty families are to settle here; the rest have continued upriver. Mr. Mitchell [the teacher] went with them. He is going to Cataraqui where there is already a school built. I will not miss him, but I wonder how long it will be until a school is built here? There is nothing at all so far. I am being called. I must help with dinner.

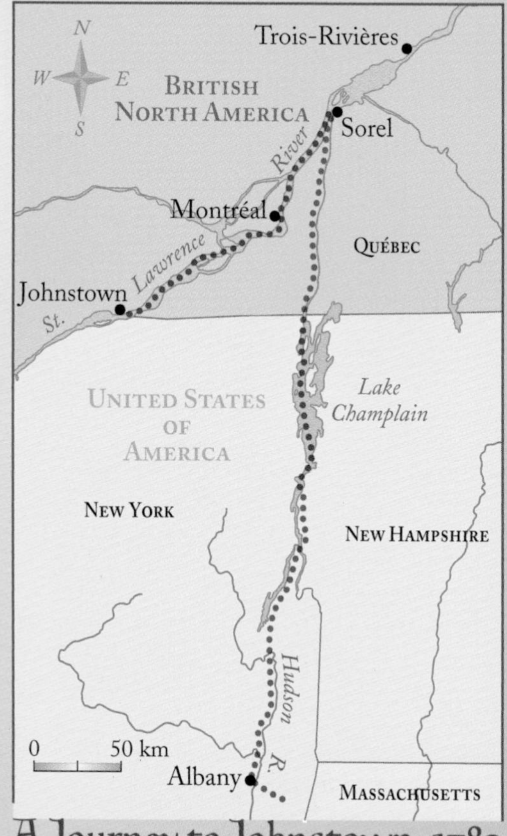

A Journey to Johnstown, 1783

The route travelled by Mary and her family is one that hundreds of other Loyalists also travelled.

After Reading

1. Working with a group of three or four students, prepare a role-play of a Loyalist family or group that is leaving the United States for British North America. In your group, prepare for your role-play by answering the questions that follow:
   a) Who are the characters (family members, friends) in your role-play? Who is leaving? Is anyone staying behind? Why?
   b) Where were you living before leaving the United States? What worries does your group have? Why?
   c) What caused you to leave?
   d) Where are you going?
   e) What possessions are you taking? What are you leaving behind?
   f) How will you travel? On foot, wagon, horse, boat, or mule? How will this affect your journey?
   g) What are some of your worries about the journey ahead of you?
2. Make notes for your dialogue. Practise it, but do not memorize. If you can speak your dialogue without memorizing, you will sound more natural.
3. Gather or make the necessary props and costumes.
4. Practise until you can do your role-play without using notes.
5. Present your role-play to your class and teacher.

Where Did the Loyalists Go?

Before Reading

1. Does your community have any Loyalist reminders? Think about street and park names or historic buildings and plaques. How could you find out about any Loyalist roots in your community? Brainstorm ideas in a small group. Contribute your group's best ideas in a class discussion.

Nova Scotia's population soared from 20 000 people before 1775, to 34 000 after the American Revolution. Almost 80 per cent of the Loyalists who moved to Québec settled in the area east of the Bay of Quinte. Haudenosaunee allies settled in the Grand River Valley.

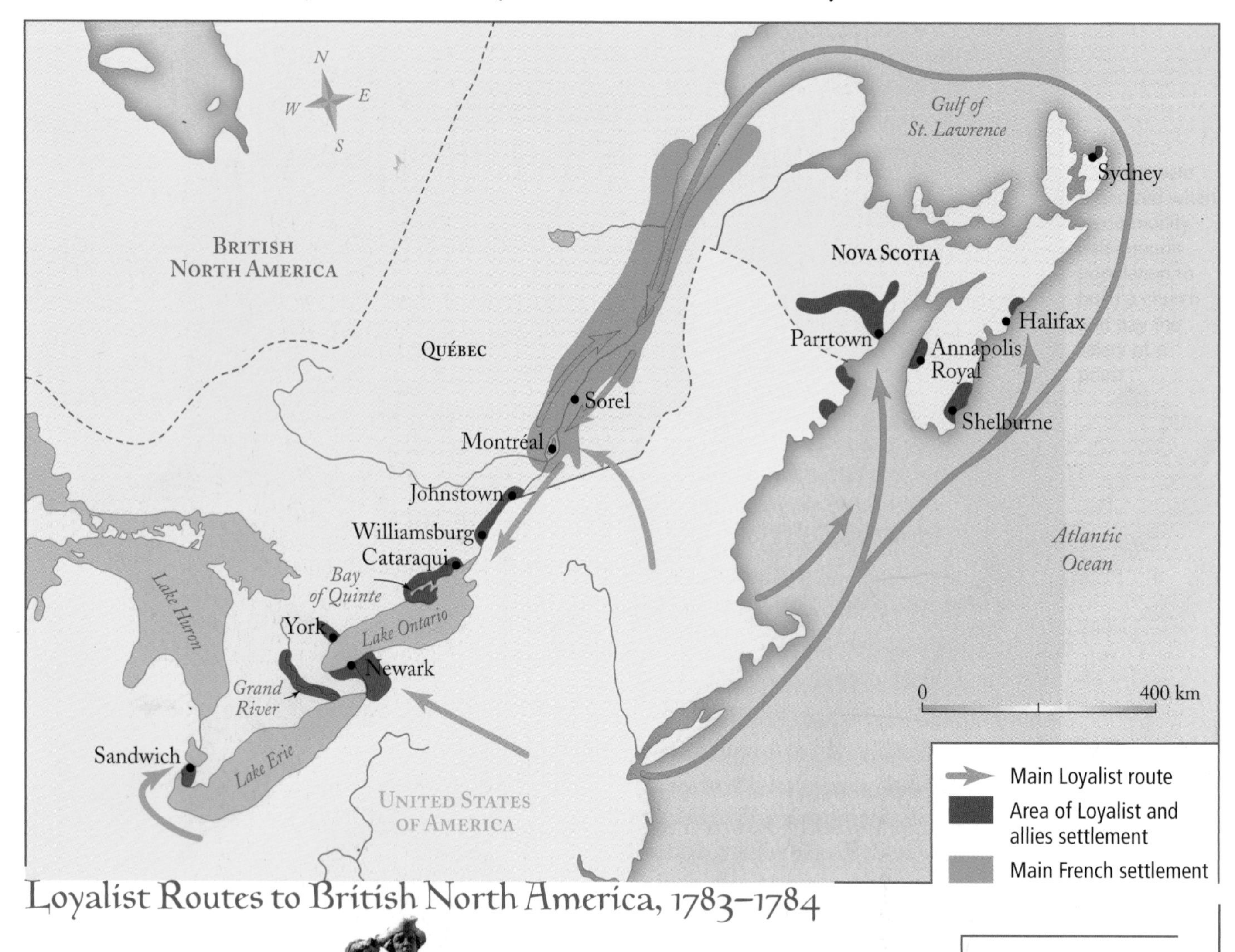

Loyalist Routes to British North America, 1783–1784

On May 24, 1929, this United Empire Loyalists statue was unveiled in front of the Wentworth County Court House in Hamilton, Ontario.

- Suggest why Loyalists settled in the areas indicated on the map.
- What positive and negative impact might the arrival of Loyalists have had on these communities?

During Reading

1. With a partner, compare the map on page 128 to a modern map of Canada. How are the political boundaries different? How does the pattern of Loyalist settlement relate to these political boundaries?
2. Look at the main routes taken by the Loyalists. If you were travelling from New York to Ontario today, what options would you have? Why do you think so many Loyalists travelled by ship?
3. What would be your first step if you needed to do research for a project about the Loyalists? Where would you turn for information? Discuss this as a class.

Evaluating Sources of Information

Whether you realize it or not, you are bombarded with information every day. You get information from obvious sources, such as books, magazines, signs, and television, but also less obvious sources, such as logos, music, and fashion.

Being able to evaluate sources of information will help you make decisions as a student, consumer, and almost any other role you take on.

One of the most popular ways to find information today is the Internet. The skills needed to evaluate a Web site can also be applied to other sources of information.

When you use a Web site for research, it is important to check whether it is a valid source of information. Anyone with a computer and small amount of technical knowledge can create a Web site, but the information provided may be nothing more than opinions. Remember that just because information is posted on the Internet, it does not mean the information is correct.

Before clicking on a Web site, look at the address. Did you know that a Web site ending in ".com" is a business? A site with "gc.ca" is a Government of Canada site, and "gov.on.ca" means it is a site published by the Government of Ontario.

Takes notes about any Web sites you use and include them with any research you give your teacher.

See more information on evaluating sources of information on the next page.

Evaluating Sources of Information, continued

Questions to Guide a Web Site Evaluation

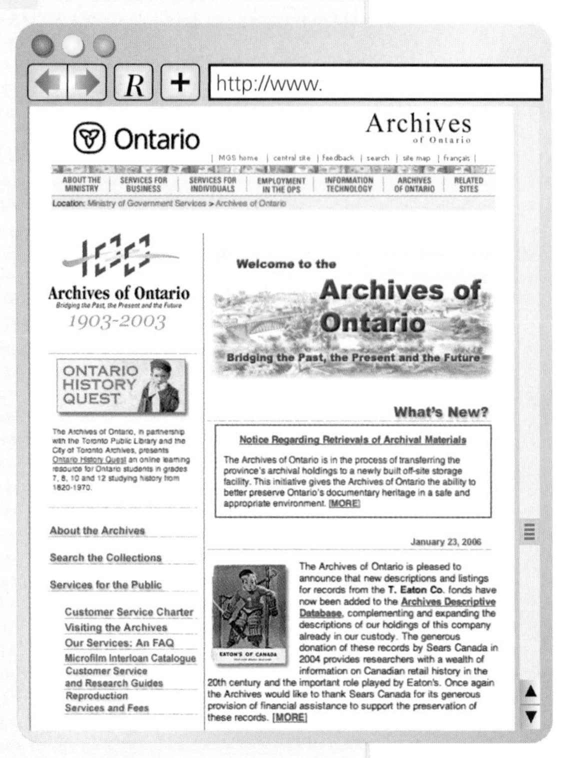

Authority

- Is the author of the Web site clearly identified?
- Does the author have a reputation as a valid source?
- Is there a publisher for the Web site? Is it a special interest group, government, individual, or business?
- Is there information on how to contact the creators of the Web site?

Objectivity

- Is the purpose of the Web site clearly stated?
- Are the sponsors of the Web site identified?
- Is the Web site free of obvious bias and stereotyping?
- Is there much advertising or many pop-ups? This is generally not a good sign. It may indicate that the information provided is influenced by the goals of the advertisers, which are generally to convince you to buy a product.

Accuracy

- Is the information accurate? Can you check the information in other sources?
- Is the information well researched? How can you tell?
- Are the links in the Web site working?
- Is there a date the Web site was created?
- Is there a date when the Web site was most recently updated? Is this date recent?

Contact

- Beware of Web sites that require information from you. Do not respond to inappropriate requests, such as your full name, picture, address, age, or phone number.

After Reading

1. Find a source of information about the Loyalists that you consider good. Write a paragraph outlining the reasons for your recommendation or reasons why you think a source should not be used by your classmates. If you prefer, give a short presentation about your source instead.

Compress

1. What groups of people were most affected by the Treaty of Paris (1763), the Royal Proclamation of 1763, and the Québec Act? Analyze the pros and cons of each document from the perspective of at least two of these groups.
2. Using a Plus/Minus/Interesting Organizer, summarize the significance of the Loyalists in the settlement of British North America.

Express

3. On page 108, you read an excerpt from Canada's Charter of Rights and Freedoms. Now that you know more about the Royal Proclamation, what rights do you think the charter refers to? Hold a discussion in a group of three or four students. Share your results with the class.
4. Write a news report as a visiting journalist from Britain on the changes happening in the colonies between 1763 and 1784. Remember that your reading audience is British people at home.

   Include the 5 Ws and 1 H and opinions or quotations from Québec or Nova Scotia residents, community leaders, and Loyalists who have just arrived. You may make up the opinions. Use what you have learned in this chapter to write fictional opinions that have some basis in facts.

Their Stories, Our History

In a group of four students, create a set of cards that could be used as a game to review this chapter's key concepts and ideas. Divide the categories that follow among your group:

a) British Rule in Québec

b) Political Changes

c) The American Revolution

d) Loyalists

Each person should prepare four questions and answers for his or her category. Use an index card for each question and answer. On one side of each of your cards, include a distinctive illustration or symbol that represents your category. On the other side, include your question and answer. Remember that your questions should touch upon key concepts and main ideas, not details.

As a group, decide on a name and write rules for your game. Design a poster advertising your game and how grade 7 students would benefit from playing it.

chapter 5
Loyalists in British North America

The Backwoods of Canada: A New Settlement, by W. Scheuer, 1874.

- What do you think the people in the illustration are doing and why?
- What challenges do you think these people face? What evidence do you have for your ideas?
- Could this be an illustration of your community in 1792? What evidence do you have to support your answer?
- Put yourself in this illustration. What are you experiencing that is different from your life today?

The United Empire Loyalists Association of Canada (UELAC) is dedicated to celebrating the contributions the Loyalists made to Canada's history and development. Many UELAC programs educate the public about Loyalist lives. In this photograph, Sarah Hurst of the Bicentennial Branch demonstrates to other students how clothing was washed by Loyalist pioneers.

The first settlers to establish a community shape its future. Their impact can often be felt hundreds of years later. This impact might be as simple as a street named after an early community member. It might be a museum housed in an important person's home. In some cases, today's institutions are the ones the first settlers established.

In Ontario, French and First Nations people have had an important influence on many communities. Loyalists have also had a major impact on the first fifty years of Ontario's development.

What challenges did early settlers face? How did the Loyalists impact other settlers? What is your local community's history?

This chapter will help you understand

- the experiences of the Loyalists when they arrived in Québec and Nova Scotia
- political changes in the British colonies after the American Revolution
- challenges faced by early settlers in British North America

Featured Skills

- Structured Note-Making
- Reading Graphs
- Researching with Various Sources of Information

Tilly McAgy steadies a log as her husband, Bill, and a student demonstrate how difficult it was to saw through logs with the two-man saw. Loyalists had to use the saw to chop down thick forests to create farmland.

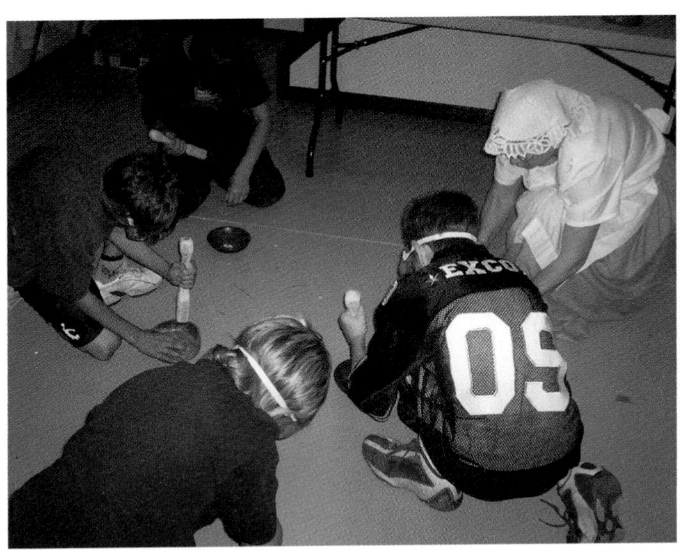

Linda Lynch of the Kingsville Historical Park teaches students how to grind corn to make bread. Until they built mills, Loyalists spent many hours grinding grain to make simple meals.

Loyalist Challenges

Before Reading

1. Have you and your family ever moved? If so, what positive and negative experiences did you have? If you have never moved, imagine that you are moving with your family to a new country. What concerns and questions would you have? Share your experiences and ideas with a partner.
2. If you were a Loyalist, what kind of reception, weather, and support would you have expected when you arrived in British North America?

Encampment of the Loyalists at Johnstown (Cornwall, Ontario) June 6, 1784, by James Peachey. Some Loyalists spent their first months living in tents.

Loyalists who arrived in Nova Scotia faced many challenges. They had to get a land grant, clear it, plant a crop, and build their home. They often did this with few tools and little knowledge of the community that was now their home. Winter was a struggle for all to survive in those early years. Food and other supplies were scarce. The British army helped people learn some survival skills and provided supplies of food, seeds, and tools.

In Québec, the experience of the Loyalists was somewhat different. Temporary refugee camps were set up at Sorel. Land was distributed through a lottery system. As in Nova Scotia, however, Loyalists in Québec faced shortages of food, tools, and clothing. The British government supported the Loyalists for three years. In 1787, the support ended. A combination of poor weather and insects created the "hungry year."

PRIMARY SOURCE 5.1

Letter from Polly Dibblee, Loyalist in New Brunswick, to her Brother in London, November 1787

May you never Experience such heart piercing troubles as I have and still labour under—you may Depend on it that the Sufferings of the poor Loyalists are beyond all possible Description…the British Government allowed to the first Inhabitants of Halifax, Provisions for seven years, and have denied them to the Loyalists after two years—which proves to me that the British Rulers value Loyal Subjects less than the Refuse of the Gaols [jails] of England and America in former Days—Inhumane Treatment I suffered under the Power of American Mobs and Rebels for that Loyalty, which is now thought handsomely compensated [well paid] for, by neglect and starvation.

During Reading

1. Make a jot-note for each challenge identified in Primary Source 5.1. Which of the challenges would you find most difficult? Why?
2. The next page includes fictional accounts of the experiences of two real Loyalists. As you read, add their challenges to your jot-notes.

Bush Farm Near Chatham, by Philip John Bainbrigge, 1838. Compared to the Thirteen Colonies, settlements in western Québec were few and far between. Families could not always depend on their neighbours for help. Many Loyalists struggled during their first years to secure the basics for survival: a home, garden, and farm.

From the Journal of Peter Van Alstine

1784—My family were Dutch immigrants to the Thirteen Colonies. After the start of the revolution, I lost my property because I would not join the rebels. I also lost my beloved wife. Now I have three children to care for on my own.

We are now in Sorel and I don't have a penny. I feel desperate, like many of the others who are here. I have to beg, even though I once lived a decent, good life. But I cannot look back. I must find work and start a new life. I will petition the governor for land. The king owes me and the other refugees at least this much.

1785— This last year was incredibly difficult. We are living in a tent in the wilderness. There are few roads and houses around us. I grew some wheat, but the mills are far from my farm. How will I get my grain to them?

Maybe I can build my own wheat mill using the nearby waterfall. I will turn my grain into flour and then we can at least have bread. It's been difficult for me and my children, but we will survive. I hope to finish my house before the winter.

Postscript—Peter Van Alstine went on to build mills in the Bay of Quinte area and became a civic leader.

From the Journal of Robert Clark

1785—I joined the Loyal Volunteers in 1776, as soon as the revolution began. I escaped north to Québec, but my wife, Isobel, and three sons had to stay behind. They had a tough time defending themselves against the rebels. They were harassed constantly.

In 1782, my family was driven from our farm in New York. They arrived in Sorel, where they spent a miserable winter. They suffered from smallpox, cold, and hunger. To make it worse, all this suffering took place among strangers who did not speak our language! To think that we are enduring these sacrifices in the name of Britain. I didn't see my family until the next year at Cataraqui. In the meantime, I continued to work for the British military as a millwright, my trade.

1786—I have built a sawmill and a gristmill for the Loyalist settlers in our area. The government paid for both. They are the first to be built between Cataraqui and Niagara. Our health improves. It's so good to have peace and I'm delighted to have my family together after seven years apart.

We're all happy we moved to this part of Québec. At least most of our neighbours speak English. Our lives have changed quite a lot since the revolution, but some things don't change, no matter where you live. I'm often impatient with the government. For example, I've yet to receive a land grant that I would like. The system for giving out land seems to favour certain people over others. In addition, we need roads to help us build our homes and transport supplies, but the government is slow to respond. We have given up a great deal for Britain and we deserve better treatment.

Postscript—From Cataraqui, the Clark family moved to Napanee, where Robert built mills for the government.

After Reading

1. How were Van Alstine's and Clark's attitudes towards Britain similar? How might their attitudes cause problems for Britain in the years following the American Revolution?

Black Loyalists

Before Reading

1. As a class, discuss how you feel if someone breaks a promise to you. Why?

One group of Loyalists was former slaves from the Thirteen Colonies. A **slave** is a person owned by another person. Slavery was legal in all North American colonies until the mid-nineteenth century.

Slaves owned by rebels had been promised freedom if they helped the British. When the American Revolution ended, approximately 3000 Black Loyalists came north to Nova Scotia.

Black Loyalist Settlements in Nova Scotia, 1783

Black Loyalists settled in and around the areas indicated on the map.

The first goal of the Black Loyalists, like all Loyalists, was to build shelter. However, tools and nails were in short supply everywhere. Black Loyalists were usually the last to receive supplies, such as cut lumber, from the British.

A Black Wood Cutter at Shelburne, Nova Scotia, by W. Booth, 1788.

Most people were forced to work for other settlers. Their wages were not much better than slavery. They often had to settle outside towns, on poor land, making their hardships even worse.

Many descendants of Black Loyalists still live in Nova Scotia. Here Elizabeth Cromwell, past president of the Black Loyalist Heritage Association, walks with former Governor General Adrienne Clarkson outside the Black Loyalist Old School Museum in Birchtown, Nova Scotia.

PRIMARY SOURCE 5.2

William Dyott's Diary, October 1788

[We] walked through the woods about two miles [3.2 kilometres] from the barracks to a Black Loyalist town called Birch Town. At the evacuation of New York there were a great number of these poor people given lands and settled here—The place is beyond description wretched [terrible], situated on the coast in the middle of barren rocks, and partly surrounded by a thick impenetrable [dark] wood—Their huts miserable to guard against the inclemency [harshness] of a Nova Scotia winter, and their existence almost depending on what they could lay up [store] in summer. I think I never saw wretchedness and poverty so strongly perceptible [obvious] in the garb [clothing] and the countenance [facial expression] of the human species as in these miserable outcasts.

Thomas Peters and the Sierra Leone Company

Thomas Peters and many other members of the Black Pioneers went to Nova Scotia at the end of the American Revolution. By 1791, many Black Loyalists were still having trouble getting farms. At most, they received less than half a hectare each. In contrast, other Loyalists received hundreds of hectares.

Peters wrote many petitions on behalf of Black Loyalists. When these were rejected, he travelled to England to present them to the Crown. Even this plea was rejected. However, while in London, Peters caught the attention of the Sierra Leone Company. The company was run by **abolitionists**, people who campaigned to end slavery. The Sierra Leone Company was trying to establish a settlement for freed slaves in Sierra Leone, Africa.

Peters and the other Black Loyalists had few alternatives. They could accept the poor land allotted to them in Nova Scotia. They could serve with the British army in the West Indies. Many chose to accept the offer of land and free transportation to Sierra Leone. They called it the "Province of Freedom."

During Reading !

1. If you were a Black Loyalist, why might you choose to go to Sierra Leone? Why might you stay in Nova Scotia?

Peters convinced 1100 people to go to Sierra Leone in January 1792. When they arrived in Africa, conditions were not much better than what they had left behind. They experienced poor weather, difficult relationships with local Africans, and delays in receiving land grants. Their settlement—Freetown—struggled with problems for many years.

However, in the nineteenth century, Black Loyalists became an elite group in Sierra Leone. Most of those who had stayed in Nova Scotia remained on the margins of society for many more decades.

After Reading !

1. Prepare a short speech in which you honour Thomas Peters' life and major contributions. If you prefer, write a paragraph on the same topic.

Think It Through

First Nations Allies

Before Reading

1. Like the Loyalists, First Nations who fought with Britain during the American Revolution found themselves unwelcome in the United States after the war. What do you think Britain should have done for its First Nations allies? Discuss this problem with a partner or small group.

Thayendanegea

Thayendanegea (tha-end-a-nee-gee) was born in Cayahoga (near Akron, Ohio) in 1742. He first served with the British in the Seven Years' War. When the American Revolution began, he remained a British ally.

In 1776, Thayendanegea travelled in disguise through rebel-controlled countryside to Haudenosaunee territory. The Haudenosaunee had a treaty of neutrality with the rebels. This treaty allowed the Haudenosaunee to remain out of the revolution.

Thayendanegea (also known as Joseph Brant)

Thayendanegea convinced them to support Britain. He believed Britain would honour First Nations rights more than the United States would. The Haudenosaunee Confederacy assisted the British in many successful battles.

However, during peace negotiations, the British ignored its allies. In the Treaty of Paris (1783), Britain transferred its claim to land as far west as the Mississippi River to the Americans. First Nations occupied most of this land. They did not believe Britain had the right to give their land to the United States.

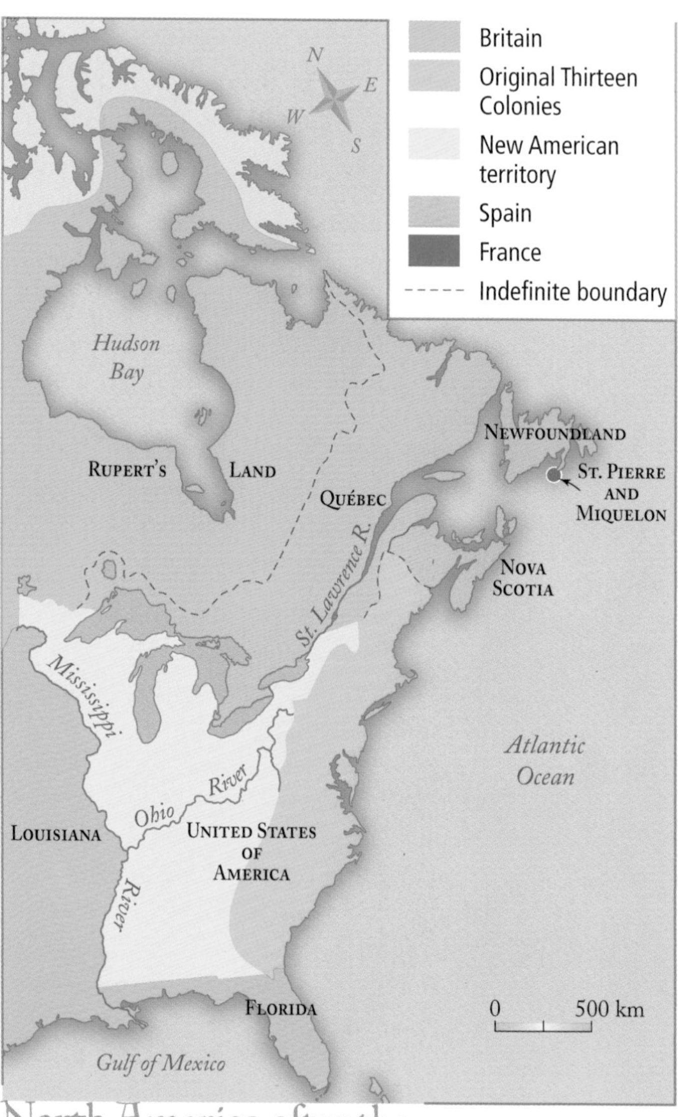

North America after the Treaty of Paris, 1783

Many First Nations felt betrayed. Thayendanegea travelled to London to petition for his people. In response, Britain finally agreed to provide land to its allies.

On October 25, 1784, Frederick Haldimand, governor of Québec, granted land to Britain's allies from the Haudenosaunee Confederacy. Now known as the Haldimand Proclamation, the grant included land six miles (9.6 kilometres) on either side of the Grand River beginning at Lake Erie. Thayendanegea and almost 2000 other First Nations people moved onto the land.

Today, many parcels of land in the original Haldimand grant are under land claims with the federal government.

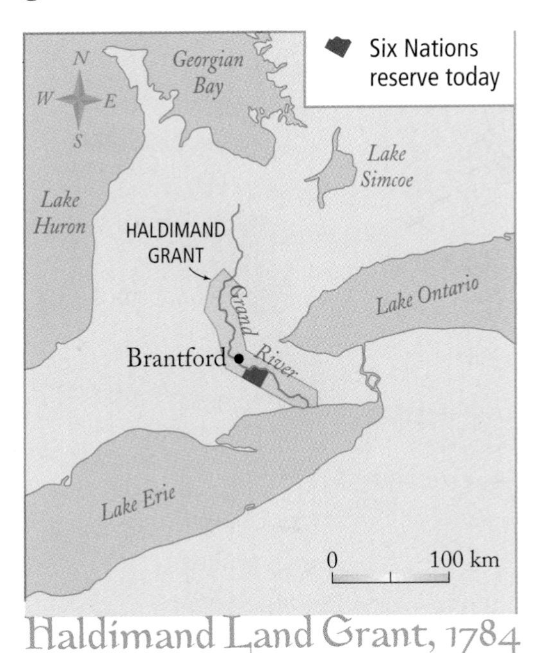

Haldimand Land Grant, 1784

- Why do you think the current Six Nations reserve is so much smaller than the original Haldimand land grant?

Structured Note-Making

In Chapter 1, you learned about split-page note-making. Other methods you have used to take notes include a K-W-L Organizer and a T-chart. You can also use questions to make notes. This is a useful method when you are assigned questions to answer while reading or researching. Using the questions to structure your notes helps you keep focused on the task.

To make structured notes, create a page in your notebook as in the example below:

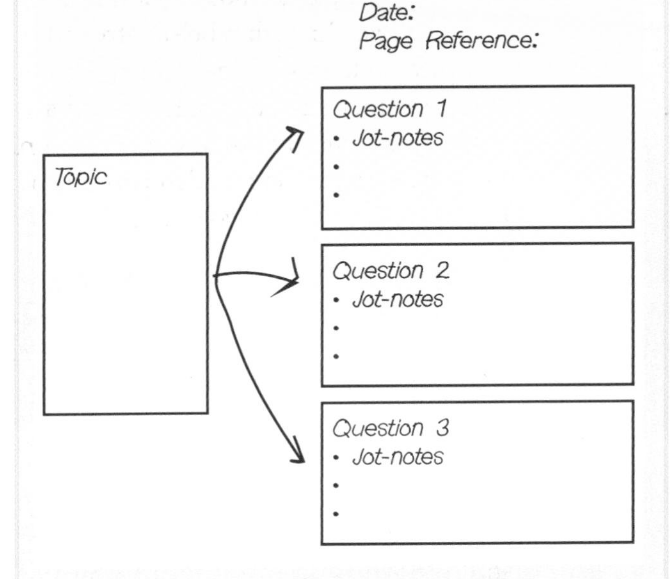

Fill in the organizer with jot-notes as you do your reading.

Pages 140–143 model how to use structured notes to answer questions from a reading. The example shows how the strategy can help you save time and stay focused on your task, without being distracted by extra information you do not need.

Although the example uses a real Web site as a source of information, you do not have to visit the Web site. Just work through the example, making your own copy of the structured notes in your notebook.

Think It Through

During Reading

1. Following directions from your teacher, answer the questions that follow:
   a) What was the Haldimand grant?
   b) Why was Thayendanegea unhappy with the grant?
   c) How was the problem resolved?

Before I begin, I'll set up a page in my notes to help me answer the assigned questions. My teacher says we should use textbook pages 138–139 and the *Dictionary of Canadian Biography* excerpts on pages 141–143. I can answer the first question using pages 138–139, so I'll fill in what I can. I'll use the 5 Ws and 1 H to make sure I get the essential information.

Date: November 7, 2006
Page references: textbook pages 138–143

Thayendanegea and the Haldimand Land Grant

What was the Haldimand grant?
- what/where: 9.6 km on either side of the Grand River from the river's mouth to Lake Erie
- who: given by Governor Frederick Haldimand to Haudenosaunee allies
- when: October 25, 1784

Why was Thayendanegea unhappy with the grant?
-

How was the problem resolved?
-

http://www.

Library and Archives Canada | Bibliothèque et Archives Canada | Canada

Français | Contact Us | Help | Search | Canada Site
Library and Archives Canada | Université Laval | University of Toronto | Links

You are here: Home | Search Results | Biography Display

DICTIONARY OF CANADIAN BIOGRAPHY ONLINE

Show printable page

THAYENDANEGEA (he also signed **Thayendanegen, Thayeadanegea, Joseph Thayendanegea, and Joseph Brant**), Mohawk interpreter, translator, war chief, and statesman; Indian Department officer; member of the wolf clan; his Mohawk name means he sets or places together two bets; probably b. *c.* March 1742/43 in Cayahoga (near Akron, Ohio), son of Tehowaghwengaraghkwin; d. 24 Nov. 1807 in what is now Burlington, Ont.

According to testimony Joseph Brant gave to John Norton*, he was "descended from Wyandot prisoners adopted by the Mohawks on both the father and mother's side"; his grandmother had been captured when the Wyandots were living in the vicinity of the Bay of Quinte (Ont.). The tradition that the Mohawk chief Hendrick [Theyanoguin*] was an ancestor of Brant has been affirmed by historian Lyman Copeland Draper. In 1879 an

I have Thayendanegea's biography, but it's long. I won't read everything, since I'm just looking for information about the Haldimand land grant. I'll scan the text, watching for words like *Haldimand, Grand River, Loyalists,* and information related to the end of the American Revolution.

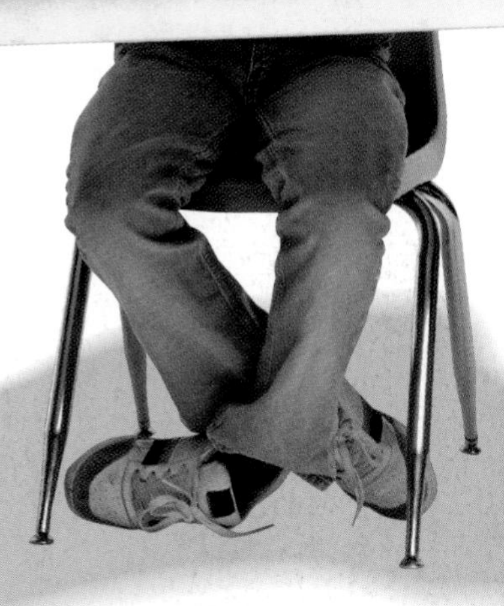

http://www.

After the outbreak of hostilities in the Thirteen Colonies in 1775, Brant remained loyal to the king. He went to Montreal with Guy Johnson in the summer and in November embarked for England with Johnson, Christian Daniel Claus*, and a few associates to present their position on First Nations affairs to the British government. Brant was generally lionized, introduced to some of the leading men in the arts, letters, and government, inducted into the Falcon Lodge of freemasons, and had his portrait painted. According to Boswell, he "was struck with the appearance of England in general; but he said he chiefly admired the ladies and the horses." He did not, however, neglect the serious side of his mission. He and his Mohawk companion, Oteroughyanento (Ohrante), presented Iroquois grievances about encroachments on their lands to Lord George Germain, secretary of state for the American Colonies. "It is very hard when we have let the Kings subjects have so much of our lands for so little value, they should want to cheat us . . . of the small spots we have left for our women and children to live on," Brant said. Germain fully agreed that the First Nations had been wronged by the Americans but stated that the government could not attend to redressing these grievances until the dispute with the king's rebellious subjects had been settled. He hoped that the Six Nations would remain loyal and could, as a consequence, be assured "of every Support England could render Them." The promise satisfied Brant and he later repeated it in a speech to the Six Nations. Indeed, as a result of discussions with numerous English leaders of varying

I've found the section of Thayendanegea's life that is about the American Revolution, but this information seems to be about his contribution to the war. I need the post-war section. I'll scan a bit slower now. Most of the information is in chronological order, so I'll probably get to the right section soon.

Think It Through

In the second line, I see the words *Six Nations' title to the Grand River land and extent of the grant.* This must be the section I've been looking for. It's a long paragraph, so I'll use chunking to work my way through it. I'll read one or two sentences at a time and make notes about anything that will help me answer my questions.

http://www.

Scarcely any problem was more enduring or more vexing to Brant than the controversy over the nature of the Six Nations' title to the Grand River lands and the extent of the grant. According to the original Haldimand grant, a tract of approximately two million acres, from the source to the mouth of the river and six miles deep on each side, had been given to the loyalist Six Nations. Later the government claimed that a mistake had been made in the original grant in that the northern portion had never been bought from the Mississaugas and the king accordingly could not grant what he had not bought. Despite repeated urgings by Brant and the other chiefs, the government never made the additional purchase. Brant also believed that the area along the Grand River was too large for the Six Nations to farm and too small for hunting. With immigrants moving into the region in increasing numbers and more land being cleared, game was becoming scarce. He therefore wanted the community to realize a continuing income from the land by sales and leases. Brant also strongly

Date: November 7, 2006
Page references: textbook pages 138–143

Thayendanegea and the Haldimand Land Grant

What was the Haldimand grant?	Why was Thayendanegea unhappy with the grant?	How was the problem resolved?
• what/where: 9.6 km on either side of the Grand River from the river's mouth to Lake Erie • who: given by Governor Frederick Haldimand to Haudenosaunee allies • when: October 25, 1784	• government later said it hadn't properly purchased the land, so the Haudenosaunee couldn't have it all as promised • grant was too large for farming, not large enough for hunting	•

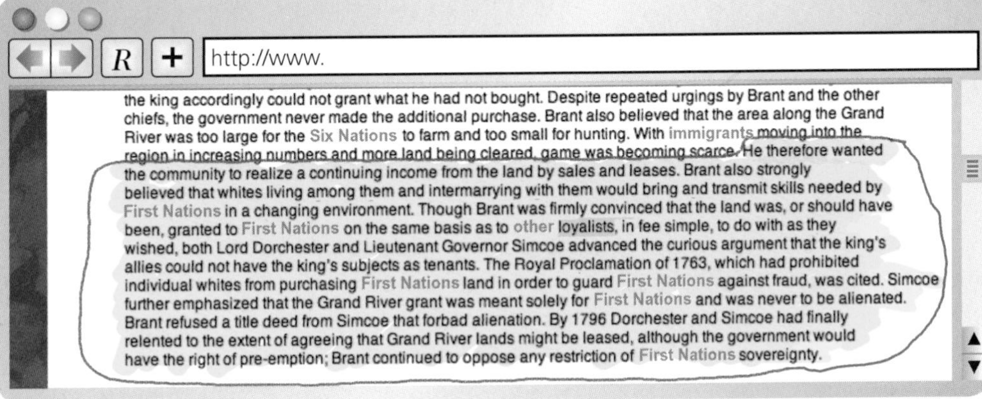

http://www.

the king accordingly could not grant what he had not bought. Despite repeated urgings by Brant and the other chiefs, the government never made the additional purchase. Brant also believed that the area along the Grand River was too large for the Six Nations to farm and too small for hunting. With immigrants moving into the region in increasing numbers and more land being cleared, game was becoming scarce. He therefore wanted the community to realize a continuing income from the land by sales and leases. Brant also strongly believed that whites living among them and intermarrying with them would bring and transmit skills needed by First Nations in a changing environment. Though Brant was firmly convinced that the land was, or should have been, granted to First Nations on the same basis as to other loyalists, in fee simple, to do with as they wished, both Lord Dorchester and Lieutenant Governor Simcoe advanced the curious argument that the king's allies could not have the king's subjects as tenants. The Royal Proclamation of 1763, which had prohibited individual whites from purchasing First Nations land in order to guard First Nations against fraud, was cited. Simcoe further emphasized that the Grand River grant was meant solely for First Nations and was never to be alienated. Brant refused a title deed from Simcoe that forbad alienation. By 1796 Dorchester and Simcoe had finally relented to the extent of agreeing that Grand River lands might be leased, although the government would have the right of pre-emption; Brant continued to oppose any restriction of First Nations sovereignty.

I don't understand everything here, but I can figure out parts of it. Thayendanegea wanted his people to be able to sell or rent out their land. This would help them make a living. I've already noted that the land grant was too large for farming and not big enough for hunting. Being able to sell or rent their land to others would help the Haudenosaunee make a living from it.

However, the government wouldn't allow them to use the land in any way they wanted. Why would it make this restriction? I'll make a note to ask the teacher later.

I think the First Nations were treated unfairly all along. First they lost their large territory to the Americans. They then received a grant of land, but were later told the government made a mistake and didn't actually own the land it gave them. In addition, they were told they couldn't do much with the land to support themselves. If it was me, I'd be frustrated with the whole situation.

Thayendanegea was a strong leader. He insisted that his people should have full rights to their land. In 1796, it looks like the government gave in a little. First Nations were allowed to rent out their land.

After Reading

1. Use the Think It Through note on this page to add to your structured notes about why Thayendanegea was unhappy with the land grant and how the problem was resolved.
2. Use an Internet search engine with the keywords *Six Nations Haldimand Proclamation* to find out if the problem was completely resolved in 1796. Add what you find to the third column of your structured notes.

Loyalists and the Constitutional Act of 1791

Before Reading

1. When you are used to playing a game one way and someone plays by different rules, how do you feel? Write your answer in your journal.

Loyalists tended to settle in areas where there was available land. In Nova Scotia, new immigrants moved to areas west of the Bay of Fundy. They quickly outnumbered the existing population. Loyalists argued that the government in Halifax was too far away to understand their needs. In 1784, a royal charter created the colony of New Brunswick. Cape Breton Island also became a separate colony.

In Québec, Loyalists tended to move west of Montréal. They settled in areas such as Cornwall, Morrisburg, Kingston, and farther west in the Niagara region. Loyalists in these areas felt that they should have the same rights as other British citizens.

Kingston, by Elizabeth Simcoe, 1793. After the American Revolution, the British government negotiated with the Mississauga First Nation to secure land for Loyalist settlers. King's Town (now Kingston) was established as the main administrative centre for Loyalists in the region.

However, Québec was still governed by the Québec Act of 1774. This act meant the colony used French civil law and the seigneurial land-holding system. The seigneurial system was especially offensive to Loyalists. In it, farmers had **tenure**, which is a right to occupy land, but did not have full **title**, or ownership.

During Reading

1. Primary documents are often easier to understand if you can imagine how you would feel in a situation similar to the person creating the document. Imagine that you are a Loyalist who suffered great losses to move to a place ruled by Britain. Now that you live there, you find the place governed by unfamiliar French laws. How do you feel? Paraphrase the excerpt from the petition in the paragraph that follows this During Reading.
2. Compare your paraphrase with a partner's to see if you both have the same main idea. Work together to complete the rest of the questions on pages 145–147.

In 1785, Loyalists sent a petition to the king of England that stated "They were born British Subjects, and have ever been accustomed to the Government and Laws of England…and they still possess the greatest Confidence, that by Your Majesty's Gracious Interposition [kind actions] they will be exempted [freed] from the Burthens [burden] of French Tenures."

The British government responded by passing the Constitutional Act of 1791. It was modelled after the system that had been put in place to create New Brunswick and Cape Breton in 1784.

Main Terms of the Constitutional Act of 1791

- Québec was divided into two separate colonies: Upper Canada and Lower Canada.
- Each colony was to have an elected assembly with the power to raise taxes.
- Lower Canada was allowed to continue its seigneurial system of land ownership.
- Upper Canada was guaranteed the English **freehold** system of land ownership. This meant farmers could fully own their land.
- One seventh of all land in Upper Canada was set aside as **clergy reserves**, which were sections of land controlled by the Anglican Church.
- One seventh of all land in Upper Canada was set aside as **Crown reserves**, which were sections of land controlled by the lieutenant-governor.

During Reading

1. Compare the 1791 map on this page to the information on the 1774 map on page 115. What are the most significant changes? How did Loyalist settlement patterns contribute to these changes?

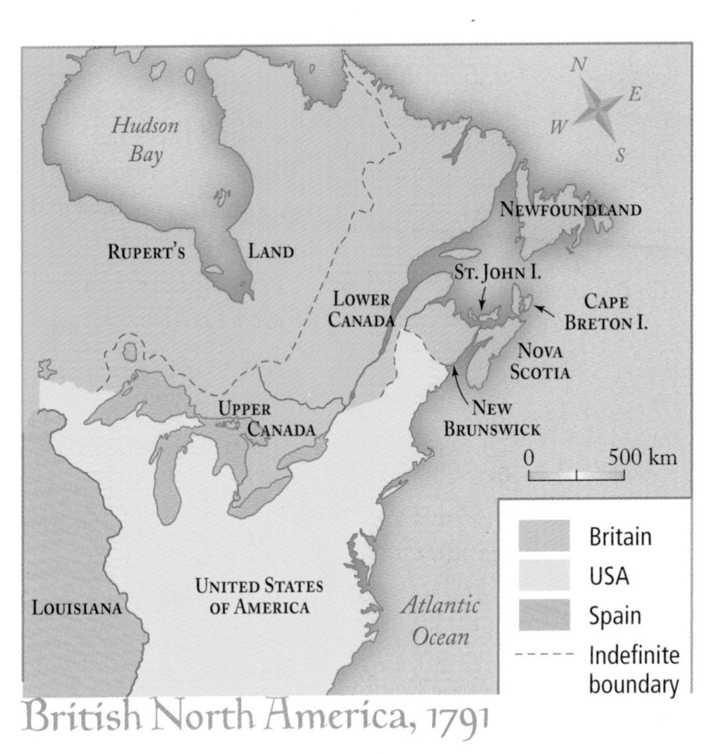

British North America, 1791

Most Loyalists settled in western Québec. The population in that area grew large enough that Britain divided Québec to create two colonies.

During Reading

1. Copy and then complete the Concept Map shown on the right. A Concept Map is a way of organizing information visually. It begins with the main topic and branches out into subtopics and details. Linking words or phrases on the lines joining the bubbles show how concepts are related.

Constitutional Act of 1791
meant
Québec divided
created
Upper Canada
created
Lower Canada
established
Elected assemblies
who had
power to raise taxes

Government Structure after 1791

From the point of view of many people in the British government, the American Revolution resulted from too much democracy. A democracy is a government in which the population elect all or some of their government. The British believed the elected assemblies in the former Thirteen Colonies had gained too much power over the appointed British governors. It was "runaway democracy," with disastrous results.

Britain now faced demands from Loyalists who wanted an elected assembly. They had proved their loyalty to Britain, but were used to having a significant voice in their government. Britain knew it owed something to these loyal subjects. However, it wanted to be sure that democracy would not lead to more rebellions. In the Constitutional Act of 1791, the elected assembly was given as little influence as possible.

During Reading

1. With a partner, compare the diagram on this page showing the 1791 government to the diagram on page 147 showing Canada's government today. What is similar? What is different?

Government Structure after the Constitutional Act of 1791

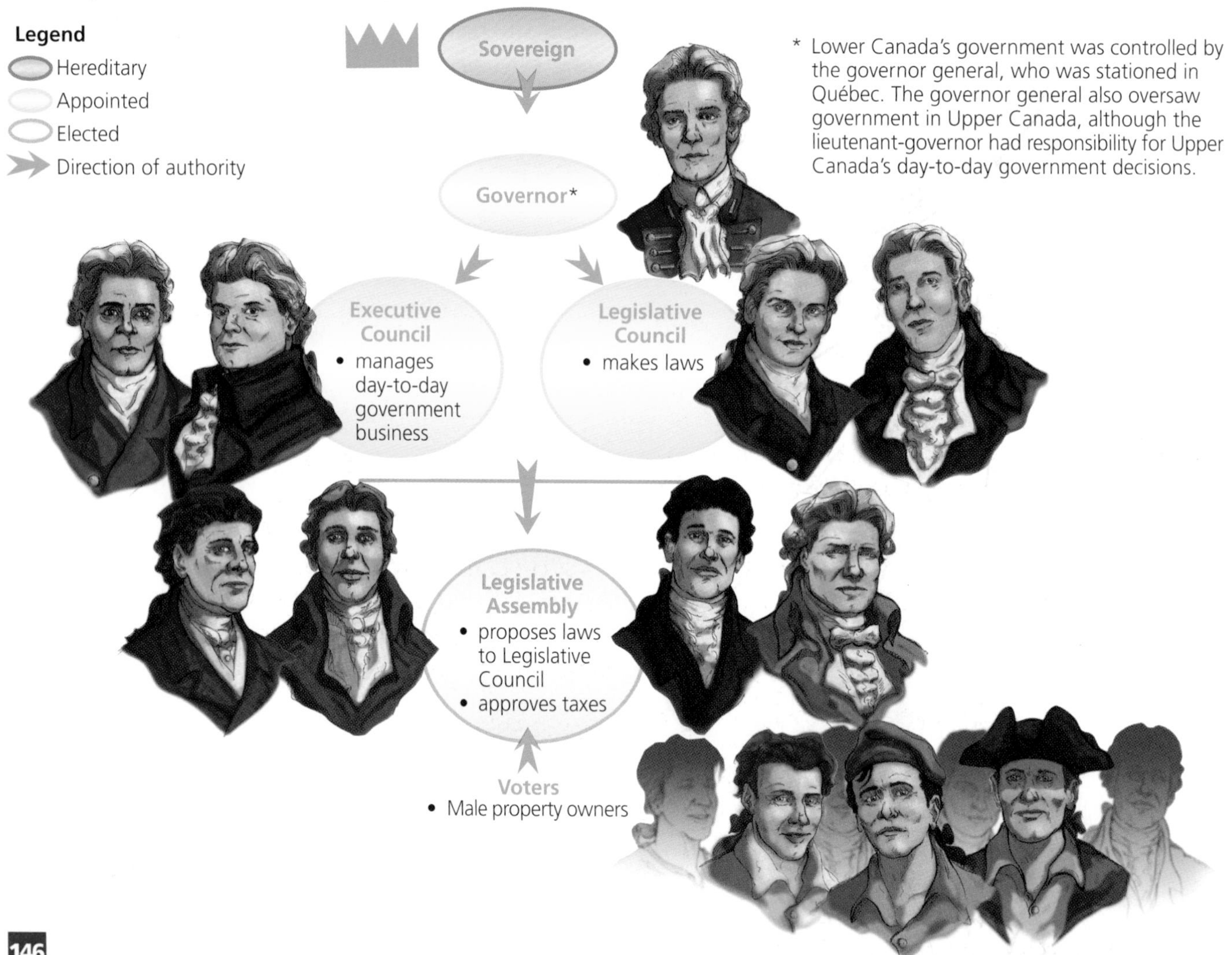

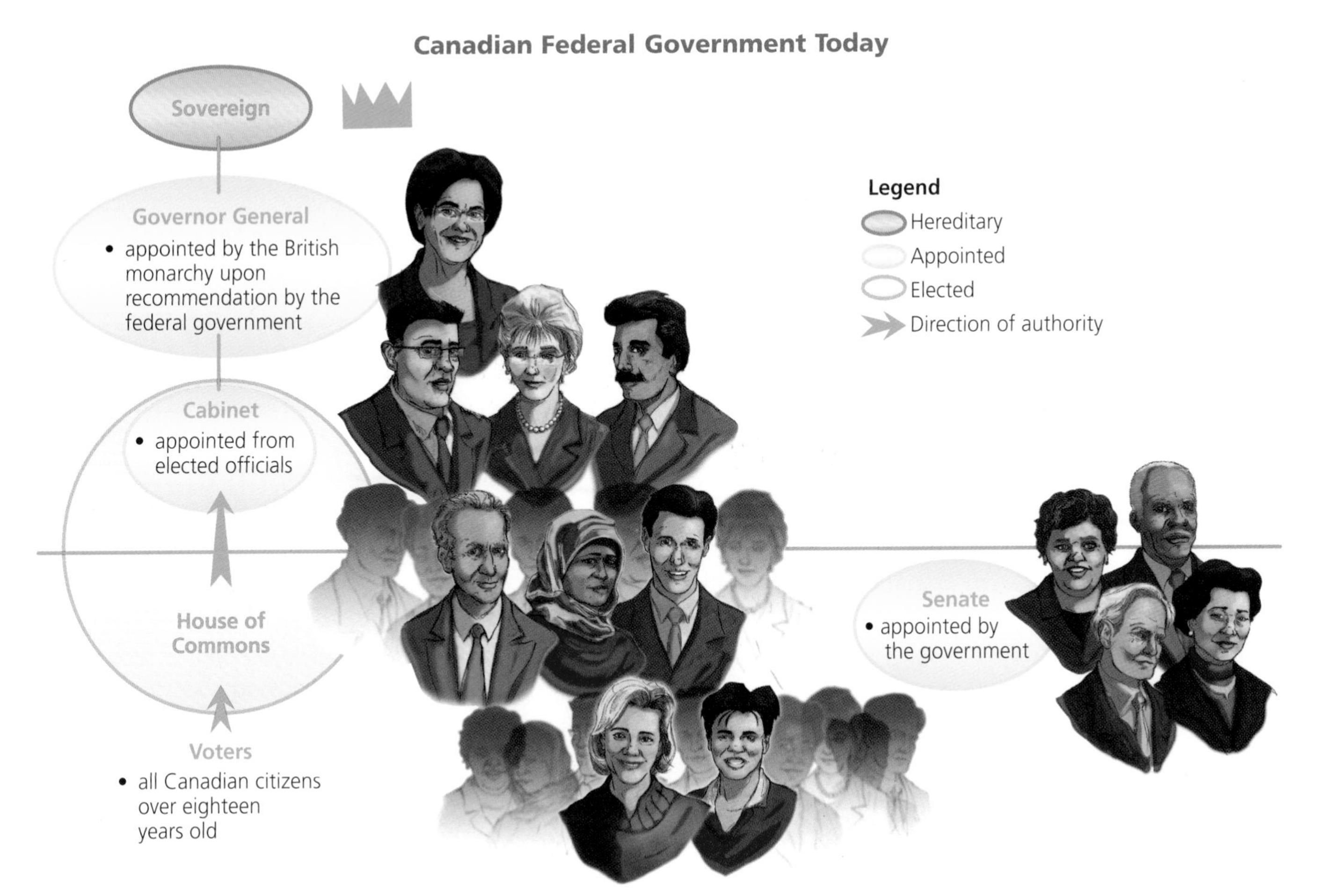

Government in Upper Canada

The government's executive branch included the main decision makers for the government: the legislative and executive councils. The Legislative Council made and approved all laws in Upper Canada. Legislative councillors were appointed to their positions for life. Positions were passed down from father to son.

The Executive Council advised the lieutenant-governor on all government matters. Councillors were also appointed, but not necessarily for life.

The Legislative Assembly formed a separate branch of the government. The Assembly was elected by male property owners. Like the Legislative Council, the Legislative Assembly made laws. The difference was that the Legislative Council or lieutenant-governor could overrule any laws made by the Assembly.

The Legislative Assembly also had the power to impose taxes. Tax money was to be used to run the government and its projects.

The lieutenant-governor could accept or reject any suggestions or advice given to him by the Assembly or his councils. The lieutenant-governor also had control of the colony's Crown reserves. This meant the lieutenant-governor did not have to completely rely on the Legislative Assembly for money to run the government.

After Reading

1. Considering what you learned on pages 144–147, what do you think are the three most important ways the Loyalists influenced British North America? Compare your ideas with those of a partner.

Simcoe and the Foundation of Upper Canada

Before Reading

1. If you are choosing members for a team, whom do you tend to pick? In your journal, write the three most important criteria you would use to create a successful team.

John Graves Simcoe had strong beliefs about class, military discipline, and the superiority of all things British. He was lieutenant-governor of Upper Canada from 1791 to 1796.

John Graves Simcoe had led a Loyalist unit called the Queen's Rangers during the American Revolution. In 1781, he was injured and returned to England.

The next year he married Elizabeth Posthuma Gwillim, a woman from a wealthy, influential family. At that time, military and government positions went to people with wealth and family connections. Simcoe's marriage advanced his career. He was appointed as the first lieutenant-governor of Upper Canada.

Choosing a New Capital

In 1792, Simcoe arrived in Newark (Niagara-on-the-Lake), the capital of the colony. He was to report to Lord Dorchester (Sir Guy Carleton), who was governor general for the two Canadas. Carleton was stationed at Québec.

Simcoe believed that Newark was an unsuitable choice as capital. Memories of the American Revolution were fresh in his mind. He was concerned about future conflict with the United States. Newark was close to the American border and would be an easy target in the event of conflict.

Simcoe's dream was to build a colony that mirrored England. He even hoped to build a capital city called London and reserved land for the future city (today London, Ontario). However, his first priority was to build a strong military base. He turned his eyes to York (renamed Toronto in 1834).

Simcoe thought York should be Upper Canada's military stronghold because it was farther away from the American border than Newark. It also had a natural harbour. At the time, the Toronto Islands were attached to the mainland by a peninsula.

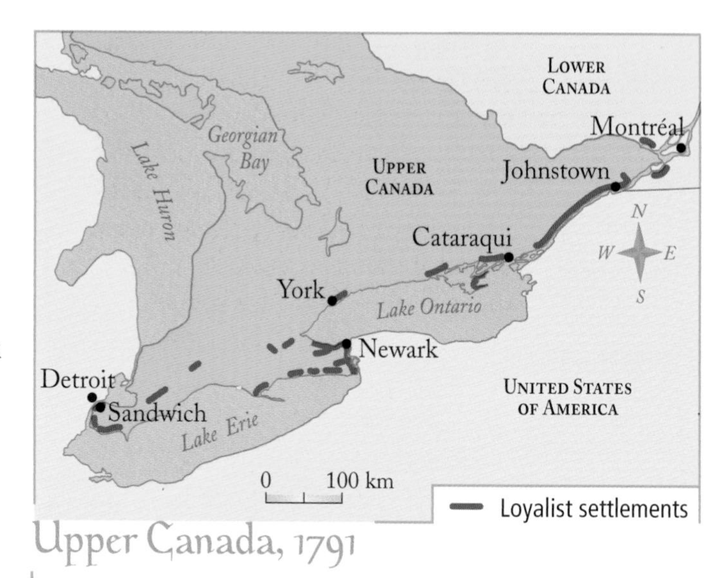

Upper Canada, 1791

- Compare the site of Newark with that of York. If you had been lieutenant-governor, which would you have chosen as the capital to ensure Upper Canada's defence?

York, by Elizabeth Francis Hale, 1804. This painting shows the view of York with Lake Ontario on the right.

Toronto before Simcoe

Simcoe was not the first to value the land Toronto sits on. The site had been an important part of transportation routes used by First Nations for many generations. When the French first travelled to the area, it was a major Seneca village called Teiaigon. Teiaigon was located at the mouth of the Humber River, in the west end of present-day Toronto.

In 1620, the French built a small fort there called Fort Rouillé. It was located on what are now the Canadian National Exhibition grounds. By the 1690s, the Mississauga had control of the area.

During Reading

1. As you read about the Toronto Purchase, use a PMI Chart to make jot-notes about how events affected the Mississauga First Nation. You may have to infer some of these effects.

The Toronto Purchase

In 1787, Sir John Johnson, the Chief Superintendent of Indian Affairs, met with the Mississauga at the Bay of Quinte. They agreed to a sale of land along the north shore of Lake Ontario, including both sides of the Humber River and Lake Simcoe. However, the exact amount of land purchased by the Crown was not clear. The deed to the sale, found many years later, was blank. It included no description of the land purchased.

When the Crown realized the mistakes made in the 1787 sale, it decided to tell the Mississauga and redo the purchase. The government said the new agreement was a confirmation of the 1787 sale. The deed, signed on August 1, 1805, indicated that the Mississauga agreed to give up a 22.5-kilometre by 45-kilometre section of land. This was far more land than the Mississauga's record of the first agreement.

Neither treaty included the Toronto Islands. Today, the New Credit First Nation (a branch of the Mississauga) has a land claim asking for compensation for the use of this land. They say the islands were never legally purchased from them.

Impressions of Upper Canada

Before Reading

1. What do you expect family life in Upper Canada was like? How would it be similar to or different from your family life today? Share your ideas with a partner and then work together on the rest of the questions on pages 152–153.

Elizabeth Simcoe helped her husband make York the new capital. Lady Simcoe's enthusiasm about York helped convince others that moving there might not be all bad. Her journal, letters, and paintings are today valuable primary resources about life in Canada at the end of the eighteenth century. She made notes on her life, as well as observations of the weather, environment, people, and events. Excerpts from her journal follow.

Lady Elizabeth Simcoe

During Reading

1. What evidence can you find from Lady Simcoe's journal that she liked her surroundings?
2. What evidence shows she sometimes feared or disliked her new home?

PRIMARY SOURCE 5.3a

From Elizabeth Simcoe's Journal

Sunday, July 1, 1792

Kingston is 6 leagues [34.7 kilometres] from Gananowui, a small Town of about fifty wooden houses & Merchants' Store houses. Only one house is built of stone, it belongs to a Merchant. There is a small Garrison here & a harbour for Ships.... The situation of this place is entirely flat, & incapable of being rendered [made] defensible, therefore were its situation more central it would still be unfit for the Seat of Government.

July 30th, 1792

I suffered exquisite pain all day from a Musquito bite, which the extreme heat increased & at night my sleeve was obliged to be cut open. I did not see any Rattle Snakes tho many Ladies are afraid to go to the table rock as it is said there are many of these Snakes near it.

August 17th, 1792

We were so cold & wet we were glad to drink tea. It was quite dark & too windy to allow of our burning candles.... The Rain & Wind did not cease [stop] for two hours, & we had no means of drying our Clothes & were obliged to sleep in a wet Tent. However we have not caught cold.

York, August 4th, 1793

We then walked some distance till we met with Mr. Grant's (the surveyor's) Boat. It was not much larger than a Canoe but we ventured into it, & after rowing a mile we came within sight of what is named on a government map, the high lands of Toronto. The Shore is extremely bold & has the appearance of Chalk Cliffs, but I believe they are only white Sand. They appeared so well that we talked of building a summer Residence there & calling it Scarborough.

PRIMARY SOURCE 5.3b

York, Tuesday, September 23, 1793

I rode on the peninsula. My horse has spirit enough to wish to get before others. I rode a race with Mr. Talbot to keep myself warm. I gathered wild grapes, they are pleasant but not sweet.

Capt. Smith has gone to open a Road to be called Dundas Street from the head of the Lake to the R. La Tranche [the Thames River]. He has 100 men with him. I hear they kill Rattlesnakes every day yet not a man has been bit tho they have been among them for 6 weeks.

York, May 1794

My Dear Mrs. Hunt

It is with pain I take up my pen to inform you of the loss we have sustained & the melancholy [sad] event of our losing poor little Katherine, one of the strongest healthiest children you ever saw.... She had been feverish two or three days cutting teeth,... I was not much alarmed; on good Friday she was playing in my room in the morning, in the afternoon was seized with fits, I sat up the whole night the greatest part of which she continued to have spasms & before seven in the morning she was no more. Our own surgeon was absent & the one present had certainly much less ability. She was the sweetest tempered pretty child imaginable, just beginning to talk & walk, & the suddenness of the event you may be sure shocked me inexpressibly....

Your sincere friend, E. Simcoe

April 24, 1795

The Gov. [Lieutenant-Governor John Simcoe] has been so ill since the 21st of March that I have not left his Room since that day. He has had such a cough that some nights he could not lie down but sat in a chair, total loss of appetite & such headaches that he could not bear any person but me to walk across the Room or speak out loud. There was no medical advice but that of a horse Doctor who pretended to be an apothecary [pharmacist].... Capt. Brant's sister [Thayandanegea's sister Molly, who was skilled at healing the sick], prescribed a Root—it is, I believe, calamus [a type of palm]—which really relieved his Cough in a very short time.

Castle Frank, by Elizabeth Simcoe, 1796. Castle Frank was the Simcoe summer home near York.

- How does this home compare to those of other Loyalists you have read about?
- What conclusions can be made about the different living conditions of early settlers in Upper Canada?

After Reading

1. What are some of the challenges the Simcoe family faced during these early years? How would your family respond to the same challenges today?
2. How do you think these problems would be similar to or different from those of people without the wealth and position of the lieutenant-governor's family? Discuss this with a partner. What evidence do you find for your answer on pages 152–153 and earlier pages in this chapter?
3. What does Simcoe's journal tell readers about how First Nations people helped settlers during these years? As a class, discuss whether you think these contributions are well acknowledged today.

Fur Trade Competition and Expansion

Before Reading

1. *Rivalry* means competition. In a small group, brainstorm examples of rivalries today. What are the benefits of having a rivalry? What can be some of the problems?

While British North America's administrators were preoccupied with the American Revolution and the arrival of the Loyalists, the fur trade continued in the background.

Since 1670, when the Hudson's Bay Company (HBC) set up shop along Hudson Bay, the fur trade had expanded. Yet it continued to follow the two systems of trading set up by the French and British. In the north, HBC traders waited at their posts for First Nations to arrive with furs to trade. In the south, rival traders used Montréal as their base to travel west across the continent in search of furs for trade.

The two systems continued, even after 1760, when New France came under British control. The Montréal-based trade was now run by small partnerships of English and Scots. They competed with one another and the HBC to find the best furs.

Competition became so intense that, in 1776, a group of traders from Montréal joined forces. They decided they could better compete with the HBC by cooperating with one another. They became the North West Company.

During Reading

1. As you read, complete a two-column chart comparing the North West Company's and Hudson's Bay Company's advantages and disadvantages in their rivalry with each other.

Coat of Arms of the North West Company.

- What symbols do you see on the coat of arms? What do you think the symbols mean?

By 1783, the North West Company dominated the fur trade. One reason for its success was its access to the rich furs near Lake Athabasca (located in what is now northern Alberta and Saskatchewan). These furs were top quality. They gave the North West Company enormous profits, even though traders had to transport the furs across the continent.

Although it cost the HBC less to transport their furs, the North West Company got the best furs. Their rivals were so successful that the HBC was forced to leave Hudson Bay to start establishing its own trading posts in the West.

A second reason for the dominance of the Nor'Westers (as the North West Company traders were called) involved the Métis. By this time, Métis traders had become a significant part of the industry. Their fathers had been French coureurs de bois or Scottish traders, and their mothers were First Nations. Métis traders had ties to both cultures and were highly successful in the fur trade. Their family ties with First Nations groups gave Métis people a strong trading advantage. Most Métis people worked for the North West Company.

The competition between the two companies was fierce. It drove the traders to explore the farthest reaches of the continent to gain advantage over their rivals.

In 1789, Alexander Mackenzie reached the Arctic Ocean. In 1793, he reached the Pacific Ocean by overland journey. Other explorers, such as Simon Fraser and David Thompson, opened new fur trade territories west of the Rocky Mountains.

The competition finally ended in 1821 when the two companies joined together under the name and charter of the Hudson's Bay Company. Although the North West Company had dominated the trade for many years, the HBC eventually beat their rivals. Hudson's Bay Company administrators kept a watchful eye on costs and profits. In the end, this concern for efficiency helped them drive the Nor'Westers out of business.

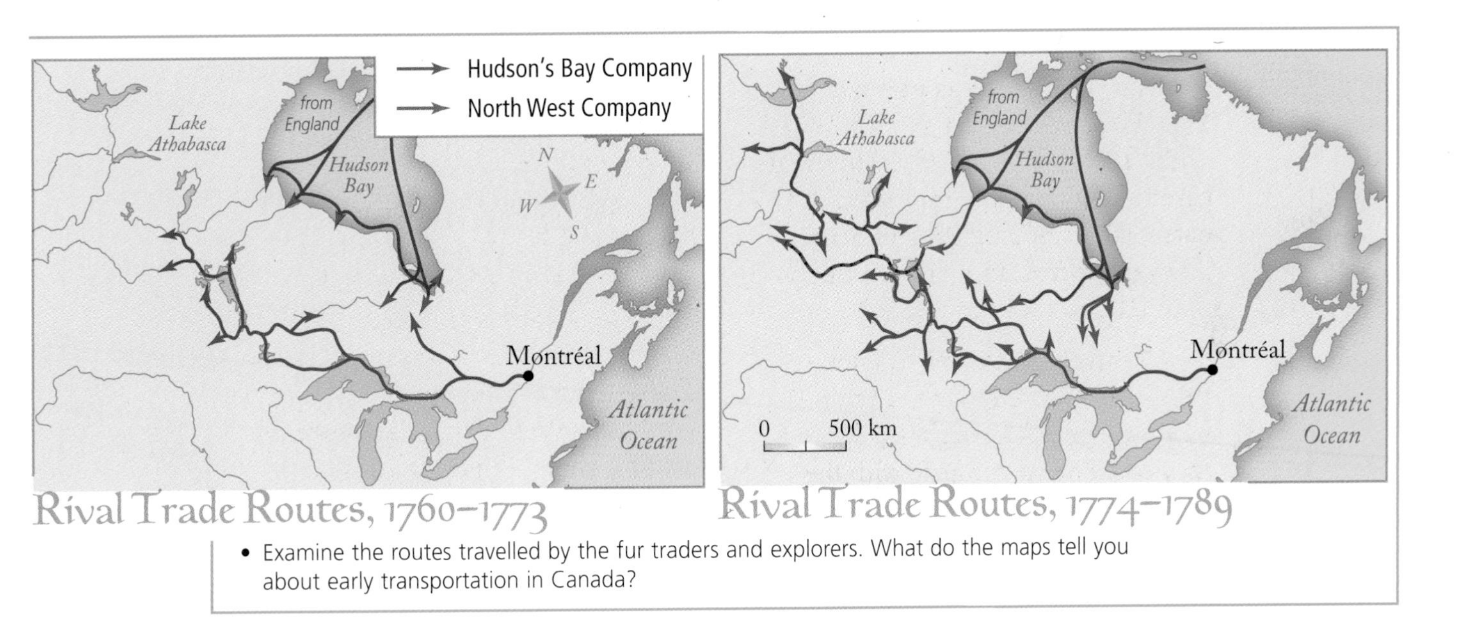

Rival Trade Routes, 1760–1773

Rival Trade Routes, 1774–1789

- Examine the routes travelled by the fur traders and explorers. What do the maps tell you about early transportation in Canada?

After Reading

1. How did competition in the fur trade affect the exploration of Canada? Use the maps on this page to help you answer the question.

Agriculture and Timber Industries Grow

Before Reading

1. Scan pages 156–159 and make a list of common jobs you think people had in Canada at the beginning of the 1800s. What clues did you use to answer this question?

In 1770, almost all of Québec's exports to Britain were furs. By 1810, furs were only 9 per cent of Lower Canada's exports. Loyalists wanting to make a living could not depend on the fur trade, even if they had wanted to.

During Reading

1. Review the pie graph and pictograph on this page. What can the information about trade and exports tell you about people's lives during this period?

Exports from Canada, 1850

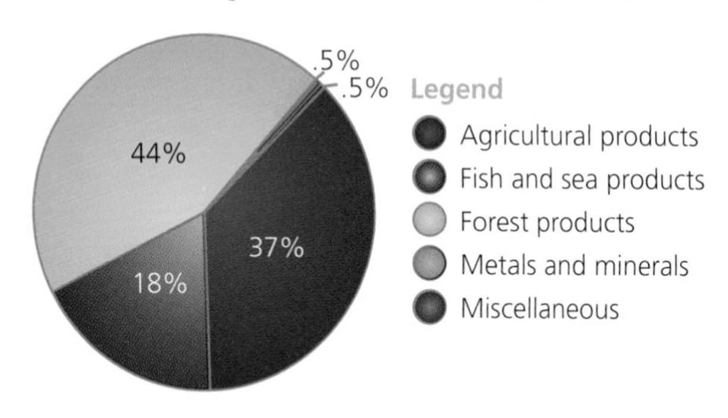

Sailing Ships Moored in the Port of Québec

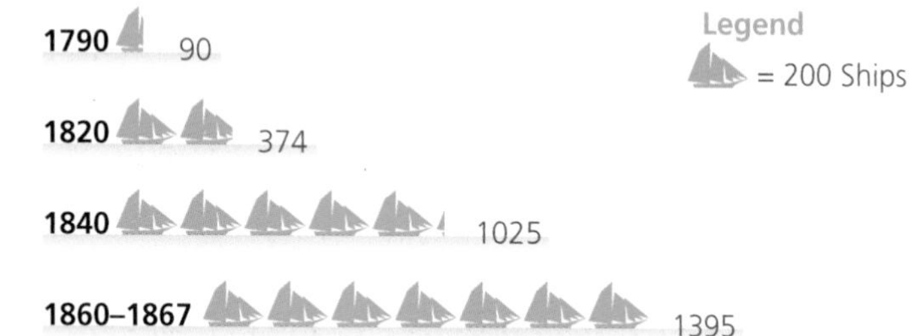

In the 1800s, British North America had a busy trade with Britain. Most of the goods shipped between Britain and British North America came through the port at Québec.

Reading Graphs

Graphs provide numerical information in a brief, visual style. In general, most are used to make a comparison.

Questions to Guide Reading a Graph

- What type of graph is it? By learning what to expect from different kinds of graphs, you can more quickly read and understand the data.

  Line graphs show trends over time, such as the value of exports from year to year.

  Circle or pie graphs compare the size of the parts to the whole, such as the number of workers in types of industry.

  Bar graphs compare data over time, such as the value of various types of beverage sold each month from the school cafeteria.

  Pictographs compare data using pictures to represent units of information being compared, such as a house used to represent every ten houses sold in a town or city.
- What does the graph title tell you about the information?
- What do captions or associated questions tell you about the graph's main ideas?
- Starting with any labels, read all the words. Check for a legend to help you understand the meaning of symbols or colours.
- How does the information relate to the chapter or pages you are reading?
- What comparisons (if any) are being made?
- What changes or **trends** (if any) are shown? A trend is a general direction or tendency.
- What is important about this information?

Agriculture

Agriculture was important to both Upper and Lower Canada. In Lower Canada, farms were relatively well established. Many families had been there since the days of New France. British settlers farmed around them. Towns and villages offered more and more services to the surrounding populations.

In Upper Canada, farms were often developed from lots covered with forest. Farmers could not clear their plot of land all at once. Usually, they felled trees on a section of land and planted wheat between the stumps. After a couple years, they could usually remove the tree stumps that had rotted and weakened. The farmers could then plant other crops, such as oats.

Wheat Production in Lower Canada, 1790–1840

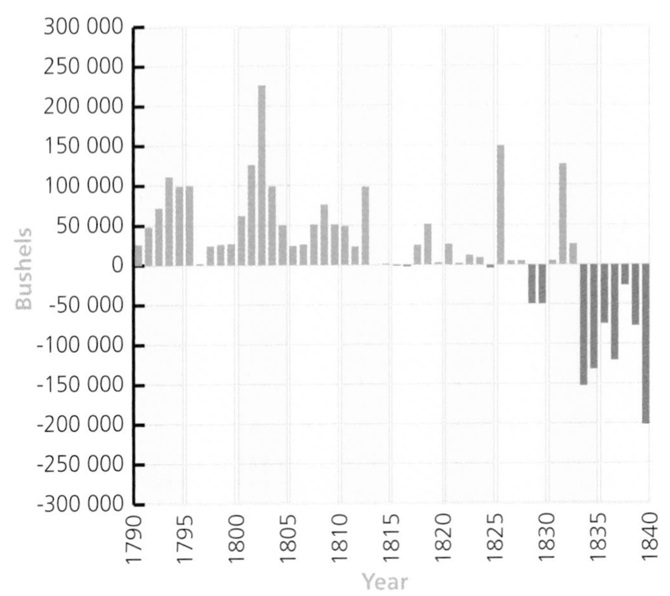

Legend

Surplus (extra) Deficit (shortage)

- What happened to wheat production around 1835? How do you think this affected farmers in Lower Canada?
- How does the bar graph help you see the trends at a glance? What would be the benefits and drawbacks of presenting this information in a chart instead?

Loyalist Settler Sowing Grain in a Rough Clearing alongside the Upper St. Lawrence, 1784, by C. W. Jefferys (1869–1951). Most of the work on farms had to be done by hand.

Process of Clearing the Town-plot at Stanley, October 1834 (New Brunswick), by W. P. Kay, 1836. The first years of settling in British North America were filled with work. Hundreds or thousands of trees had to be felled and cleared. Some of the lumber was used for homes and furniture. Other trees were burned.

Timber

By the end of the eighteenth century, the timber industry was booming in British North America. England needed wood to build ships and houses, and to make paper for the newspaper industry. At this time, wood was also used for shoes, eating utensils, furniture, wagons, and jewellery. Because of war in Europe, Britain's usual supply of timber was cut off. British North America stepped in to fill the gap.

Sometimes, logs would become jammed at narrow points in the river or stream. Workers had to climb onto the jam, find the log that was holding back the others, and chop it free. They then had to race to safety before the jam broke loose, carrying them down the river under a mountain of rushing logs.

Lumbering in the Backwoods, 1858. During the winter, loggers felled trees and hauled them to the edge of frozen rivers to wait for the spring thaw.

The lumber industry made heavy use of the Saint John, St. Lawrence, and Ottawa Rivers. Workers lived in isolated labour camps along rivers or streams. They felled trees and cut them into square logs. These square logs were easier to pack in ships to transport across the ocean. Then they moved the logs downriver in huge rafts. A constant stream of ships loaded with timber left Saint John and Québec. Most went to Britain and the West Indies.

Many farmers worked part time in the timber industry, especially in the winter months, when they could not work their land. While the men were away, the women took care of the house, barn, animals, and children.

During Reading

1. Why did British North America's lumber industry use rivers and streams so extensively?
2. What challenges would the lumber industry present to family life?

Lumberers on the Miramichi River, New Brunswick, by James Fox Bland, 1880. Loggers used the river system to move logs from where they were cut to ports where they could be shipped.

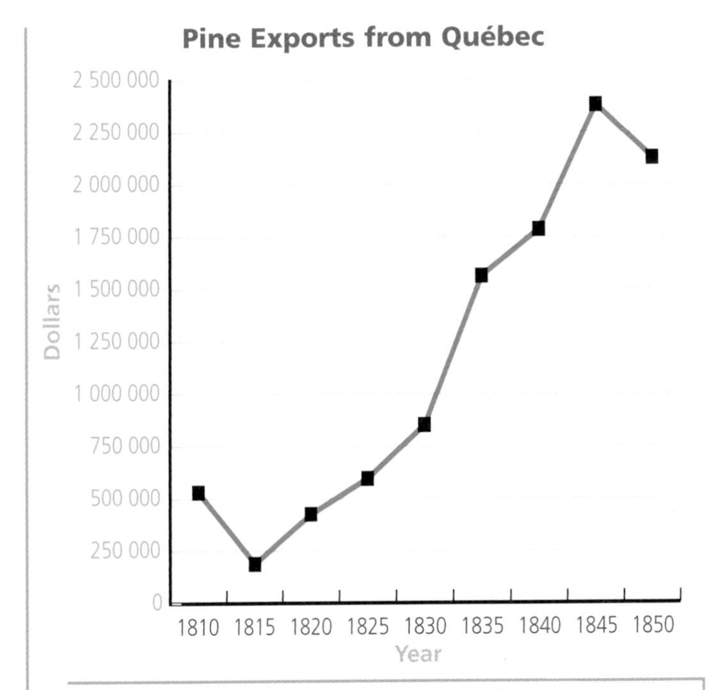

- In one sentence, describe the general trend in pine exports from Québec between 1810 and 1850.
- How does the line graph help you see this trend? What other form of graph could you use that would still highlight the trend?

Mill on the Gananocoui, by Elizabeth Simcoe, around 1792.

- Based on what you have read, why do you think mills were an important part of communities in Upper Canada?

After Reading

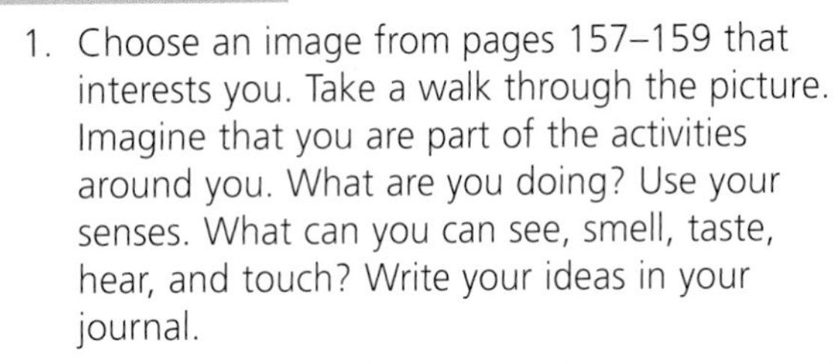

1. Choose an image from pages 157–159 that interests you. Take a walk through the picture. Imagine that you are part of the activities around you. What are you doing? Use your senses. What can you can see, smell, taste, hear, and touch? Write your ideas in your journal.
2. Use an Important/Interesting Chart to summarize information from pages 154–159 about the fur trade, agriculture, and timber industries. Using at least four ideas from your chart, write a short story about one of the paintings or illustrations in this chapter. Consider using the image you "walked through" in question 1 of this After Reading.

Discovering the Foundations of Your Community

Before Reading

1. With a partner or small group, brainstorm any evidence that indicates the history of your local community. Consider your community's name, the names of major streets, local landmarks, historical plaques, heritage buildings, statues, and so on.

What do you daydream about? You probably think about things you want or look forward to. You may also recall events from your past. You might **commemorate**, or celebrate, past events by keeping photographs. Perhaps you have a T-shirt or some other souvenir from a concert or event you attended.

Why do you want to remember people or events from the past? Why do you keep things that remind you of them? The answers to these questions are similar to reasons why communities commemorate people, events, and places that are significant parts of their history.

During Reading

1. With your partner or group, brainstorm ways that key historical events and people are commemorated or ways you would like to see them commemorated.

Stamp commemorating the 200th anniversary of a war hero's birthdate

Plaque recording the accomplishments of the Fathers of Confederation

Eternal Flame symbolizing the strength of Canadian unity

Statue honouring Thayendanegea's leadership

Researching with Various Sources of Information

An excellent way to learn about the history of your area is to ask an expert to visit your classroom. First Nation Elders and local historians can often provide valuable information that is not easily available from other sources. In particular, much First Nations history is unpublished. The only way to learn about this history is through an Elder or another individual a community recognizes as being a keeper of its oral history.

Sources such as libraries, museums, journals, paintings, personal records, Web sites, photographs, newspaper archives, county atlases, town council minutes, and street directories can provide much historical information. Goad's insurance atlases give information about the types and locations of buildings that once existed in cities such as Toronto and Vancouver.

Almost all cities and towns have one or more historic sites. Visiting one of these places can provide you with some of the best, most interesting research possible on your topic.

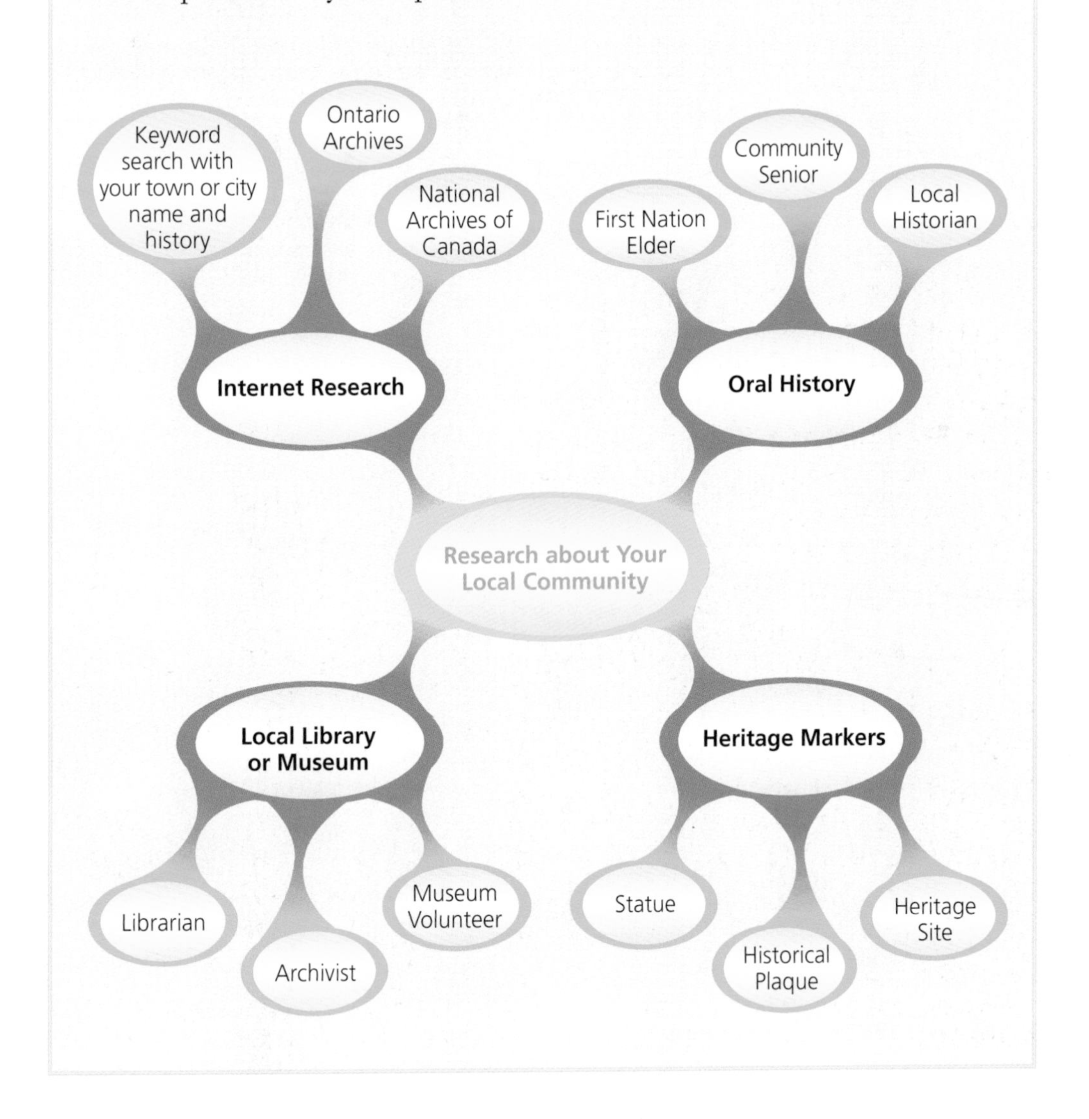

After Reading

1. Imagine that you have been asked to commemorate an individual or group needing greater recognition as a community founder.
   a) Establish criteria for your selection of who to commemorate.
   b) Research your local community's history using any or all of the sources suggested in the feature on page 161. Begin with the first people to live in your region—usually one or more groups of First Nations.
   c) Select a person or group to be recognized.
   d) Choose and design a form of commemoration. Consider a statue, plaque, historic site designation, Web site, television commercial, anniversary celebration, scholarship or award, or another form.
   e) Prepare a written justification for your choice to present to your local historical society or town council.
2. Consider presenting your research at a Historica Fair. Students' presentations range from tabletop displays to performance pieces and Web-based projects. More than 250 000 Canadian students participate in Historica Fairs at their schools every year. Go to www.duvaleducation.com/canadasearlyyears. For more information, click on the link to the Historica Fairs Web site.

Students from across the country celebrate Canada's history by participating in Historica Fairs.

Chapter 5 Review

Compress

1. Prepare a Concept Map with the title *Early Ontario*. Include the concepts and individuals that follow: Loyalists, Black Loyalists, First Nations allies, John Simcoe, Elizabeth Simcoe, Thayendanegea, Thomas Peters, and the Constitutional Act of 1791. Include subtopics and appropriate linking words.
2. Prepare a timeline of the key events from this chapter using either *settlement* or *politics* as your theme. Include a title, dates, and brief descriptions of events. Add visuals, if you wish.
3. Prepare a three-circle Venn Diagram to compare the challenges experienced by the groups of people who moved to British North America after the American Revolution: Black Loyalists, other Loyalists, and First Nations allies.

Express

4. Which of the problems faced by early settlers to British North America were the most challenging? What evidence do you have? Select one person who lived at this time and tell his or her story in your own words. This could be done as a presentation to peers or with a partner.
5. Write a letter to one of the individuals you learned about in this chapter. Include information about your community today and how it has changed since the time of the person to whom you are writing. Identify any themes or changes that would be of special interest to the person.

Their Stories, Our History

Identify a person or event in your school's history worth commemorating. Research the details and determine how and where to commemorate this person/event. Prepare a proposal for your principal.

Grade 7 History (Mrs. Fortney)

November 21, 2006

Dear Principal,

I'm writing to propose a plan to commemorate two former students of our school. They graduated 10 years ago, and have dedicated their young lives to help the less fortunate people of the world. They are working with the local people in less developed countries. Currently they are working together to build schools and hospitals in Africa. They are positive role models for the students in our school, who also want to make a difference.

I suggest that there are many ways to recognize their efforts. These ideas include: a display with photos and a map in the library; a garden of hope for the future; or a plaque in the lobby of our school. I think we should contact the former students to ask for their accomplishments, current projects, as well as any photos they might contribute.

I am willing to organize this commemoration for our school. I hope you will consider this idea as enthusiastically as I do.

Sincerely,

chapter 6

The War of 1812

The Death of Brock at Queenston Heights, by C. W. Jefferys, around 1908.

- What questions come to mind as you look at this painting?
- Is this a primary or a secondary source of information? How do you know?

Meeting between Laura Secord and Lieutenant Fitzgibbon, June 1813, by Lorne Kidd Smith (1880–1940).

- What seems to be happening in the painting?
- What do you notice about Laura Secord's clothes? What might have caused this?

Like earlier wars in North America, the War of 1812 had both European and North American roots. Unlike other wars, all the battles for the War of 1812 were fought on North American soil. Most happened along the border between British North America and the United States. For over two years, Canadians, Americans, and First Nations suffered loss of property and life.

In the end, the War of 1812 had a lasting impact on both sides of the border. The war resulted in famous treaties, the United States' national anthem, many monuments, new transportation routes, and the development of national myths and heroes.

Historical records on the war are inconsistent. Sometimes, both sides claim the same battles as victories. Even the outcome of the war is controversial. At various points, both Americans and Canadians have said they won.

In this chapter, you will learn about the causes, events, and impact of the War of 1812. You will then decide for yourself who won. What kind of evidence will help you make your judgment? How does a historian weigh evidence to reach such a conclusion?

This chapter will help you understand

- the causes of the War of 1812
- the roles of key individuals in the war
- key battles in the War of 1812
- effects of the war on different groups of people
- long-term effects of the War of 1812

Featured Skills

- Analyzing Newspaper Editorials
- Understanding Organizational Patterns
- Debating a Question

Primary Causes of the War of 1812

Before Reading

1. As a class, discuss some of the reasons countries go to war. Would you risk your life for any of these reasons? Why or why not?

The Treaty of Paris that ended the America Revolution was signed in 1783. However, tension between Britain and the United States did not end. Many issues continued to cause problems in their relationship. Some of the most significant are described on pages 166–167: impressment, Britain's blockade of Europe, First Nations alliances, and the influence of the War Hawks.

Action between USS Chesapeake *and* HMS Leopard, *22 June 1807,* by Fred S. Cozzens, 1897. The British boarded the American ship and forced a number of American sailors to serve on British ships.

Impressment

Napoleon Bonaparte was a successful military leader in France in the late eighteenth century. In 1793, Britain went to war with France to stop Napoleon's plan to conquer all of Europe.

By 1793, war against France was Britain's main priority. The British feared that French troops led by Napoleon might cross the English Channel and invade England. They needed a strong navy to protect their shores.

However, conditions on British ships were poor. Many sailors deserted and joined the American **merchant navy**, where pay and conditions were better. A merchant navy is used for trade and business, not war. Britain began stopping American ships at sea in search of deserters. Sometimes, the British impressed, or forced, American sailors into service in the British navy. **Impressment** caused enormous anger in the United States.

Blockade

As part of its war strategy, Britain used its navy to **blockade** Europe. The blockade prevented countries from trading with France. It was supposed to hurt Napoleon's war effort. However, the American economy also suffered because they lost a major market for their goods.

During Reading

1. Was Britain justified in boarding American ships in search of deserters? Why or why not? Write your thoughts in your journal.
2. In your opinion, did impressment or the blockade justify a declaration of war? Explain your answer in your journal.

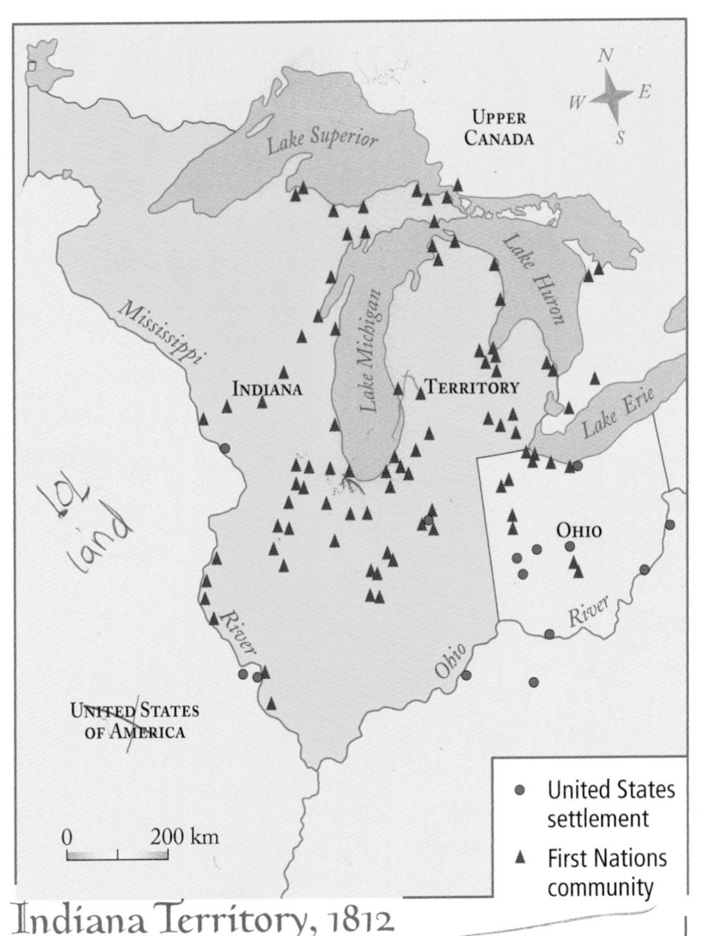

Indiana Territory, 1812

- How did it suit British interests for First Nations to control the Indiana Territory?

First Nations Alliances

After the American Revolution, Britain encouraged First Nations in the West to keep a large territory for their own use. This territory kept the Americans from expanding.

The Americans accused the British of encouraging First Nations to be hostile towards them. In particular, they believed Britain supported Tecumseh's (ta-kum-suh) efforts to protect First Nations land. Tecumseh was an influential First Nations leader from the Ohio and Indiana territories. He opposed the western movement of settlers onto First Nations land. To stop further settlement, he created an alliance of First Nations. He advised his allies not to sell any more land to the Americans.

War Hawks

A more immediate cause of the War of 1812 was the **War Hawks**. This was a group of American politicians from the southern and western states. They believed that the United States should expand its borders. They saw British North America and First Nations in the Ohio Valley as obstacles in their way.

The War Hawks believed they should simply take over these territories. In a famous statement from 1812, former U.S. president Thomas Jefferson wrote, "The acquisition of Canada this year, as far as the neighborhood of Québec, will be a mere matter of marching, and will give us experience for the attack of Halifax the next, and the final expulsion of England from the American continent."

President James Madison was especially influenced by the War Hawks. On June 19, 1812, he declared war on Britain.

After Reading

1. Which of the causes of the War of 1812 presented on pages 166–167 seems the most significant? Why?
2. Based on the information provided here, do you think the Americans were justified in declaring war? Work with a partner to make a Both Sides Now Organizer to prepare your answer. Look back to page 91 to review how to make this type of organizer.

Invasion!

Before Reading

1. In a small group, discuss how you would feel if another country invaded yours. What would your response be? How would you expect your government and military to respond?

On July 12, 1812, William Hull, commander of the Northwestern Army of the United States, invaded Canada with a force of 2000 men. He stationed himself in Sandwich (present-day Windsor). There, he distributed a proclamation to convince residents not to oppose his invasion.

General William Hull

During Reading

1. As you read the primary sources on pages 168–169, list examples of facts, opinions, and arguments. Use a chart or table to organize your notes.
2. According to Hull's proclamation, how did he view Britain's First Nations allies? Why do you think he issued such a strong warning about working with First Nations?

PRIMARY SOURCE 6.1

From General Hull's Proclamation Flyer, July 12, 1812

Inhabitants of Canada!

After thirty years of peace and prosperity the United States have been driven to arms....

I come to find enemies, not to make them. I come to protect, not to injure you....

I promise you protection to your persons, property, and rights; remain at your homes, pursue your peaceful and customary avocations [activities]; raise not your hands against your brethren [brothers]....

If, contrary to your own interests and just expectations of my country, you should take part in the approaching contest you will be considered and treated as enemies, and the horrors and calamities [disasters] of war will stalk before you....

If the First Nations are let loose to murder our citizens, and butcher our women and children, this war will be a war of extermination.... No white man found fighting by the side of any First Nations person will be taken prisoner; instant destruction will be his lot [fate].

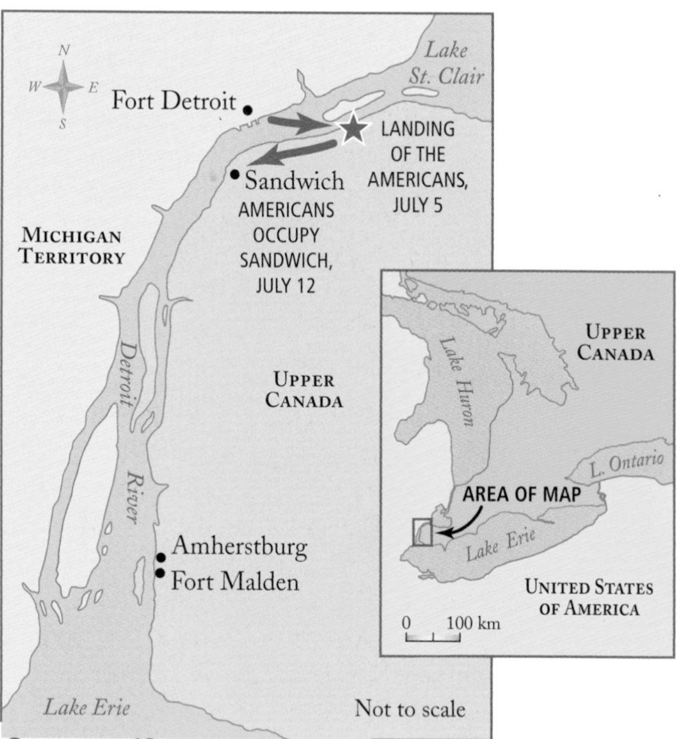

Detroit Frontier, 1812

- Why do you think Sandwich was the first target for invasion by the Americans?

Major General Isaac Brock

Isaac Brock and the Defence of Canada

When the war began in 1812, Isaac Brock was a major general and the administrator of Upper Canada. For a number of years, Brock had asked the British government for a command in Europe. He wanted to join the fight against Napoleon. However, when war with the Americans broke out, he was determined to defend the colony.

Brock's concern about Napoleon showed in his response to Hull's proclamation. In it, he reminded the people of Upper Canada of the benefits they had enjoyed under British rule. He hinted at the dangers of siding with the Americans. France had helped finance the American Revolution against the British. Brock suggested that if Britain were to lose the war, America's debt might be repaid by returning Canada to the French.

PRIMARY SOURCE 6.2

From Isaac Brock's Response to Hull's Proclamation, Published in the Kingston Gazette on July 28, 1812

Proclamation

The unprovoked [uncalled-for] declaration of war, by the United States of America against the United Kingdom of Great Britain...has been followed by the actual invasion of this Province....

Settled not thirty years by a band of Veterans exiled [sent from] from their former possessions on account of their loyalty, not a descendant of these brave people is to be found, who...has not acquired a property and means of enjoyment superior to what were possessed by their ancestors....

Are you prepared inhabitants of Upper Canada, to become willing subjects or rather slaves to the Despot [unfair ruler, meaning Napoleon] who rules the nations of Europe with a rod of iron?

If not, arise in a Body, exert [use] your energies, co-operate cordially [in a friendly manner] with the King's regular forces to repel [turn back] the invader, and...[do not part] with the richest inheritance of this Earth—a participation in the name, character and freedom of Britons.

A Question of Loyalty

In 1812, British North Americans and their leaders were concerned about their ability to fight off an American invasion. British troops were busy fighting Napoleon in Europe. Few could be spared for Canada.

Brock was not sure how many people in Upper Canada would fight the Americans. In the years since the American Revolution, many American settlers had moved to Upper Canada. Late Loyalists now formed a larger part of the population than the original Loyalists. No one was sure whether the recent arrivals had strong feelings of loyalty to Britain. Many suspected they had come north only to get land. Some people feared they might welcome the American invasion.

After the invasion, some militia members deserted British forces. A few deserters joined the Americans, which seemed to prove there were feelings of disloyalty among the population. The mood in Upper Canada was generally negative. Few thought Upper Canada could be defended. Brock refused to listen.

During Reading

1. As you read Primary Source 6.3, written a week after Brock's response to Hull's proclamation, summarize Brock's main ideas.
2. What challenges does Brock face? How can he overcome these challenges?

PRIMARY SOURCE 6.3

Letter from General Brock to Colonel Baynes, July 29, 1812

My situation is most critical, not from any thing the enemy can do, but from the disposition [mood] of the people—the Population, believe me is essentially bad—A full belief possesses them that this Province must inevitably succumb [give in]. This prepossession [idea] is fatal to every exertion [effort] —Legislators, Magistrates, Militia Officers, all, have imbibed [accepted] the idea, and are so sluggish and indifferent [uncaring] in their respective offices that the artful and active scoundrel [villain, meaning hull] is allowed to parade the Country without interruption, and commit all imaginable mischief....

What a change an additional regiment would make in this part of the Province! Most of the people have lost all confidence. I however speak loud and look big.

Militia Training on the King's Birthday, by C. W. Jefferys (1869–1951). All able-bodied men were enrolled in the militia. Their main training day was on June 4, King George III's birthday. Most militia trained with only sticks, pitchforks, and umbrellas. Few had uniforms.

Analyzing Newspaper Editorials

Newspapers have editorials in addition to news articles. Editorials are short articles that state the opinion of the newspaper on a topic. The editor of the paper usually writes them to persuade the reader to agree with the paper's opinion. The sample editorial in this feature is fictional, but it is based on real attitudes towards British North America in some parts of the United States before the War of 1812.

Characteristics of Editorials

- Editorials are usually clearly identified. Most appear on a special page. Occasionally, they may appear on the front page. They present a reaction to a major story the newspaper has covered elsewhere or in previous editions.
- The first sentence states the point of view to be developed in the editorial.
- The paragraphs in the body of the editorial use facts, opinions, and arguments to develop the point of view.

Washington, D.C. **Columbian Centinal** June 1, 1812

EDITORIAL

It is time to expel the tyrants!

The time has come to banish Britain from North America once and for all. Our sons and fathers gave their lives during the War of Independence. We won that war, but Britain is blind to the new reality. Now is the time to show them what our independence means. We will no longer be bullied to serve Britain's benefit.

British arrogance knows no bounds. They repeatedly board our ships and take our sailors to serve as slaves in their war with France. To serve their own cause in the war, they block our right to trade in Europe. And they wage a secret war with us by supplying First Nations with military support.

We must invade British North America. Our greater population and military experience can easily overtake its small population of farmers. They may welcome their chance to throw off British shackles and gain their freedom. We would then settle the question of ownership of the western territory for good. The continent is ours. Now is the time to exercise our rights.

- The concluding or summary paragraph is a strong restatement of the opinion or a call to take action.
- Editorials use strong, direct language.

Questions to Analyze Editorials

1. What is the point of view expressed in the editorial?
2. Where are the editorial's facts, opinions, and arguments?
3. What is the editorial's call to action?
4. Are there examples of strong, direct language? Does this language make the editorial more or less convincing?

After Reading

1. Should colonists in Upper Canada support Brock's appeal? Working with a partner, make a T-chart that lists support for and against supporting Brock's ideas.
2. On your own, write an editorial for the *Kingston Gazette* that takes a position on how colonists should respond to the invasion.

Leaders of Action

Before Reading

1. With a partner, make a list of the kind of information you would you expect to find in a biographical profile of a famous person from history.

Sir Isaac Brock

Isaac Brock was born in 1769 in the Channel Islands, England. He chose a military career and was sent to Canada in 1802. Brock's assignment was to improve the colony's ability to defend itself, especially against the United States. To do this, he helped train militia units. In 1811, he became the head of British forces in Canada.

Brock was not excited about his job in Canada. He wrote to his brother in 1811, "You can hardly imagine the uninteresting and boring life I am doomed to lead in this position." However, his life would not be boring for long. When the War of 1812 started, Brock had a war to fight.

After his invasion in July, General Hull had retreated from Sandwich to Detroit because of supply problems. Brock joined forces with Tecumseh to plan an attack on the American fort.

On August 16, they boldly approached Detroit from across the river. The force of 1300 included about 600 First Nations people led by Tecumseh. Hearing First Nations war cries outside the fort, General Hull grew anxious. He surrendered almost immediately, even though he had a force of 2000 men at his disposal.

The early victory built support for Britain. The mood in Upper Canada improved. More people began to believe they could beat the Americans. The victory also gave Brock a reputation as a strong military leader.

However, Brock did not lead for long. He died in October 1812, early in the Battle of Queenston Heights. Despite their leader's death, his troops went on to win the battle.

Brock was made a Knight of Bath for his victory at Detroit, but he was killed before he learned of this honour. Today, Brock University, in St. Catharines, Ontario, is named in his honour. He is buried beneath a monument near the place he was killed.

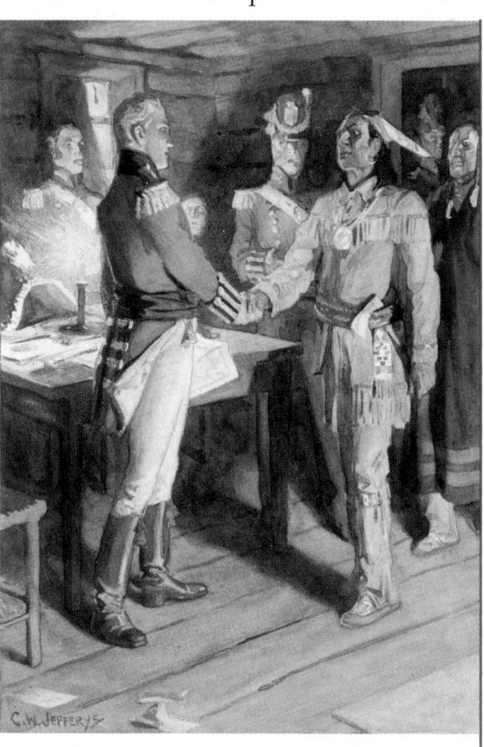

Meeting of Brock and Tecumseh, 1812, by C. W. Jefferys (1869–1951).

- Does this picture of Brock and Tecumseh show them as equals? Explain your answer.
- What might have motivated the artist to paint this picture?

During Reading

1. Was Brock a hero? Some historians argue that he was not. They say his military successes relied more on American failure than his own skill. Use the information on pages 168–172 to find evidence for and against this point of view.

Tecumseh

Tecumseh's fight against American settlers merged with British interests during the War of 1812.

Chief Tecumseh was born in 1768, a member of the Shawnee (shaw-nee) nation. With his brother Tenskwatawa (tens-kwa-ta-wa), he built an alliance of First Nations to resist the settlement of what is today the western United States. The brothers encouraged First Nations to protect their traditions.

Tecumseh raged against the sale of lands long held by First Nations: "Sell a country! Why not sell the air, the clouds, the great sea as well as the earth? Did not the Great Spirit make all for the use of his children? Our fathers from their tombs reproach us. I hear them wailing in the winds. We are determined to defend our land, and if it be the Creator's will, we wish to leave our bones upon it."

During Reading

1. Is the quotation in the second paragraph a primary or secondary source? Why might a biographer include this kind of information?

Tecumseh allied with Britain against the United States in the War of 1812. In return, Britain promised to support Tecumseh's claim to the western territory.

Tecumseh first met Brock near Detroit on August 13, 1812. The two leaders immediately admired each other. Of Tecumseh, Brock wrote, "A more sagacious [wise] or more gallant [brave] warrior does not, I believe, exist. He was the admiration of every one who conversed [spoke] with him." Together, Tecumseh and Brock planned the invasion of Detroit. Many historians argue that without First Nations participation, the battle would not have been won so easily.

On October 5, 1813, Major General Henry Proctor was in charge of British and Canadian forces west of Burlington. His forces and Tecumseh's were fighting the American troops near Lake Erie. However, when Proctor ran short of supplies, he retreated to Moraviantown. The British retreat left Tecumseh and the First Nations to fight alone. In the Battle of the Thames (Moraviantown), they were outnumbered. During the battle, Tecumseh was shot and died.

Proctor was court-martialled and suspended for six months. His decision to retreat made many First Nations believe that the British would lose the war.

Tecumseh and his allies helped the British win several battles in the War of 1812. His death marked the end of this alliance with the British. It was also the end of the major First Nations resistance to American settlement in the West. Today, there is a town in southwestern Ontario named after Tecumseh.

After Reading

1. What questions do you have about Brock or Tecumseh? Where might you find this information? Use a K-W-L Organizer to format your response.

Who's Who in the War of 1812

Before Reading

1. Scan the subheadings on pages 174–175. Which names do you know? What did they do? Share your knowledge with a partner.

Pages 174–175 include profiles of three people who helped British North America in the War of 1812.

Richard Pierpoint

Richard Pierpoint was born in 1746 in Bondu (now Senegal), Africa. He was taken into slavery as a teenager. During the American Revolution, he joined the Butler's Rangers, a regiment based at Fort Niagara. Along with a few other Black soldiers, he became an expert in First Nations-style warfare. When the revolution ended, he settled in the Niagara area.

After the revolution, Americans sometimes raided Canada to bring former slaves back to the United States. Pierpoint petitioned the government to allow all the Black people in the region to settle together. He thought this would help them defend themselves against raids.

When the War of 1812 began, Pierpoint organized a Black military company called the Coloured Corps. Pierpoint was sixty-eight years old at the time. The Coloured Corps fought in the battles of Queenston Heights and Fort George.

During Reading

1. Why do you think Pierpoint decided to fight in the War of 1812?
2. Why do you think there is no image of Pierpoint on this page?

Laura Secord

Laura Secord was born in 1775 in Massachusetts. She moved with her husband and family to Queenston, Upper Canada, in 1795.

During the War of 1812, her family was forced to house American soldiers. She overheard the men discussing plans of an American attack on the British at Beaver Dams (today Thorold, Ontario). Secord knew that if the Americans won at Beaver Dams, they would gain control the Niagara Peninsula, a key region in the war.

On June 13, 1813, Secord set off to warn the British of the attack. She walked 32 kilometres through heavy forest until she met a group of Haudenosaunee people who were allied with Britain. They brought her to General Fitzgibbon, leader of British forces in the area. The British and their allies fought off the Americans, taking all but six as prisoners.

In the 1860s, Secord received a £100 reward from the Prince of Wales. She died in 1868 in Niagara Falls, at the age of ninety-three.

Laura Secord on Her Journey to Warn the British, by C. W. Jefferys, around 1921. Secord's journey included a six-hour climb over the Niagara Escarpment.

John Strachan

John Strachan was born in 1778 in Scotland. He immigrated to Upper Canada in 1799. He was a teacher and then became an Anglican priest.

During the War of 1812, he was chaplain for the troops. On April 27, 1813, the British had retreated from York and American soldiers were looting and burning the town. Strachan was the only leader to step forward to meet with American General Henry Dearborn. Strachan negotiated the surrender of York with better terms for its citizens.

After the war, Strachan helped found and lead the Loyal and Patriotic Society. It raised funds to help disabled militia and their families.

After the war, John Strachan became a member of the Legislative Assembly in Upper Canada. Strachan encouraged Canadians to feel proud of their war effort. Like many other people, he believed the local militia, not the British soldiers, had saved the colony from the Americans.

The Loyal and Patriotic Society gave out this medal to recognize "extraordinary instances of personal courage" from the War of 1812.

- What do you think the lion, beaver, and eagle represent?

After Reading

1. Imagine that the Government of Ontario is building a park dedicated to the War of 1812. The park will have several statues of people who played key roles in that war. Nominate one of the people on the list that follows as a candidate for a statue:
   - Septimus Clarke
   - Matilda Ridout
   - Samuel Ridout
   - Sir Roger Sheaffe
   - Sou-neh-hoo-way (Thomas Splitlog)

   To make your nomination, write a profile of the individual and his or her role in the War of 1812. Be sure to include the 5 Ws and 1 H. Begin and end your profile with a reason why the person should be the subject of a statue.

Think It Through

Events of the War of 1812

Before Reading

1. Does the most skilled team always win? What other factors can affect whether a team wins or loses? Discuss your answer with a small group.

As you read earlier in the chapter, many American leaders thought it would be easy for the United States to conquer British North America. In Thomas Jefferson's words, it would be "a mere matter of marching."

They had good reasons for their opinion. First, the population of the United States was far larger than that of British North America. Second, Britain was busy with the war against Napoleon. It could not spare many troops for North America. And finally, nobody was sure the settlers in Upper Canada would rush to fight the Americans.

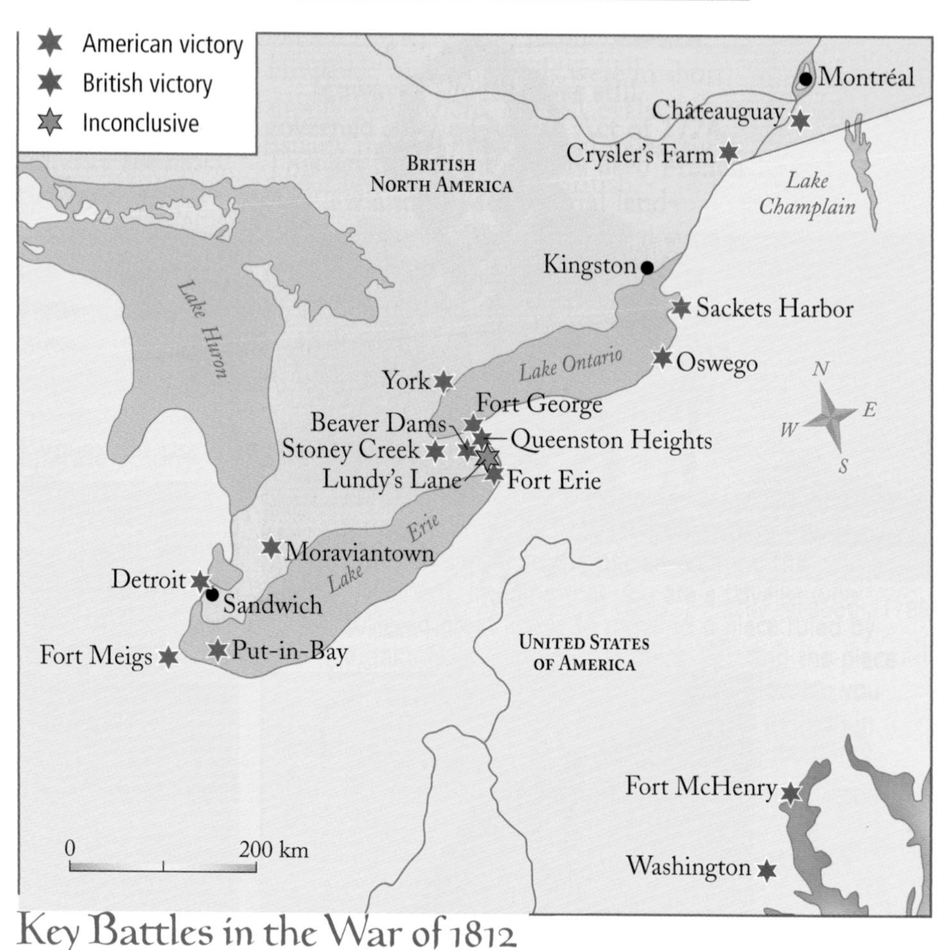

Key Battles in the War of 1812

During Reading

1. Use the Understanding Organizational Patterns feature on page 177 to identify as many organizational patterns as you can on this page.

However, Jefferson was mistaken. The War of 1812 lasted two-and-a-half years and was fought on land and water. Battles raged from Detroit and Windsor in the southwest, through the Niagara Peninsula, to Châteauguay in Lower Canada.

Understanding Organizational Patterns

Information can be organized a number of ways. Recognizing different organizational patterns can help you find the most important ideas in what you read. Certain words and phrases can signal when a particular organizational pattern is being used. The chart below includes some of the most common patterns.

Organizational Pattern	Signal Words and Phrases
Chronological Order	after, before, during, first, finally, following, immediately, next, then, when
Cause/Effect	as a result of, because, consequently, effects of, leads to, therefore
Compare/Contrast	although, as well as, compared with, however, similarly, yet
Order of Importance	beginning, first, following, most important, next, finally, significantly, important
Generalizations	additionally, because of, for example, in fact, seldom, therefore

Sometimes, a section of writing will have one pattern and sometimes, more than one. You have already encountered some of these patterns in this textbook.

Think It Through

During Reading

1. As you read pages 178–181, use a Spider Organizer to make notes about the most important information. Include a maximum of three points for each battle.

Major Battles in the War of 1812

Battle of ______
- ______
- ______
- ______

Battle of ______
- ______
- ______
- ______

Battle of ______
- ______
- ______
- ______

Battle of ______
- ______
- ______
- ______

Deciding what to put on the Spider Organizer will be the most difficult part. There isn't much space. I guess you have to decide what is most important. A Spider Organizer would be a good way to take notes or study.

The Battle of Queenston Heights

Major General Isaac Brock left Fort George at four o'clock in the morning on October 13, 1812. He had been awakened by the sound of heavy guns 11 kilometres away at Queenston Heights. Although he did not have a full force to deal with the invasion, he took action. As Brock led his small force up the hills, he was shot in the chest by a musket ball and died. His troops withdrew to wait for reinforcements to arrive.

By mid-afternoon, the second phase of the battle began. This time Major General Roger Sheaffe led British troops and militia. Joining them were a number of Haudenosaunee led by Ahyouwaighs (ah-yoo-way), also known as John Brant. Ahyouwaighs was the youngest son of Thayendanegea (Joseph Brant). Together, Sheaffe's and Ahyouwaighs's forces made the invading Americans withdraw.

The American cause was not helped when their militia from Buffalo, New York, refused to fight on the Canadian side of the border. Many American citizens did not support the war as strongly as the War Hawks.

British losses were light and 958 Americans were taken prisoner. The battle was an important defensive victory for the British allies.

Battle of Queenston Heights, by James B. Dennis (1796–1855). The artist was the senior British officer at Queenston during the Battle of Queenston Heights.

Battle of Lake Erie, by Percy Moran, around 1911. Many battles in the War of 1812 were fought on the Great Lakes. The Americans were confident they could defeat British forces by land. The British were just as confident they could conquer the Americans at sea. As the war went on, both were proved wrong. The Battle of Lake Erie (or Battle of Put-in-Bay), shown here, gave the Americans dominance on the Great Lakes.

As I'm reading about these battles, I see that the first information I am given is the date. This signals that this section is in chronological order. The date is followed by background information about which side had an advantage or where they were positioned.

I'm most interested in the information about the battle itself. In discussions of both battles so far, the last sentence told me the most important information. I read signal words, such as *important* and *finally*, which told me who won and the importance of the win.

The Battle of Put-in-Bay

In September 1813, the British at Amherstburg (near Detroit) were facing a winter with supply problems. The Americans had an advantage on the Great Lakes because the British navy was busy blockading the American coast. They could not send many ships to the Great Lakes.

Forces at Amherstburg could not depend on supplies getting past the Americans. On September 10, six British ships fought nine American ships. The sea battle raged from early in the morning until late afternoon. The Americans finally captured the British ships and control of Lake Erie.

Jul 12, 1812 Americans invade Canada at Sandwich

Aug 16, 1812 Detroit surrenders to the British

Oct 13, 1812 Americans repelled at Queenston Heights

Apr/May 1813 British lay siege to Fort Meigs, Ohio, but fail to take fort

Apr 27, 1813 Americans invade York; British troops retreat to Kingston

May 27, 1813 Americans capture Fort George

Jun 6-7, 1813 British stop American advance at Stoney Creek

Sep 9, 1813 British fleet on Lake Erie defeated at Put-in-Bay

JUL AUG SEPT OCT NOV DEC JAN FEB MAR APR MAY JUN JUL AUG SEPT

Think It Through

PRIMARY SOURCE 6.4

A Civilian's Concerns: A Letter from Cathe Lyons, October 16, 1814

We are all alarmed here, the Americans are the other side of the Chippawa Creek.... Appearances are very much against us here, if the fleet does not come, there is not a man to defend this place should the enemy attempt to cross at the same time they make an attack above.... I cannot get even a place to put my things in near the Forts every one is so full, if the enemy is successful, I shall lose everything.

The Battle of Châteauguay, by Henri Julien, before 1884. During the Battle of Châteauguay, the Canadians blew horns in the woods and used other tactics to convince the Americans that the Canadian force was much larger than it was. This strategy helped them win the strategic battle.

The Battle of Châteauguay

The Battle of Châteauguay was fought on October 25, 1813. The British force included soldiers and militia from Lower Canada and First Nations. All were commanded by a French Canadian, Lieutenant Colonel de Salaberry (de sal-a-bree).

The battle began with an American plan to invade Montréal. The Americans wanted to cut off the supply line between Montréal and Kingston. This would hinder the British war effort in Upper Canada.

However, the Americans had poor leadership and communications. At one point, they shot at and killed some of their own advance guard as the men were returning through the forest. In addition, the Americans consistently overestimated the size of the British force. In reality, the American force outnumbered British troops by about eight times. However, believing themselves outnumbered, the Americans retreated.

This was not a major battle in terms of casualties. Nevertheless, it was a significant strategic win. Montréal was still in British hands. Even more significantly, soldiers from both Upper and Lower Canada had fought off a common enemy. For the first time, French and English shared a bond.

In this last paragraph, I see an example of information arranged in order of importance. I noticed it because of the signal phrase *Even more significantly*. I think the authors have decided this point is the most significant because it had long-term consequences. Winning or losing a battle is one thing. Changing attitudes and the way people think is much more difficult.

Think It Through

The Battle of Lundy's Lane

The Battle of Lundy's Lane was fought in 1814, over a period of five hours. Historians have sometimes described it as the defining battle of the War of 1812. Both sides suffered approximately 800 casualties and were exhausted by the effort.

Much of the battle was fought in darkness, with Niagara Falls thundering in the background. Confusion dominated the battlefield. The British fired on their own men. American soldiers accidentally bayoneted their own forces in the dark forest.

The Americans withdrew the next day and built up their defence at Fort Erie. The British prepared for a second attack that never came. Both sides claimed victory because neither side clearly lost or won.

In this case, the significance of the battle came in the first and last paragraphs. If this battle defines the War of 1812, then I know why both Canadians and Americans claim to have won the war! It's probably hard for anyone to be clear on who really won.

The Battle of Lundy's Lane, by C. W. Jefferys, around 1921. This illustration attempts to capture the passion of the fight, with bayonets fixed during a charge towards the guns.

- Imagine that you are part of this illustration. What sounds and smells surround you? How would you be feeling?

After Reading

1. Use books, encyclopedias, or the Internet to research three other battles from the War of 1812. Look for locations of battles on the timelines on pages 179 and 181 or the map on page 176. Add your research to your Spider Organizer. Remember that you want just the three most important points about each battle.
2. How would you define a victory in war? Based on all the battles you have learned about, can you identify who won the War of 1812? Explain why or why not in a class discussion.

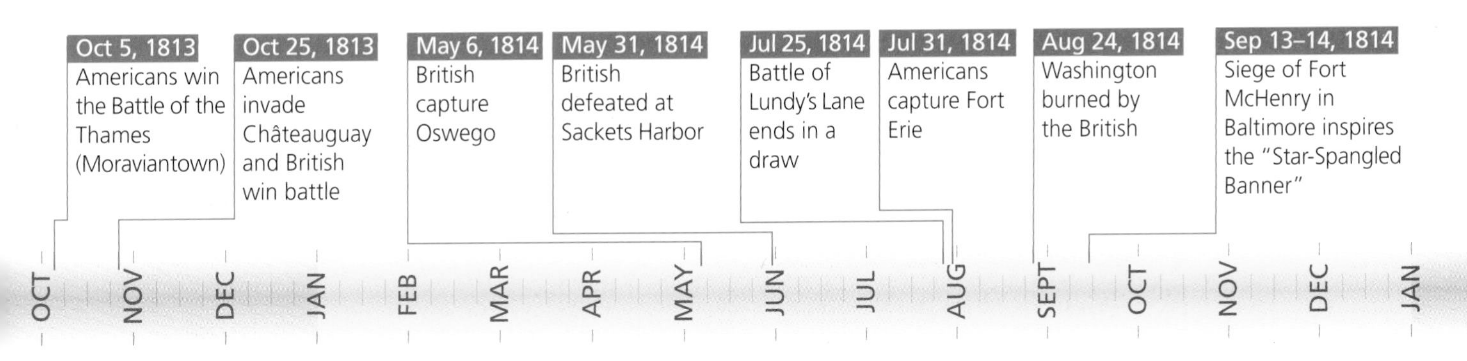

The War Ends

Before Reading

1. Would you help defend your community if it was threatened by war? How would you help?
2. At the end of the war, how should those who were loyal to Britain have been rewarded?
3. What should happen to British North Americans who helped the Americans?

Soon after the Battle of Lundy's Lane, the War of 1812 came to an end. Britain had finished fighting Napoleon. The Americans were worried that more soldiers would be sent to fight in North America. In addition, Britain had stopped the impressment of American soldiers before the war began and had since ended the blockade of Europe. For the Americans, most of the reasons for war were gone.

The Treaty of Ghent

The war officially ended with the signing of the Treaty of Ghent in Belgium on December 24, 1814. The treaty took five months to negotiate.

In the treaty, impressment and the blockade were not mentioned, even though these had been among the major reasons the United States had declared war.

Boundaries between the United States and British North America went back to the way they were before the war. In the Convention of 1818 (Convention of Commerce), the two countries agreed that the forty-ninth parallel of latitude would be a guideline for their international boundary.

Britain agreed to drop its goal of a First Nations territory. The British and Americans also agreed that they would never use First Nations as allies in war again.

During Reading

1. Recall the causes of the War of 1812. Does the Treaty of Ghent reflect the causes of the war? Does the treaty show who won the war? Explain your answer.

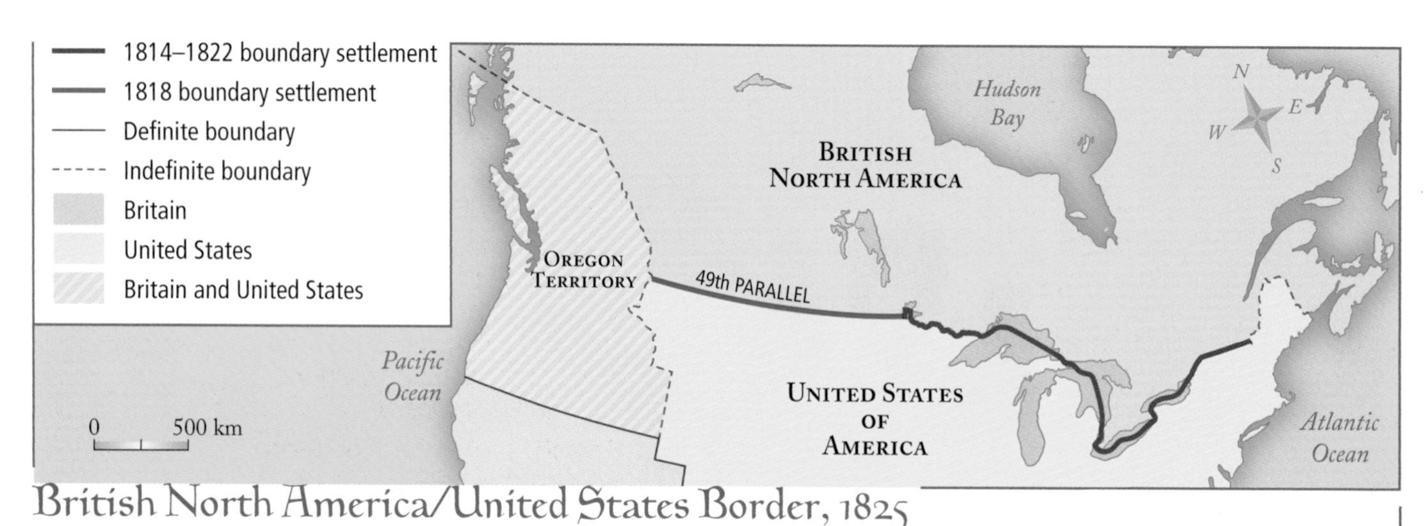

British North America/United States Border, 1825

- After the War of 1812, why do you think Britain and the United States wanted to make a formal agreement about the international boundary?

Aliens and Treason

After the war, the British colonies had to decide how those who helped the Americans should be punished. In March, Upper Canada's Legislative Assembly passed the Alien Act. Alien is another word for foreigner. The Alien Act applied to people with strong connections to the United States. This act made it illegal to have gone to the United States after the war began in July 1812.

Fifteen people were convicted of high treason, which is a serious crime against the government. People found guilty had their property taken away and were sentenced to death. In the end, eight people were hanged. Some were deported.

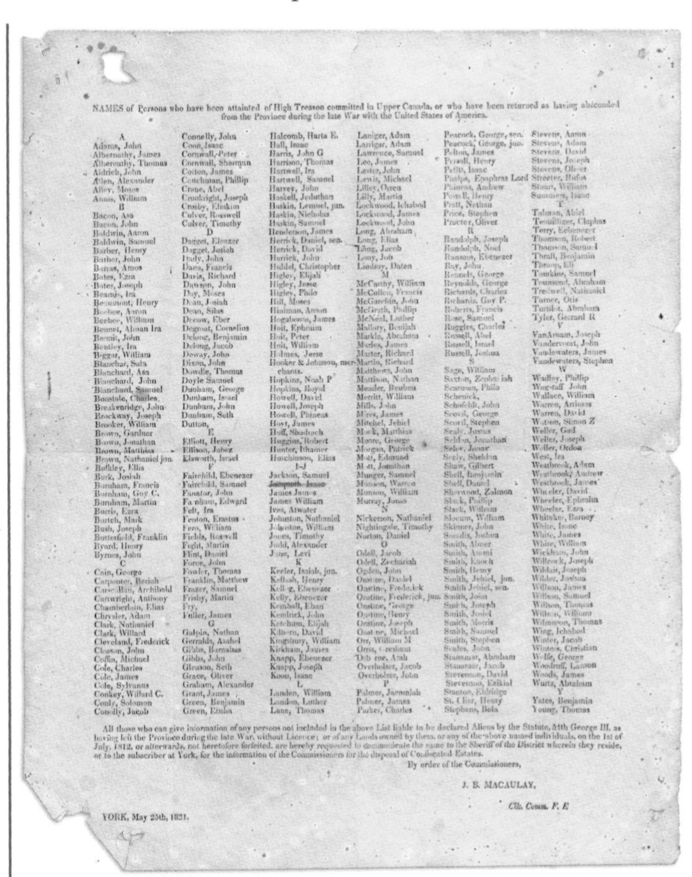

NAMES of Persons who have been attainted of High Treason committed in Upper Canada, or who have been returned as having absconded from the Province during the late War with the United States of America.

All those who can give information of any persons not included in the above List liable to be declared Aliens by the Statute, 54th George III. as having left the Province during the late War, without Licence; or of any Lands owned by them, or any of the above named individuals, on the 1st of July, 1812, or afterwards, not heretofore forfeited, are hereby requested to communicate the same to the Sheriff of the District wherein they reside, or to the subscriber at York, for the information of the Commissioners for the disposal of Confiscated Estates.

By order of the Commissioners,

J. B. MACAULAY,

Clk. Comm. F. E

YORK, May 25th, 1821.

This poster lists the names of people charged with treason after the War of 1812. Most of the people listed were never caught and brought to trial.

- Why do you think this poster was distributed? How do you think it would affect the local population?

During Reading

1. Why do you think the government of Upper Canada passed the Alien Act? Do you think the act was unfair? Why or why not?

Recognition for Loyalty

Militia members and their families wanted to be recognized for their loyalty to Britain. Those who survived were eligible for land grants. Some of the land they received came from people found guilty of treason, whose property had been taken away. The amount of land a militia member received depended on his rank. Most received land near the border with the United States. If another invasion occurred, they could be called back to fight.

Widows of the militia members who had died or wives of those injured in the war received a small pension. How much each received depended on the rank of her husband and the length of his service. The Loyal and Patriotic Fund started by John Strachan also helped widows and orphans.

As for First Nations, the British had peace and no longer needed its allies. First Nations had fought for Britain with the promise of a territory of their own. The Treaty of Ghent removed that hope.

During Reading

1. Working in a small group, consider how Britain, Canada, First Nations, and the United States were affected by the War of 1812. Who gained the most from the war? Who gained the least?
2. Does this analysis help you decide who won the war? Explain why or why not.

Debating a Question

A debate is a formal way of discussing a question. When participating in a debate, you and a partner take a side in response to a question. You then work together to find evidence to support your side, referring to your notes and the textbook. Sometimes, you might also use other sources, such as the library.

Formal debates follow set rules and steps. For example, usually each side speaks for a limited amount of time on the question. Your teacher will help you with other rules of debating.

It is important to also find evidence that supports the other side, so you can prepare for the rebuttal stage of the debate. During the rebuttal, you briefly repeat the other side's argument, adding your own argument as to why it is not valid.

You may want to organize your research as follows:

Arguments for Our Side	Evidence for Our Arguments	Arguments for the Other Side	Counter-arguments (how their arguments are less valid)

After your research is complete, plan your debate. Prepare an introductory and concluding statement and organize your arguments. Think about the benefits of presenting your ideas from most important to least important or from least to most. Determine who will present each of your arguments and the evidence.

Practise with your partner until you can make your arguments without reading.

After Reading

1. The question of who won the War of 1812 is still argued by historians on both sides of the border. After studying this chapter, who do you think won the War of 1812? Why?
   a) In groups of four, divide into two pairs. You will be debating the question *Who won the War of 1812?*
   b) Determine which side each pair of students will support. One pair should argue that Britain won and the other should argue that the United States won.

Long-Term Effects of the War of 1812

Before Reading

1. How does war affect a country? Who benefits from war? Who suffers?
2. What are some of the similarities and differences between Canadians and Americans today? What evidence do you have for your opinion?

During the War of 1812, the St. Lawrence River had come under attack. The Rideau Canal was built to ensure a more secure transportation route in case of another war with the United States. The canal was one of many long-term effects of the war.

- What questions do you have about the building of the Rideau Canal or its route, as shown on this map?

During Reading

1. Before reading the fictional news report on pages 185–186, prepare a T-chart. As you read, note long-term effects of the War of 1812 in the first column. In the second, indicate whether or not you think the effect is still important to Canada and why.

May 1827

Rideau Canal furthers post-war plans

York—Led by Lieutenant Colonel John By of the Royal Engineers, workers began construction of the Rideau Canal this spring. The workers—mostly Irish immigrants and French Canadians—have a mighty task ahead of them. Fifty dams and forty-seven locks will be built along the 200-kilometre stretch. Most of the route is heavy forest, rock, and swampland.

The canal was first proposed at the end of the War of 1812. It will form part of a transportation link between Montréal and Kingston.

"The St. Lawrence River has always been our main transportation route. During the war, the Americans tried to cut off our supply route from Montréal to Kingston. That would have been a disaster. The Royal Engineers were hired in 1825 to design and build the Rideau Canal. It will offer a more protected transportation route in times of peace and war," stated John Official, a government spokesperson, this afternoon.

Lieutenant Colonel By has set up his headquarters at the junction of the Rideau and Ottawa Rivers. A settlement has started there to support the project. People call it Bytown in his honour.

The canals are just one part of a massive improvement in British North America's ability to defend itself from American aggression. Other projects include a naval base at Penetanguishene, the construction of Fort Henry in Kingston, and expansions to the forts at York, Mississauga, and Amherstburg.

The colonies are also expanding roads that could help move supplies and troops in case of another war. Transportation experts say that any future railways in the colonies will be built at a safe distance from the border.

continued on page 186

unit 3
Conflict and Change

Chapter 7: Roots of Conflict

Chapter 8: Social Change

1825 Erie Canal completed

Feb 25, 1832 Quarantine station established in Lower Canada to prevent the spread of cholera

Nov 2, 1832 Reformer William Lyon Mackenzie expelled for the third time from the Upper Canada Assembly

Mar 6, 1834 York becomes the first city of Upper Canada

Aug 1, 1834 Slavery abolished in the British Empire due to law passed in 1833

1835 Sir Francis Bond Head appointed lieutenant-governor of Upper Canada

Nov 23, 1837 Patriote rebels in Lower Canada turn back British army at Saint-Denis

1825 1826 1827 1828 1829 1830 1831 1832 1833 1834 1835 1836 1837 1838 1839

Chapter 9: Economic and Political Change to 1856

Key Questions for Unit 3

- What caused the Rebellions of 1837?
- What was the outcome of the Rebellions of 1837?
- What challenges did different groups of people face in nineteenth-century British North America?
- How did transportation affect people and businesses in British North America?
- How did Britain's decisions about its empire affect people in British North America?
- How were minority groups treated in the past?
- What strategies can people use to resolve conflict?

Dec 8, 1837 Mackenzie's rebels in Upper Canada defeated at Montgomery's Tavern

Dec 14, 1837 Rebels in Lower Canada defeated at Saint-Eustache

Feb 4, 1839 Lord Durham recommends uniting Upper and Lower Canada

1848 Responsible government achieved in British North America

1848 St. Lawrence River deepened

1849 Rebellion Losses Bill; Houses of Assembly burned by mob in Montréal

1850 Robinson-Superior and Robinson-Huron treaties signed

1850 Fugitive Slave Act signed in Washington, D.C.

1853 Grand Trunk Railway completed

1841 1842 1843 1844 1845 1846 1847 1848 1849 1850 1851 1852 1853 1854 1855

chapter 7
Roots of Conflict

Back View of the Church of Saint-Eustache and Dispersion of the Insurgents, by Charles Beauclerk, 1840. At the Battle of Saint-Eustache, 70 **Patriote** (pa-tree-ut) rebels from Lower Canada were killed and 118 others were taken prisoner. In the days that followed, militia volunteers hunted down other rebels, looting and burning French-Canadian homes as they went.

- There are two groups shown fighting in this painting—the British infantry and the Patriotes of Lower Canada. How can you tell the groups apart?
- What does it mean to be a *patriot*? Why do you think people become patriots?
- Which group do you think will win the battle? What evidence do you have?
- What questions might help you understand the event in this painting?

The Constitutional Act of 1791 set up governments for Upper and Lower Canada. Each colony had an elected Legislative Assembly. Each also had an appointed executive. The executive worked closely with the governor. Together, the executive and governor controlled the government.

By the 1820s and 1830s, many people were unhappy with this system. Executive members made many decisions that benefited themselves or their friends and family. The executive often ignored the wishes of elected Assembly members.

Some people wanted to change, or reform, the government. These people—the **reformers**—were tired of appointed officials making most of the decisions. They demanded **responsible government**. With responsible government, the main decision makers for the government would be responsible (that is, accountable) to elected officials. The Assembly, not the governor, would control the government.

However, ideas about responsible government were new at this time. They frightened some people. Many resisted the proposed changes. Those who wanted responsible government had to oppose many powerful people who did not. Eventually, the disagreement led to violent conflict in the form of armed **rebellion**.

What do you think would make a farmer or merchant choose violence as a way to resolve a conflict with the government? Could the issues have been resolved peacefully?

This chapter will help you understand

- issues leading to the Rebellions of 1837
- how different leaders' personalities affected the crisis
- events in the Rebellions of 1837
- how the British government tried to resolve the conflicts that had led to the rebellions
- how people resolve conflicts through negotiation

Featured Skills

- Negotiating a Conflict of Interests
- Writing a Report
- Asking Questions for Research: The Inquiry Question

Issues in Upper and Lower Canada

Before Reading

1. With a partner, study the diagram on page 193 showing the government established by the Constitutional Act of 1791. Which groups do you think would be most satisfied with the government? Which would be least satisfied? How might unhappy groups resolve their grievances?

A Political Meeting at "The Corners" in 1837, by C. W. Jefferys (1869–1951).

- What does this illustration tell you about politics in 1837?

A conflict occurs when people disagree about what should be done in a given situation. In Upper and Lower Canada in the 1820s and 1830s, people disagreed about who should make decisions for the colony. Should decisions be made by a small elite? Or, was it better to involve a wider group from society?

After the War of 1812, many people from Britain and the United States moved to British North America. Many were drawn to British North America's particular form of democracy. As you may recall, a democracy is a government in which power rests with the people. At this time, *the people* meant the people who could vote in elections. These were property owners—mostly men with European backgrounds. People who could not vote had no formal way to influence the government.

After the American Revolution, the United States had become a **republic**. In a republic, the highest power is held by elected officials, not a monarch who inherits power. To British Loyalists, American-style democracy was extreme. It meant a rejection of British values, culture, and religion. It meant revolution.

In contrast, British North America had a limited form of democracy. In Upper and Lower Canada, voters could elect their Legislative Assembly (also referred to as the Assembly). However, the Assembly was not very powerful. The Crown was still at the head of the government. Any laws the Assembly passed could be stopped by the Executive and Legislative Councils (together with the governor called the executive).

Even so, the executive did not have all the power. It depended on the Assembly to approve taxes needed to pay for projects. This meant the executive and Assembly were in frequent conflict. The Assembly often refused to support executive projects with tax money. In turn, the executive often refused to approve laws passed by the Assembly.

A small class of wealthy, influential families dominated the executive. These people and their friends had the best jobs and opportunities. In Upper Canada, this elite class was known as the **Family Compact**. In Lower Canada, it was known as the **Château Clique** (shah-toe klik).

Government Structure and Operations, 1830s

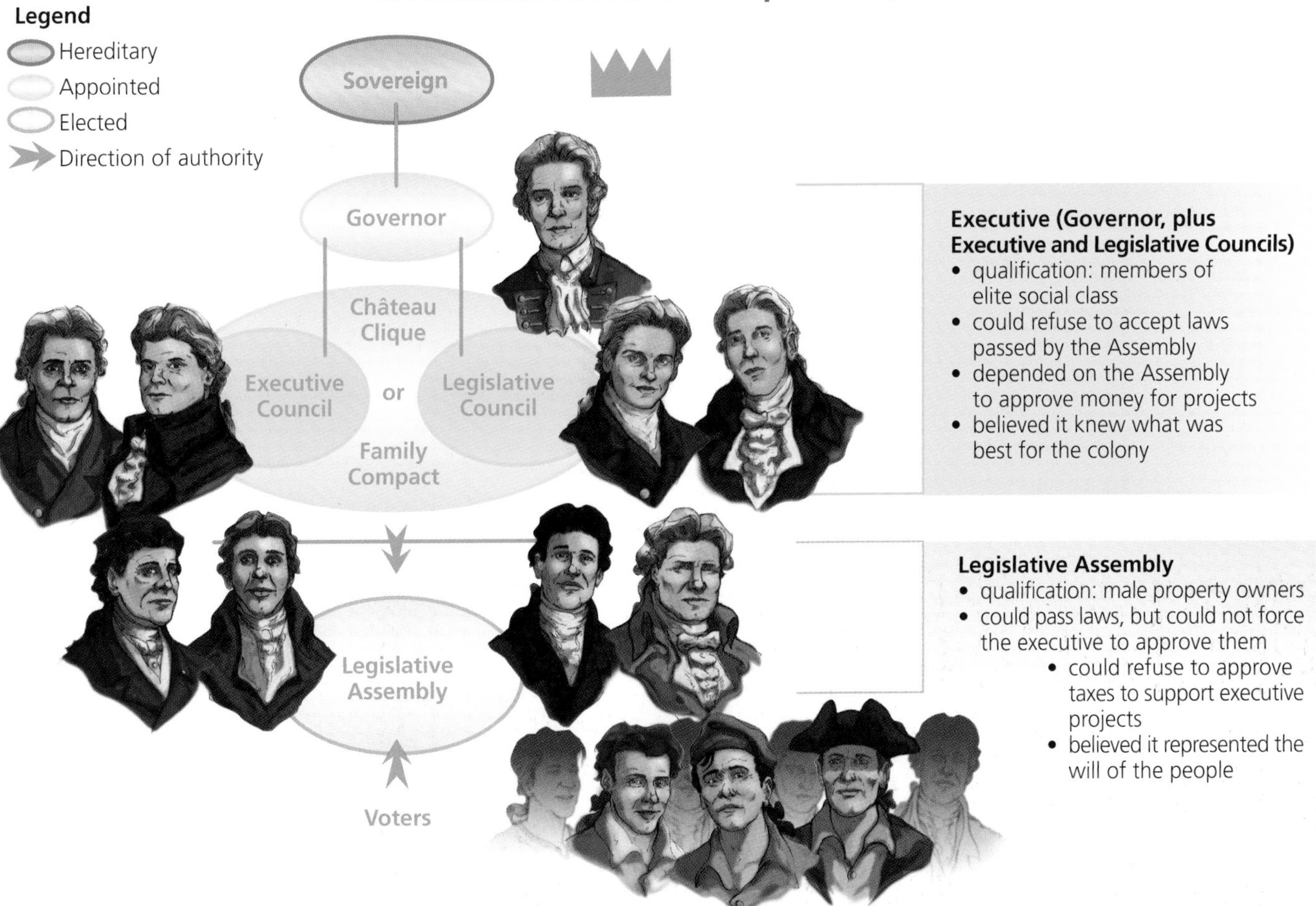

Executive (Governor, plus Executive and Legislative Councils)

- qualification: members of elite social class
- could refuse to accept laws passed by the Assembly
- depended on the Assembly to approve money for projects
- believed it knew what was best for the colony

Legislative Assembly

- qualification: male property owners
- could pass laws, but could not force the executive to approve them
    - could refuse to approve taxes to support executive projects
    - believed it represented the will of the people

During Reading

1. Each of the fictional characters that follow represents an issue in Upper and Lower Canada in the years leading to the Rebellions of 1837. Create an organizer that includes the name of each person and the issue or concern the individual represents:

Name of Person	Issue or Concern	Options
Charles Robson		

Include a third column labelled *Options*. Leave it blank for now. You will use it for your analysis on page 195. As you read pages 193–195, use jot-notes to fill in the first two columns of your chart for each person.

I came to Upper Canada seeking my own piece of land, but all the land near roads or easy access to water is owned by the Canada Land Company or by government officials. These people want me to rent the land from them.

I can only afford to buy land in the wilderness. It would take years for my family and me to clear enough land to make a good living.

Before I came to this country, I read many advertisements in British newspapers about land in Canada. These ads showed roads and schools, but the land I can afford doesn't have these services.

Charles Robson

I came to Upper Canada from Scotland to marry, but I'm a Methodist and only the Anglican Church can marry people in this colony. I have to convert and become an Anglican if I want a legal marriage and to have my children go to school. I had heard this was a new world here. I thought there would be more religious freedom.

Anne McCrae

I am an engineer with training and experience. The government of Upper Canada is expanding the road and canal systems, but every time I offer my services, I am turned down. Jobs are given to friends and family members of the Executive Council. This so-called Family Compact gets all the best jobs and appointments. In this colony, skill and hard work are not as important as your family's connections to government officials.

Adam Cook

My family has worked the same piece of land in Lower Canada for over forty years. The seigneur who owns it has no more land that my four sons can work. The Anglican Church has large reserves of land, but they will not release it. What are we going to do? My sons can't live with me forever.

Times are hard right now. Some of my neighbours are on the verge of starvation. They can't make enough money from their farms to live. I've appealed to a local government official, but he won't listen. I've heard that he is a member of the Château Clique and favours the Anglican Church and the rich British merchants, not habitants like me.

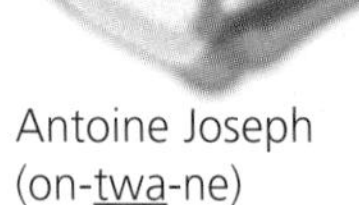

Antoine Joseph (on-twa-ne)

The lieutenant-governor has told me that our people, the Anishinabé (a-nish-i-nah-bay), would be better off if we moved north, away from new colonial settlements in Upper Canada. He says this will protect us, but I think he's protecting his own plans to expand his settlements. We were promised the lands we currently live on by earlier treaties—does this man have no honour?

Wichkewan (wich-kay-wan)

What is wrong with the French? My family has been in Montréal for two generations and my trading business provides twenty jobs for young men. We are entering a modern age and need changes that will improve public works, such as canals. A better canal system will help our businesses grow. However, the French dominate our Assembly and block projects that will make these changes. Why must they cling to their old ways of life?

Wilson Maloney

My old teacher, Reverend John Strachan, is right. Our colony needs order and leadership from the Anglican Church. We must not be influenced by the rabble from the United States who want to give more people a vote. The Americans call this democracy, but Reverend Strachan calls it "mob rule." Educated people can make the best decisions for everyone.

Stuart Michaels

I've worked on the land with my father and brothers my whole life. Three days ago, my father died and his farm will be divided between my two brothers. Under the laws of New France, daughters and sons inherited equal shares of their parents' property. Now, the government is moving us towards British laws. These laws allow fathers to will away their property in any way they wish and they do not allow married women to own property. Why are women treated like second-class citizens?

Isabel Boucher (ee-za-bel boo-shay)

Our leader, Monsieur Louis-Joseph Papineau (loo-wee-zho-zef pa-pee-noe), is correct. The French are the majority in this colony. We can use this to our advantage in the Legislative Assembly. But we must take our control further. We need to control the head of the government. The executive should answer to the French majority, not the English minority.

Gaining this control is our only chance to protect our language and culture. British immigrants are flooding into our colony. I fear we are losing our majority in the cities. We cannot allow this to happen. If we lose our majority, we lose any hope of preserving our culture. We must control the government in the best interests of French citizens.

We've asked Britain to change our colony's government, but they ignore us. I believe they might someday give responsible government to the minority English in Lower Canada, but not the French.

Armand Bourdages (ar-mon boor-dazh)

My family came to Upper Canada from the Thirteen Colonies at the end of the American Revolution. We had to swear allegiance to King George III of England. In return, we received land and the protection of British law.

Thirty years later, some people are calling us traitors and aliens. They want to take away our right to vote, hold office, and even to own the land we settled and cleared when I was a boy. They point to the War of 1812 and say we didn't help defend the colony—although many of us did!

Those of us who came from the Thirteen Colonies make up over half of the population. We are demanding that the government stop trying to steal our rights. We are tired of this unfair treatment and want to reform the way the government works. We're becoming a stronger voice in the colony.

Duncan Oliver

After Reading

1. Stuart Michaels presents a view that is different from the others. How is it different?
2. With your partner, suggest two or three methods each character might use to resolve his or her issue or concern. Write them in the third column of the chart you started on page 193. What are the pros and cons for each option?

Tensions Grow in Upper Canada

Before Reading

1. Skim pages 196–197. How is the information organized?

As time passed, few changes were made in response to reformer demands. In Upper Canada, the reformers grew more vocal. They believed responsible government could solve many of the colony's problems.

Against the reformers were the Conservatives, or Tories. The Tories were members of the Family Compact. They did not like the reformers' demands. The proposed reforms seemed to threaten public order and stability, along with their own power.

Front St. W. Looking NW from Front and Simcoe Streets, by John George Howard, 1834. Upper Canada's parliament buildings on Front Street in Toronto were the site of many demands for change in the years leading to the rebellion. Most reformers believed that change could happen legally, within the rules of the constitution.

During Reading

1. As you read about the key events leading to the rebellions, watch for examples of how people tried to resolve conflict. Place a check beside any methods you suggested in the chart from pages 193–195.

Escalating Conflict

1819 Robert Gourlay, a Scottish immigrant, distributes a questionnaire on problems in the colony. He suggests a general meeting to find solutions. The Executive Council calls his questionnaire an act of treason and deports him.

1820 The Executive Council takes over a school funded by tax revenues. It runs the school under Anglican principles and values.

1821 The Executive Council expels Barnabas Bidwell from the Assembly as an alien because Bidwell had held office in the United States. The Executive does not want anyone associated with American political movements to influence the government in Upper Canada.

1824 The Legislative Council (under the leadership of Anglican Reverend John Strachan) throws out a law passed by the Assembly (under the leadership of Methodist Egerton Ryerson). The law would have allowed non-Anglican ministers to perform marriage ceremonies.

1825 The army pension of Captain John Matthews, a reform politician, is suspended. His offence was asking an American orchestra to play "Yankee Doodle" on New Year's Eve.

1825 Charles Fothergill votes against the executive in the Assembly. He loses his contract to print government publications.

1826 Executive Council supporters destroy the printing press of reformer and newspaper publisher William Lyon Mackenzie.

In 1826, the sons of a group of Family Compact members broke into reform newspaper publisher William Lyon Mackenzie's home and office. The young men wrecked Mackenzie's printing press and then threw some of his equipment into the Toronto harbour. Mackenzie sued the offenders and won his case. He received much public support and a financial settlement. This money helped his newspaper continue to publish.

1827 Led by John Strachan, the Executive Council tries to establish the colony's first university, King's College, as an Anglican institution. The Assembly blocks the project.

1828 William Lyon Mackenzie becomes a member of the Legislative Assembly.

1830 Mackenzie claims that the colony's executive is a closely knit clique. He calls them the Family Compact.

1831 A reform petition demands change. A petition is a request to the government that is signed by many people. Issues include

- Anglican Church privileges
- the government's control of Crown and clergy reserves
- land-granting practices
- more Assembly control of government revenue
- favouritism by the Bank of Canada (the colony's only bank)
- the practice of allowing judges and clergy to hold seats in the Legislative and Executive Councils

The Executive Council ignores the petition.

1831–1834 Mackenzie repeatedly attacks the government for refusing to act on the 1831 reform petition. His demands become more violent. He is expelled from the Assembly several times. Each time, voters re-elect him.

1835 Mackenzie produces the "Seventh Report on Grievances." It includes demands from the 1831 petition and more.

1836 The newly appointed lieutenant-governor, Sir Francis Bond Head, dissolves the Assembly. During the next election, Head portrays all reformers as disloyal and anti-British. Tories win most of the seats in the Assembly.

1836–1837 Mackenzie and others decide they must take drastic action to resolve their grievances.

After Reading

1. Refer to your chart from pages 193–195. With a partner, discuss which of the following statements each person would use to describe what was done about his or her grievance:
   - It was taken up in government and improved.
   - It was taken up in government and left the same or made worse.
   - It was ignored.
2. How do you think each person would feel as a result of how his or her grievance was handled (or not handled)?

Leadership and Conflict in Upper Canada

Before Reading

1. As a class, identify the skills needed for leading a small group of students, a school team, or a country. Keep your list for an activity later in this chapter.

As you have learned so far in this chapter, Upper Canada had many problems during the 1820s and 1830s. People tried to address these problems by running for political positions, trying to change or pass laws, and writing petitions to the government. In the end, however, some people chose armed rebellion as their solution to the conflict.

Some historians argue that the personalities of two leaders, in particular, made rebellion more likely. These leaders were William Lyon Mackenzie and Sir Francis Bond Head.

William Lyon Mackenzie

William Lyon Mackenzie

People who wanted responsible government in Upper Canada looked mainly to two men for leadership: Robert Baldwin and William Lyon Mackenzie. Baldwin tended to be moderate in his approach. He petitioned the government and worked through the Assembly to bring about change.

COLONIAL ADVOCATE,

And Journal of Agriculture, Manufactures, and Commerce.

The *Colonial Advocate* was published every Tuesday. Each issue carried Mackenzie's fiery political views and opinions.

Mackenzie was a different story. At first, he just wrote about reform issues in his newspaper, the *Colonial Advocate*. One of his main complaints was the Family Compact's power in the Executive Council.

In 1828, he was elected to the Legislative Assembly. There, he worked with other reformers to demand change. However, as time passed without significant reform to government, Mackenzie became a **radical**. A radical is more extreme than a reformer. A radical wants change by any means, including revolution.

During Reading

1. Primary Source 7.1 is an example of **rhetoric**. Rhetoric is the art of using words effectively to
   - present an argument or point of view
   - persuade others to take an action.

   To analyze the rhetoric in Mackenzie's proclamation, copy and complete the organizer that follows:

Analysis of Rhetoric in William Lyon Mackenzie's Proclamation of 1837	
Structure of Argument	**Example**
Paragraph one: State what is wrong.	
Paragraph two: Give an example of what is wrong.	
Paragraph three: State an action that must be taken to deal with the problem.	
Powerful language used in • paragraph one: • paragraph two: • paragraph three:	

2. In your opinion, does Mackenzie's use of rhetoric make his argument more or less convincing? Why?

PRIMARY SOURCE 7.1

Proclamation by William Lyon Mackenzie, December 13, 1837

Inhabitants of Upper Canada!

For nearly fifty years has our country languished [suffered neglect] under the blighting [harmful] influence of military despots [cruel rulers], strangers from Europe, ruling us, not according to laws of our choice, but by the capricious [unpredictable] dictates of their arbitrary [not fixed by rules] power.

They have taxed us at their pleasure, robbed our exchequer [national treasury], and carried off the proceeds [money] to other lands—they have bribed and corrupted ministers of the Gospel, with the wealth raised by our industry...they have spurned [turned away] our petitions, involved us in their wars....

We are wearied [tired] of these oppressions [abuses], and resolved to throw off the yoke [heavy burden]. Rise, Canadians, rise as one man, and the glorious object of our wishes is accomplished.

PRIMARY SOURCE 7.2

From the Colonial Advocate, Thursday, November 22, 1832

Huzza [hooray] for Mackenzie!!!

To the Poll! To the Poll!

Gentlemen—We expect to see you next Monday at the election! Herein fail not!! Huzza for the County of York!!! Wake up! and awaken your sleepy neighbours!! Your rights are invaded!!! To the Poll! To the Poll!

- What is the purpose of this notice?
- Who is the intended audience?
- Would a similar notice in a newspaper today be effective? Why or why not?

An Election During the Struggle for Responsible Government, by C. W. Jefferys (1869–1951). In the 1830s, people had to vote by shouting their choice for all to hear. Arguments would often erupt between supporters of opposing sides. These arguments could quickly turn to violence.

During Reading

1. As you read Primary Source 7.3, make notes to describe Mackenzie's personal qualities. Which of these qualities might people find alarming?
2. What were Mackenzie's leadership qualities? Do you think others would have followed him in his attempt to change the government? Explain why or why not.

PRIMARY SOURCE 7·3

Letter from Edward O'Brien to his Friend Dr. Anthony Gapper, College Green, Bristol, England, July 6, 1832

We have just had our first general meeting of the Agricultural Society.... Mackenzie was in attendance and the treasurer, Mr. Jarvis, asked him to subscribe [pay his membership]. This he refused to do.

In the first place I should mention that this meeting was a meeting of the subscribers [members].... That meant, of course, that, though the meeting was in public and any person might witness the proceedings, none who was not a subscriber and a member of the Society could be allowed to interfere [clash] with the business.

Mackenzie, with his accustomed impudence [rudeness], got up to make a speech, but Mr. Elmley, the secretary, and Mr. Jarvis interrupted him and tried to persuade him to be quiet. He persisted. I was standing near him at the bottom of the table and asked if he were a subscriber. On being told that he was not I said, "Then he has no right to speak here." He said he would. I stepped inside the bench above him and said he should not. I then moved that the Chairman leave the chair, and, on Mackenzie insisting on being heard, backed him over the bench. There was then a great cry of "Turn him out!" Elmley came up and laid hold of him but let him go again on their saying, "Try him again and he will remain quiet!"

However, the moment he got to the table he began again. Elmley and Richard laid hold of him. Between us then we shoved him to the door and out of it....

The little blackguard [villain] then, like a spoilt and ill-behaved baby, kept thumping on the door. Some time afterwards one of the members, a Mr. Denison, proposed that the door should be opened as there were many farmers outside who might wish to come in. He said he would undertake to keep Mackenzie quiet. Upon being asked how, he replied, "By giving him a slap in the chops to be sure!" However, when the door was opened again, he was gone. Had he come in a second time, a tumble from the window of the Grand Jury room would certainly have been his fate.

Sir Francis Bond Head

People wanting leadership by an elite group supported Lieutenant-Governor Sir Francis Bond Head. Head was appointed lieutenant-governor for Upper Canada in December 1835.

Sir Francis Bond Head

PRIMARY SOURCE 7·4

From the Writings of Sir Francis Bond Head, 1839

The "family compact" of Upper Canada is composed of those members of its society who, either by their abilities and character have been honoured by the confidence of the executive government, or who, by their industry and intelligence, have amassed [built up] wealth.

PRIMARY SOURCE 7·5

Proclamation by Sir Francis Bond Head

To the Queen's Faithful Subjects in Upper Canada.

In a time of profound peace, while every one was quietly following his occupation, feeling secure under the protection of our Laws, a band of Rebels, instigated [started] by a few... disloyal men, has the wickedness and audacity [daring] to assemble with Arms [weapons], and to attack... to Burn and Destroy Property... to threaten to Plunder [rob] Banks... and to fire the City of Toronto....

Let every man do his duty now, and it will be the last time that we or our children shall see our lives or properties endangered, or the Authority of our gracious Queen insulted by such treachery and ungrateful men.

During Reading

1. As you read Primary Sources 7.4 and 7.5, compare Head's views of the elite and the radicals to Mackenzie's views. Use a chart to organize your responses:

Group	Head	Mackenzie
Elite		
Radicals		

Fill in Head's views first, using Primary Sources 7.4 and 7.5. To find a comparison for Mackenzie's views, return to Primary Source 7.1. You may need to infer some of their views from evidence you read in these selections.

After Reading

1. Your teacher will label each corner of the classroom with one of the viewpoints that follow:
   - I support William Lyon Mackenzie.
   - I support Sir Francis Bond Head.
   - Both are poor leaders.
   - I am undecided. I need more information.

   Move to the corner that represents your view at this point. In your group, select a leader, recorder, and speaker. You have ten minutes to list reasons for your point of view. Share your ideas in a class discussion.
2. In your journal, write about your opinion of Mackenzie and Head as leaders. Indicate whether you changed your mind after the group or class discussion. Why or why not?

Changing History in Lower Canada

Before Reading

1. As a class, suggest definitions for the word *negotiate*.
2. What conditions do you think help a negotiation to be successful?

While tensions in Upper Canada heated up, a similar situation was developing in Lower Canada. There, reformers were led by Louis-Joseph Papineau and his political party, the Parti Patriote.

Like reformers in Upper Canada, reformers in Lower Canada also wanted responsible government. However, they had an extra reason. Papineau and his followers were **nationalists**. They believed French-speaking people should control their own future. They did not want to be governed by an English-speaking minority.

The French were the majority in the colony. This gave them the most seats in the Assembly. Responsible government would give them control of the executive as well.

A Political Meeting in Lower Canada, by Fergus Kyle (1876–1941). This painting shows Louis-Joseph Papineau giving a speech.

- Imagine you are a member of the Château Clique. Why might this scene alarm you?

Unrest in Lower Canada grew during the fall of 1837. In response, Sir Francis Bond Head sent in troops from across British North America to stop a full-blown rebellion. Rebels in Upper Canada took advantage of the troops' absence. Their rebellion began shortly afterwards.

The activity on page 207 will allow you to change the course of history. Your task will be a role-play about preventing the rebellion in Lower Canada. Your strategy will be **negotiation**. A negotiation is a discussion that results in an agreement. Your negotiation will include the three major parties involved in the conflicts leading to rebellion: the French-speaking residents of Lower Canada, the English-speaking residents of Lower Canada, and the British government.

Lower Canada before the Rebellions of 1837

British Government
- represented by the governor general and executive

English Residents of Lower Canada
- mainly business people
- a minority in the Assembly, but a majority in the executive

French Residents of Lower Canada
- mostly farmers
- represented in the Assembly by a growing class of French professionals, such as teachers, lawyers, doctors
- held a majority in the Assembly

During Reading

1. Set up split-page or structured notes in your notebook. Title the notes *Viewpoints in Lower Canada before the Rebellions of 1837*. Use the headings *Position of the English Minority, Position of the French Majority* and *Position of the British Government* to structure your notes. As you read the points of view on pages 204–206, use point form to write a maximum of three goals each group believed it must achieve. You will use these notes for your negotiating activity.

Negotiating a Conflict of Interests

A conflict can be as minor as a disagreement between a brother and sister about what television show to watch. It can also be as major as a war between nations. Today, schools, businesses, and governments spend a great deal of time and money training people how to resolve conflicts.

Everybody has a way of dealing with conflict and confrontation. Some people walk away if they feel threatened or if they cannot get their own way. Some people face conflict directly. They challenge the ideas that others hold important. Other people try consensus building. They negotiate until there is an agreement among everyone involved.

As you read the steps to conflict resolution that follow, discuss with a partner or small group why each step is significant. How does it move participants closer to a peaceful resolution?

Six Steps to Conflict Resolution

- What appears to be happening in this picture?
- How could the steps to conflict resolution on this page be used in this situation?
- Do you think the steps would work to resolve the situation peacefully? Explain your answer.

1. Each side describes how it feels.
2. Each side describes what it wants.
3. Each side gives reasons for what it wants and how it feels.
4. Each side paraphrases the other side's perspective or way of thinking about the conflict.
5. All participants consider options for a solution. Solutions should benefit both sides to some extent, although no side will get everything it wants.
6. Reach a **compromise**, which is an agreement that meets some needs of all groups involved in the conflict or issue.

The viewpoints that follow set out the major goals and attitudes of each of the three main groups involved in the conflict in Lower Canada. Although each viewpoint is fictional, the concerns, ideas, and individuals associated with each viewpoint are real.

The First St. Lawrence Canal, by Rex Woods, 1955. Merchants in Upper and Lower Canada wanted more canals. Most canal projects were paid for with government money. Meanwhile, farmers struggled with muddy roads that were nearly impassable part of the year.

Position of the English Minority in Lower Canada

The French are the cause of Lower Canada's problems.

They use their majority in the Assembly to block our efforts to improve the colony's economy. For example, they refuse to approve money to deepen Lake St. Peter, to extend Montréal's docks, or to build canals on the St. Lawrence River. These projects would improve shipping into and out of Upper and Lower Canada.

The French insist that government income should come from a tax on goods moving in and out of the colony. This kind of tax just increases the cost of our goods and makes them more expensive than those of our competitors.

Why can't they see that a land tax is the best way to fund government projects? For example, the French always want more roads. These should be supported by a local land tax, not general government income. The people who use the roads should pay for them.

The habitants are living in the past. They want to live on their farms, growing little more than will feed themselves. They ignore the future, which is based on business and industry. Worse, they actively oppose people who are trying to bring economic success to the colony.

For example, the French oppose our efforts to get rid of the seigneurial system, even though it's hopelessly outdated. We want to invest in land and put together larger, more efficient farms. They continue to break up their farms into smaller and smaller parcels. These overused parcels of land are becoming less fertile.

The French also fiercely protect their hold on the Assembly. They don't want English speakers to take away their majority. They consider anyone who is British, Irish, or American a foreigner. How can I be a foreigner when I'm living in a British colony? They seem to forget that Britain won the war in 1760!

Their concern for their majority means they oppose any hint of uniting Upper and Lower Canada. Even though a union would allow us to be more efficient and modernize our colonies, they won't consider it. They know they might lose their precious majority.

John Molson was an important business leader in Montréal. Like many businesses in the colonies, his relied on the ability to transport goods as efficiently and inexpensively as possible.

Position of the French Majority in Lower Canada

Make no mistake. Lower Canada's problems are caused by the English leadership of this colony and the British government.

Think about it. Of the 600 000 people in Lower Canada, English speakers make up about 75 000. That is only about 12.5 per cent. Yet this small minority controls the government. How is this fair?

The English have most of the seats in the Executive and Legislative Councils, have the ear of the governor, and have far too much control over day-to-day government decisions. They frequently refuse to pass laws proposed by the Assembly, even though these laws reflect the will of the majority.

Even worse, the English use their position to favour themselves and their friends. For example, they receive most government appointments. English people become judges, justices of the peace, government printers, surveyors, and tax collectors. There are many qualified French people who could do those jobs, but they don't get the chance. In 1832, 157 out of 204 such positions—almost 77 per cent—were held by the English minority.

The problems with this system are obvious. Our government does not reflect the needs of the majority. As another example, more than three-quarters of French people are farmers, but the English increasingly control the land. They are buying up seigneuries at prices we cannot afford. French people can't even borrow what they need. The English control the banks, too!

Many habitants have been reduced to poverty. English landowners have raised rents to prices the habitants cannot pay. This is a clear attempt to force them off the land. Don't forget that these farms were created from the back-breaking work of generations of French people! Why should we give the fruits of that work to the English?

The English are clever—I have to give them that. Because they control the executive, they also control the Crown reserves. It is their loophole to get around the Assembly. The Executive Council can decide when to sell Crown lands and what to do with the money once the land is sold. For example, in 1834, the British American Land Company received a grant of 400 000 hectares of Crown land. This is land we French desperately need. In return, all the company had to do was promise to build roads on the land and make annual payments to the Crown. The Executive Council then used these payments so it would not have to depend on money approved by the Assembly. They simply bypassed the democratic process! They took away the only bit of power the Assembly has.

An Old Man of '37, by Henri Julien (1852–1916).

- What adjectives would you use to describe this Lower Canadian rebel?
- What details tell you the rebel is from Lower Canada, not Upper Canada?

Louis-Joseph Papineau was trained as a lawyer, like many of the professionals leading the reform movement in Lower Canada. He and the Parti Patriote listed their demands for responsible government in a document called the "Ninety-two Resolutions." When the British government rejected these demands, reformer outrage helped fuel the rebellions.

Position of the British Government

The French demand too much control of the government and are not willing to compromise. I admit that we were not especially willing to compromise at first. For years, we rejected most reform demands. But since 1828, we have made many changes. For example, we gave the Assembly greater control of how money is spent in the colony. In return, we asked only for a guaranteed sum to pay the salaries of government employees and the other costs of government.

However, the Assembly refused to cooperate. Demands grew stronger, until it passed the "Ninety-two Resolutions" in 1834. After that, they refused to approve money to pay for the government. Everything ground to a halt because employees weren't paid. We couldn't allow the situation to continue.

The governor must have the power to raise money for the government. If the Assembly won't agree, the governor needs the authority to raise money by any means necessary. Britain cannot turn the governing of its colonies over to a bunch of locals. This discontent in Lower Canada proves the point! Locals do not understand the full needs of His Majesty's global empire.

Lord John Russell was governor general at the time of the rebellions. In March 1837, he wrote the "Ten Russell Resolutions," which the British parliament passed. The resolutions rejected all Patriote demands.

1. As you read the feature about Writing a Report, make a checklist of the characteristics of a report. You can use this checklist for the activity on page 207.

Writing a Report

A report is a way of providing information. Reports can present scientific data, a business analysis, an evaluation of an event, or various kinds of research. How a report is organized depends on its audience and purpose.

Tips for Writing a Report

- Reports are based on facts and research, not just opinions.
- Reports have an introduction that should be targeted to the audience. You might use a less formal introduction in a report for fellow students. You will need a more formal introduction for your teacher.
- The introduction is followed by several related topics. Each should be clearly linked to your main topic so the reader knows why they are there. Many reports use subheadings to organize different sections.
- A conclusion includes your recommendation or a summary of the main points you are making.
- A report should also include an explanation of how you found your information, or an alphabetical list of the resources you used.

After Reading

1. With your teacher's direction, form a negotiating team of two to four students. Your teacher will assign your team to one of the three groups you just read about: the French, the English, or the British government.
2. Work with your team to prepare a list of goals you feel you must achieve. Also list what you may be willing to give up to reach a peaceful agreement. Remember that the conflict will probably be resolved through a compromise.
3. Join with a negotiating team representing each of the other viewpoints. Share your list of goals with one another. Take notes so you will remember what the other groups most want. Listen carefully so that you understand the problems from their perspective.
4. Once you know each group's main goals, return to your negotiating team and prepare a settlement proposal. To make this happen, each group will have to give up some demands. Your proposal should have the following components:
   - a paraphrase of each group's main goals and why the group wants them. This shows that you understand the other groups have reasons for their points of view.
   - a proposal for a resolution, along with an explanation of how your proposal will meet the needs of the other groups

To reach a negotiated settlement, your group's resolution must somehow benefit all parties.

5. Join with the negotiating teams you met with in step 3. Following your teacher's direction, share your settlement proposals and attempt to reach an agreement. Remember that failure to reach an agreement will lead to rebellion.
6. With your team, write a one-page report about the outcome of your negotiations. Your report should include the sections and subheadings that follow:

   Introduction

   Explain how negotiation can resolve conflicts. Explain how negotiation was used in this activity.

   Sides in the Negotiation

   Include a summary of each side's goals in the negotiation.

   Analysis of Negotiation

   Include your analysis of what went well during negotiations and what could have been done better. State the resolution that was accepted and give an explanation of why it worked. If no resolution was reached, give your opinion why.

   Conclusions

   Conclude with a sentence or two that explains how and why you avoided rebellion or why you were unable to avoid rebellion.

Think It Through

Key Events in the Rebellions of 1837

Before Reading

1. Quickly scan pages 208–209. What predictions can you make about the information you are going to read? What clues do you have? Discuss your ideas with a partner.

Saint-Denis, by Henri Julien (1852–1908). In one of the first battles of the rebellion, rebels defeated government troops at Saint-Denis. When news of the rebel victory reached Upper Canada, more people were encouraged to join the rebellion.

Attack on Saint-Charles, by Charles Beauclerk, 1840. The Battle of Saint-Charles lasted two hours. Government troops outnumbered the rebels and defeated them.

Drilling in North York, by C. W. Jefferys, 1898. Many reformers were angry with the government, but reluctant to break the law in a rebellion. William Lyon Mackenzie convinced many to join his march down Yonge Street by telling them it was an armed, but peaceful demonstration.

Pages 208–211 include a list of some of the major events and battles during the Rebellions of 1837.

During Reading

1. As you read, write questions related to the Rebellions of 1837 in your notebook. Think of some open-ended and some closed questions. Look back to page 66 if you would like to review the Forming Questions skill feature.

March 1837 Unrest in Lower Canada grows. The Patriotes organize protest rallies. Patriote women's groups boycott British goods. Sir Francis Bond Head sends troops from Upper and Lower Canada to stop the unrest.

November 16, 1837 Government troops try to arrest Patriote leaders at Longueuil. Patriotes resist in the first open violence of the rebellion.

November 23, 1837 Patriote rebels in Lower Canada turn back the British army at Saint-Denis.

November 25, 1837 The British kill forty rebels at Saint-Charles and defeat the Patriote force. The town is looted and burned. Rebel leaders flee to avoid capture.

December 4, 1837 While colonial troops are dealing with the rebellion in Lower Canada, William Lyon Mackenzie and his supporters hold a meeting at Montgomery's Tavern, north of Toronto. There they form a plan to take advantage of the troops' absence.

Death of Colonel Moodie, by C. W. Jefferys (1869–1951). Colonel Robert Moodie and some friends were riding towards Toronto to warn of the rebellion when they exchanged fire with rebels outside Montgomery's Tavern. Moodie became the first death in the rebellion.

View of W. Powell Escaping from Armed Pursuers on Horses, by William Bengough, 1885. Alderman John Powell had heard rumours of a rebel gathering and rode north to find out if they were true. On his way, he was captured by Mackenzie and a group of rebels. He then escaped and raced to Government House to warn Sir Francis Bond Head.

Battle of Montgomery's Farm. After government supporters fired into the roof at Montgomery's Tavern, rebels fled into the woods.

December 4, 1837 Colonel Robert Moodie is shot by rebels as he tries to ride to Toronto to warn people of the gathering rebels.

December 4, 1837 Alderman John Powell reaches Toronto and warns the government. The rebels lose the element of surprise.

December 5, 1837 Rebels armed with rifles and pitchforks march south down Yonge Street. They meet a smaller force of people loyal to the government, who open fire. The rebels retreat.

December 7, 1837 Government supporters from around the colony arrive in Toronto to fight the rebels. Close to 1000 militia are ready to support Sir Francis Bond Head.

December 8, 1837 Government militia march to meet Mackenzie's force of approximately 700 to 800 men. The battle at Montgomery's Tavern lasts less than thirty minutes. Mackenzie flees the scene. In spite of a $5000 reward for his capture, he is protected by supporters and avoids arrest.

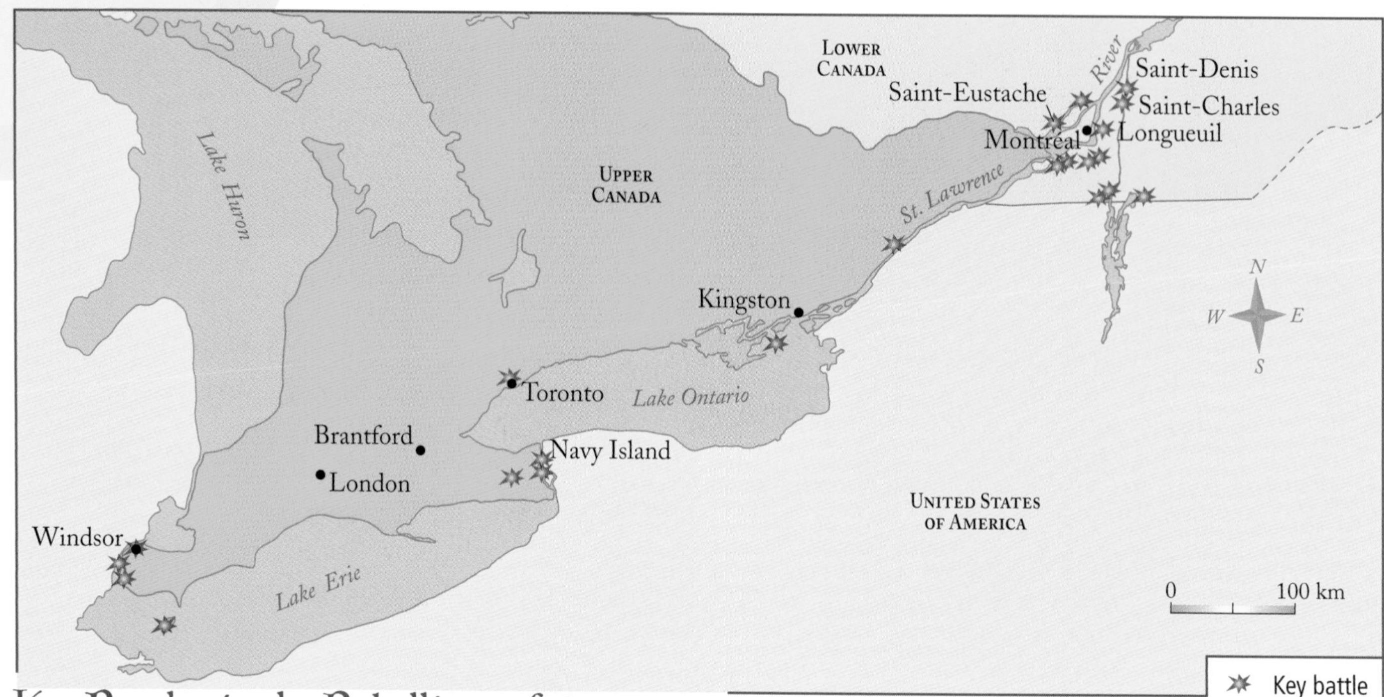

Key Battles in the Rebellions of 1837–1838

December 11, 1837 Mackenzie takes refuge on Navy Island on the Niagara River. He declares himself president of the "Republic of Canada."

December 13, 1837 Around 300 rebels from the Brantford-London area hear of Mackenzie's defeat and of 2000 militia members marching towards them. They decide to disband. Some reports say First Nations in the area kill three or four rebels as they leave Brantford, but reports are inconsistent.

December 14, 1837 British troops in Lower Canada capture Saint-Eustache after a fierce battle. The first rebellion in Lower Canada is over. British troops and militia again loot and burn French-Canadian homes.

Front View of the Church of Saint-Eustache Occupied by the Insurgents. The Artillery Forcing an Entrance, by Charles Beauclerk, 1840. A government force of about 2000 faced 400 rebels at Saint-Eustache, 31 kilometres northwest of Montréal. It was the largest fight in the rebellions. Finding many rebels hidden in the village church, soldiers bombarded it with artillery for hours and then set it on fire. Rebels trying to escape the burning church were shot.

April 12, 1838 Rebel leaders Samuel Lount and Peter Matthews plead guilty to treason for their actions in the Upper Canada rebellion. They are hanged.

Execution of Lount and Matthews. Samuel Lount and Peter Matthews were hanged from a scaffold on the corner of King and Toronto Streets for their parts in the rebellion.

1838 Rebels organize raids from across the United States border. They are joined by American republicans, who want to see Britain pushed out of North America. These republicans want Canada to become a republic, or even part of the United States. The border is in turmoil. Britain and the United States reach the brink of war.

May 29, 1838 Lord Durham is appointed governor general. He arrives from England to restore harmony.

June 28, 1838 Durham orders eight Patriote leaders to be exiled to Bermuda. Patriots who plead guilty to treason are pardoned and released.

November 1838 The British government is unhappy with how Durham is handling the rebels. He resigns and returns to Britain.

November 1838 Shortly after Durham leaves, the Patriotes launch a second rebellion from across the American border. One group of rebels is captured by the Haudenosaunee at Caughnawaga.

November 9, 1838 The second rebellion in Lower Canada is defeated, mostly by militia. Militia groups loot and burn homes across Lower Canada to discourage further rebellion.

mid-December 1838 All raids from the United States have been crushed. The rebellions are over.

71st Regiment, Highland Light Infantry: Heavy Marching Order 1840–1844, by James Henry Lynch. When Lord Durham arrived in the colonies, he found the jails full of rebels such as these on their way to jail in Montréal. To calm the tense situation, he decided to free many of the prisoners. His decision angered many government supporters and the British government.

During Reading

1. With a partner, discuss the questions you wrote while reading pages 208–211. Make sure you understand which are closed and which are open-ended.
2. Which of your questions might make a good research project? Read the feature on page 212 and then work with your partner to develop at least one potential inquiry question.

Think It Through

Asking Questions for Research: The Inquiry Question

In Chapter 2, you learned about the 5 Ws and 1 H: Who, What, When, Where and Why (or How). You learned that who, what, when, and where questions are closed. Closed questions usually have one answer. The why and how questions are open. This means they can have more than one answer. Answering an open-ended question requires analysis and evaluation.

To prepare a good research project, you have to start with a good open-ended question. This is sometimes called an inquiry question.

General topics, such as *The Rebellions of 1837* or *Achieving Responsible Government in Canada*, are too large to make good research topics. There is far too much information about them. If you chose one of these general topics, you would likely waste a lot of time reading and gathering information that you do not need. You might end up with a project that just restates facts and lacks analysis and originality.

Your teacher will sometimes give you an inquiry question or choice of questions. However, sometimes you might be asked to form your own.

Forming an Inquiry Question

1. **General Topics:** If you were to study the period 1800 to 1820, general topics might include
   - Loyalists
   - Government Relations with First Nations
   - War of 1812
   - Life in Upper Canada

   You might find ideas by scanning the main headings in your textbook.

2. **Specific Focus:** Choose one of the general topics that interests you. Break it down into more specific ideas. For example, the War of 1812 might be broken down into
   - Causes of the War
   - Major Events of the War
   - Life of Soldiers
   - Results of the War

   Ideas for specific topics might come from headings, subheadings, photograph captions, or questions and activities.

3. **Inquiry Questions:** Develop several inquiry questions for the specific topics that most interest you. An inquiry question should be open-ended enough that you have the opportunity to develop and communicate your own ideas. However, an inquiry question does not try to cover all information about your specific focus. It should touch on only one aspect of your focus.

General Topic	Specific Focus	Inquiry Question Example
War of 1812	Life of Soldiers	What kind of adjustments would a Canadian have to make if he or she went back in time to defend Upper Canada in 1812?

   Think of several questions. Choose the best one for your project.

I think the closed questions are pretty easy to recognize. Many begin with *who, what, why,* and *where.*

That's true. For example, I wrote the question *Who were the rebels?* Were they landowners? Were they educated? I'm guessing they might have been farmers since they had to use pitchforks as weapons! But did all farmers rebel? I wonder if other factors, such as a farmer's personality, influenced whether he joined the rebels or not.

Your question about farmers could become an inquiry question. Remember the first section of this chapter? It had all those perspectives of people discussing the issues in the 1830s. I wonder which of those people would have grabbed a pitchfork and headed to Montgomery's Tavern. How about a question like *What causes people to use violence to change their society?*

I like your question, but it might be too broad. I mean, we could use the same question to do an inquiry about terrorists today or wars in ancient Rome. We should make the question more specific. We could try *What caused people to use violence in the Rebellions of 1837?* I don't think the answer would be simple and straightforward, so I think it would qualify as an inquiry question.

Good idea. I have another question. It says in the timeline that Mackenzie and the other rebels took advantage of the situation in Lower Canada to launch their rebellion. A closed question might be *Were the rebellions in Upper and Lower Canada connected?* I think the answer to this one should be pretty clear. Either Mackenzie and his group were in contact with the Patriotes or they weren't. An inquiry question might be *Would the rebellion in Upper Canada have taken place if people in Lower Canada had not rebelled?* This seems more open to opinion and debate. Nobody could really say for sure what would have happened.

After Reading

1. On your own, choose your best inquiry question and complete a K-W-L Organizer.

Viewpoints on the Rebellions

Before Reading

1. When you see a picture of a world event on the front page of a Canadian newspaper, what questions or concerns might you have? Discuss your ideas as a class.

Cameras were not widely used until the middle of the 1800s. Until then, historical events were recorded with drawings and paintings. Artists travelled to the site of significant events or battles. There they recorded events quickly on a sketchpad or in notes. Much detail was left to an artist's memory.

Sometimes, an artist arrived after an event was over. In that case, he or she used interviews to shape a painting or sketch. Many artists accepted a commission, or fee, to paint a picture of an event. The person paying the artist often became part of the painting.

Other people create artwork showing events from previous eras. For example, Dr. Charles W. Jefferys (1869–1951) produced hundreds of paintings and sketches. His work reflected his interpretations of key events in Canadian history. Pages 214–215 include two of his sketches and other pages of this textbook include more.

Rebels Marching Down Yonge Street to Attack Toronto, December 1837, by C. W. Jefferys (1869–1951).

- Imagine that you are marching alongside these men. What do their facial expressions tell you about their state of mind?
- How would you feel to be part of this group?
- What questions would you like to ask the other marchers?
- What clues suggest that the march might not end well for the marchers?

Arrival of Government Supporters at the Parliament Building, Toronto, by C. W. Jefferys (1869–1951).

- Who are the people in this illustration? Do they support the people marching down Yonge Street?
- Why might these people win in a confrontation with the Yonge Street group?

During Reading

1. Primary Source 7.6 is part of a letter written by Fanny Bridgman to her friend Fanny West in England. Bridgman was the governess for Sir Francis Bond Head's daughter. How does Bridgman portray the rebels? As you read, watch for words and phrases that will help you infer the answer to this question.

PRIMARY SOURCE 7.6

Letter from Fanny Bridgman to Fanny West, Government House, December 15, 1837

I have no doubt you will be astonished to hear that our peaceful Province has been threatened with civil war, and that an insurrection [uprising of people] has actually broken out and been crushed it is hoped for ever, or at least for a very long time.... There were rumours that the radicals were assembling at Newmarket, a place at a considerable distance up Yonge Street.... On Saturday the 2nd there was also a report that they intended to attack Toronto.... Things were in this state till Monday night, the 4th, when about 12 o'clock a Mr. Powell came breathless to Government House and told Sir Frances that the rebels were in great force... and intended to attack us that night. He had a very narrow escape and had he not acted with great courage and determination we should not have been aware of their approach and had they got possession of the town our situation would have been dreadful as it was their intention to burn it to the ground.

After Reading

1. In a group of three or four students, discuss how Bridgman's ideas about the marchers are different from C. W. Jefferys' ideas as shown in the illustration on page 214.
2. Does your group consider Fanny Bridgman's letter a reliable source of information about the Rebellions of 1837? Why or why not? What biases might she have?
3. How reliable does your group consider C. W. Jefferys' drawings as a source of information?
4. As a group, discuss the benefits and drawbacks of each source.

First Nations in the Rebellions

Before Reading

1. Imagine that a confrontation is taking place in the schoolyard between two people you know, but are not friends with. Heated words are exchanged. It looks like the confrontation could become more than angry words. You know the school's anti-violence policy: both students will be suspended if the conflict escalates. What are reasons for getting involved and not getting involved in this situation? What would you do? Why? Write your answers in your journal.

Since the beginning of the 1800s, First Nations territory in Upper Canada had rapidly declined. When European settlements first began in the region, there was plenty of land available. First Nations were able to move away from areas that became too crowded.

By the end of the War of 1812, finding acceptable land was becoming more difficult. Immigration increased quickly. Most of the good land was taken. The only available land was far from traditional territories. First Nations did not want to leave the land their people had used for generations.

Led by Sir Francis Bond Head, leaders in Upper Canada established **reserves** as a way to solve the problem. Reserves are land set aside for the exclusive use of First Nations. Some reserves were close to colonial settlements. In these cases, First Nations were usually expected to adopt the lifestyle of colonial farmers. Other reserves were in isolated areas. Government administrators believed these reserves would "protect" First Nations from the colonial population.

Lieutenant-Governor Head was not popular among First Nations people. Many did not trust him. For example, in 1836, Head signed a treaty with four Saugeen (sahk-een) River Ojibwa (oh-jib-wah) people. In the eyes of some First Nations in the region, these individuals did not have the authority to make this agreement. In Head's eyes, he had fairly purchased 1.5 million acres (607 028 hectares) of land.

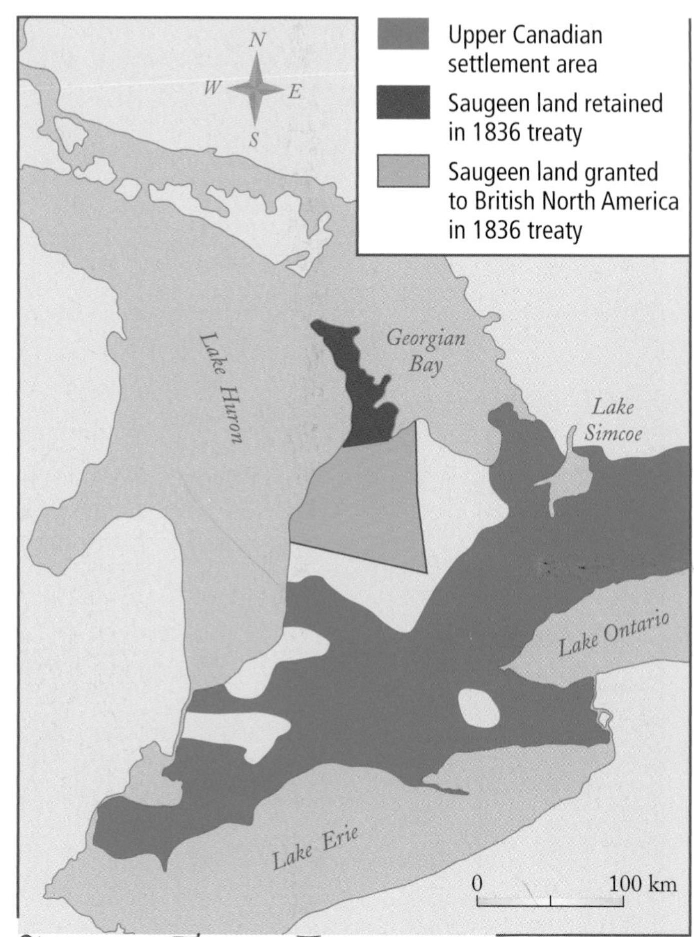

Saugeen Treaty Area, 1836

By 1837, the colony was on the verge of revolt. First Nations throughout the colonies knew of the trouble. If Head was defeated, would First Nations find more support for their claims to the land? As Primary Source 7.7 demonstrates, First Nations leaders considered their options cautiously.

During Reading

1. Why might First Nations support the rebellion against Sir Francis Bond Head?
2. What is the main idea of Primary Source 7.7?
3. How do the First Nations leaders support their argument?

PRIMARY SOURCE 7•7

Letter from Chiefs Joshua Wawanosh (wow-won-oos), Edward Ogeebegun (o-jee-bi-gung), and Gordon Megezeez (meg-a-zee), St. Clair Mission, December 14, 1837

Dear Brothers,

We last evening received a letter bringing us bad news respecting the troubles which exist in our country, of which we were sorry to hear.

You enquire whether we think it best to take any part in these affairs. We can inform you that we consider it best to spread our matts to sit down & smoke our pipes and to let the people who like powder & ball fight their own battles.

We have some time ago counseled with the First Nations around us & we are all agreed to remain quiet and we hope that all the First Nations will do so, as we can gain nothing by fighting, but may lose every thing.

We should be glad to see you but cannot come at present, we send this by one of our Chiefs who will have a talk with you on the subject.

We have no fear that you who are wise will go astray [in the wrong direction], but we fear that some of those who are in the west on Lake Huron may be misled by designing [scheming] white men & should such as are yet foolish be induced [persuaded] to commence [start] war on the whites of any party, we should all be more hated by the whites than we are now.

We would just observe [watch] that we cannot be compelled [forced] to go & fight for any party, we mention this fact in order that should you be called on you may know that you are free men & under the control of no one who has authority to make you take up arms.

In the end, most First Nations in the colonies remained neutral, although some Haudenosaunee helped British forces in Lower Canada.

After Reading

1. What do the chiefs mean when they say, "we consider it best to spread our matts to sit down"?
2. Explain the chiefs' argument, "we can gain nothing by fighting, but may lose every thing."
3. With a partner, use a Discussion Web to analyze the decision facing First Nations: Should First Nations get involved in the Rebellions of 1837? Record reasons for both sides of the question on your web:

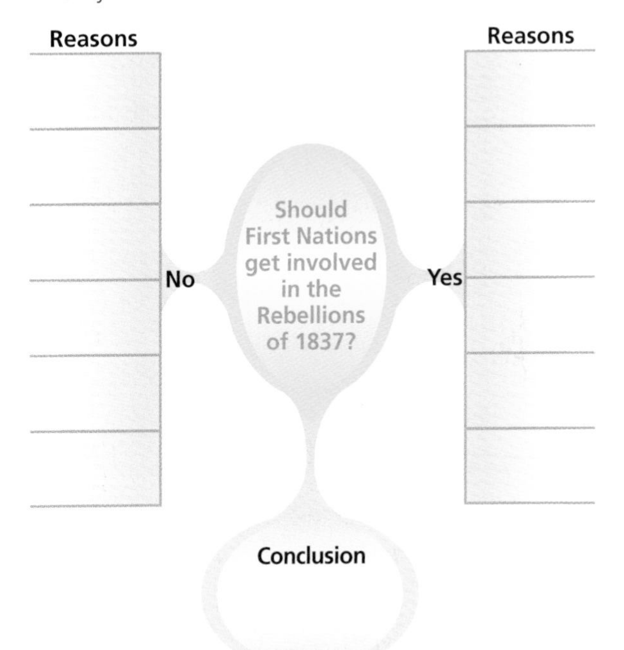

4. Join with another set of partners and compare your webs. If necessary, add reasons to your web. Which do you think is the most convincing viewpoint? Write your conclusion at the bottom of your web.

The Act of Union

Before Reading

1. In your opinion, what is the best way to resolve a conflict that has resulted in a crisis? Should those with authority punish those involved? Or, should they try to repair the damage by being sympathetic and understanding? Discuss as a class.

After the end of the rebellions, the British government wanted to fix the problems that caused the uprising. They asked Lord Durham, who had been in Upper and Lower Canada towards the end of the rebellions, to make some recommendations. Durham had a reputation for supporting reform causes, such as responsible government. Durham presented his report in 1839.

The Earl of Durham

During Reading

1. As you read, think of how each of the groups listed below would have responded to Durham's report:
   a) the British in Lower Canada
   b) the French
   c) reformers in Upper Canada
   d) Family Compact in Upper Canada

   Use a chart or Spider Organizer to organize the different points of view.

Report on the Affairs of British North America (The Durham Report)

Lower Canada

Problem: Durham wrote that the French Canadians are "an old and stationary society in a new and progressive world.... They are a people with no history, and no literature.... In any plan, which may be adopted for the future management of Lower Canada, the first object ought to be that of making it an English Province.... I believe that tranquility [calm] can only be restored by subjecting the Province to the vigorous [strong] rule of an English majority."

Recommendation: Unite Upper and Lower Canada and encourage British immigration to outnumber the French.

Upper Canada

Problem: Durham's report stated that the Family Compact is "a petty, corrupt, insolent [rude] Tory clique."

Recommendation: Give more power to the elected representatives of the people. Select the lieutenant-governor's councils from people elected to the Assembly.

In 1840, the British government passed only one of Durham's recommendations. The Act of Union came into effect in 1841.

The Act of Union

- joined Upper and Lower Canada into one colony, the Province of Canada, with two parts: Canada West (formerly Upper Canada) and Canada East (formerly Lower Canada)
- placed the capital of the new colony in Kingston, Canada West (the English-speaking part of the colony)
- combined Upper Canada's large debt with Lower Canada's small debt (Upper Canada's debt was more than twelve times that of Lower Canada.)
- gave Upper and Lower Canada the same number of seats in the new Assembly, even though there were 650 000 people in Lower Canada and 450 000 people in Upper Canada
- made English the only language allowed in the new parliament
- suspended some French institutions related to education and civil law

Response to the Act of Union in Canada East

French people were outraged at the Act of Union. First Durham insulted their culture and then the British government attacked their political power. The fictional statements at the bottom of this page summarize the range of opinions in Canada East following the Act of Union.

During Reading

1. Discuss the opinions with a partner. Briefly suggest
   a) how much support each would likely have among French Canadians
   b) its possible strength(s) and/or weakness(es)
   c) your personal reaction

We should rebel and become a separate state or join the United States.

We should boycott the new Assembly and refuse to send any delegates.

We should send delegates to the Assembly, but use our votes to destroy all efforts to make the government work.

We should send delegates to the Assembly, but have them stick together on all votes. We can force the English to support our goals if they want any support from us for theirs.

We should insist that all new laws be passed with a double majority—the support of a majority of French-speaking representatives and a majority of English-speaking representatives.

We should accept the union. We can make it work for us by working together with English-speaking reformers.

United Reformers

As you learned on page 219, French Canadians were outraged at Durham's report and the Act of Union. However, the insults just strengthened their resolve to preserve their culture. Many leaders in Canada East wanted to destroy the Act of Union.

However, one prominent leader disagreed. Louis-Hippolyte LaFontaine (loo-wee-hi-po-leet la-fon-tay-ne) had been a reformer under Louis-Joseph Papineau. Like Papineau, he had called for responsible government in the 1830s. However, when reformers turned to rebels in 1837, LaFontaine backed away. He did not support the use of violence.

LaFontaine was elected to the first Assembly of the united Province of Canada in 1841. He joined forces with reform leaders from Canada West: Robert Baldwin and Francis Hincks. Together, they formed a political party that united reformers from Canada East and West. The Reform Party's goal was responsible government for Canada.

Sir Louis-Hippolyte LaFontaine

Robert Baldwin had been neutral during the rebellions. He met with Lord Durham in July 1838 and gave him a detailed report on reformers' demands for responsible government. Many people believe this report influenced Durham's recommendations.

Francis Hincks

After Reading

1. Based on your readings in this chapter, make a prediction about government in the Canadas in the 1840s. Would it be based on peace and stability or conflict? Explain your response.

Compress

1. In this chapter, you read about many different methods of conflict resolution:

   - petitions
   - voting
   - running for office
   - rebellion
   - negotiation
   - boycotts

   Other ways of dealing with conflict included ignoring problems or silencing people who demand change with deportation or violence. Find and list at least one example of each of these ways of addressing conflict.

2. As a class, use the list of qualities of good leaders you developed in response to the question on page 198. Create a scale for evaluating leaders that ranks them from 1 (poor) to 5 (outstanding). Agree upon how many leadership qualities a leader needs for each number.

   a) Working with a small group, use this set of criteria to analyze the role played by an individual from the time of the rebellions. You want to determine whether this person was a good leader. Your teacher will assign your group one of the people listed below:

   - William Lyon Mackenzie
   - Sir Francis Bond Head
   - Lord Durham
   - Louis-Joseph Papineau

   b) Keep your own record of your group's discussion.

   c) Form new groups among the class so that each group has a student representing each of the four leaders.

   d) Share your previous group's discussion with your new group.

Express

3. You are throwing a historical dinner party. Your five guests must be chosen from the people discussed in this chapter.

   a) Who would you invite? Why?

   b) How would you arrange your guests around the table? Why?

   c) Who would you sit beside? Why?

   d) Write a dialogue for two of your guests or work with a partner to perform a dialogue for the class.

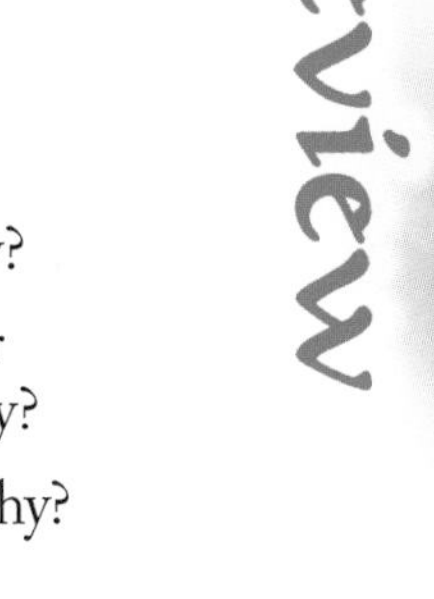

Their Stories, Our History

Select a picture from this chapter that shows an artist's interpretation of the rebellion. Prepare a thirty-second news report for television as though you are a reporter who has stepped into the illustration to give a live report to today's audience.

a) Include an interesting opening to your story. This opening statement is often called a lead. You might watch a news program on television to get a feel for the kinds of leads reporters use.

b) Include some background information to the story and a description of what you are witnessing.

c) Connect what you see to a current event for viewers. You may have to read the newspaper or watch television news for ideas.

d) Conclude with a statement that indicates the significance of the connection between past and current events. Give your report to the class or a small group of students.

chapter 8
Social Change

- What conditions are shown in this illustration that you might find unusual on a voyage over the ocean?
- Based on what you see, what would you infer about the passengers' economic background?

On Board an Immigrant Ship in the Thirties, by C. W. Jefferys (1869–1951).

Ahyouwaighs, Haudenosaunee leader

- What traditional First Nations clothing do you see in this portrait? What non-traditional clothing do you see? What does this suggest is happening to First Nations cultures at this time?
- How does the artist portray Ahyouwaighs? Based on this painting, what adjectives would you use to describe him?

During the Rebellions of 1837, reformers expressed their grievances in demands for political change (responsible government). However, the issues challenging British North America at this time were not all political. From the 1830s to the 1850s, British North America also experienced many social changes. For many people, these changes were positive. Immigrants from Europe hoped life in North America would give them more opportunities.

Yet immigrants frequently arrived with few or no resources. Many struggled to make a living, often in one of the growing cities in the colonies. Conditions in these urban areas became difficult as populations grew faster than services.

These were also decades of disease. Deadly illnesses, such as **cholera**, swept through the colonies. People did not understand the causes of cholera. Immigrants from Europe often arrived with the disease and were sometimes blamed for spreading it. Tensions and conflict between groups of people in British North America sometimes resulted.

Not all people in British North America had European roots. These other groups faced additional problems. For example, Britain ended slavery in its empire in the early 1830s. However, a legal end to slavery did not mean Black people had a full and equal place in British North American society.

First Nations also had problems. The land's first inhabitants faced an unhappy prospect as immigrants outnumbered and surrounded them. First Nations faced constant demands for their land. Many were pressured to abandon their traditions and assimilate into non-First Nations society. Some signed treaties to protect their land, but even these did not always guarantee their rights.

This chapter will help you understand

- causes of social conflict and change before and after the Rebellions of 1837
- how immigrants' ideas about social class changed in North America
- how people's problems from the nineteenth century compare to people's problems today
- conflict and change affecting British North America's Black population
- how growing settlements affected First Nations

Featured Skills

- Using a SEARCH Strategy for Analyzing Problems
- Conducting an Interview

Immigration and Urban Growth

Before Reading

1. With a partner, brainstorm a list of advantages and disadvantages of living in a city in Ontario today.
2. Share your list with another pair. As a group, make three recommendations about how the quality of life might be improved for people living in urban areas. Explain why each recommendation is important.

From 1830 to 1850, immigrants came to Canada with high hopes for a better life. After the Rebellions of 1837, political stability returned to the colonies. Many Europeans saw British North America as a place where they could increase their wealth and opportunities.

The Embarkation, Waterloo Docks, Liverpool, was published in the *Illustrated London News* on July 6, 1850.

Immigrants often left their home countries because of hard economic conditions. Many Europeans were unemployed at this time. New inventions had reduced the need for workers in factories and on farms.

In Ireland, a series of famines had made even survival difficult. A famine is a food shortage so severe that many people starve. The famines in Ireland at this time were caused by a disease that damaged potato crops, a main food source. Between 1845 and 1850, over 300 000 Irish people came to Canada to find land and employment.

Point of Departure for Immigrants to Québec, 1829–1851

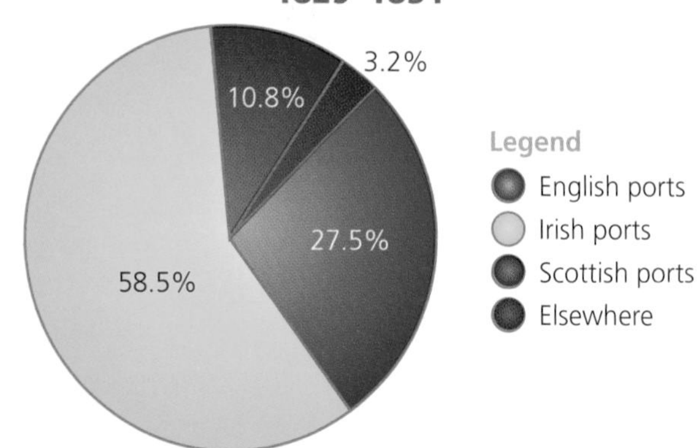

Between 1829 and 1851, 696 129 immigrants arrived in Québec. The nationality of immigrants was not always recorded. All that is known for sure is what port they came from. Many Irish immigrants left from English ports, so their numbers are likely even higher.

British Immigration, 1815–1849

Year	British Immigrants to Upper/Lower Canada
1815	700
1818	15 000
1832	66 000
1849	109 000

- Prepare a bar or line graph to show changes to immigration in Upper and Lower Canada.

Most immigrants were crowded into ships like cargo. Timber ships that emptied their goods in Britain returned to North America with their holds packed with people. Fees collected from these "below deck" passengers made the return trip more profitable for ship owners.

However, these passengers could not prepare for a trip that might take as long as two months. North Atlantic storms, rats, poor sanitation, and rotting food combined to give passengers a variety of illnesses. Many died before they ever saw North America.

As immigrants flocked to Canada West, there was enormous population growth in the countryside. Many immigrants were attracted to the idea of owning their own farms. Wheat farming and lumbering flourished.

Most immigrants had to purchase their land, but the cost was low. People could earn the purchase price by working on the farms of those who had arrived earlier. In their home countries, it was nearly impossible to buy land. Compared to that, Canada was a land of opportunity.

Urban Growth

Setting up a new farm in the wilderness took years of labour. As a result, many people decided to build their future in towns and cities. In 1841, Toronto had a population of 15 000 people. By 1851, it had doubled to 30 000.

During Reading

1. While reading Primary Sources 8.1 and 8.2 (on the next page), list three urban problems citizens and politicians faced in the 1840s.

PRIMARY SOURCE 8.1

Letter to the Mayor of Toronto, June 26, 1841

The earnestness [seriousness] of my desire to advance the prosperity [wealth] of the City, as well as to promote the health and comfort of the inhabitants, and to aid in improving its general appearance to the eyes of strangers, will be my excuse for offering the following suggestions....

No Soapsuds, or other dirty water, ought to be allowed to be thrown into the kennel [sewer] in any of the streets:—they there accumulate in pools, deepened by the feet of cattle and the wallowing [rolling around] of pigs, and become exceedingly offensive....

The surface drains from yards, passing beneath the footpaths, and emptying into the street, are exceedingly offensive and deleterious [harmful]; in like manner pigs when kept in a small yard, not regularly cleaned, become a nuisance to the neighborhood and passengers....

Tanners and Limekilns [places where people tan hides and destroy the remains of animals], in neighborhoods where a dense population is gathering, are very disagreeable, and injurious [harmful] to the health.

The sweepings from the shops, particularly those of Tailors and Shoemakers, give a very slovenly [sloppy] appearance to the streets....

Blacksmith's waste or rubbish, carts and other carriages under repair, empty carts and wagons or sleighs left in the streets after the day's work is over; furniture, barrels, ploughs, stoves... encumbering [all over] the paths; some of which remain for weeks and months without removal, may prove the cause of very serious accidents at night....

View in King Street (looking eastward), City of Toronto, Upper Canada, by Thomas Young, 1860.

- How does this painting compare to the descriptions of urban life in Primary Sources 8.1 and 8.2? What might be some reasons for these differences?
- Compare what you see in this painting with what you would see today on a Toronto street. What are the differences?

PRIMARY SOURCE 8.2

Letter from W. B. Jarvis to W. H. Boulton, Mayor of Toronto, August 28, 1847

To the inhabitants of Toronto it is a novel [new] sight to witness families lying under the shelter of fences and trees, not only in the outskirts, but within the very heart of the town,—human beings, begging for food, having disease and famine depicted [shown] in their countenances [faces], and without a shelter to cover them. That there will be many amongst them incapable of labour is beyond a doubt, but it is equally certain that there will be very many able and willing to work who will be unable to procure [find] employment. The expense of sustaining these people should not fall upon individual charity or uncertain means [chance]. Funds should be provided.... I beg permission therefore to request that you would please suggest to the Corporation [City of Toronto] the propriety [appropriateness] of making an application to the Government to advance, by way of loan, such sum of money as may be considered necessary, and that improvements tending to the well being of the City should be undertaken, which would give employment to those able to work.

Livestock roamed freely on urban streets, such as Sparks Street in Ottawa, shown here in the mid-nineteenth century.

Using the SEARCH Strategy for Analyzing Problems

The SEARCH strategy gives you an organized system for analyzing or researching issues and problems.

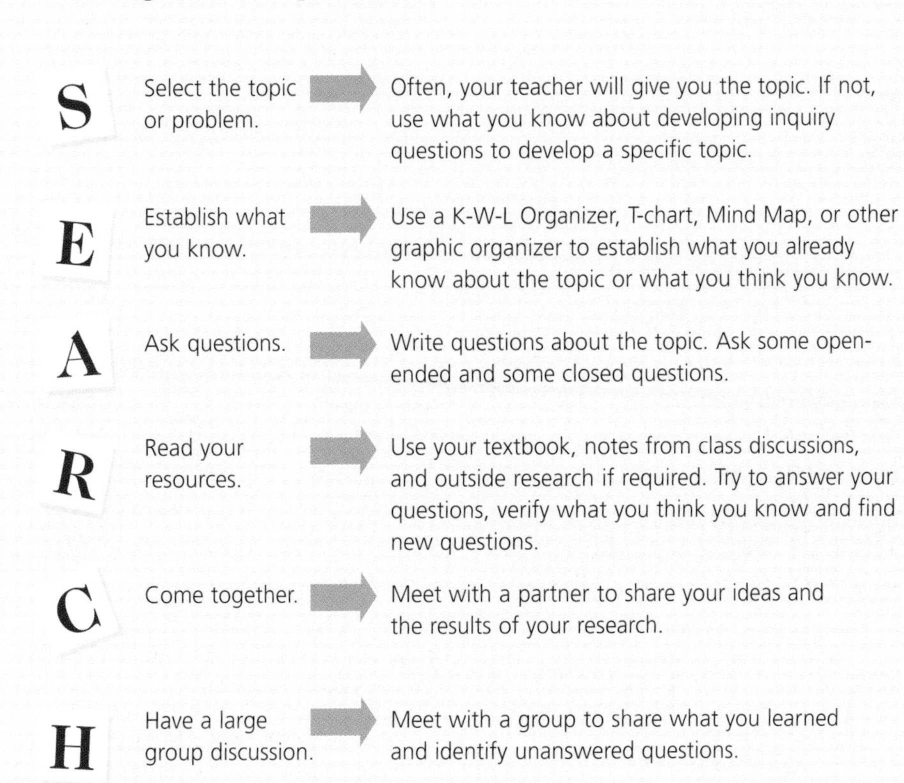

After Reading

1. Use a SEARCH Strategy to analyze the topic *Was it easier to live in urban areas in the 1840s than it is today?*
   a) Establish what you know: Use the readings and your own knowledge to write down three aspects of urban life that might help you compare past and present, such as safety, convenience, and pollution. Use jot-notes to record your ideas about each point of comparison for the 1840s and today.
   b) Ask questions: Write questions that will help you verify what you know or think you know.
   c) Read your resources: Go over your notes from the Before Reading and During Reading activities to try to answer your questions.
   d) Come together: Meet with the same partner you had for question 1 in the Before Reading activity on page 224.
   e) Have a large group discussion: Meet with the group of four that you had for question 2 in the Before Reading activity. Review your unanswered questions on the topic to see if anyone in the group can respond.
2. Which of the two statements that follow best reflects your opinion?
   - *I would rather live in the 1840s than today.*
   - *I would rather live today than in the 1840s.*

   Write it in your notebook. Use the three aspects of urban life you listed in step a) to write three sentences to support your preference.

Social Class and Settler Life

Before Reading

1. Would you consider moving to a place that has fewer services and comforts than you are used to? Explain why or why not in your journal.
2. If you were considering such a move, how would you prepare for it?

Today, in answer to the question, *To what social class do you belong?* most people would probably answer, *I don't know* or *middle class*. Their choice of *middle class* would likely be based on factors such as their job, income, and maybe education. In nineteenth-century Europe, attitudes to class were very different.

For most of European history, social class affected almost every part of a person's life. Class was rooted in land ownership. The upper class had huge estates. Sometimes these estates included large sections of a country. Land was passed down to the oldest son in a family.

The middle class also owned land. They had great amounts by our standards today, but less than the upper classes. Land owned by the middle class was also passed down through the oldest sons.

Younger sons of both the upper and middle classes had to make careers in areas such as the military, clergy, or government. Most women from these classes had to marry to make their way in the world, although a few had employment.

In comparison, people from the lower class did not own land. Most worked on other people's land and paid rent. They had no way to purchase or find their own land because all of it was owned and passed down through families.

In North America, however, plenty of affordable land was available. As a result, Europe's strict class attitudes began to change in North America. This was one of the reasons that North America was sometimes called "the new world." It presented a new start for many people from the lower classes. However, recent immigrants from Europe were still conscious of class status. It sometimes took them time to adjust to the rules of their new environment.

One such arrival was Mary Gapper. In 1828, Mary Sophia Gapper travelled from her home in England to Upper Canada. She was from the middle class. This meant her crossing was quite comfortable. She travelled by cabin in a better quality ship than thousands of other emigrants making the trip.

Mary Gapper married in Upper Canada and became Mary O'Brien. Her journals give historians a look at life on Yonge Street in the late 1820s and early 1830s.

- Why do you think historians value the information in primary sources such as journals?
- What kinds of primary sources will future historians use to learn about your society?

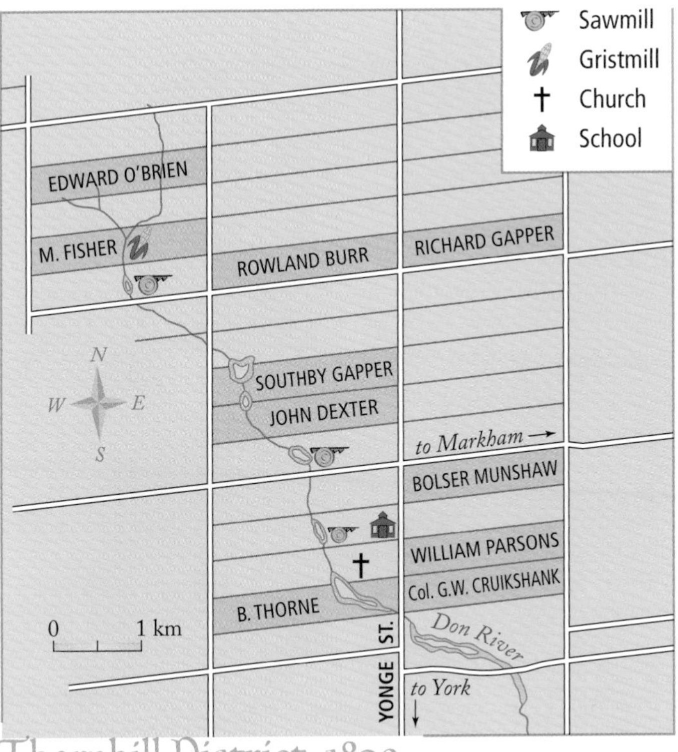

Thornhill District, 1830

Mary and Edward O'Brien settled in the village of Thornhill, about 22.5 kilometres north of York down Yonge Street.

During Reading

1. As you read Primary Sources 8.3a (on this page), and 8.3b and 8.3c (on the next page), note how Mary reveals her middle-class background and attitudes.
2. Find evidence of tension between people of different classes in her writing. Why do you think this tension exists? How might it lead to conflict in the colonies?
3. Copy the graphic organizer below into your notebook. As you read the excerpts from Mary O'Brien's journal, fill in the appropriate column.

Topics	Middle-Class Woman (Mary O'Brien)	Lower-Class Woman (Eliza Stacey)
Responsibilities		
Concerns		
Leisure activities		

Complete the chart after reading Primary Source 8.4 on page 231.

PRIMARY SOURCE 8.3a

From the Journals of Mary O'Brien

November 1, 1828: Southby's man McMullen, who is an Irishman, has been ten years in Canada. He has a wife, two children, and three cows. He has also bought some wild land about fifteen miles up the Street. However, not liking to go so far, he is about to get himself some more nearer where he will settle himself. He is a very good servant but no respecter of persons. He came into the room where we were watching Richard at his work and, whilst we were talking to him, took out his little pipe and lit it. After this he very coolly sat down and began smoking....

January 25, 1829: The new Parliament [in which reformers, for the first time, had a majority in the Assembly], it seems, is very radical and very stupidly so.... Four hundred acres [160 hectares] of land, wild or cultivated, form the requisite [required] qualification for a member, and they are paid for their attendance. Some of them are sad raffs [disreputable characters] without any sort of qualification but their acres, and the government let the editors of the two radical papers [one of whom was W. L. Mackenzie] write away after their own fancies [wishes] without employing anyone to write against them....

Two of the most radical members are returned [elected] for this county, but our party think that it was done more through the ignorance of the voters as to the real state of things....

February 5, 1829: Mary [her sister-in-law] and I both set to work on our books till dinner time.... Mr. Thorne came to tea and we passed the evening gaily [happily] enough. We put the finishing touch to the arrangement of our Book Society [Book Club], though the books cannot be issued till the autumn.... Our canvass [recruitment] for members is not quite concluded but I believe we have secured [collected] seven.

PRIMARY SOURCE 8.3b

From the Journals of Mary O'Brien, continued

August 14, 1829: Spent the morning as usual. By the way, I might as well tell what that usual is. I get up at six, half dress myself, and go to the dairy to see the milk, etc., put right. Then I dress the baby [her brother's child] and myself, walking once or twice into the kitchen to see that the servants do not forget to put on the teakettle, etc.

After breakfast I take orders for dinner and go with Bill into the garden to get vegetables, and, if there be any meat-cutting which the cook cannot manage, I get him to do it. All the while I take all convenient opportunities to look into the kitchen to see that the cook is doing the right thing at the right time.

Unaccustomed to the routine, I am myself obliged to ask Mary almost everything about cookery each time I go into the kitchen. This continues till dinner time. There are two dinners to be dressed [prepared] before one o'clock, and our own generally includes something more than roasting or boiling as Mary has a taste for cookery.

May 21 and 22, 1830: On Friday morning after breakfast we came home [Mary has been married for a week and this is her new home] and remained till Saturday night. I was very busy arranging my odds and ends and establishing the due limits between kitchen, parlour, and bedroom. Unluckily, however, there is no fireplace in the parlour (it being designed only for summer use). Considering that the only furniture of my parlour is two chairs, a sort of makeshift [temporary] table, two guns, a whiskey keg and a beer barrel, a box of nails, a few carpenter's tools, a bottle of ink, a few books and drawings of Edward's, and that two sides are composed of whitewashed logs and the other two of planed planks, I think I am very smart [stylish] and genteel [upper class]....

June 5, 1830: Our new man cannot milk very well. I proposed taking the pail and trying to do better. The cow greeted my first attempt with a kick and a race. Before I tried again Edward attempted to tie her legs with our pocket handkerchiefs, but with another kick at him she set off again with the handkerchief round her leg and would not stop till she had succeeded in disengaging [freeing] herself. The third attempt was more prosperous and I completed my job very dexterously [skillfully].

This museum worker at Bellevue House National Historic Site in Ontario works in a kitchen similar to one that Mary O'Brien may have had in her home.

PRIMARY SOURCE 8.3c

From the Journals of Mary O'Brien, continued

July 1, 1830: I have been very busy today. I have made two puddings and a pie, baked two loaves and a cake, and made two pounds of butter. Besides this I have done the usual routine duties of preparing two dinners and keeping my house in order. I should not have been ashamed to receive not only Lady Colborne [wife of the lieutenant-governor] but Aunt Sophy herself during the two hours' leisure when I was reading and writing.

January 31, 1831: We came home as early as we could and found a damsel [girl] from the Isle of Mull [an island off the west coast of Scotland] waiting to offer me her services. I held a consultation and, finding that there was a chance of her being more efficient than the child [current servant], I have determined on going straightway...to make arrangements.

Mary O'Brien's concerns and daily activities may have been typical for a middle-class settler, but not for all settlers. Many of the immigrants who came to North America faced challenges as they established themselves.

In Primary Source 8.4, a woman writes about significantly different concerns than those of Mary O'Brien. Eliza Stacey's father-in-law had saved her husband, George, from debtor's prison in London, but then sent the couple to British North America. It was common practice at this time to send troublesome family members to the colonies. As Stacey writes her letter, her husband has again been taken to prison.

The Whitecross Street Prison for Debtors, London, 1843. The top image shows the ward for woman and children and the bottom shows the ward for men.

- What mood does the illustration portray? How?

PRIMARY SOURCE 8.4

Letter from Eliza Stacey to her Father-in-law, Edward Stacey, in England, 1847

March 1847

My dear Father-in-law,

Some time ago George was sued by a man of the name of Crosby for a debt of 12 pounds which he had been owing a long time, and as he had not liquidated [paid] it they sent a bailiff [officer of the court] to put an execution [seize property to pay bills] on the house and seized what comforts we were blessed with.

Last Wednesday after supper the bailiff arrived in a sleigh, arrested George and took him to Sherbrooke gaol [jail]. You can imagine my distress and tears, and poor George was distraught at leaving me suddenly with everything to do, and my baby due in about two weeks' time. No entreaty [pleading] served to bring mercy, and George was driven away in the bitter cold to the prison he had been condemned to once before.... And now we are told that our debt, with the interest and legal expenses, might come to near 100 pounds....

I expect to [have my baby] in two weeks' time, and Fred [their young son] cannot carry the whole farm upon his young shoulders. I have worked very hard all the time of my pregnancy. I now never lay my weary body full of pain on my bed....

During the winter we have brought our bed into the kitchen, the cold being so intense that our bedroom was icy.... how long George will be held in prison I do not know, but at least they are not seizing everything we have, so perhaps it is the lesser of two evils....

Adieu, my dear Father. I dare not dwell longer on our serious situation for fear of distressing you too much, and causing myself upset just at this time when I can least sustain it. I must keep calm for the babe's sake.

After Reading

1. In your opinion, do social classes and attitudes about social class still exist today? Discuss as a class.
2. What do you think happened to Eliza? In a class discussion, suggest ways that society today might help someone in a similar position.

The Cholera Epidemic

Before Reading

1. On February 23, 2003, a new virus was reported in Canada. SARS (Severe Acute Respiratory Syndrome) killed twenty-four people in less than three months. By September of that year, 438 SARS cases had been identified in Canada. In a small group, discuss how you would respond to people who showed symptoms of a deadly new illness. What would you do to protect yourself?

In June 1832, a ship from Ireland docked in Québec. It was the first of many over the next decade that carried the deadly disease *cholera morbus*. A week after that ship landed, 1200 people were sick. A month later, 4500 people in Lower Canada had died. At that time, no one understood the causes of the disease, how it spread, or how to treat it.

Cholera is caused by an infection in the intestine. A person may get cholera from eating food or drinking water contaminated with *cholera bacterium*. The disease spreads rapidly where there is poor sewage for human and animal feces or if the bacteria enters the water system. Conditions on the boats carrying people to British North America were ideal for the spread of the disease.

During Reading

1. You might be reading about cholera for the first time. As you read the accounts that follow, keep a list of the things you find alarming about the illness.
2. How might this illness cause conflict in the colonies?

Symptoms include diarrhea, vomiting, and leg cramps. A person with cholera rapidly loses body fluids, which leads to dehydration and shock. Without treatment, they die within hours.

This nineteenth-century medicine chest includes a treatment for cholera, as seen on the label of the bottle. In desperation, people would try anything to save themselves. One popular treatment was made of maple wood ash, pig fat, and maple syrup.

PRIMARY SOURCE 8.5

Letter from C. Beadle and L. Cross to Rev. James Clarke, President of the Board of Health, St. Catharines, July 4, 1842

About forty minutes before we saw him he said he was taken suddenly ill with Pain and Cramp in the Stomach and Cramp in his limbs—accompanied with vomiting and purging [diarrhea] —At the time we saw him the Spasms were extremely severe—he was vomiting a thick gray mucus, without colour. The dejections [material] from the bowels were frequent—watery and apparently without bile—Lips livid [blue]—Extremities [hands and feet] cold—Pulse small, quick but not frequent.—Perspiration profuse [plentiful]—Thirst excessive—

PRIMARY SOURCE 8.6

Letter from John Capelain, Huron Tract, Upper Canada, August 28, 1832

My Dear Brother

I take the opportunity of writing these few lines to you, to inform you of our distress and trouble. After a very rough passage of twelve weeks, by the help of the Almighty God, we arrived safe to land, except the loss of two babes....

There was 32 of us that came up into the woods together, and there is twelve of the 32 dead. The complaint was the cholera morbus; they all died in the space of a fortnight [two weeks]. There [was] none laid ill but a few days. Dear brother, I should like to know what my brother in law should like to be done with poor Bob's things: he had no money.

PRIMARY SOURCE 8.7

Practical Views on Cholera, by Dr. Wolfred Nelson, 1854

As a general rule, it may be said that [cholera] first invades the miserable, filthy, and cheerless haunts of the poor, vicious and depraved.... (It is well it should be understood that in the visitation [epidemic] of 1849, and during the present year in England, cholera has been more frequent among the comfortable and wealthy classes than formerly. Hence, let those of every station [class] take heed [pay attention] in time.)

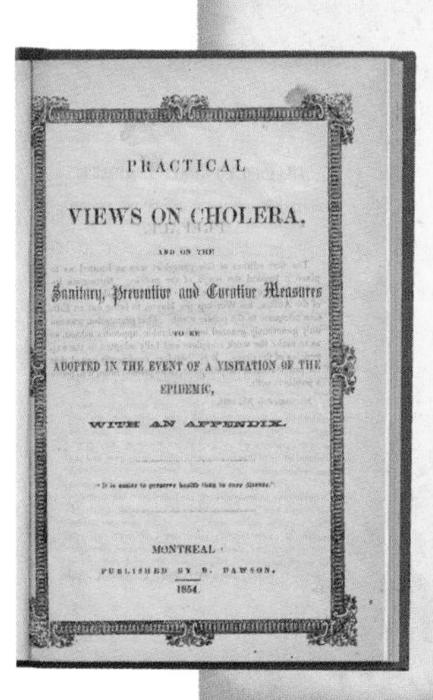

PRACTICAL

VIEWS ON CHOLERA,

AND ON THE

Sanitary, Preventive and Curative Measures

TO BE

ADOPTED IN THE EVENT OF A VISITATION OF THE EPIDEMIC,

WITH AN APPENDIX.

MONTREAL:

PUBLISHED BY B. DAWSON.

1854.

PRIMARY SOURCE 8.8

Letter to Isaac Lundy from Lardner Bostwick Jr., Toronto, August 15, 1834

Read this to yourself before you read it loud

Dear Grandmother Uncle Aunt and Cousins—

Never did I set down to write such unwilling news as what I have to communicate to you I must do it as briefly as possible

Dear Grandmother your Son is no more. My Father was seized night before last with Cholera and in 14 hours was in his grave he died happy and resigned [at peace]. Mother and the rest of family are as well as can be expected.... I cannot allow myself to make any remarks—judge of my feelings we done anything which lay in our power to cure him but it would not do the times are truly awful—our friends are dying all around us—business is at a stand—many are leaving the city. David Lackie the Baker is dead—God only knows who next—40 or 50 are dying a day....

Lardner Bostwick Jr.

Uncle Isaac – be careful how you communicate this news to Grandmother. I would advise you not to come to the city till the plague is over—the Doctors are completely baffled they cannot cure it at all.

National Gallery of Canada, Ottawa/#7157

Cholera Plague, Québec, by Joseph Légaré, around 1832. The fires in the streets were believed to be a protection from cholera.

Grosse Île

In 1832, officials established Grosse Île as a **quarantine** station to help control the spread of diseases such as cholera. A quarantine is a period of isolation for a person or animal that has (or has come in contact with) a contagious disease. Grosse Île was 48 kilometres downstream from Québec on the St. Lawrence River. Officials hoped to prevent people with the illness from infecting other people in the colony.

However, Grosse Île could not keep up with all of the ships. Some reached their final destinations without the approval of health officials. The diseases spread. Many people began to fear new immigrants, who often carried the disease. In Lower Canada, some French people grew angry with British immigrants. This anger contributed to the tensions causing the Rebellions of 1837.

Historians are not sure how many people died aboard the ships waiting for health clearance or while hospitalized at Grosse Île. Many people were buried at sea or in mass unmarked graves.

During Reading !

1. Parks Canada's Web site for Grosse Île shows the huge task that faced doctors who tried to control the spread of diseases, such as cholera, smallpox, and typhus. Go to www.duvaleducation.com/canadasearlyyears. Click on the link to the Parks Canada Web site to read more about Gross Île. Find out why 1847 has been called the "Tragic Year at Grosse Île." You could also use the phrase *tragic year at Grosse Île* in an Internet search engine.

A View of the Quarantine Station at Grosse Île, by Henri Delattre, 1850.

- Who is the person in the foreground of the painting?
- Why do you think he is there?
- Based on what you have read about Grosse Île, how historically accurate is this painting?

The quarantine station at Grosse Île was closed in 1947. Today, it is a National Historic Site.

Conducting an Interview

An interview is a conversation where one person (the interviewer) asks questions to learn something from another person (the interviewee). Historians and other researchers often use interviews to gather or clarify information.

Tips for Conducting a Successful Interview

- Always ask permission to talk to your interviewee a few days ahead of time. Outline the purpose of your conversation so he or she can be prepared.
- Write down your questions and give them to the interviewee. A good place to start is the 5 Ws and 1 H. Begin with a question that makes the interviewee feel comfortable. This is often a closed question that is fairly easy to answer.
- Include some open-ended questions. Ask the interviewee to clarify what he or she thinks about the topic. One way to begin these questions is *How do you feel about...?*
- Plan your questions ahead of time, but listen carefully to the interviewee's answers. Additional questions may come to you as the interview takes place.
- Plan a method to record your interview. You might write notes or use a recording device.
- Show the interviewee you are interested in what he or she is saying. Make eye contact, smile, or nod your head.
- Give the interviewee time to think about his or her responses. Count to five before you repeat or rephrase the question.
- Be on time for the interview and thank the interviewee when you are finished.
- Write your report of the interview as soon as possible. This will ensure the responses are still fresh in your mind. Send a copy of your report to the interviewee.

After Reading

1. With a partner, think of a person you can interview who has either faced a major change in his or her life or who has witnessed a major change in Canadian society.
2. Develop seven questions for your interviewee and then conduct your interview.
3. Prepare a summary of your interview. You might write a news report, editorial, or report for your class. If you prefer, prepare an oral summary for the class. It might take the form of a television or radio news report or talk show interview.

Think It Through

Upper Canada and the End of Slavery

Before Reading

1. Working in a small group, brainstorm what you know about slavery. Use the points that follow to help you generate ideas:
   - images of slavery
   - times and places that allowed slavery
   - reasons to have slaves
   - conflicts and problems with slavery

The Land of the Free and the Home of the Brave (Slave Market, Charleston, South Carolina), by Henry Byam Martin, 1833. Martin was a British military officer travelling in the United States.

- What do you think is the artist's opinion about slavery? What are your clues?

Slavery is the ownership of one person by another. The main reason for owning slaves is economic. Slaves are not paid for their work, so they are the most inexpensive labour possible (after the expense of purchasing them). Before the 1800s, slavery was practised in most countries around the world, including British North America.

Slavery was an important part of the economy in the southern United States. These states produced mainly tobacco and cotton, which required large numbers of workers. The capture, sale, and use of slaves from Africa allowed these crops to be profitable. However, these profits came at a great human cost. Slavery involves many injustices, including the denial of basic human rights.

Upper Canada limited the growth of slavery in 1793. Legislation stated that no new slaves could be brought to the colony. People who had slaves at the time were allowed to keep them. The children of slaves were to be freed at the age of twenty-five. The law was a way of phasing out slavery. It was a compromise between those who wanted to keep slavery and abolitionists, such as Lieutenant-Governor John Simcoe.

During Reading

1. You have learned many strategies in this textbook that can help you become a better reader. Usually, you learned one new skill at a time. However, real reading situations are often more complicated. You will often have to use more than one strategy to get the most out of what you are reading. Your skills as a reader grow as you learn when to use your skills.

   As you read pages 236–241, use at least four of the strategies listed below. Challenge yourself by using at least one strategy that you are not confident using. If you want to refresh your memory of these skills, use the page numbers listed.

   - Reading Techniques (page 7)
   - Compare and Contrast (page 11)
   - Identifying Main Ideas (page 45)
   - Finding Facts, Opinions, and Arguments (page 77)
   - Determining Cause and Effect (page 81)
   - Paraphrasing (page 102)
   - Making Inferences (page 110)
   - Understanding Organizational Patterns (page 177)

   Keep notes about how you use these strategies in your notebook.

I already know how I'll use one of these skills! I use what I learned about reading techniques all the time. I've already scanned pages 236–241, so I know how much I have to read. There are six pages with different kinds of information on them: paragraphs, primary sources, questions, and a map.

I'll also use chunking—another reading technique. I find chunking helps me stay focused. There aren't many subheadings on these pages, so I think I'll use each page as one chunk. After each page, I'll stop and think about whether I can use one of the other skills listed in this activity.

I'll start by rereading page 236.

Reading Techniques

scanning: 6 pages
→ primary sources, paragraphs, questions, map

chunking: will stop after each page

On page 236, I can make an inference. The second paragraph explains that slavery was important to the economy in the southern United States. I can infer that because slavery was so important to the economy, the southern states wouldn't want to give it up.

I can make another inference. The last paragraph explains that Upper Canada decided to limit slavery. I can infer that slavery was not as important to Upper Canada's economy. From what I've learned earlier in the textbook, the economy was based on fur trading, fishing, lumber, and agriculture. I guess none of these industries required as many workers as cotton and tobacco farms.

Making Inferences

page 236: One reason the southern U.S. wanted slavery was because its economy depended on it. Places like Upper Canada were more willing to abolish slavery, possibly because their economies did not need it.

Think It Through

Upper Canada's position on slavery led to conflict with the United States. Escaped slaves sometimes fled to British North America in search of safety. However, escaped slaves were often followed by American slave owners. If found, the former slaves were sometimes kidnapped and returned to slavery in the United States.

Primary Sources 8.9 and 8.10 are letters on this issue exchanged between political leaders in the United States and Upper Canada.

During Reading

1. In Primary Source 8.9, John Quincy Adams, an official with the United States government, writes to G. Crawford Antrobus, a British official in Washington. What is Adams requesting?
2. Why is Adams writing to a British official, rather than an official from Upper Canada?

PRIMARY SOURCE 8.9

Letter from John Quincy Adams, Department of State, Washington, D.C., to G. Crawford Antrobus, Charge' d'Affaire from Great Britain, June 11, 1819

Representations have been received at this Department that several Black Slaves ran off last Fall from their Owners in the State of Tennessee, and have taken refuge at Malden in Upper Canada. The Owners are anxious to know if any arrangement can be made by which permission could be obtained for them to go to Canada, and re-obtain possession of their Property.

I have therefore the honor to address this letter to you, to enquire, if you can inform me, whether the Owners of these Slaves can obtain such permission, and restitution [giving back to rightful owner] of them, by the interposition [assistance] of the Government of Canada.

The activity directions say to use one skill that I'm not confident using. For me, I think this is paraphrasing. Reading some of these primary sources is challenging because the writing style is so different from today. I find it easier to paraphrase if I jot down phrases or words that seem important as I read. I then put the notes together at the end.

Paraphrasing, Primary Source 8.9 page 238

- *Black slaves ran off from Tennessee*
- *living in Malden, Upper Canada*
- *owners want to come to Canada to get the slaves back*
- *asking → Can owners have permission? Will the government help?*

Main idea: Adams is asking Antrobus if slave owners from Tennessee can come to Upper Canada to capture some escaped slaves.

During Reading

1. Antrobus passed Adams' letter along to the attorney general of Upper Canada, John B. Robinson. In the letter that follows, Robinson's response sets out Upper Canada's position. Paraphrase his opinion.
2. What reasons does he give for his response? What other reasons might he have?
3. What does he say could happen if people from the United States try to take back their slaves? To whom can the former slaves turn for help?

The Honourable John Beverly Robinson

PRIMARY SOURCE 8.10

Letter from Jno. B. Robinson, Attorney General, to the Governor General of Upper Canada, York, July 8, 1819

In obedience to Your Excellency's commands I have perused [looked over] the accompanying letter from G. C. Antrobus Esquire, his Majesty's Charge d'Affaires at the Court of Washington....

I beg to express most respectfully my opinion to Your Excellency that the Legislation of this Province having adopted the Law of England as the rule of decision in all questions relative to property and civil rights, and freedom of the person being the most important civil right protected by those laws, it follows that whatever may have been the condition of these Black people in the Country to which they formally belonged, here they are free—For the enjoyment of all civil rights consequent [resulting from] to a mere residence in the Country and among them the right to personal freedom as acknowledged and protected by the Laws of England in cases similar to that under consideration....

The consequence is that should any attempt be made by any person to infringe upon this right in the persons of these Black people, they would most probably call for, and could compel [force] the interference of those to whom the administration of our Laws is committed and I submit with the greatest deference [regard] to Your Excellency that it would not be in the power of the Executive Government in any manner to restrain or direct the Courts or Judges in the exercise of their duty upon such an application—

Fugitive Slave Act

In 1833, the British parliament passed a law abolishing slavery in all parts of the British Empire. The law took effect in 1834. In contrast, the United States became divided over whether to end slavery or not. Slavery continued in the southern states. The northern states abolished it. Black people living in the northern states were considered free.

However, in 1850, the United States passed the Fugitive Slave Act. The act stated the following:

- All citizens of the United States were required to help return escaped slaves to their owners. Refusal to do so could result in a $1000 fine. (The average wage at the time was about $300 per year.)
- There would be no jury trials to hear the complaints or stories of escaped slaves. This included those who lived in a free part of the United States.
- Anyone helping an escaped slave could be fined $1000 and sent to jail.

The Fugitive Slave Act meant even Black people living in the free part of the United States could legally be returned to slavery in the South.

After 1850, many former slaves left the northern United States to live in British North America. Slaves escaping the South went directly to Canada. Many took the **Underground Railroad**, a network of safe houses that helped slaves escape.

I can make another inference here. In the last paragraph on this page, it says that after 1850, many former slaves left the United States to come to British North America. Since 1850 is the date the United States passed the Fugitive Slave Act, I can infer that the act caused Upper Canada's Black population to increase. I'll write my note in the form of a Cause and Effect Organizer.

Cause
U.S. passes Fugitive Slave Act

Effects
former slaves leave the U.S. for Canada
some tension between U.S. and Canada?

In 1860, eleven southern states declared their independence from the United States and the American Civil War began. Slavery in the United States ended after the war in 1865.

Josiah Henson was an escaped slave who helped found a settlement and school for escaped slaves at Dawn, near Dresden, Canada West.

Harriet Tubman was one of the Underground Railroad's most famous "conductors." Most of her trips north with escaped slaves ended in St. Catharines, Ontario.

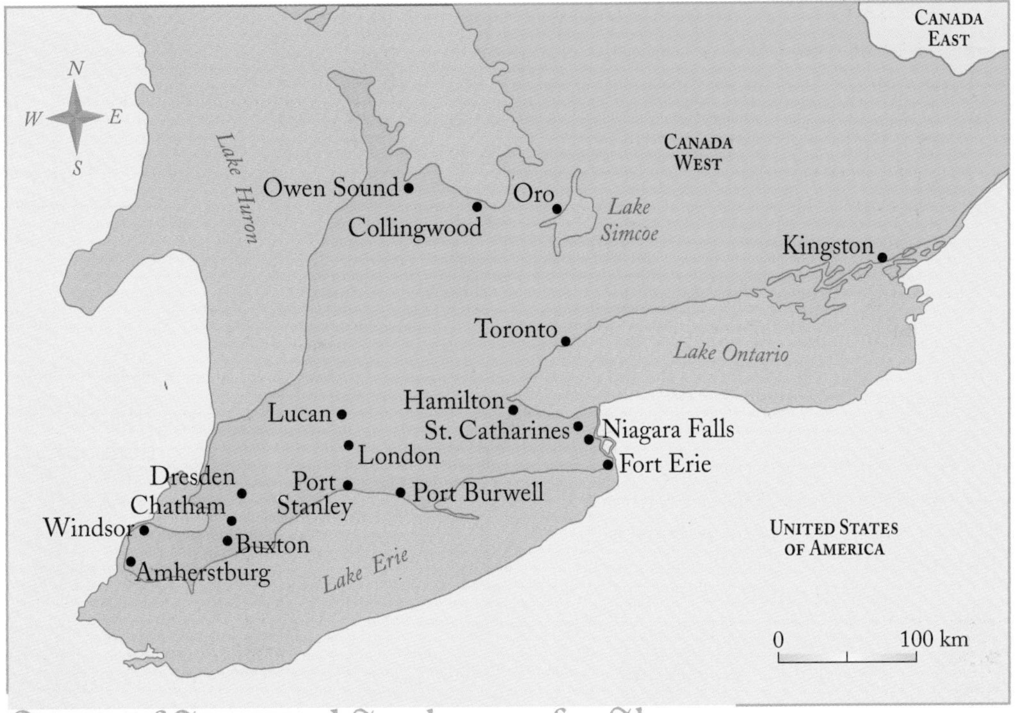

Points of Entry and Settlement for Slaves on the Underground Railroad, 1850–1865

After Reading

1. With a partner, discuss how the Fugitive Slave Act affected British North America. How was the United States affected by Britain's decision to abolish slavery?
2. How was slavery a cause of conflict and change? Discuss with your partner and then write your answer in your notebook on your own.

Free, but Not Always Equal

Before Reading

1. Imagine a situation where someone is treating you poorly. What options do you have in dealing with this person? With a partner, brainstorm alternatives, along with positive and negative consequences for each option.

In the 1790s, the Black population in Upper Canada was estimated at several hundred people. By the early 1850s, it had reached 30 000 to 35 000 people.

At this time, Black people in Upper Canada had many freedoms not available to most Black people in the United States. They could move freely throughout the colony, own property, and vote if they were property owners. Despite these freedoms, Black people and other minorities experienced much **prejudice** and **discrimination**.

In 1850, the Common Schools Act established separate elementary schools for Black children in Canada West. Schools were established at Amherstburg and Windsor. They operated until the early twentieth century. This photograph shows teacher John Alexander and his students at the King Street School in Amherstburg around 1890.

Prejudice: a rigid (usually unfavourable) opinion about a group of people that is applied to all members of that group. The term comes from the word *prejudge*.

Discrimination: when a person is denied full participation in society because of his or her membership in a particular social group.

Prejudice is an attitude. Discrimination is an action. Discrimination is often based on a prejudiced attitude.

Throughout the British Empire, slaves gained their freedom in 1834. However, the laws of freedom were not applied equally to all people in British North America. For example, Black people who applied for lots along Yonge Street were refused, even though there was no legal reason for the refusal. In addition, if a community had a separate school for Black people, Black children had to attend it. They were not free to choose any school they liked.

Some Black people made good lives for themselves in British North America, in spite of prejudice and discrimination. Rose Fortune, shown in this painting, was the child of Black Loyalists. She turned a job carrying luggage in Annapolis Royal into a shipping business that is still operated by her descendants today.

During Reading

1. Work with a partner to determine what the writers are requesting in Primary Source 8.11.
2. What reasons do the writers give for the government to support their request?
3. What is the tone of the petition? What clues did you use to infer the tone?
4. How is requiring Black students to attend a separate Black school an example of discrimination?

PRIMARY SOURCE 8.11

Petition of the Coloured People of Hamilton, October 15, 1843

We the people of colour in the Town of Hamilton have a right to inform Your Excellency of the treatment that we have to undergo. We have paid the taxes and we are denied of the public schools, and we have applied to the Board of Police and there is no steps taken to change this manner of treatment, and this kind of treatment is not in the United States for the children of colour go to the Public Schools together with the white children, more especially in Philadelphia, and I thought there was not a man to be known by his colour under the British flag, and we left the United States because we were in hopes that prejudice was not in this land.... I am sorry to annoy you by allowing [telling you about] this thing, but we are grieved much.... I have left property in the United States and I have bought property in Canada, and all I want is justice and I will be satisfied. We are called [names] when we go out in the street, and sometimes brick bats [a piece of brick] is sent after us as we pass in street. We are not all absconders [thieves] now we brought money into this Province, and we hope never to leave it.... May my God smile upon your public life and guide you into all truth, which is my prayer and God bless the Queen and Royal Family.

A Community Divided

During the 1840s and 1850s, Black community leaders proposed different ways of dealing with discrimination and prejudice. Some recommended **segregation**. This meant setting up separate Black communities, where Black people could live free of discrimination.

One of the most successful communities was the Elgin settlement, also known as Buxton. Reverend William King established the settlement in 1843.

Reverend William King

During Reading

1. What options do you think Black people had for dealing with prejudice and discrimination at this time? Discuss with your partner.
2. Why do you think segregation was an attractive option for some people?

PRIMARY SOURCE 8.12

Presbyterian Church of Canada Circular

There are upwards of 30 000 colored people in this Province— most of them living in that degraded [poor] condition, in which Slavery has left them. With a view to their moral and social improvement, "THE ELGIN ASSOCIATION" was formed and incorporated, and has purchased a Tract of Land in the Township of Raleigh, for the settlement of Colored persons of approved character, on which about ninety families are already established.

The Presbyterian Church of Canada donated funds for the Elgin settlement.

The land the Elgin Association bought was 19 kilometres south of Chatham. Settlers at Buxton had to follow strict rules. All had to purchase their land and agree to live there for a minimum of ten years. They also had to build a house and maintain their yard to set standards. The community flourished. In 1856, it had 800 settlers. By the 1860s, it was home to 2000 people.

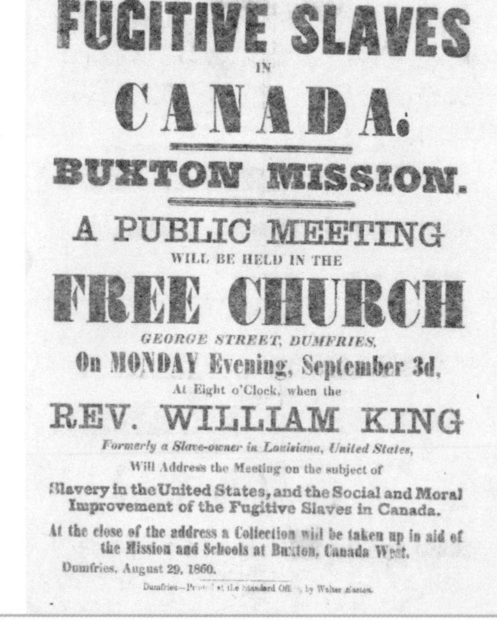

- Based on what you see in this poster, how did organizers try to attract settlers to Buxton?

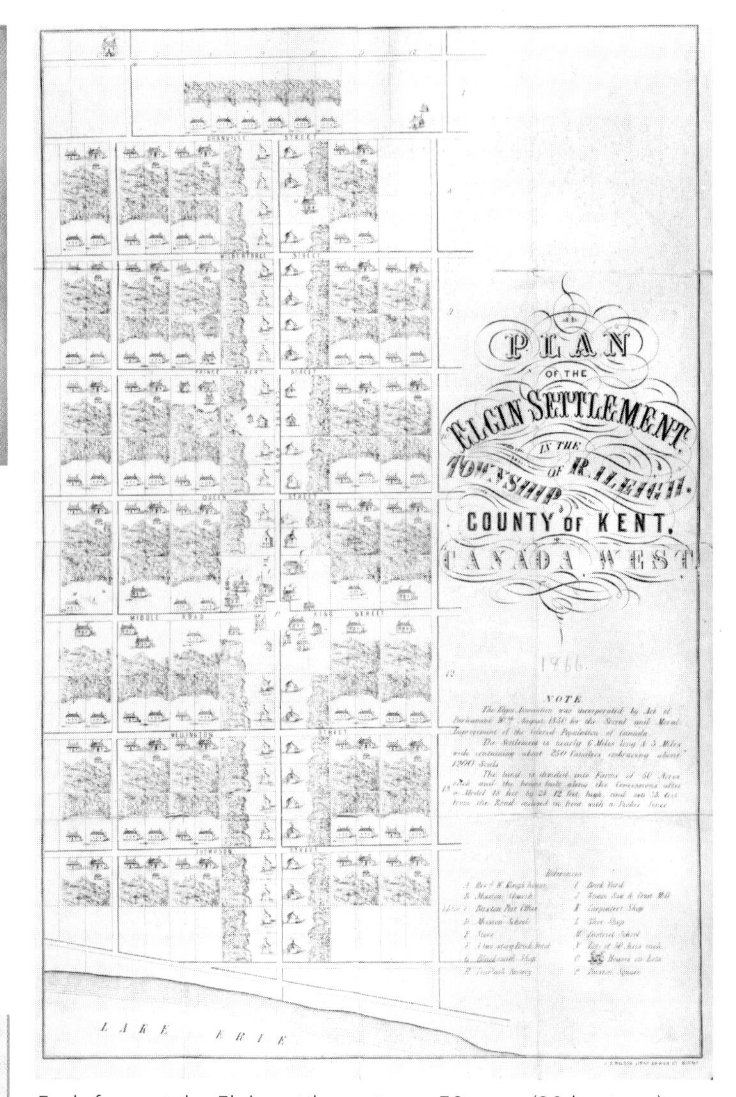

Each farm at the Elgin settlement was 50 acres (20 hectares).

Some residents of the area had opposed the settlement when it was proposed. However, by 1856, most agreed that Buxton was a success. King's school on the settlement was especially well regarded. Settlers from the surrounding area even asked to close their school and send their children to the school at Buxton. It became one of the first schools in North America to educate Black and white students together.

Mary Ann Shadd and Henry Bibb

Mary Ann Shadd

Despite the success at Buxton, some Black leaders disagreed with the idea of separate settlements. They believed the best way to prevent prejudice and discrimination was **integration**. This meant Black people would live among other settlers. A well-known supporter of this approach was Mary Ann Shadd.

Shadd was born in Wilmington, Delaware, the first of thirteen children. Her father had been active in the Underground Railroad and his experiences influenced his daughter. In particular, he taught her that hard work, thrift, and education were the keys to equality for Black people.

In 1850, Shadd came to Canada to see if it could be a safe place for escaped slaves. By the next year, she was working as a teacher near Windsor.

In 1853, Shadd became the first Black woman to establish a newspaper in North America, the *Provincial Freeman*. The motto of the paper was *Self-Reliance Is the True Road to Independence*. Shadd encouraged Black people to start businesses and to develop their skills in building trades such as masonry and carpentry. She argued that such skills allowed Black people to integrate and become part of the surrounding society.

Shadd strongly objected to another Black leader, Henry Bibb, and his organization, the Refugee Home Society. Bibb supported segregation. He believed that integration could happen later, once Black people were established on their own. To build segregated communities, the Refugee Home Society raised funds among white people in the United States.

Henry Bibb

Shadd objected to Bibb and his methods for many reasons. In particular, she disliked the idea of asking white people for help. She believed Black people could find equality on their own.

Shadd and Bibb had a furious debate about each other's point of view. Bibb voiced his views in his own newspaper, *Voice of the Fugitive*. Shadd wrote hers on the pages of the *Provincial Freeman*. The newspapers became a forum for their debate until Shadd returned to the United States after the civil war.

After Reading

1. Do you think integration or segregation was the best approach to dealing with discrimination and prejudice in the mid 1800s? Use the SEARCH Strategy you learned about on page 227 to analyze the two approaches.
2. As a class, discuss any programs or activities your school uses to prevent discrimination and prejudice. In your opinion, how effective are these programs?
3. Today, the Ontario Human Rights Code states, "it is public policy in Ontario to recognize the dignity and worth of every person and to provide for equal rights and opportunities without discrimination." What is public policy? As a class, give examples of how public policy can "recognize the dignity and worth of every person."

First Nations in Canada West

Before Reading

1. As a class, discuss how the following situations might have impacted First Nations in Canada West:
   - Natural resources found on First Nations land, especially copper, become increasingly valuable.
   - The number of immigrants to Canada West increases sharply.

First Nations in Canada West faced many challenges between 1830 and 1850. Many First Nations wondered how to best protect their culture, rights, and freedoms. Should First Nations people become part of the non-Aboriginal society around them? Or, should they live on reserves, apart from non-Aboriginal society, in order to protect their traditional ways?

By the 1840s, First Nations people made up about 10 per cent of Canada West's population. As the non-Aboriginal population grew, the settled part of the colony moved closer to First Nations lands. Although many groups had treaties to secure their land, some First Nations found the treaties were being ignored.

The government was under pressure to open more First Nations land for settlers and miners. However, many people did not wait until treaties were signed. Some settlers simply moved onto First Nations land and began clearing it for farms. Canada West's administrators even gave out mining licences for land the colony did not legally own. First Nations leaders turned to the government, asking it to enforce earlier treaties.

In response, Captain Thomas G. Anderson, the Superintendent of Indian Affairs, summoned First Nations leaders from the Lake Simcoe area to a meeting. Primary Source 8.13 is part of his speech to the First Nations at that meeting.

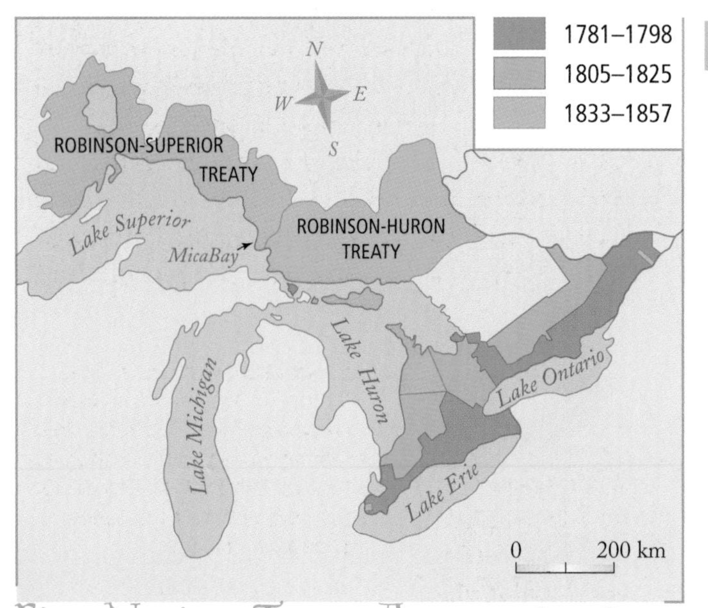

First Nations Treaty Areas, 1781–1857

During Reading

1. With a partner, discuss the difference between being invited and being summoned to a meeting.
2. How is the tone of Anderson's first sentence different from the rest of his remarks?
3. How did Anderson make his speech sound like he was thinking of First Nations' best interests?
4. Reading between the lines of Anderson's speech, what had the government decided was in First Nations' best interests? How might First Nations people disagree? You and your partner might use an I Read/ I Think/ Therefore Chart to prepare your answer.

PRIMARY SOURCE 8.13

Speech by Thomas Anderson to a Meeting of First Nations at Orillia, July 1846

BRETHREN [brothers]... As great changes are taking place in your condition, and your Great Mother, the Queen, having directed the Indian Department to make arrangements for your future benefit and guidance....

Firstly—That the First Nations shall use every means in their power to abandon their present detached little Villages, and unite, as far as practicable [practical], in forming large Settlements—where,

Secondly—Manual Labour Schools will be established for the education of your children; and the Land, to which you may now, with the consent of the Government, remove [move], the Government will secure, by written documents to you and your posterity [descendants] forever.

Thirdly—That you shall devote one-fourth of your annuities [annual payments promised by the government in treaties], which many of you promised me last fall that you would do, for a period of from twenty to twenty-five years, to assist in the support of your children of both sexes, while remaining at the Schools...

Fourthly—That you give up your hunting practices...

Fifthly—That the present practice of paying for putting up your houses [as per previous agreements] shall cease, and that each man shall put up his own Buildings....

It has, therefore, been determined that your children shall be sent to the Schools, where they will forget their First Nations habits, and be instructed in all the necessary arts of civilized life, and become one with your White brethren...

The Management of the Manual Labour Schools will be entrusted to your Missionaries, under the direction of the Great Father, the Governor General, who takes a deep interest in your prosperity.

During Reading

1. Situations such as that faced by First Nations at Orillia occurred all over the colony. The following newspaper article is a fictional account of two significant treaties in Canada. Divide a page in your notebook into two columns. Title the page *Robinson-Superior and Robinson-Huron Treaties, 1850.* At the top of one column, write *Terms that Helped Government/Miners/Settlers*. At the top of the second column, write *Terms that Helped First Nations.* As you read the article, work with your partner to fill in the details of the treaties under the appropriate heading.
2. Does the newspaper article appear to be biased? Discuss why or why not.

Robinson treaties sell land rights to British

September 9, 1850

NORTH SHORE OF LAKE HURON—Commissioner William B. Robinson has concluded the second of two treaties with the Ojibwa First Nations living north of Lake Superior and Lake Huron. Under the terms of the treaties, the Crown obtains title to 129 500 square kilometres of land between the lakes and the height of land to the north. Negotiations were prompted by the recent discovery of valuable minerals near Sault Ste. Marie.

The Robinson-Superior and the Robinson-Huron treaties—as they are known—grant the First Nations twenty-one reserves, a lump sum payment of £4000 pounds sterling, as well as annual payments of 96 cents per person. Also, the Crown admits the right of the First Nations to continue to fish and hunt throughout the territory named in the treaties. These are the first treaties with First Nations in the northern part of Canada West.

William Robinson had a reputation as a fair man when he worked in the fur trade. This reputation helped him negotiate treaties with First Nations along the northern shores of Lakes Superior and Huron.

During Reading

1. How do the points on this page affect your impression of the news article? Does the information change your idea about bias in the article?
2. In the text that follows, identify three ways in which the Ojibwa and the government used conflict resolution strategies. Rate the success of each method as successful or unsuccessful. In your opinion, was this conflict properly resolved? Why or why not?

The Story behind the Story

1845 A mining boom hits Canada West due to an increased demand for copper. Without permission from the Ojibwa, Canada West's Crown Lands Department issues licences for mines on Ojibwa land north of Lake Superior and Lake Huron.

1845–1849 Mines continue to open on First Nations lands. Shantytowns, open pits, and piles of dirt dot the landscape. Ojibwa leaders ask the government to remove miners from their land. The government does not respond.

Mining operations greatly disturbed the surrounding environment. Most left garbage and pollutants as a result of the mining process. This mica mine, shown here around 1900, was located on the shore of Buck Lake in northern Ontario.

1848 Local Ojibwa people attack the Québec Mining Company's site at Mica Bay. During the conflict, the mine and surrounding townsite are burned. The First Nations capture the mining superintendent, along with 100 crew. Governor General Elgin sends troops from Montréal to arrest the "rebels." The uprising's leaders are arrested, jailed for several weeks, then released.

1849–1850 Elgin sends William B. Robinson north of Lake Superior and Lake Huron with orders to purchase as much First Nations land as possible. Robinson negotiates the Robinson-Superior and Robinson-Huron treaties. Reserves are established in the treaty areas.

1854 Robinson tells First Nations leaders from the Saugeen Peninsula that the government cannot protect their people from settlers moving into the area. First Nations there feel pressured into giving up their land and signing the Robinson-Huron treaty.

After Reading

1. What do you predict will happen to First Nations cultures if Captain Anderson's plan is put into effect? As a class, discuss current issues that give you evidence to support your predictions.
2. In your journal, explain why the government may have a difficult time trying to balance First Nations rights with miners' and settlers' interests.

Compress

1. The statements of opinion that follow were raised by the readings in this chapter:
   - North America was a land of opportunity for European immigrants.
   - It is better to live in a city today than in a city in the 1840s.
   - Canadian governments of the 1840s and 1850s treated First Nations unfairly.
   - Discrimination towards various groups was greater in the past than today.
   - Women lived more difficult lives in the 1840s than today.

   Copy and complete the following graphic organizer to develop your point of view on one of the opinions:

Topic: *(Write the opinion you are working on.)*	
Strongest Reason	*(Example or fact to support your reason)*
Second Reason	*(Example or fact to support your reason)*
Third Reason	*(Example or fact to support your reason)*
Other people might argue...	**I say...**

   You can agree or disagree with the opinion.

   Write a supported opinion paragraph using the information from your graphic organizer.

Express

2. Prepare a time capsule for the period 1830 to 1850. The purpose of the time capsule is to show people from the future that this was a period of conflict and change for people in British North America.
   a) Write a journal entry for someone living at this time. The person can be real or fictitious. Include the name of the person, something significant about his or her background, and a short entry of three or four sentences to show how life is changing for this person.
   b) Draw a picture of an event or situation that shows a major conflict or change during that period. If you do not wish to draw, write a detailed description of what would be in your picture. Explain why you have included this particular drawing.
   c) Write a summary of a primary source from this chapter that you think is key to understanding the period. Explain why this reading shows conflict or change during this period of history.
   d) Create one other item of your choice. You might consider including a news article, letter to the editor, poem, poster, or artifact. Explain why you would put this item in the time capsule.

Their Stories, Our History

Many current issues deal with treaties signed in the nineteenth century. Research what happened to Dudley George in September 1995 at Ipperwash, Ontario.

Why was Dudley George at Ipperwash at that time? How might a different treaty have prevented George's death? Write a news article about this story.

Dudley George's brother joins a demonstration about Ipperwash.

chapter 9

Economic and Political Change to 1856

- What kind of traffic is shown using the Rideau Canal in this painting?
- What kind of traffic do you think uses the canal today?

Entrance of the Rideau Canal, Bytown, Upper Canada, by Henry Francis Ainslie, 1839. The Rideau Canal was one of the first canals built in British North America. Here the canal is shown in 1839.

BELL'S PREMIUM "HORSE REAPER."

The above is a representation of one of the most useful of modern inventions. In this country, where labour is, and for some time must continue dear, labour-saving machines are objects of great importance to the Agriculturist. There is no period of the year when the farmer is more harrassed and put about for want of help than the time of harvest. Everybody just then requires an unusual number of hands, and the demand becomes immediately greater than the supply. The highest prices must be paid for inferior workmen, and the work is either done badly, or not done at the proper time. Loss is thus sustained, sometimes of considerable amount. Now, if a machine could be made, which with the complement of hands already on the spot would reap 15 or 20 acres in a day, two or three farmers, by joining together in its purchase, would probably save the price (if not too high) in one year, besides getting rid of much anxiety and annoyance. The machine made by Mr. Bell is, in our opinion, just the thing that is wanted. The principle has been fully tested in Canada, we believe, as well as the United States, and has been found to work well.

This advertisement promotes a horse-drawn reaper, to be used when harvesting wheat. Before this period in history, such work would have been done completely by hand. Machines revolutionized farming in the nineteenth century.

- How does this advertisement show the relationship between old technology and new technology in the mid-nineteenth century?
- What would be considered new technology today? How is this technology changing the way people live and work?

The issues that erupted into violence during the Rebellions of 1837 were not resolved through the Act of Union. However, the Act of Union made new political action possible. Political leaders from Canada East and West now worked together to achieve responsible government.

In the meantime, the population grew and the economy expanded. Roads, canals, and railroads were built. Trade goods moved more efficiently and the economy grew.

Better transportation also helped immigrants access more land. Settlements spread to new areas. Many small towns of the 1820s became cities.

Most people saw their old ways of life challenged and changed. Some people did not welcome change. They wanted their lives to stay the same. Others saw these challenges as opportunities. They welcomed change with a sense of **optimism**, which is a positive feeling about the future. These people saw new technology as a way to achieve a better life.

These decades also saw a shift in Britain's relationship with its empire. Britain's economic success no longer depended on its colonies. Britain began to give its colonies more independence. The shift encouraged British North America to develop new trading relationships, especially with the United States.

The growing economic independence was also reflected politically. In 1849, Canadians finally achieved responsible government. It was the end of a long struggle that had begun in the 1820s. Political leaders, such as Louis-Hippolyte LaFontaine, Robert Baldwin, and Joseph Howe, welcomed the new era of government.

This chapter will help you understand

- how responsible government was finally achieved in British North America
- how transportation affected the economy
- the history of Toronto's growth
- how French-English relations in the 1850s evolved
- how and why British North America developed stronger economic ties with the United States
- economic issues facing British North America in the mid-nineteenth century

Featured Skill

- Preparing an Independent Research/Inquiry Project

An Interview with Louis-Hippolyte LaFontaine

Before Reading

1. Nationalism is an attachment to and sense of identification with a country or people. The attachment can be mild or it can be intense and emotional. With a partner, recall how nationalism fueled the Rebellions of 1837. How did nationalism affect French responses to the Act of Union? Review pages 202–206 and 218–220 if you want to refresh your memory. Do you think these were mild or intense forms of nationalism? What evidence do you have for your answer?

In the years following the Act of Union in 1841, Louis-Hippolyte LaFontaine faced much anger from other French Canadians. Many saw LaFontaine's wish to work with English Canadians as a rejection of his French roots.

The following fictional interview brings Louis-Hippolyte LaFontaine to the present to answer some of the questions he faced during his time as leader. Although the interview is fiction, what he says is historically accurate.

During Reading

1. As you read, watch for LaFontaine's arguments against nationalism. Paraphrase his opinion in your notes. Do you agree? Why or why not?

Interviewer: Welcome, Monsieur LaFontaine. I'm glad you could talk to us today.

LaFontaine: Thank you. It's certainly interesting to be in twenty-first-century Canada.

Interviewer: Our most pressing question is one that I'm sure you faced many times in the 1840s: Did you not, like most Canadiens of that time, see Lord Durham's statements about your people as an insult and attack?

LaFontaine: Of course! Not only was Durham's report outrageous, but the way the British government responded—the Act of Union—clearly intended to make that attack succeed.

Interviewer: How?

LaFontaine: There were several fronts to this new war against the French. First, you'll recall that the new capital was to be Kingston, in English-speaking Canada West. This was a clear strategy to ensure the power of the government was on the English-speaking side of the province.

Second, they attacked our economy. The Act of Union combined our government's debt with that of Upper Canada, even though our debt was less than one tenth of theirs!

Third, the first lieutenant-governor, Lord Sydenham, tried to make English the only language of debate in the new government.

And if all that wasn't enough, Sydenham also threatened our education and religion. It's no wonder Canada East exploded in anger from one end to the other.

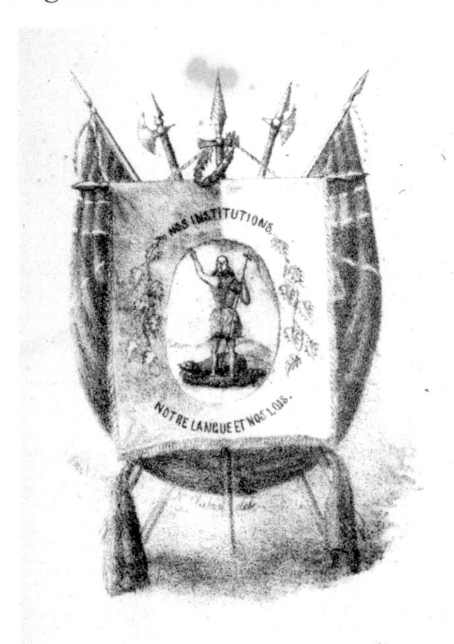

The St. Jean Baptiste (sehn-t zhawn ba-tees-te) Society was founded on June 24, 1842. Its mission is to protect French-Canadian institutions, language, and laws. Today, June 24 is a provincial holiday in Québec celebrating the saint, French culture, and Québec patriots.

Interviewer: So you agree that this situation was an attack on your people. Yet you, almost alone among Canadien leaders, accepted the Act of Union. Why?

LaFontaine: I'm pleased you say "almost alone," because I had some excellent company in Étienne Parent (ay-tee-n pa-rawn). He was editor of *Le Canadien*, the newspaper that had been defending our rights since 1800. I took my stand because I thought the alternatives could lead us to an even worse disaster.

Interviewer: Would you explain?

LaFontaine: Many leaders wanted to boycott the entire Assembly. Others wanted to make it unworkable. You see, Canada East and West had the same number of votes. If all representatives from Canada East voted the same way, we had power. The government would have trouble passing any laws without our cooperation.

Interviewer: Why did you disagree with this approach?

LaFontaine: I thought it would anger the British and turn them against us. Even worse, it might alienate the English-speaking Canadians who were sympathetic to our rights. We would lose all hope of making allies in the Assembly.

I was also afraid of what it would do to us as a nation. I disliked a constant focus on our interests as French-speaking people. It sends a message that nothing is more important than our cultural identity. I was afraid it would turn everything into an emotional "us versus them" situation. It might lead people to believe that only *our* ways, *our* customs, *our* way of thinking are "good." Everybody else's ways and ideas would become "bad."

Even one of our own who dared suggest that some "foreign" idea could help us might be treated as a traitor. Is this the kind of freedom we wanted?

Interviewer: I know you didn't have an easy time of it. It must have been difficult to keep to your plan when so many people around you were so angry. To many, it looked like you were a traitor.

LaFontaine: I did not, as some people claim, "accept" what was being proposed. I just chose to work on change from within the system. I think my goals were the same as those of my critics. I just chose a different path.

For example, when I joined the Assembly, I ignored the rule against speaking French. I just spoke in the Assembly using my mother tongue and made them scramble to understand me. I eventually forced the government to change its law. In my case, resistance and persistence worked better than rebellion.

Interviewer: Why did you think your approach would work?

LaFontaine: Like Étienne Parent, I thought we could make the Act of Union work for us in spite of what it was intended to do.

What we had to do was find people in Canada West who wanted local self-government—what you call responsible government—as much as we did. So that's what we did. We made an alliance with Canada West leaders Robert Baldwin and Francis Hincks. Our alliance was strong. It helped us withstand many setbacks. For example, after one election, I lost my seat in Canada East. This proves how unpopular my views were at this time. Baldwin then convinced people in Canada West to elect me so we could continue our work.

The key to our success was that we worked together—all for one and one for all. Today, I believe you call this **party discipline**. It meant we stuck together. If the lieutenant-governor invited one or two of us to join the Executive Council, we refused. He hoped this offer would satisfy us. We feared that agreeing would divide us. We held out until we gained our prize.

James Bruce, the Earl of Elgin was governor general of Canada from 1847 to 1854. He was the first governor general to believe responsible government was the best way to solve political tension in the colonies.

Interviewer: We know today that you were eventually successful. Can you explain how you did it?

LaFontaine: Through the 1840s, our Reform Party won more and more support from the voters. In 1848, we won a clear majority of seats in the Legislative Assembly.

We insisted that our party's majority in the Assembly gave us the right to fill all the seats in the Executive Council. The confidence of the voters gave us this right.

We would govern in the name of the people of the Canadas. If another party won a majority of seats, then we would resign and they would govern. That's what responsible government meant. The voters would ultimately decide who would form the government.

In 1848, Governor General Elgin at last agreed. He asked me to form the government. For the first time, elected members of the Assembly filled the Executive Council.

Yes, it was a long, hard, and, at times, dangerous struggle. I was shouted down when I tried to explain my stand at public meetings. Fights often broke out. Even church leaders opposed me. I had to convince my people that my positive approach was best. It took years.

At times, convincing the British government to give us control of our own affairs seemed almost impossible. When they finally agreed to responsible government, the British had their own agenda.

Government Structure with Responsible Government

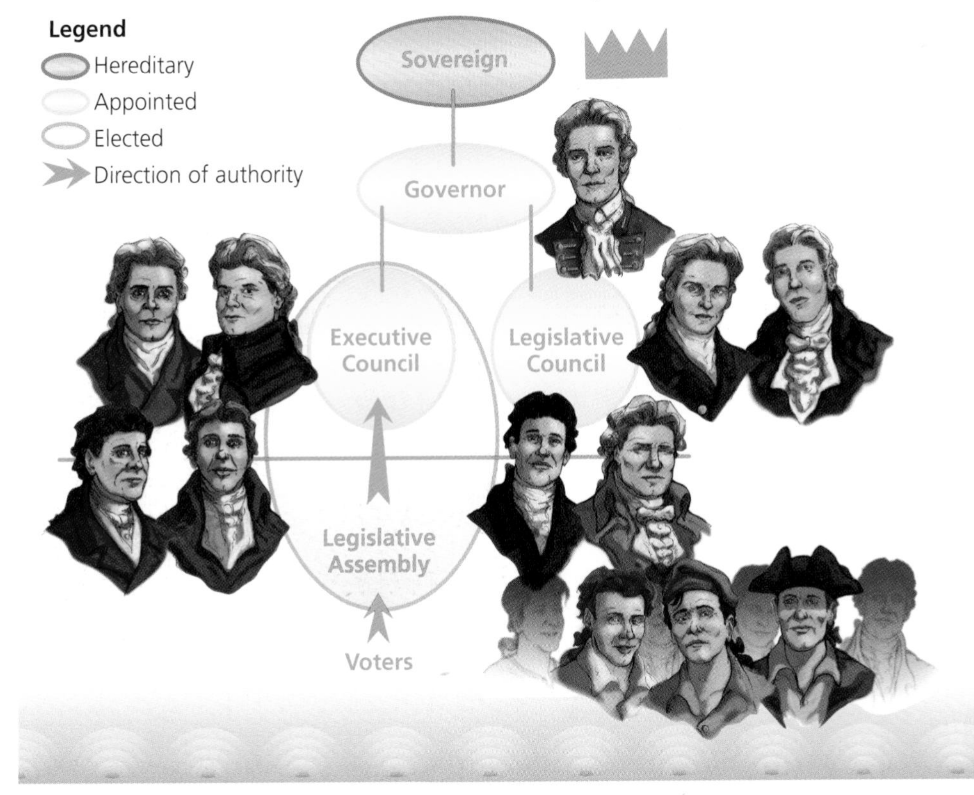

Interviewer: What do you mean?

LaFontaine: First, let me say there is no doubt in my mind that the moderate approach we took was why we succeeded where others failed. We worked within the British system and made the British comfortable enough to give us control of local matters. In their minds, rebellion just confirmed that we weren't ready to control the government.

By the late 1840s, however, giving us more control also suited Britain. By that time, Britain had adopted a policy of free trade. This meant every country could trade its goods in Britain without paying an extra tax. Before this, only British colonies were not taxed. This had given the colonies a trading advantage for many years.

Britain's colonies were no longer as essential to its economy. Once this happened, was there still a need to control the colonies politically? By 1848, the answer was no. Agreeing to responsible government was one result.

Interviewer: Your leadership and the principle of responsible government were tested almost immediately.

LaFontaine: You're referring to the Rebellion Losses Bill of 1849. My government was able to pass a bill that would repay innocent people in Canada East who suffered losses during the Rebellions of 1837. The bill was similar to one passed in Canada West in 1845. Payment would be made to people whose homes had been burned or looted by British troops.

Interviewer: Not everyone looked at this bill the same way you did.

LaFontaine: That's for sure. Many English Tories opposed it. They viewed the bill as rewarding traitors. In their minds, if you were French-speaking, you could not be the innocent victim of a British army out of control.

Interviewer: The Tories certainly pressured Governor General Elgin to defeat the bill. Although the Assembly had passed it, the bill needed his signature to become law. If he had refused, responsible government would have been defeated as well. His refusal would have meant Britain was not willing to give control of colony decisions to elected officials.

Were you surprised at Elgin's decision to sign the bill?

LaFontaine: I knew Elgin disagreed with the bill personally, so there were no guarantees. However, he ultimately upheld the right of the elected Assembly to make law in the colony. Britain stepped back from directly controlling our government.

Interviewer: Did you expect the violence that occurred after he signed the bill?

LaFontaine: I expected a demonstration of some kind, but not the level of violence that occurred. Some 1500 Tories stormed the Assembly buildings, destroying symbols of responsible government. My home and those of other reform leaders were attacked and looted. Even Elgin's carriage was pelted with rocks and rotten eggs!

Burning the Houses of Assembly in Montréal was an act of criminals. The crowd even prevented the fire department from putting out the fire by cutting their hoses.

And why? Because we wanted a form of government that would benefit all people in Canada East and West.

Lord Elgin and Staff Leaving Government House for Parliament, April 1849, Francis Augustus Grant (1829–1854).

Interviewer: What can be learned from this episode in our history?

LaFontaine: To me, I think it shows that violence is not the answer. It had not worked for the radicals in 1837 and it did not work for the Tories in 1849. Working together in a spirit of compromise was the path to success.

Interviewer: I believe many people today believe your cooperation was a model for successful government in this country. Thank you.

This statue of Robert Baldwin and Sir Louis-Hippolyte LaFontaine stands outside the Parliament Buildings in Ottawa.

After Reading

1. With your partner, explain what *responsible government* means in your own words.
2. Discuss as a class how the Rebellion Losses Bill was significant to responsible government.

Responsible Government in the Maritimes

Before Reading

1. Upper and Lower Canada fought a rebellion over the right to responsible government. Yet Nova Scotia had responsible government first, just months before the Province of Canada. Predict why Britain gave Nova Scotia responsible government peacefully. Discuss your answer with a partner.

Mackenzie and Papineau had their methods of achieving responsible government for Upper and Lower Canada. In Nova Scotia, a young newspaperman used a different approach. Joseph Howe has been called the "Father of Responsible Government" in Nova Scotia.

At that time, Nova Scotia was one of British North America's most thriving colonies. It had a busy international harbour, Halifax. It also had a strong economy based on fishing, lumber, and steam shipping. As in Upper and Lower Canada, the government was controlled by an elite group of business people.

Joseph Howe's father, John, had been a Loyalist. He passed on his love of Britain and British institutions to his son.

- How do you think Howe's Loyalist upbringing might influence his approach to political change? Would he be more or less inclined to use violence?

During Reading

1. Like Robert Baldwin, Howe has been called a *moderate reformer.* As you read pages 258–259, work with a partner to decide whether his actions and words justify the use of this term. Why or why not?

The Career of Joseph Howe

1827 Howe buys a Halifax newspaper and renames it the *Novascotian.* He begins to publish accurate transcripts of all Assembly debates.

1830 Howe uses the *Novascotian* to attack the colony's Family Compact. He accuses them of serving themselves and of being too secretive about their business interests.

PRIMARY SOURCE 9.1

From a Letter Signed The People, Published in the Novascotian, January 1, 1835

From the pockets of the poor and distressed at least £1000 is drawn annually, and pocketed by men whose services the country might well spare [do without].... During the lapse of the last thirty years, the Magistracy [judges] and Police have, by one stratagem [plan] or other, taken from the pockets of the people, in over exactions [taxes], fines etc. etc., a sum that would exceed in the gross amount of £30,000.

1835 Howe is sued for **libel**, which is the act of publishing false statements that damage a person or group's reputation. He is threatened with having his newspaper shut down. Howe is acquitted and becomes a hero of the people.

Joseph Howe after a Halifax Triumph, by C. W. Jefferys (1869–1951). Howe had defended himself in his libel case in a six-hour speech to the jury before celebrating his acquittal.

1835–1839 Howe continues to demand reform to government. He argues, "we seek for nothing more than British subjects are entitled to, but we will be contented with nothing less."

PRIMARY SOURCE 9.2

From Writing by Joseph Howe, 1835–1837

I have been called the Papineau of Nova Scotia, ...and a connection is attempted to be shown between the Reformers of this Province, and the agitators of Canada. It has been said that we have been holding treasonable correspondence with traitors in Canada.... [On the contrary] in these matters, my feeling has ever been...keep the peace, never break it, use the means within the law and the Constitution,—and these, after patient perseverance [persistance], will procure [obtain or get] every needful reformation [change].

1837–1838 Howe condemns the rebellions in Upper and Lower Canada.

1839–1840 Howe supports Lord Durham's recommendations for more responsible Executive and Legislative Councils.

1841 Howe is criticized by his own supporters for joining a **non-partisan** Executive Council. This meant the council included both reformers and conservatives and was not dominated by either group. Howe hoped he could achieve the changes he wanted from within the executive.

1843 Howe resigns from the Executive Council after seeing that no changes were being made. He focuses on building a strong political party of reformers.

1847–1848 The Reform Party, led by Howe and James Boyle Uniacke, a former conservative, win a majority of seats in the Assembly. Howe boasts that they did it without "a blow struck or a pane of glass broken." Uniacke becomes the first premier and Howe the provincial secretary. It is the first responsible government in British North America.

After Reading

1. William Lyon Mackenzie and Joseph Howe were newspaper editors before they became politicians. Why might their jobs at their papers have led them to a second career as politicians?
2. In your journal, describe a television personality or writer you think would appeal to voters today if he or she decided to run for political office. Would this person be a good choice as political leader? Why?

A Night to Remember

Before Reading

1. This story takes place at the end of the 1840s, just after Robert Baldwin and Louis-Hippolyte LaFontaine had achieved their goal of responsible government. As a class, discuss which group or groups in Canada East may not have been pleased about responsible government. Explain why. Would the situation in Canada West be the same? Why or why not? Discuss as a class.

Preferred customer is a common phrase today. The management of a store or business will often give regular customers this status. It usually means the customers get a discount off the regular price. They get a special deal in return for their business.

At the beginning of the 1800s, British North America had a kind of "preferred customer" status in Britain. All British colonies received a special deal when they sold their goods in the mother country. This special status was called **imperial preference**. Countries not in the British Empire, such as the United States, did not receive this deal.

In the following story, which takes place in 1849 in Montréal, one of the main characters, William Price, is a wealthy business person. His business depends on selling goods in the British market.

In the story, Price is angry because Britain has decided to end the colonies' preferred status. This means Price, along with other colonial merchants, will lose their special deal. They will be forced to compete with stronger, wealthier American merchants on what is often called today a *level playing field*. It means no countries have a special advantage.

The characters in the story are fictional, but the historical events described are real.

It was going to be a wonderful night, Henri (awn-ree) thought as he left work for home. It was a night he would remember for the rest of his life.

What he didn't know—what he couldn't know—was that it would indeed be such a night, but not for the reasons that filled his head and heart. As he hurried along the crowded street that fateful Montréal evening, April 25th, 1849, all Henri could think about was his daring plan.

Henri Couture (koo-tur) was twenty-five and a proud Canadien. The older of the two Couture brothers, he had trained in the law, as had his father, Guillaume (gee-yome). His brother, Gilles (zh-il), had chosen journalism and was a reporter for *Le Canadien,* edited by the influential Étienne Parent.

The paper had stood by Louis-Hippolyte LaFontaine through the rocky years since the union of the Canadas. Henri's brother was passionate about the need for responsible government. Gilles defended LaFontaine with enthusiasm and would argue his cause to anyone who would listen. Since LaFontaine became prime minister last year, the brothers had speculated what it might mean. Had LaFontaine achieved his goal?

Henri's mother, Jeanne, doted on both her sons. She thought they were brilliant and was sure there was no limit to what they could accomplish. But they were French. Even though they were completely fluent in English, this was Canada East. *Les Anglais*—the English-speakers accounting for about 20 per cent of the population—ran the province. They always had. They were sure they always would.

How far could a young Canadien go in this world? His father had found out. He had made a good life for his family, but what did Papineau say? *The English get not only all the bread, but all the butter and jam as well. Les Canadiens, all we get are the crumbs!*

But that world, Henri's world, had been turned upside down today. Just after three o'clock, he had been summoned to Government House. Monsieur LaFontaine's principal secretary wanted to see him immediately. After the two-hour meeting, Henri had left the building in a daze. He couldn't even remember how he got back to his office. All he could think was that now, after three years of hoping, worrying, praying, but never really believing, maybe the beautiful Stephanie Elizabeth Price could be his wife.

During Reading

1. What history have you learned from the story so far? In your notebook, list at least three parts of the story that you believe are based on historical fact.

Now, as Henri dressed for a meeting that he hoped would see his dream fulfilled, his mind slipped over his pursuit of the impossible.

He had met Stephanie at a music recital three years ago. Not only was she *une Anglaise* (oon awn-gleh-ze), but she was the only daughter of William Price, one of the richest, most powerful English merchants in Canada East. Price was probably the best symbol of everything that Papineau had fought against in the rebellion.

Gilles had argued long and hard that Henri was out of his mind to think that he could win Price's permission to court his daughter. Price and his clique had only contempt for the likes of Henri Couture. Their attitudes went back generations, and the rebellion had only hardened their feelings.

The rebels had been passionate, but unprepared to take on the British army. The rebellion had been a disaster. Worse, it prompted Durham's report and the Act of Union. Both seemed designed to wipe the French from the face of Canada East.

But the French were not about to disappear. Far from wiping out French culture, Durham's report had caused a surge of cultural pride. Throughout the 1840s, there was an outpouring of books and poetry across Canada East. Literary clubs that promoted reading, writing, and discussion sprang up everywhere.

His people's determination to thrive mirrored Henri's own determination to win Stephanie's hand. He smiled to himself as he thought of how hard he had worked. After their first introduction, he had found as many ways as possible to be where she would be. Slowly, he had built the acquaintance into a friendship. Gradually, the friendship had grown into something more.

He had found himself relaxing in her company. Fluent in French, she had a wide range of interests. They discussed everything from life in Canada East to slavery in the United States and the latest news from Europe. Henri wanted to make this relationship permanent and he knew Stephanie felt the same.

Her father, of course, was a different story—a *very* different story. William Price may not have shared all of the prejudices of the English against the French, but Stephanie was his only child. Anything beyond an acquaintance with someone like Henri was…well, it was unthinkable.

But Henri had refused to quit. He was proudly French. In his mind, his people were survivors. They had overcome many British efforts at turning Canadiens into Englishmen since 1760. Henri was determined to be a survivor too.

After this afternoon, Henri felt it was time to test his dream. Stephanie said her father would be in that night and would be expecting his call. Would Price be ready to put aside his reservations? Perhaps. After this afternoon, at least Henri had something to offer.

As he carefully inserted the studs into the cuffs of his new shirt, he recalled his meeting with the principal secretary. He, Henri Couture, just two generations removed from the farm at St. Lin, was about to become the chief prosecutor in the Office of the Attorney General of the Province of Canada! At his age, it was unheard of. Never mind that! For his people, it was unheard of—at any age.

And it was all because of Louis-Hippolyte LaFontaine. For years LaFontaine had promised that something like this would be possible. He had been screamed at, dismissed, and attacked, even by his own people. Even Papineau, one LaFontaine's friends, had turned on him.

But LaFontaine had persevered. He and his English colleague, Robert Baldwin, had slowly won over most of the people, French and English, in both parts of Canada. And they had won! This afternoon had been, for Henri, the final proof of what LaFontaine had long promised. With power would come all that rebellion had not been able to achieve: Access to power. Jobs. Opportunities. Appointments for people like Henri Couture.

• • •

Henri was not the only one affected by the events of the afternoon. To the English elite of Montréal—people like William Price—the afternoon had been positively infuriating.

For Price, it was the last straw. As Price paced back and forth in his Westmount home, he realized that this disaster had been in the making for many years.

His import-export business had been carefully built on one foundation: imperial preference. Imperial preference meant the British gave their colonies better access to their own market, which was the most valuable in the world. It meant companies like Price's paid a lower tax when they imported their goods to Britain. Outsiders, such as the Americans, had to pay more taxes and therefore charge higher prices for their goods. Imperial preference guaranteed Price could compete against wealthier American companies.

Over the years, imperial preference had been gradually stripped away. The British government now believed the preference was no longer necessary. British manufacturers produced more of everything at the best price. No one could compete against them. If Britain adopted free trade, it could argue that other countries should do the same. Britain would have access to the world. The markets for its goods would multiply again and again.

During Reading

1. Before continuing, write definitions for *free trade* and *imperial preference* in your notebook. Note any questions you have about the terms for discussion at the end of the class.

Fine for them, fumed Price, but what about us? We've played by all the rules. We've spent millions building canals along the St. Lawrence River. This improved the movement of goods and lowered shipping costs. And we've done it in spite of wild-eyed radicals like Papineau. And this is our reward—betrayal.

Burning of the Houses of Assembly at Montréal, around 1849.

His thoughts raced to the events of the afternoon. Now the betrayal was not just economic. It was political, too. The British had given up control of local politics. Here, in Canada East, that meant the French ruled the government. And this afternoon, Governor General Elgin had added insult to injury. He had signed the Rebellion Losses Bill into law. Price was furious. This was proof of the chaos that would result from French control over the government.

The Rebellion Losses Bill was a joke. It would pay people for damages they received in the Rebellions of 1837. In effect, it could end up paying rebels for damages they had caused! It would pay rebels for treason! The Montréal *Courier* had it right: "let the Governor sanction it if he pleases, but while there is an axe and rifle on the frontier and Saxon [English] hands to wield them these claims will not be paid."

• • •

"Henri! Henri! Have you heard?" Gilles was shouting from the entry to their home. Henri heard the door slam and Gilles's feet pounding up the stairs.

"The Houses of Assembly are burning! An English mob attacked the governor's carriage and then set the Houses of Assembly on fire! Can you believe it?"

A cloud crossed Henri's mind. But he set it aside. After calming Gilles, he set out for the Price home to fulfill his dream.

A Night to Remember *continues on page 278.*

After Reading

1. What do you think happens when Henri arrives at the Price household? Discuss this as a class.
2. From Henri's point of view, what was the real importance of LaFontaine becoming prime minister?
3. Why did William Price think his business interests were threatened?

Transportation and Colonial Life

Before Reading

1. In the 1830s, people across Canada West pressured the government to improve roads and canals. Both were expensive investments. Whose priority would roads be? Who would want canals? Explain your reasoning in a small group discussion.
2. If you were a government representative, which would be your priority? Why?

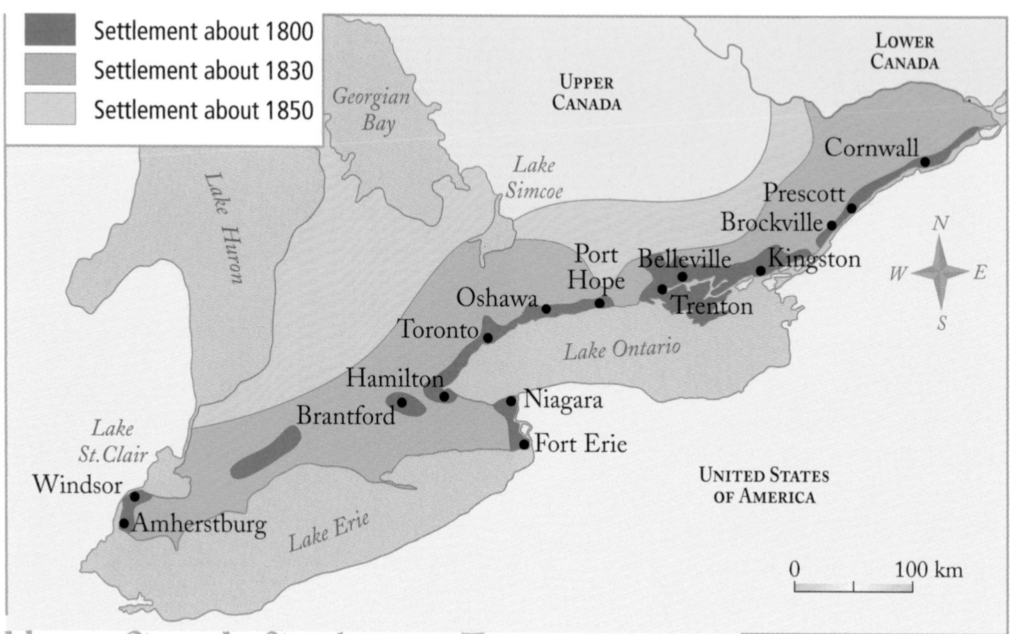

Upper Canada Settlement Area, 1800–1850

Despite the conflict over the Rebellion Losses Bill in 1849, the period following the Rebellions of 1837 was generally one of political stability. British North America became an increasingly attractive place for immigrants.

In 1790, approximately 10 000 settlers lived in what was about to become Upper Canada. By 1851, the population of Canada West was 952 000. In just over sixty years, the population had increased by over 95 per cent.

Such rapid growth meant the colony had growing pains. Transportation was one of the most significant. The colony had to be able to move people and goods between farms in the outlying areas and the cities and ports.

Early settlers had adopted First Nations methods of moving through the heavily forested country. In the summer, people travelled by canoes. In the winter, they travelled along frozen streams and rivers. The first settlements were almost all on rivers and lakeshores. People wanted and needed to live close to the only practical way of moving from place to place in the colony.

The Ice Pont [Bridge] Formed between Québec and Point Levi, by L. Stewart. Improving roads through Canada West took a long time. Early settlers did much of their travelling in winter, when the ground was frozen and sleighs drove smoothly over the snow and ice.

However, as the population grew, people wanted faster, more convenient methods of travel. Farmers had produce they wanted to take to the cities to sell. Merchants had goods they wanted to sell to farmers in remote areas. Canoes were no longer enough. Everywhere there were cries for better transportation.

During Reading

1. Although roads are one of the most common forms of transportation today, they were not common in early nineteenth-century Canada. Roads were the last form of transportation to be improved in the colonies, after canals and railroads. Why do you think this was the case? Discuss in a small group.

Roads

In 1734, a person could travel by road from Québec to Montréal. The journey of 267 kilometres took almost five days.

Most roads were short paths used for local traffic, such as a farmer's movements from his home to the nearest river or lakeshore. Settlers often had homemade vehicles, with wheels made from the trunks of oak trees. Riding these vehicles on roads that were little more than muddy paths was very uncomfortable. It meant most people chose other ways of getting around the colony.

Road between Kingston and York, Upper Canada, by James Pattison Cockburn, around 1830. Travelling by cart or wagon was so uncomfortable that many people preferred to walk.

The Royal Mail, by C. W. Jefferys (1869–1951).

- How would the condition of these roads affect the economy?

In 1793, people called pathmasters were put in charge of road construction. Pathmasters could require settlers to work up to twelve days per year building roads. Roads that had military importance were the highest priorities. For example, people who received a lot along Yonge Street had to build a road along the front of their property in return.

As roads improved in the first half of the nineteenth century, the stagecoach became more common. Coaches offered regular transportation along some major routes in British North America. As road traffic increased, **tolls** appeared. Toll are fees that pay for road improvements. They are charged to people using the road. On some roads, even people travelling by foot had to pay a toll.

Bilking [Cheating] the Toll, by Cornelius Krieghoff (1815–1872).

- Look closely at the action in the painting. What is happening?
- Based on what you see, how do you think some settlers felt about toll roads?

Most early roads were simply cleared paths through the forest. Some had planks or corduroy, which were logs laid side by side as shown in this painting from the late nineteenth century.

During Reading

1. As you read Primary Source 9.3, consider with your group whether you think tolls would lead to having better roads sooner. Why or why not?
2. Should individual farmers have been required to build the part of the road that went past the front of their property? Why or why not? What are the hazards of making different people responsible for sections of the same road?

PRIMARY SOURCE 9·3

From the Journals of Mary O'Brien

October 24, 1828: In the present state of the roads they drive into York [from Thornhill down Yonge Street] in two hours and a half. They set out today at ten and returned by a little after seven. The distance is from fourteen to fifteen miles [24 kilometres].

March 11, 1829: After dinner rode with Anthony to my friend Mr. Miles on the concern of the Book Society. had a pleasant enough ride and the road was covered with mud four or five inches [about 13 centimetres] deep....

March 5, 1830: Then I went to old Munshaw who started from his dying pillow to tell me he had forty-three grandchildren. Then he went on to describe the state of Yonge Street when he settled here thirty-six years ago. Then there was barely a road chopped through the forest, and York contained only two stores and not a single frame house.

June 11, 1830: Edward took me round his fields and then I went to my household work while he went to superintend [supervise] the making of the road past our lot. I went afterwards to see what they were doing and found them placing logs across a swamp to make a corduroy.

January 29, 1831: Mama has just called me to the window to look at something that was passing. I do not know any road where there is so much travelling except near a very considerable [large] town in England. A hundred and twenty-five waggons passed Gordon's Tavern, twenty miles [32 kilometres] up the Street from York, in one day.

February 16, 1831: It is high time to do something on Yonge Street...[but] there is such a fear of innovation, more especially of tolls, that there are numerous petitions pouring against improvement. This fear of tolls is no great wonder, for in the States and in Lower Canada the tolls are as common as the roads are wretched.

Canals

Until the middle of the nineteenth century, most newcomers to British North America came as far as they could by steamship up the St. Lawrence River. Others landed in New York and came north along the Hudson and Mohawk Rivers.

However, the water routes had problems, such as rapids. Business owners quickly realized that canals would smooth out problem areas and could help them ship goods quickly and cheaply. Canal building boomed in the 1820s and 1830s.

People were already using the water system as the main transportation route. Canals just made the routes faster and more efficient. In 1848, the St. Lawrence River was deepened. This completed the major canal phase of Canada's transportation development.

During Reading

1. Why were the Rideau, Welland, and St. Lawrence Canals so important to the area shown by the map?
2. In 1852, if people wanted to make the 290-kilometre journey from Montréal to Kingston, what were their options? What were the costs of each option?

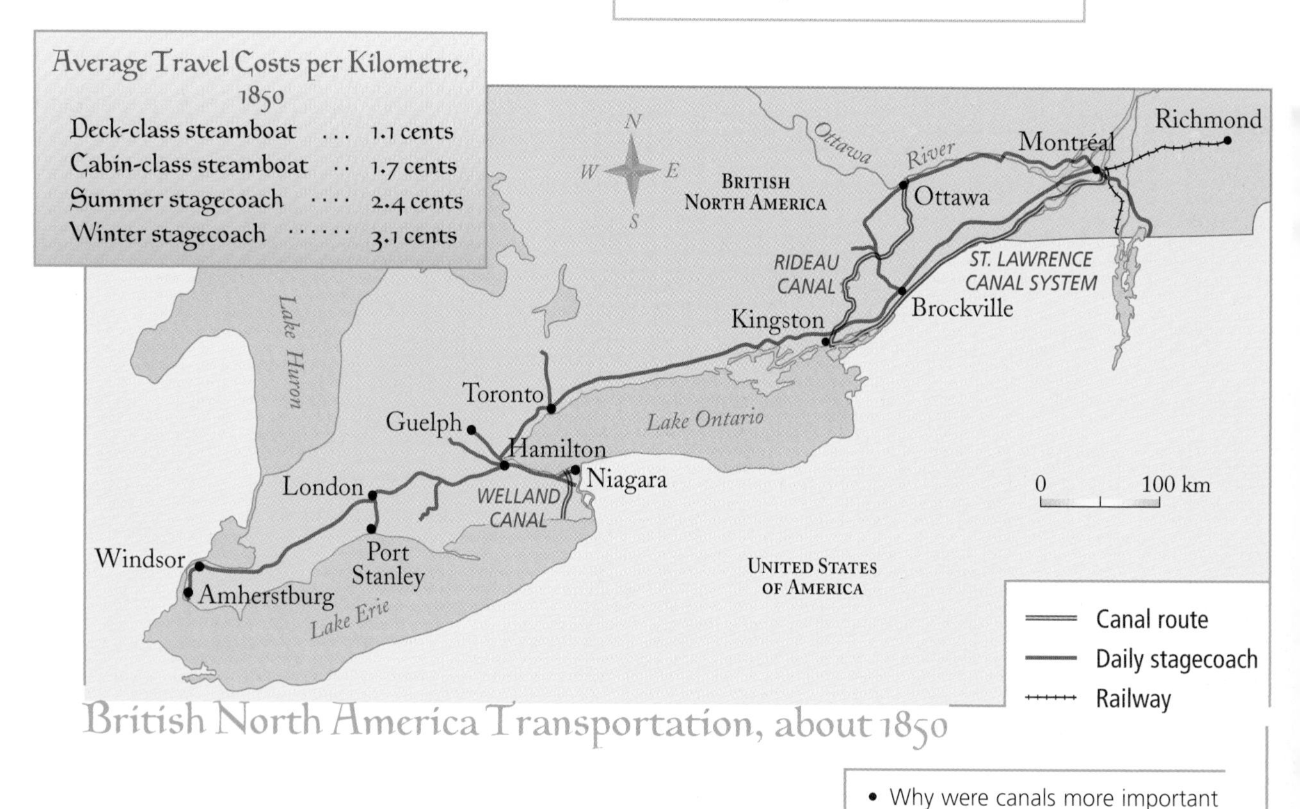

Average Travel Costs per Kilometre, 1850

Deck-class steamboat	1.1 cents
Cabin-class steamboat	1.7 cents
Summer stagecoach	2.4 cents
Winter stagecoach	3.1 cents

British North America Transportation, about 1850

- Why were canals more important than roads for improving the economy in Canada East and West in the 1830s and 1840s?

Long Sault Rapids on the St. Lawrence River, Canada West, 1849. The use of steamboats in North America peaked in 1852. On the St. Lawrence River, most steamers ran the rapids when heading downriver towards Montréal. On their way upriver, they used the canal system.

Welland Canal Cargo, 1844

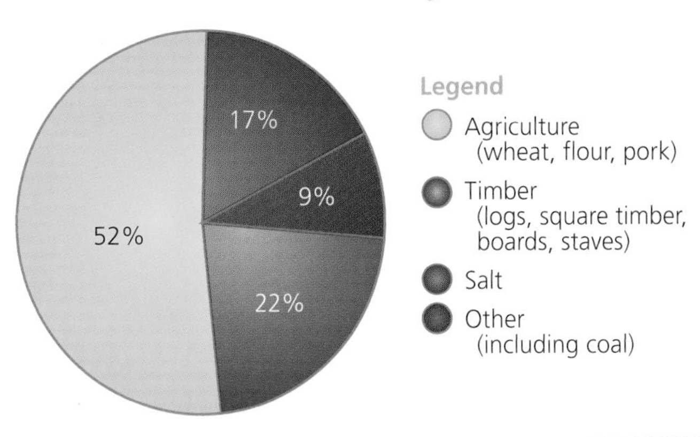

- How can this data help you make an inference about the lives of people in British North America in 1844?

Cargo Shipped through the Welland Canal

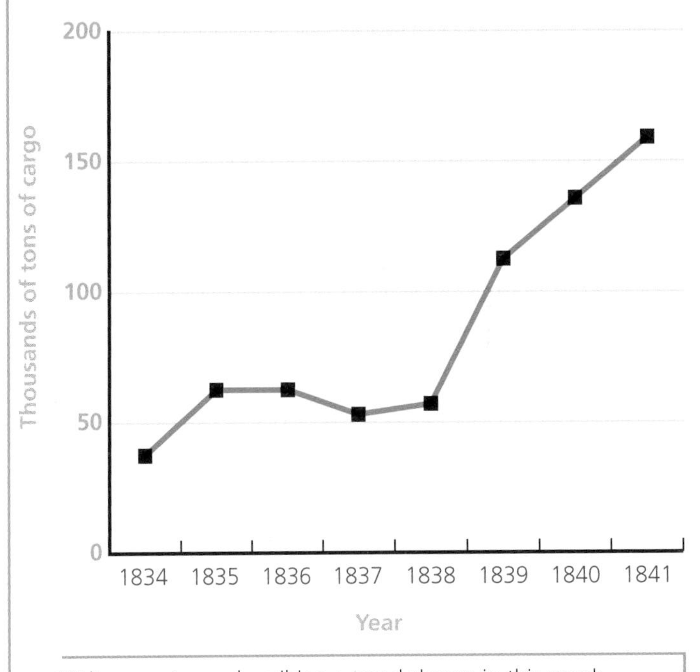

- Write a sentence describing a trend shown in this graph.

Today, the Welland Canal still plays a significant role in the movement of goods through Canada. Here, a ship enters the Welland Canal at Port Colborne.

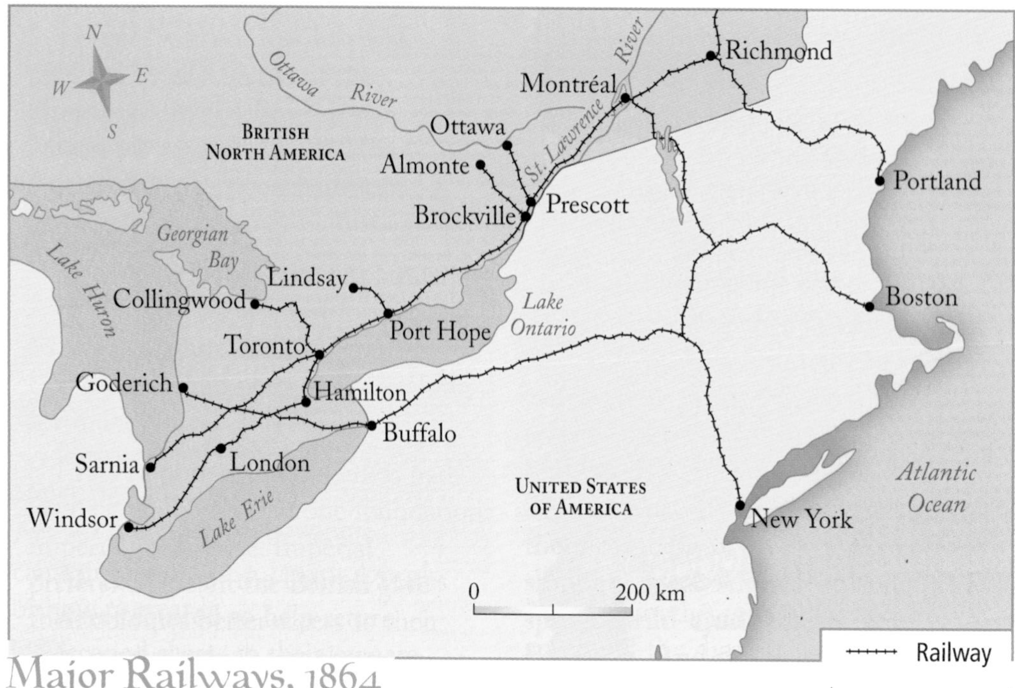

Major Railways, 1864

- In the year 1850, there were only 120 kilometres of railway track laid in all of British North America. By 1865, over 3300 kilometres had been laid. What might have caused this tremendous growth in railway construction?

Railroads

By the end of the 1840s, railways began to take over from canals. Trains were faster than steamboats. They were also more flexible. Train tracks could be built anywhere, not just along waterways. As the population grew and settled farther from rivers and lakeshores, people needed more transportation options. Railways seemed the perfect answer.

The first steam-powered railway was built in England in 1830. It began a frenzy of railway construction in that country that has been called "The Mania." The British enthusiasm for railways spilled over into North America. The rapid expansion of railways that began in the 1840s became a symbol of the era's great optimism.

Many people at this time believed that human technology could conquer the forces of nature. They believed in progress. In this sense, *progress* meant that human inventions would ensure that society would constantly improve. Each generation would live a better life than those before them.

For many people, the railway became a symbol of progress. Railway locomotives seemed to give humans the upper hand over nature. Railways solved many challenges: distance, time, weather, and physical obstacles, such as rivers and mountains. It seemed to be the key to progress.

During Reading

1. As you read Primary Source 9.4, answer the questions that follow in your notebook:
   a) What words and phrases does Keefer use to describe Canada in the winter?
   b) What does he say are the problems with steamboat and stagecoach travel in the winter? What are the benefits of rail travel?
   c) According to Keefer, how does winter affect Canada's economy?
   d) Summarize Keefer's argument in one sentence.

PRIMARY SOURCE 9·4

From The Philosophy of Railroads, by Thomas C. Keefer, Engineer, 1850

Old winter is once more upon us, and our inland seas are 'dreary [depressing] and inhospitable [unwelcoming] wastes' to the merchant and to the traveller—our rivers are sealed fountains—and an embargo [suspension of trade] which no human power can remove is laid on all our ports.... The animation [life] of business is suspended, the life blood of commerce is curdled [sour] and stagnant [still] in the St. Lawrence—the great aorta [a major artery of the heart] of the North. On land, the heavy stage [stagecoach] labours through mingled frost and mud in the West—or struggles through drifted snow, and slides with uncertain track over the icy hills of Eastern Canada.

Far away to the South [in the United States] is heard the daily scream of the steam-whistle—but from Canada there is no escape: blockaded and imprisoned by Ice and Apathy [lack of interest], we have at least ample [lots of] time for reflection.

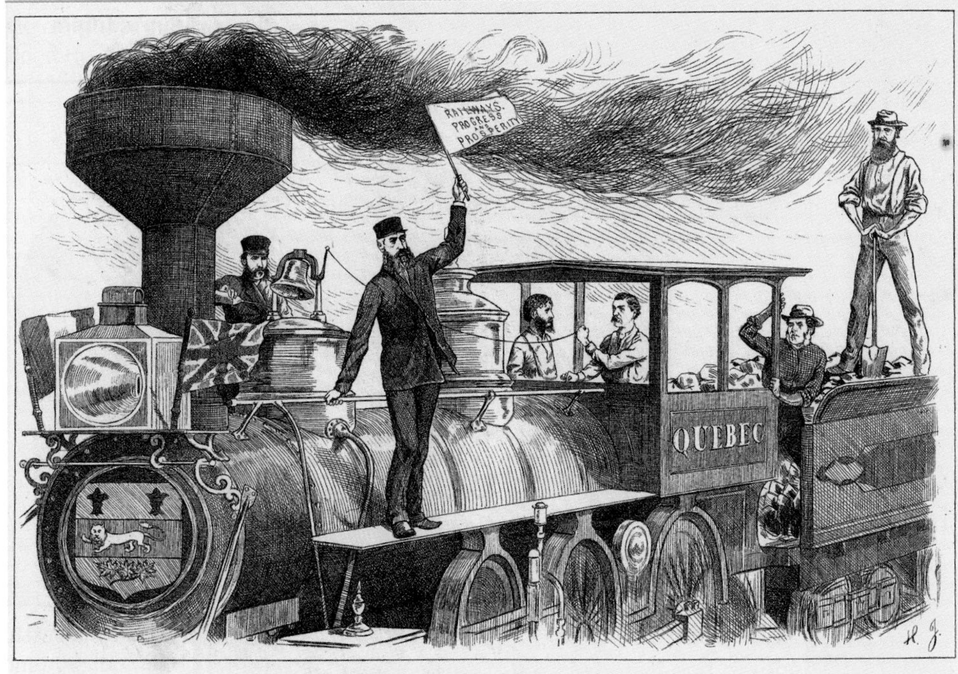

- How does this illustration show the belief in railways and progress?

The Québec Railway Policy: "All Aboard for the West!", by Henri Julien, 1875.

After Reading

1. Does Keefer believe in progress? What evidence do you have? Discuss your ideas as a class.
2. On your own, write in your journal about which form of transportation you would rather have used at this point in history and why.

An Autobiography of Toronto's Early Years

Before Reading

1. What makes a town or city important?
2. What would your town or city need in order to grow? In your opinion, would growth be good or bad? Discuss as a class.

If you could go back in time to 1800, you would see few people in what is now southern Ontario, but you would see lots of trees, trees, and more trees.

By 1850, you might recognize the outline of modern Ontario. There was settlement from Windsor to the Québec border and from the north shores of Lake Erie and Lake Ontario to Georgian Bay and Lake Simcoe. Many of the towns you know today had been founded and were busily growing. Improved transportation stretched the limits of settlement each year.

The story of how this growth took place can help you better understand what is happening in Ontario's cities, towns, and villages today.

During Reading

1. The following story is what the city of Toronto might tell of its own beginnings and early life. As you read, keep a list of the factors that influenced its growth.

A Tale of a City

Getting off to a good start is as important to a future city as it is to a person. I got off to a good start because of my location. I'm on the shore of Lake Ontario, one of a great chain of lakes that reaches west into the North American continent. I also have an excellent natural harbour. Other places along the lake, such as Hamilton, think they have a better harbour. But my location was always a top choice.

Although my founders didn't know it at the time, I was at the head of a long-established First Nations trading route. For generations, First Nations had used the rivers that run through me—the Humber and the Don—to travel to Georgian Bay and what the First Nations called the Upper Lakes (especially Lake Huron and Lake Superior).

This colour engraving shows the Toronto harbour in 1793, around the time that Lieutenant-Governor Simcoe and his family arrived to establish York.

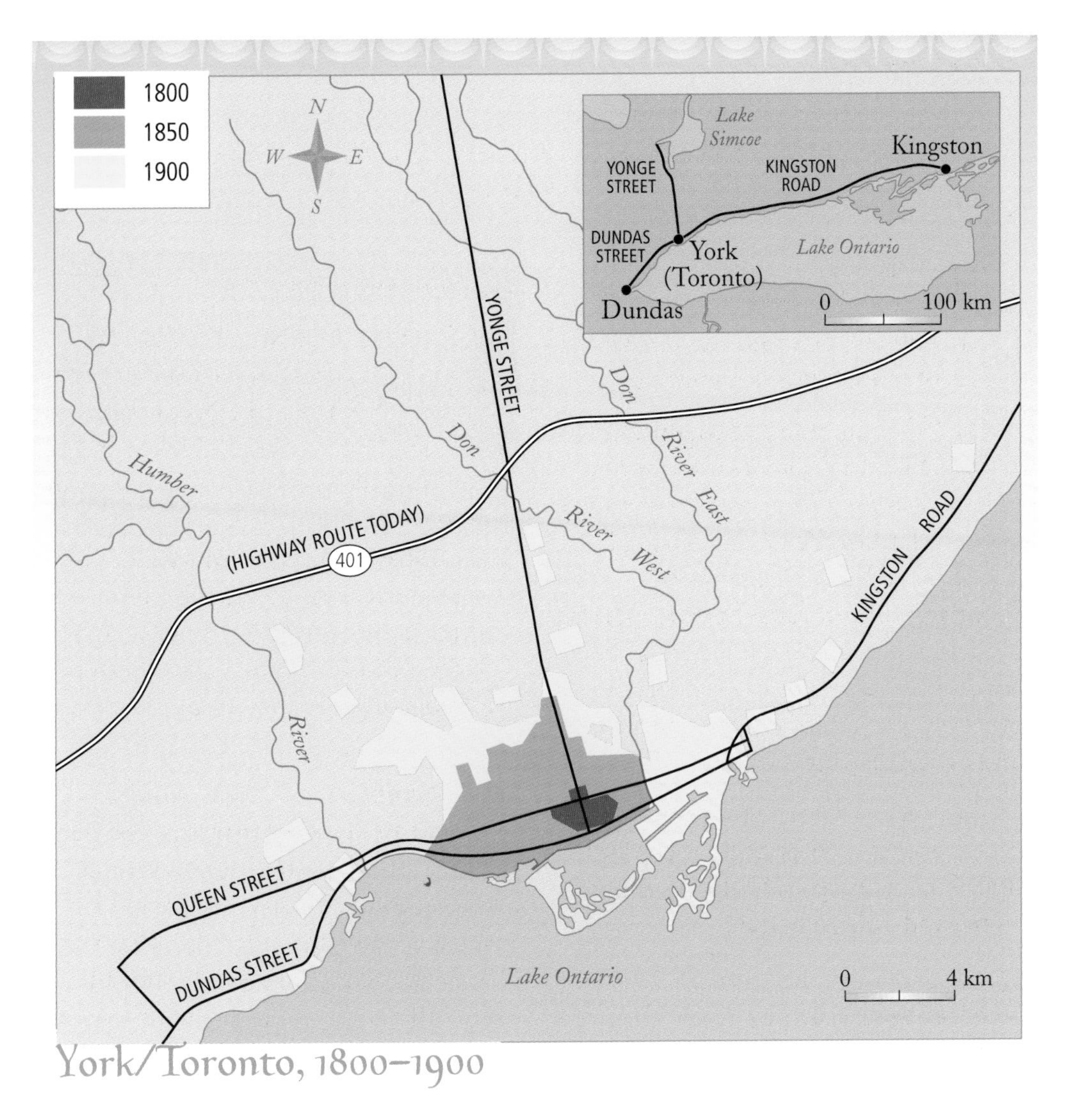

York/Toronto, 1800–1900

Like humans, cities grow with the help of people around them. An important person in my life was the first lieutenant-governor of Upper Canada, John Graves Simcoe. He chose me to be his capital and named me York. All the towns along the lake were jealous. They knew being capital would make me grow faster than them.

If you look at an early map of my area, you will see how Lieutenant-Governor Simcoe helped me grow. Because I was the capital, he built roads leading out from me in all directions. You see, the War of 1812 was just over. Many people worried about the possibility of another war. The roads would help militia and soldiers reach all parts of the colony quickly if necessary.

Of course, when I say *roads*, you shouldn't think of the roads I have today. I think the only thing people complained about more than the horrible state of the roads were the trees that were everywhere!

Dundas Road went west, while Kingston Road went east along the shore of the lake towards that town. Yonge Street went north. These roads really helped me grow, especially when so many new people began arriving after 1820.

During Reading

1. How do you think the combination of roads and immigration benefited Toronto?

By the 1840s, I dominated the area around me, my **hinterland**. My hinterland was far less developed. People in the hinterland looked to me for leadership, goods, and services. I was at the centre of everything.

By this time, there were a number of **metropolitan centres** like me in British North America. Access to water transportation was important, so all metropolitan centres were port cities. We were like hubs on a wheel, with trade lines as spokes that extended out from us. The Atlantic colonies had four metropolitan centres: Halifax in Nova Scotia, Saint John in New Brunswick, St. John's in Newfoundland, and Charlottetown in Prince Edward Island.

Sometimes, there was competition when two hubs tried to control the same hinterland. For example, Halifax and Saint John both tried to control the coast of the Bay of Fundy and the north shore of New Brunswick. This competition sometimes caused resentment. Competition was especially a problem if one hub controlled the main trade line to the other. That was what happened between me and Montréal.

My competition with Montréal was caused by many factors. Montréal was older and bigger. It saw itself as the hub, with me as an upstart from its western hinterland. It didn't like having its position as the main trading centre for the West challenged.

I gained the upper hand in 1825. Until then, my merchants and settlers were at a disadvantage. Montréal's traders purchased goods directly from Britain. My merchants and settlers had to buy the goods from Montréal traders, at greater cost, of course.

Montréal profited by supplying my merchants and settlers and then again as we shipped our goods through Montréal to Britain. This ability to control our trade allowed Montréal to maintain its position as the most important metropolitan centre.

Then, in 1825, New York completed the Erie Canal. Some Upper Canadians sneered at it and called it "the ditch." In some ways, it was a ditch. It wasn't very wide and it had barges pulled along by horse or donkey. Some barges were pushed through the water with long poles. Compared to later canals, the Erie was pretty basic.

View on the Erie Canal, by John William Hill, 1829. The Erie Canal was a feat of engineering. The 585-kilometre canal was longer than any other canal in Europe or America at the time.

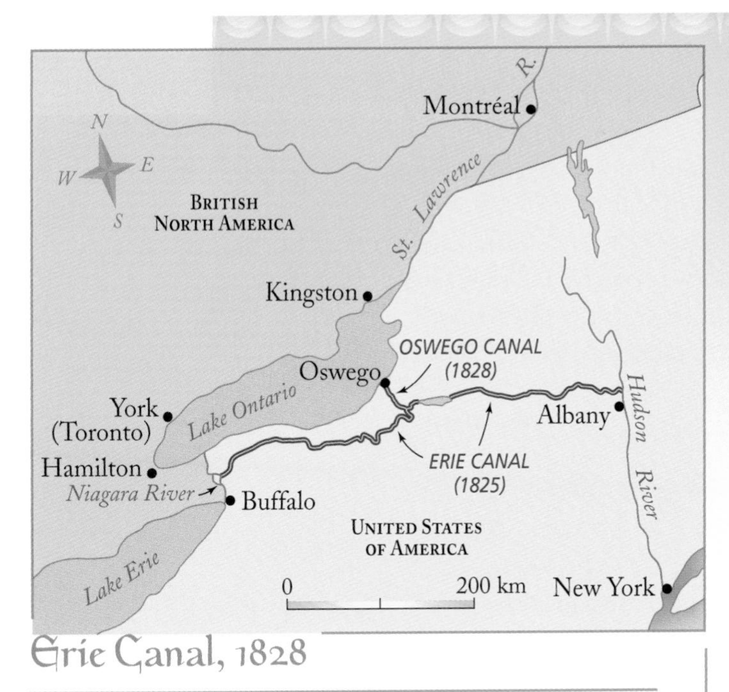

Erie Canal, 1828

- With a partner, use the map to understand why the Erie Canal was so significant for Toronto's businesses.

However, the Erie Canal linked New York City to Buffalo and Niagara. It cut huge amounts of time off the transportation of goods. Faster transportation meant lower shipping costs. Lower costs greatly improved my economic development. My merchants finally had a choice. They no longer had to rely on Montréal to ship or receive goods. Many of my merchants took advantage of the new canal to ship goods to and from the United States.

But Montréal was a partner, as well as a competitor. We were both hurt when Britain cancelled its imperial preference. It really pulled the rug out from under our merchants. It was a tough time for Montréal and me.

However, with setbacks came opportunities. The 1850s was the decade of the railway and I had plans! I was determined to get access to every corner of my hinterland, but I wasn't going to stop there. My Northern Railway ran to Collingwood. That line gave me access to the West, using the Great Lakes. There were no limits to my growth!

After Reading

1. The relationship between a metropolitan centre and its hinterland brings mutual benefits, but also resentment. As a class, suggest why resentment might develop. What are the benefits?

Toronto, Canada West, from the Top of the Jail, by Edwin Whitefield, 1854. By the mid-nineteenth century, Toronto was well on its way to becoming a major metropolitan centre.

A Night to Remember: Five Years Later

Before Reading

1. Imagine you have a conflict with another person and you have decided to confront the person to try to resolve the problem. How would you prepare for the confrontation? In your journal, describe what you would do.

A Night to Remember *continues from page 265.*

As Henri Couture climbed the steps to the Price household, he felt a sense of déjà vu. Five years ago, he had taken the same steps. That night, Henri hadn't even gotten in the door. William Price had been in a rage and refused to see him. Worse, he had forbidden Stephanie to see or talk to Henri again. Her tears had only fuelled Price's anger. He felt the French were taking over the country and his own household.

After that terrible night, Henri hadn't seen Stephanie until three months ago. They had accidentally met again and found their feelings for each other were unchanged. The couple was now determined to receive William Price's blessing on their match.

The young man who had approached William Price's door in 1849 was now far more confident. Since then, Henri had become a man of some influence. He was now an advisor for government contracts and was currently involved in delicate trade negotiations.

As he knocked on the door, he took a deep breath. He hoped he was ready. Ready, he thought with a smile to himself, to meet the lion in his Westmount den. Price had reluctantly agreed to receive Henri at home this evening. At precisely eight o'clock, Henri Couture presented himself—once again—at the grand residence.

As the butler took his coat, Henri got his nerves under control. Over the past few years, he had dealt many times with powerful English businessmen. He was no longer as intimidated. Of course, none of those meetings carried the personal consequences of this one. He might once again be shown the door. But tonight he would at least have his say.

Henri was shown into the library, a room with solid oak furniture and floor-to-ceiling bookshelves with glass doors. Seated behind the desk, cigar in hand, was a grim looking William Price. He nodded towards an uncomfortable-looking, straight-backed chair in front of the desk. So, thought Henri. He wants to demonstrate his power. I'm supposed to sit in front of him like a schoolboy in front of the principal.

"I'll stand, if you don't mind, Mr. Price," Henri said, drawing himself up to his full height in front of the seated figure.

"Please yourself," replied Price gruffly. "What is your business with me? I don't believe we've met." He didn't give any indication that he remembered Henri.

Henri felt his nervousness flutter, but stuck to his strategy.

During Reading

1. As you read, think about how Henri builds his case to Price. What is his strategy?
2. How does Henri's argument reflect the conflict resolution strategy you learned about on page 203? Discuss with a partner.

"First of all, I wish to thank you for receiving me in your home, sir. I hope you will allow me to say my piece without interruption. I have no desire to provoke you, but I have urgent business that involves you...and your family."

The room was silent for several seconds as Price watched Henri with a level gaze. Price then closed his eyes and heaved a great sigh.

"Well, get on with it," he said.

Perhaps it was only wishful thinking, but it seemed to Henri that Price seemed a little less gruff. He plunged in.

"First of all, although I am not English, I come from a proud family and a people with a long history. It is true, as you English have said, my family came from many generations of farmers. And, although I firmly believe we have many legitimate complaints..."

At this Price started forward, as if to interrupt.

"If you please, sir," Henri said quickly, warding Price off. "I recognize that you English have complaints too. I early on decided there was no reason why our peoples could not work together for our mutual benefit. That's the reason I learned English. That's the reason I supported Monsieur LaFontaine rather than Monsieur Papineau. I could see that the way of Monsieur Papineau was a dead-end street leading only to destruction."

Henri could not tell if he was getting through to Stephanie's father. Price sat stiffly in the chair, his gaze fixed on Henri. Henri felt strangely calm. He knew he had to build his case brick by brick. Rushing to the true purpose of this meeting would surely ruin it all. There was too much at stake to let his emotions run out of control. It was time to play his strongest cards.

"I know you expected that responsible government would lead to chaos. But sir, that has not happened. In fact, the government has taken a number of steps recently that will greatly strengthen our economy and, I might add, your business interests."

Was he mistaken, or was Price now leaning slightly forward, paying more attention?

"I have actually played a small role in this matter." There was no doubt now, Henri had William Price's full attention.

"Through my position in government, I helped ensure the construction of the St. Lawrence and Atlantic Railway from Montréal to Portland, Maine. As you know, this transportation route—so important to Montréal businesses—was completed last year." Don't stop now, he told himself.

"I have worked in a similar way on a new project that will link the entire province: the Grand Trunk Railway. Now, with the alliance between Monsieur Cartier and that well-regarded countryman of yours from Canada West, Monsieur John A. Macdonald, we have a stable government. This government's policy is to promote equality between our peoples and, above all, to expand business opportunities. This will ensure our wealth and prosperity." He sucked in his breath and braced himself. He had one more card to play—his ace.

But before he could, Price sat back in his chair and said thoughtfully, "What you say, Monsieur, is true. In 1849, I thought my world was over. I thought Britain was washing its hands of us and that we'd all be ruined. But I have come to see that we may have prosperity, even without imperial preference. If only we can get a free trade deal with the Americans!"

Mon Dieu! Henri thought, with a rush of excitement. He's playing my card for me. "Monsieur Price, I have been a part of Lord Elgin's negotiation team with the Americans." He now felt in control of the interview.

"I am sure, Monsieur Price, that I can rely on you to keep this information to yourself. Although it is not yet public knowledge, the Reciprocity Treaty with the United States will be completed and signed next week, on June 6, 1854. Free trade with the Americans will be ours," Henri smiled.

What might have been the beginning of a smile appeared at the corners of Price's mouth. There was no doubt that Price was now happier than when the interview began.

It's now or never, thought Henri.

"Sir, there's one more thing and, again, I beg you to hear me out. I have told you all this to demonstrate that, like you, I am a man of the modern age and a man of no small standing in our community."

Price nodded. Henri went to the heart of the matter.

"Sir, I am in love with your daughter, Stephanie." He hurried on, hardly daring to watch Price's reaction. "I have been in love with her for the past seven years."

"What?" Price started, loudly.

"Please, sir, I beg you. Let me finish. We have done nothing to bring dishonour or disgrace to Stephanie or to your family. I'm here because we both realize that it is wrong to meet without your blessing." There, he had said it.

"Monsieur Couture, what do you want from me?" Price asked sternly.

That must be some kind of victory, thought Henri. At least he hasn't called the butler to throw me out! "I—we—ask only this: That you and your wife allow me to court your daughter, under your supervision, of course. You will set the rules and I will observe them. If after a length of time—of your choosing—you decide that I must no longer see her, then I will go." He had said his whole piece. His future happiness was in William Price's hands.

Without a word, Price rose and walked to the window. He looked out at the street for what seemed like an hour, yet it could only have been a minute or two. "I will send a note to your residence tomorrow evening with my answer. Good evening, sir." With that, he turned and left the room.

After Reading !

1. What do you think will be on the note Henri receives that evening? Write the note from William Price's perspective.
2. As a class, discuss Henri's strategy for breaking down William Price's prejudice against him. Considering Price's prejudices and business interests, why was this a good strategy?

Think It Through

Conflict, Change, and Nineteenth-Century Canada

Before Reading

1. A picture gallery, such as the one on pages 282–283, can be a creative way to present ideas and information about a topic. What are other interesting ways of presenting information? Share your ideas with a partner.

The pictures and captions on pages 282–283 may help you generate ideas for an independent research/inquiry project on conflict, change, and nineteenth-century Canada. You might also review Chapters 7–9 to find other topics.

During Reading

1. As you read, take a walk through any pictures that interest you. Think of how each might relate to topics of conflict and change. Start to develop potential inquiry questions for your project.

March of Intellect, by William Elliott, 1845. Elliot was a district superintendent of schools for Middlesex County.

The Underground Railroad, by Charles T. Webber, 1893. Although slaves found freedom from slavery in British North America, they encountered many challenges in their new home.

Circus acts were popular entertainment in the nineteenth century. In 1859, a performer named Blondin (blon-dane) crossed the 395-metre span of the Niagara Falls both ways on a rope. Thousands of people watched.

In the mid-nineteenth century, people began to wear fur clothing with the fur on the outside. Before this, it was commonly worn next to the skin. Part of the reason for the change was that people with wealth wanted to show it off by wearing rare furs for others to see.

Think It Through

The Fire in the Saint-Jean Quarter, Seen Looking Westward, 1845, by Joseph Légaré (1795–1855). In the mid-nineteenth century, at least forty major fires destroyed large sections of cities in British North America.

Beginning in the 1830s, the government in Upper Canada began to set up reserves for First Nations. William Armstrong painted this picture of the Wikwemikong Reserve on Manitoulin Island in 1856.

Curling Match at Montréal, Canada East, by W.S. Hatton, 1855–1864. The sport of curling was imported from Scotland by immigrants.

Kingston Convicts at Work in the Yard of the Penitentiary, 1873. The Kingston Penitentiary was the first prison in Canada when it opened in 1835.

It says in the caption that curling was imported by Scottish immigrants. I wonder what other parts of Canadian culture were imported by immigrants? I wonder how these imports were adapted to Canadian life?

I wonder what kinds of crimes were most common in the nineteenth century? How would punishments then compare to punishments today?

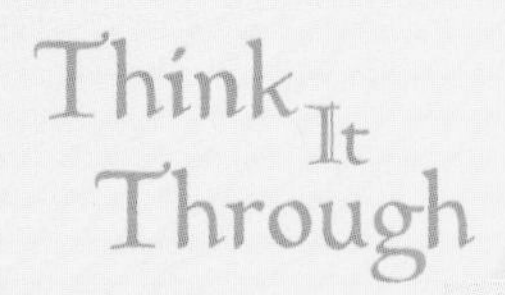

Preparing an Independent Research/Inquiry Project

As you have worked through this textbook, you have learned many useful research skills, such as taking notes, developing inquiry questions, kinds of research sources, paraphrasing, and scanning and chunking information. An independent research/inquiry project gives you the chance to use them all. Often, your teacher will specify how and what you should research, but sometimes, you might get to choose your own project. The steps that follow will guide your independent work.

Stage 1: Understand the Assignment

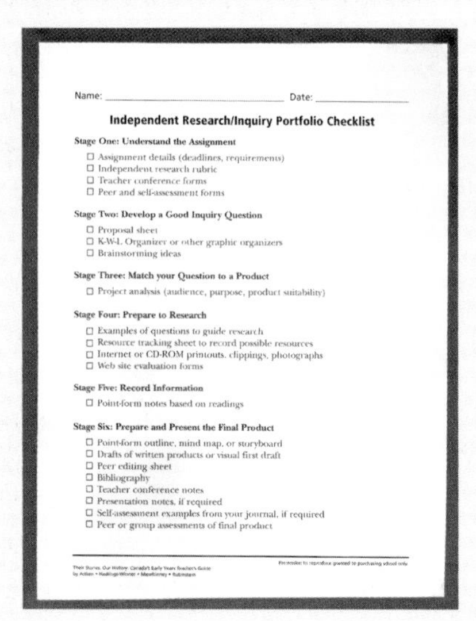
Name: ____________ Date: ____________

Independent Research/Inquiry Portfolio Checklist

Stage One: Understand the Assignment

- ☐ Assignment details (deadlines, requirements)
- ☐ Independent research rubric
- ☐ Teacher conference forms
- ☐ Peer and self-assessment forms

Stage Two: Develop a Good Inquiry Question

- ☐ Proposal sheet
- ☐ K-W-L Organizer or other graphic organizers
- ☐ Brainstorming ideas

Stage Three: Match your Question to a Product

- ☐ Project analysis (audience, purpose, product suitability)

Stage Four: Prepare to Research

- ☐ Examples of questions to guide research
- ☐ Resource tracking sheet to record possible resources
- ☐ Internet or CD-ROM printouts, clippings, photographs
- ☐ Web site evaluation forms

Stage Five: Record Information

- ☐ Point-form notes based on readings

Stage Six: Prepare and Present the Final Product

- ☐ Point-form outline, mind map, or storyboard
- ☐ Drafts of written products or visual first draft
- ☐ Peer editing sheet
- ☐ Bibliography
- ☐ Teacher conference notes
- ☐ Presentation notes, if required
- ☐ Self-assessment examples from your journal, if required
- ☐ Peer or group assessments of final product

Their Stories, Our History: Canada's Early Years Teacher's Guide

Permission to reproduce granted to purchasing school only.

Be sure you understand the assignment and how it will be evaluated. A good way to check is to explain the project to another person. If you can explain it clearly and answer questions, you probably understand what you need to do. Consider making a timeline of when various stages of your project are due. You might also create a research portfolio to keep your project information organized. A list of what you need to do on the outside of the portfolio can help you keep focused on your task.

Stage 2: Develop a Good Inquiry Question

You might begin with a photograph, event, person, or other general topic that interests you. Consider using a graphic organizer for your ideas. You might also meet with a small group to brainstorm ideas about one another's topics. Refer to page 212 of your textbook to review Asking Questions for Research.

Stage 3: Match Your Question to a Product

What are you going to do with your research? Match your question to the type of product you are going to create. For example, a report might be better for an analysis of an issue. A dramatization might be best for a project about an event or person. Also consider how you will work: alone, with a partner, or in a small group. Writing a report or making a storyboard might be projects you do on your own. Performing a play may be better for a small group.

Keep the audience for your product in mind. Your teacher and classmates will often be your audience, but not always. Some projects might ask you to prepare a project as if for a specific audience, such as the historical society of your community. An audience that knows nothing about your topic will require a different presentation than an audience with some or a great deal of understanding.

Stage 4: Prepare to Research

Break down your inquiry question into more specific parts or develop questions to guide your research. To complete this step, you may need to do some background reading. Brainstorm ideas about the kind of information you will need to answer your inquiry question. Create a list of keywords to guide your library and Internet searches. Be sure you consult a variety of resources: print, on-line, and media. Ask your teacher and school librarian for suggestions.

As you learn more, you may want to refine your inquiry question. Keep notes about how and why you changed your question to discuss with the teacher.

Complete a quick skim of the available resources, looking for helpful information. Learning how to find the most valuable resources for your topic is like detective work. At this point, you are not making notes. You are only looking for the best and most reliable information. Do not forget to include a space in your research to record your own thoughts and ideas.

If you have not already done so, meet with your teacher to get feedback on your plans.

Stage 5: Record Information

Next, use the resources you identified in stage four to find the information you need. Make notes. Be sure to record each source of information carefully using the format provided by your teacher.

Stage 6: Prepare and Present the Final Product

Before beginning work on your final product, answer your inquiry question with one sentence. Does this answer include your own ideas or point of view on the topic? If not, think about your question and research some more. You might also talk to someone to see if you can refine your answer to include your own ideas.

Create a point-form outline, Mind Map, or storyboard to develop the first draft of your product. Get feedback on your plan from another student or your teacher.

Prepare your final work. Check it over before handing it in or presenting it. Make sure your portfolio includes all required material.

Think It Through

Stage 1: Understand the Assignment

I've reread the During Reading question carefully and listened to the teacher's directions. I need to follow the steps on pages 284–285 to create a project. The topic can be anything that relates to a conflict or change in nineteenth-century Canada.

Name: ______________________ Date: ____________

Independent Research Rubric: Conflict, Change, and Nineteenth-Century Canada

Student Reflection:

Criteria	① Limited	② Basic	③ Very Good	④ Excellent
Knowledge/ Understanding Demonstrates awareness of a conflict or change in nineteenth-century Canada using supporting evidence	Demonstrates **beginning** awareness of a conflict or change related to life in nineteenth-century Canada using a **limited** amount of supporting evidence	Demonstrates **satisfactory** awareness of a conflict or change related to life in nineteenth-century Canada using **some** supporting evidence	Demonstrates **effective** awareness of a conflict or change related to life in nineteenth-century Canada using a **considerable** amount of supporting evidence	Demonstrates **outstanding** awareness of a conflict or change related to life in nineteenth-century Canada using a **thorough** amount of supporting evidence
Thinking Develops a question for research to help shape a topic	Develops a question to direct research with **limited** clarity	Develops a question to direct research with **some** clarity	Develops a question to direct research with **considerable** clarity	Develops a question to direct research with **outstanding** clarity
Plans and supports a point of view by analysing a variety of sources	Plans and supports a point of view using a **few** sources with **limited** effectiveness	Plans and supports a point of view using **some** sources with **some** effectiveness	Plans and supports a point of view using **many** sources with **considerable** effectiveness	Plans and supports a point of view using a **wide variety** of sources with a **high degree** of effectiveness
Communication Communicates ideas and information with clarity and attention to audience and purpose	Communicates ideas and information with **limited** clarity and attention to audience and purpose	Communicates ideas and information with **some** clarity and attention to audience and purpose	Communicates ideas and information with **considerable** clarity and attention to audience and purpose	Communicates ideas and information with a **high degree** of clarity and attention to audience and purpose
Application Transfers knowledge and skills with respect to a conflict or change in nineteenth-century Canada to new contexts	Transfers knowledge and skills related to conflict or change in nineteenth-century Canada to new contexts with **limited** effectiveness	Transfers knowledge and skills related to conflict or change in nineteenth-century Canada to new contexts with **some** effectiveness	Transfers knowledge and skills related to conflict or change in nineteenth-century Canada to new contexts with **considerable** effectiveness	Transfers knowledge and skills related to conflict or change in nineteenth-century Canada in new contexts with a **high degree** of effectiveness

Student Comments: Please notice: ______________________

Their Stories, Our History: Canada's Early Years Teacher's Guide
by Aitken • Haskings-Winner • Mewhinney • Rubinstein

Permission to reproduce granted to purchasing school only.

My teacher gave me a rubric that will be used to evaluate the project. I've read it a couple times. I think I understand what I need to do to get an "excellent" mark. There are four parts to my grade. For *Knowledge and Understanding*, I need to be sure my project discusses a conflict or change and that I have good evidence from my research to back up my ideas.

Thinking is about my inquiry question and how I answer it. I need to be sure my inquiry question is strong. This means I need an open-ended question that is still quite specific. After my research, I need to be sure my answer to the inquiry question includes my own ideas, not just information I find in other resources.

To get a good *Communication* mark, I need to make sure my project is organized and clear. *Application* seems the trickiest. I need to be able to relate what I'm saying about conflict or change in nineteenth-century Canada to another situation. My first thought is that I will relate a conflict or change in the nineteenth century to something happening today. I'll see if that works once I've written an inquiry question.

Stage 2: Develop a Good Inquiry Question

I think I'd like to do a project about the role of women. I can see from the photo and caption about this woman that she must have been from the upper class, or at least she had some financial wealth. I wonder what roles she played in society? She doesn't look like she's dressed to work on a farm, like Mary O'Brien from pages 229–230, or worrying about how she'll survive, like Eliza Stacey on page 231. Maybe she would be more like Stephanie Elizabeth Price, from the story *A Night to Remember*, which starts on page 260.

I'll use the organizer shown on page 212 to brainstorm some inquiry questions.

General Topic	Specific Topic	Questions
Conflict, Change, and Nineteenth-Century Canada	Women's Roles	What roles and responsibilities did women have in the 1850s? -closed
		Which social class placed more responsibility on women? -open
		What other factors affected women's responsibilities? Education? Culture? -closed

I like the first question the most, but it's a closed question. I know I'll need an open-ended question to do a good job on this project. Another problem is that it doesn't include conflict or change, which the directions for this project say I have to include. Maybe I could work on a project about how women's roles and responsibilities changed over time. My inquiry question could be *How did women's roles in Canada change between the early days of New France and the 1850s?*

However, I don't think this question will fit the Application part of the rubric. Maybe I can show how the changes in women's roles relate to changes in Canada. I'll be applying what I learn about women's roles to what I've learned about changes in Canada over time. For example, I know the economy in Canada changed a great deal from the fish and furs of New France to the agriculture and timber of the nineteenth century. Maybe I can relate these changes to changes in women's roles. My inquiry question could be *How did women's roles in Canada reflect societal changes between the early days of New France and the 1850s?*

Think It Through

Stage 3: Match Your Question to a Product

My teacher says written projects will be handed in to him and presentation projects will be displayed in our classroom or presented to the class.

I could present my project on a piece of Bristol board with a line drawn down the middle. I'll paste a piece of paper in the middle for my question and conclusion. On one side of the line, I'll have illustrations showing famous women or kinds of women's work in New France. I'll do the same on the other side for Canada in the early nineteenth century. Each illustration will have a caption relating the illustration to women's roles in that period.

I know my audience is my teacher and classmates. I'll use information I've learned from this textbook to show I know my audience, but I'll expand it with my own research.

Stage 4: Prepare to Research

I used my textbook to select a graphic organizer to keep my research focused. I made a page for New France and one for Canada in the nineteenth century. I've listed helpful textbook pages as my first resource and a few key terms to try for my research.

Topics for Research	Potential Resources
New France, 1534–1763	
• First Nations women, fur trade roles	• pp. 24-29, 72 •
• Women indentured servants?	• p. 19 •
• Settlers' wives, Marie Rollet?	• pp. 22, 52-57, 70 •
• Missionaries-Marie de l'Incarnation?	• pp. 34-36 •
• Filles du roi	• pp. 49, 62, 70 •

Key Terms to Try
- New France women
- New France missionaries
- women roles history
- fur trade women
- women history

Now I'm ready to check my work with my teacher. I have my research portfolio prepared for the meeting and I've filled in the planning sheets my teacher gave the class.

Use any feedback from your teacher conference to adjust your project plan. Next, move on to stages 5 and 6 of the research/inquiry process.

After Reading

1. Research and prepare an independent research project on an aspect of conflict or change in nineteenth-century Canada.

Compress

1. Make jot-notes about how each of the following changes affected the lives of people in British North America in the mid-nineteenth century:
   a) Britain's move from imperial preference to free trade
   b) improvements to transportation
   c) achieving responsible government

Express

2. Use your answers from question 1 to write a newspaper article that sums up the ways people's lives changed in British North America from the 1830s to the 1850s.

> A decade of change ends for British North Americans — December 30, 1859
>
> Toronto—

3. On page 273, engineer Thomas C. Keefer argues in favour of technological progress brought about by railroads. Write a paragraph that supports or disagrees with Keefer's argument for progress, using examples from today.
4. Write a brief editorial for the Montréal *Courier* discussing the governor general's acceptance of the Rebellion Losses Bill and the burning of the Houses of Assembly. Remember that the *Courier* is an English-language newspaper.

   or

   Write an editorial that Gilles Couture, Henri's brother, might have written on the same topic for the leading French newspaper, *Le Canadien.*

Their Stories, Our History

In the fall of 2004, the Canadian Broadcasting Company (CBC) ran a poll to see who Canadians felt were the 100 Greatest Canadians. Visit www.duvaleducation.com/canadasearlyyears. Click on the link to CBC's Greatest Canadians Web site to find out who received strong support. Make a list of criteria Canadians used in finally choosing Tommy Douglas as the greatest Canadian.

Tommy Douglas was a twentieth-century politician known as the "Father of Medicare."

Select an individual from Unit 3 and write a nomination letter stating why the person should be on the list. Make your letter no more than three paragraphs long.

a) The first paragraph should clearly state what criteria you used to decide to nominate this person. One of your criteria must be how the individual can teach today's Canadians something valuable.
b) The second paragraph should give some historical background and issues this person had to deal with.
c) The third paragraph should show how this person specifically meets your criteria for being considered a "great Canadian."

Conclusion: Cross-Colony Roundup

Before Reading

1. How many newspapers, radio stations, and television stations are in your community? Name as many as you can.
2. Compare newspapers, radio, and television in terms of how well they communicate news. What are the advantages and disadvantages of each? Use a three-circle Venn Diagram to format your response.

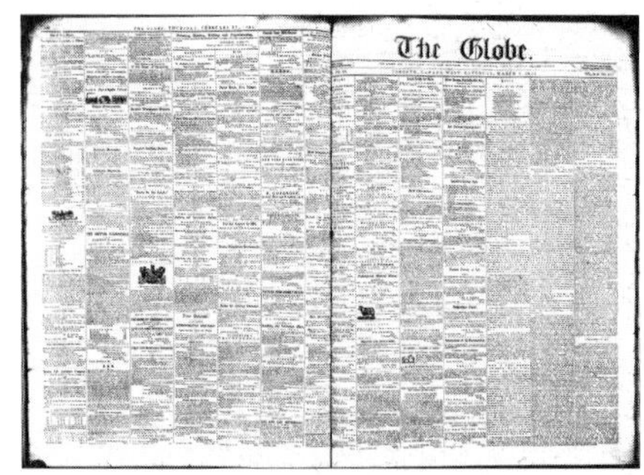
The Globe.

Newspapers in the 1840s and 1850s were published weekly. It took several days for papers to be distributed, so news could be a week or more old before people read about it.

George Brown

In the mid-nineteenth century, people did not have radio, television, computers, or telephones to get their news. Other than word of mouth, newspapers were the only way to find out what was happening in other parts of the colony, continent, or world.

Most newspapers showed a strong bias on issues. Newspaper publishers or owners used their paper to communicate their own points of view. For example, in the 1830s, the most popular newspaper in Toronto was the *Globe*. The *Globe* was owned and run by George Brown. Brown's pro-American, anti-French sentiments were well known to his readers.

It can be more difficult to see the bias of a newspaper today. Most aim to appear completely objective and bias-free. However, many people believe it is impossible to be completely free of biases. Sometimes, a bias becomes clear if you ask yourself what is *not* said. What side of the story is *not* presented?

The *Colonial News* is not a real newspaper, but the clippings that follow cover real events and issues from the years 1853 to 1856.

During Reading

1. Like all newspapers, the *Colonial News* contains a combination of facts, opinions, and arguments. As you have learned earlier in this textbook, it is not always easy to tell the difference between them.
   a) Copy the chart below into your notebook:

Story Title	An Example of a Fact in the Story	An Example of an Opinion in the Story	An Example of an Argument in the Story
Seigneurial system abolished			

   b) Meet in a group of five students. This will be your base group. Your teacher will assign your group two articles from the *Colonial News*.
   c) With your group, fill in your organizer for your assigned articles.
   d) Next, make a new group with one member from each base group. Share your notes from the articles you analyzed. All students should have notes for all articles on pages 291–297 when this process is complete.

The Colonial News

News from British North America

November 23, 1854

Seigneurial system abolished

Montréal—The seigneurial landholding system was abolished by parliament today. Investors, city officials, and land speculators applauded the change. They say the seigneurial system prevents economic development in Canada East.

Abolishing the seigneuries will help open more land for railways and industry. Experts say more land will help Canada East stay competitive with Canada West and the United States.

More than two centuries old, the seigneurial system was a unique part of life in Canada East. About 80 per cent of the population in Canada East will be affected by the change.

Parliament has set aside close to $1.5 million to pay seigneurs for their land.

Pierre Bouchard (boo-shar), a local habitant, greeted this news with anger. "The seigneurs have been unfair to us for generations. We have paid heavy fees and given them free days of work. Now they are being paid for the loss of their land. What's in it for people like me?"

The father of ten is worried that he will be forced from his land and home. "Already most seigneuries have fallen into the hands of English merchants. This law will finish off the French landowner in this colony," said Bouchard.

Political leaders promise that all people will be treated fairly.

Special courts will hear claims for compensation from seigneurs.

The Colonial News

News from British North America

July 30, 1853

Financial troubles surround rail expansion

Montréal—This month, a 450-kilometre rail line between Montréal and Portland, Maine was completed. Officials in both communities see the St. Lawrence & Atlantic Railway as a great opportunity. Montréal will now have access to an ocean port that does not freeze in the winter. Merchants can ship goods to American or European markets all year round.

The St. Lawrence & Atlantic Railroad station at Longueuil, Canada East, was built in 1848 to house trains. Railway officials predict that future stations will focus on passengers and cargo.

Yet these opportunities come at great cost. John Poor, the Portland businessman who developed the project, is well named. Poor put all his money into the ten-year project, but ran into trouble. He had to be bailed out by the Parliament of Canada. In 1849, Parliament passed the Guarantee Act to protect investors. The act guaranteed that investors would not lose their money.

Other railways have similar problems. The Great Western Railway has had financial problems for almost nineteen years. It will open in December. The line will link Hamilton and London.

The most ambitious project of the decade is the Grand Trunk Railway (GTR). This line will provide service from Québec and Montréal to Sarnia. From Sarnia, goods can be sent by ship to the United States.

Critics say the GTR will never be profitable. Stories of terrible working conditions, poor pay to immigrant workers, and outbreaks of cholera surround the project. Some critics say the government's money is helping a few private investors become wealthy.

However, the government of Prime Minister Francis Hincks is not deterred by the criticisms. It pushes the GTR forward. Prime Minister Hincks says the GTR will open a golden age of economic development.

Some investors and politicians would like to see the GTR extended to the Maritimes. However, discussions have stalled. Negotiators for each colony cannot agree upon a fair division of costs.

SHERIFF'S SALE!

IN THE COMMON PLEAS
John Heaton, vs. William Henry Morgan.
IN THE QUEEN'S BENCH
Philip Cady VanBrocklin, vs. William Henry Morgan

By virtue of Executions issued in the above Causes, and to me directed and delivered against the Goods and Chattels of the above named defendant, I have seized the whole stock of Goods and other property in the defendant's Store and Dwelling House, on Colborne Street, in the Town of Brantford, consisting of

DRY GOODS
GROCERIES, AND
SHOP & HOUSE FURNITURE,

All of which I will sell by Public Auction, on
Monday, 21st day of May
Instant, at the hour of 2 o'clock, P. M.

The stock of Goods will be offered in one lot, on which the bidding will be so much on the Pound, upon cost prices, as per stock Book. A credit of 3, 6, 9, 12, and 15 months will be given by furnishing Notes endorsed to the full satisfaction of the above named Plaintiffs, with interest

Further particulars will be made known on the day of sale. The Goods may be inspected on any day previous to the sale, by applying at my office.

JOHN SMITH, Sheriff C. B.

Sheriff's Office,
Brantford

Herald Job Press, Brantford.

The Colonial News

News from British North America

June 6, 1854

Canada–U.S. trade deal signed

Toronto—Today, Governor General Elgin signed a trade agreement with the United States. The Reciprocity Treaty will end taxes on many goods exchanged over the border. The treaty took more than ten years to complete. It will affect all British North American colonies.

Governor General Elgin stated that he is proud of the treaty and what it represents. "When Britain ended imperial preference in 1840, we faced an uncertain future. Our exports of wheat, lumber, and other materials such as coal had dropped to almost half," Lord Elgin told reporters.

"Our wheat exports fell from 628 000 bushels to 238 000 bushels in one year. But we survived. We found another market and worked hard to open it. The Americans were tough negotiators. Many of their leaders wanted to protect their industries from imports. But they finally saw the benefits of gaining access to our raw materials. Farmers, lumber companies, fishers, and miners will benefit from this ten-year deal."

Despite the governor general's optimism, a few negative voices were heard on Toronto's streets. William Blake, a blacksmith, questioned the wisdom of the deal. "We supported the British for decades. But as soon as the Brits thought they had better options, they abandoned us. We can't rely on any one market too much," Blake commented. He continued, "Maybe the answer is freer trade between the colonies of British North America."

Macdonald confirms French role in government

Kingston—Canada West politician John A. Macdonald confirmed that French-Canadians will play a strong role in any future governments he might lead.

John A. Macdonald is a Kingston lawyer who leads the Liberal-Conservative Party. Tories in Canada West call him a promising new leader.

Parti bleu (par-tee bluh) leader George-Étienne (zhor-zhe-ay-tee-n) Cartier welcomed the announcement. "This colony is big enough for English and French. Both may preserve their cultures and traditions. Each has something to offer," he stated.

The leaders are united against demands for a more American political system.

In the United States, representation by population plays an important role in the political system. With representation by population, voting districts with roughly the same of number of people each elect a representative. The system means that areas with larger populations have more representatives in government.

George-Étienne Cartier leads the *Parti bleu* in Canada East. The *Bleus* have support from the powerful Catholic Church.

"The timing of interest in 'rep by pop' is no coincidence," says Jean Tremblay (trom-blay), a member of the Parti bleu. "In 1852, the population of Canada West finally became larger than the population in Canada East. Suddenly people cry that the Act of Union is unfair! Where were the cries of 'rep by pop' when Canada East had the larger population?"

The Colonial News

News from British North America

July 10, 1854

Experts study census

Québec—Experts are meeting in Québec this week to discuss the recent census.

The 1851 census is the most reliable in the history of British North America. Its data will make it easier to analyze population patterns. This will help political leaders make decisions about government policies and programs.

Earlier census data was too inconsistent to be useful. Each colony gathered its own data. Each used its own time frame and system. The results often had many irregularities.

This year's census is already a topic of wide discussion. Analysts from Canada East are concerned about the jump in Canada West's population. Some believe this growth will fuel demands for representation by population. Political instability could result.

British North America, 1854

Population in British North American Colonies		
	1851	Earlier data
Canada West	952 004	725 879 (1848)
Canada East	890 261	765 797 (1848)
Nova Scotia	276 854	202 575 (1838)
New Brunswick	193 800	156 162 (1840)
Prince Edward Island	62 678	56 678 (1848)
Assiniboia	5 391 (1849)	4 871 (1846)
New Caledonia	55 000	No earlier numbers available

The Colonial News

News from British North America

May 11, 1856

Maritime economies booming

Halifax and Fredericton—Leaders in Nova Scotia and New Brunswick applauded their recent economic statistics. All information points to a strong future for their colonies. Halifax is one of the busiest ports on the eastern seaboard. New Brunswick's ship-building industry is flourishing.

When Britain ended imperial preference, business leaders had concerns about their future. However, those fears can now be put to rest. Economic ties with Britain remain strong.

The 1854 Reciprocity Treaty with the United States has also helped. From New Brunswick, agricultural products and lumber now flow across the border to the United States. From Halifax, cod exports are booming. Close to half the male population in the colony works in the fishing industry.

However, all is not good news. Trade with the other colonies in British North America remains slow. In New Brunswick, intra-colonial trade is less than 5 per cent of the colony's total trade. Business leaders hope to reopen talks of extending Canada's railway lines to the Maritimes.

December 18, 1856

The news comes to Newfoundland

St. John's—This year saw the island of Newfoundland linked with the rest of British North America for the first time. Earlier in the year, Engineer Frederic Gisborne laid an underwater telegraph cable from Cape Breton to Newfoundland. It was the first such cable in North America. The cable has allowed news to be sent to Newfoundland more regularly.

The connection excited some residents of the island. However, Willie Smith, a local fisher, summed up the general public opinion, "Who do I know in the other colonies who would send me a message?"

Smith, a third generation fisher, only leaves "the Rock" to fish. "We are a poor people here, so who wants to waste money on a cable, unless it makes good nets."

In other parts of North America, Gisborne's project was watched with interest. Plans are underway to install a cable across the Atlantic Ocean.

The laying of the electrical cable between Newfoundland and Cape Breton last year proves that trans-Atlantic telegraphs may soon be a reality.

The Colonial News

News from British North America

August 31, 1856

Prince Edward Island farmers meet

Charlottetown—Tenant farmers from across Prince Edward Island met this week in Charlottetown. At the meeting, farmers voiced concerns about the amount of money being sent to absentee landlords in Britain.

Many island landowners live in England. Most have never even visited the colony. Other issues include the farmers' lack of opportunity to buy the land they have worked for generations.

Currently, about 60 per cent of island farmers rent their land. Speaker after speaker insisted that the lieutenant-governor take the farmers' demands to London. The crowd demanded their right to buy their farms at fair prices.

Alex Coles, a tenant farmer, spoke for many, "We are the lifeblood of the island because we supply food for all. We even have enough produce to trade with other colonies and the United States. Yet we are poor, because every profit we make goes to the landowners in London. We are independent people, who do not wish to be controlled by anyone."

September 20, 1856

Douglas warns colonial office

Victoria—Governor James Douglas warns the British colonial office that his government will not ignore First Nations land rights. He affirmed today his wish to sign more treaties in the colony of Vancouver Island.

Vancouver Island's first Legislative Assembly meeting was held in Victoria this year.

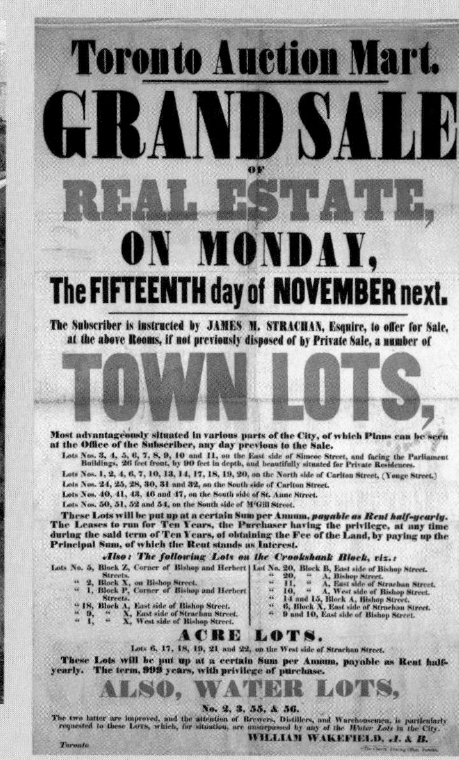

Between 1850 and 1856, Douglas signed fourteen treaties with First Nations. The treaties cover only about one-fortieth of the land on the island. Douglas believes the treaties work for both First Nations and settlers. "Treaties ensure that First Nations are protected by the government. Treaties also make more land available for settlers and miners," Douglas reports.

Other colonial leaders disagree. A British House of Commons committee recently issued a report that recognized only a few First Nations land rights. Already some settlers are asking the government to limit First Nations rights. They argue that First Nations are entitled to only their homes and farmland.

The Colonial News

News from British North America

November 12, 1856

Canada West businessmen sent packing

Toronto—Two businessmen from Canada West were ordered out of Red River, a Métis settlement near Fort Garry, last week. Community leaders there told Orin Henry and Felix Wilson to return to Toronto or face a hanging.

Henry and Wilson were in the area to investigate the possibility of a railway from Toronto to Red River. Politicians in Canada West would like western areas of the continent, such as Assiniboia and Rupert's Land, to become part of their colony. Otherwise, they fear the territory might fall into American hands. A railway would bring more settlers to the area. More settlements would strengthen their claim.

Henry and Wilson tried to sell their plan to the Métis community. They warned the Métis that Red River would be "much better off casting in its lot with Canada West than waiting for Americans to spill into the territory."

However, the community may have other ideas about its future. It has traditional ties with settlements just south of the border. In addition, it is far easier to travel south from Red River than it is to travel east.

Few residents could see the benefit of joining with Canada West.

The unwelcome visitors were given food and water and told to go home.

Original Selkirk grant, 1811–1818

Main Métis settlement

Lake Winnipeg
Assiniboine River
Fort Garry
Lake of the Woods
Pembina
Red R.
Rupert's Land
Fort William
Grand Portage
Lake Superior
Canada West
United States of America
Lake Michigan
Lake Huron
Toronto
Windsor
Lake Erie
0 200 km

Red River Settlement, about 1850

The Red River settlement was formed from a land grant given to Lord Selkirk in 1811. The settlement was divided in 1818, when Britain and the United States agreed to the 49th parallel as the border. Settlers in Red River still have family and community ties across the border.

After Reading

1. With your base group, make a list of four issues that appear in the *Colonial News*. For each issue, develop a focus question. An example might be

   Issue: Trade

   Focus question: What kind of trading relationship should British North America have with the United States?

2. With your base group, discuss which of these issues are still in the news today. Why do you think these issues are unresolved?

3. In your journal, write four or five sentences in which you predict what issues will be most difficult for British North Americans to deal with between 1857–1867. Why?

Pronunciation Guide

The accented syllable is underlined. All vowels are short except the following:
ay = long a (make)
y = long i (like)
oo = long u (mule)
ee = long e (equal)
oh = long o (rope)
ah = a as in father

A

Agona (a-goh-nuh)
Ahyouwaighs (ah-yoo-way)
Algonquian (al-gong-kwin)
André (on-dray)
Anishinabé (a-nish-i-nah-bay)
Antoine (on-twa-ne)
Armand (ar-mon)

B

Blondin (blon-dane)
Bouchard (boo-shar)
Boucher (boo-shay)
Bourdages (boor-dazh)
Bourgeoys (boor-zwa)
Briand (bree-an)
Brûlé (broo-lay)

C

Carignan-Salières (ka-ree-nyan-sa-lee-air)
Cartier (kar-tee-ay)
Catherine (kat-rin)
Château Clique (shah-toe klik)
Chouart (shoo-ar)
Claire (kl-air)
Cliche (kli-sh)
Colbert (kul-bear)
Compagnies Franche de la Marine (kum-pa-nyay fran-se de la ma-ree-ne)
Couture (koo-tur)

D

Dames de la Sainte-Famille (dahm de la sane-t-fa-mee-yuh)
de Buade, Compte de Frontenac (de boo-ad, kon-te de front-nak)
de Champlain (de sham-playn)
de Chomeday (de shum-day)
de Courcelle (de kur-sel)
de Laval (de la-val)
de Lévis (de lay-vee)
de l'Incarnation (de lin-car-na-see-on)
de Maisonneuve (de may-zoh-nuh-ve)
de Salaberry (de sal-a-bree)
de St.-Augustin (de sayn-o-gus-tin)
Des Groseilliers (day groh-zay-yay)
Domagaya (doo-mag-u-yuh)
Donnacona (do-na-koo-nuh)
Du Gua de Monts (dew goo-a de mon)
d'Youville (dee-yoo-vil)

E

Étienne (ay-tee-n)

F

filles du roi (fee-yuh dew rwa)
Françis (fran-sis)
François (fran-swa)

G

Gabriel (ga-bree-el)
George (zhor-zhe)
George-Étienne (zhor-zhe-ay-tee-n)
Gilles (zh-il)
Gosselin (gos-lin)
Guillaume (gee-yome)

H

Habitant (ha-bee-tawn)
Haudenosaunee (hoh-den-oh-shoh-nee)
Hébert (ay-bear)
Henri (awn-ree)
Hôtel-Dieu de Québec (hoh-tel dyew de kay-bek)

I

Inuit (in-oo-weet)
Isabel (ee-za-bel)

J

Jacques (zhawk)
Jean (zhawn)
Jean-Baptiste (zhawn-ba-tees-te)
Jean-Olivier (zhawn-oleev-yay)
Jeanne (zhawn-ne)
Jérôme (zhay-rohm)
Jesuit (zhe-zuit)
Jolliet (zho-lee-yet)
Joseph (zho-zef)

L

LaFontaine (la-fon-tay-ne)
Lalemant (la-le-mawn)
LaSalle (la-sahl)
les Anglais (lay zawn-gleh)
Louis (loo-wee)
Louis-Hippolyte (loo-wee-hi-po-leet)
Louis-Joseph (loo-wee-zho-zef)

M

Madeleine (ma-de-lane)
Mance (mon-se)
Marguerite (mar-gu-rit)
Marie (ma-ree)
Marie-Aimée (ma-ree-a-may)
Marquette (mar-ket)
Marquis de Montcalm (mar-kee de mon-calm)
Megezee (meg-a-zee)
Métis (may-tee)
Michel (mee-shel)
Mi'kmaq (mig-mah)
Miséricorde de Jésus (mi-zay-ri-kord de zhay-zoo)
Mississauga (mis-sis-sah-guh)

N

Neuville (noo-vil)

O

Odawa (o-dah-wuh)
Ogeebegun (o-jee-bi-gung)
Ojibwa (oh-jib-wah)
Ouendake (owen-du-gee)
Ouendat (owen-dah)

P

Papineau (pa-pee-noe)
Parent (pa-rawn)
Parti bleu (par-tee bluh)
Passamaquoddy (pa-zim-a-kwah-dee)
Patriote (pa-tree-ut)
Paul (pol)
Pierre (pee-yair)
Pontiac (pon-tee-yak)

R

Radisson (ra-dee-son)
Récollet (ray-koh-lay)
Richelieu (ree-sha-lee-uh)
Robert (roh-bear)
Rollet (roh-lay)

S

Samuel (sa-myoo-el)
Sarrazin (sa-ra-zin)
Saugeen (sahk-een)
Savignon (sa-vee-nyon)
Shawnee (shaw-nee)
Sieur Lannard (see-yur la-nar)
St. Jean Baptiste (sehn-t zhawn ba-tees-te)

T

Taignoagny (tag-nog-nee)
Talon (ta-lun)
Tecumseh (ta-kum-suh)
Tenskwatawa (tens-kwa-ta-wa)
Thayendanegea (tha-end-a-nee-gee)
Tremblay (trom-blay)

U

une Anglaise (oon awn-gleh-ze)
Ursuline (ur-siew-lin)

V

Vaudreuil (voh-dray)

W

Wawanosh (wow-won-oos)
Wichkewan (wich-kay-wan)

Glossary

A

aboiteau: a hinged valve in a dam that allows water to drain from farmland

abolitionists: people opposed to the practice of slavery

Aboriginal peoples: the original inhabitants of a land and their descendants. The Canadian Constitution Act, 1982 recognizes three groups of Aboriginal peoples: First Nations, Métis, and Inuit.

absentee landlords: landowners who do not live on their land, but collect rent or revenue from the land

absolute monarchs: kings and queens who may rule their subjects without limit

Acadians: the first French inhabitants of Nova Scotia and New Brunswick and the descendants of these people

alien: a foreigner

artifact: an object made by people

assimilate: when a person or group adopts a new culture, usually one that surrounds them

B

bias: a stake or goal in an issue; a point of view that makes no attempt to include other perspectives

blockade: to block access to a country so that it cannot trade with other groups

boycott: a rejection of a product or service by a wide group of people in order to achieve a change

C

Canadiens: French people living in New France around 1763, at the fall of New France; the ancestors of these people

capitulation: surrender

Château Clique: an elite class of families that dominated politics and business in Lower Canada in the early nineteenth century

cholera: a contagious disease caused by an infection in the intestine

chronological: in the order in which things occurred

clergy reserves: land put aside to support the Anglican Church

colony: a country that is controlled by another which is sometimes called the mother country. The colony's land, population, and resources are used to benefit the mother country.

commemorate: to celebrate or remember a past event

compromise: an agreement that meets some of the needs of all sides to a conflict or issue

consensus: a decision that best addresses all points of view, reached through discussion and common agreement

converting: convincing people to adopt a new set of religious beliefs

coureurs de bois: young French men who lived and travelled with First Nations in order to trade for furs. These furs were transported to the French colonies along the St. Lawrence River.

Crown reserves: land put aside for the monarchy; used to support the government in the colony

D

democracy: a government in which power rests with the people who can vote in elections; a system in which the population elect all or some of the government

discrimination: when a person is denied full participation in society because of that person's membership in a particular group

dowry: property a woman brings to a marriage, usually provided by her family

E

engagés: people hired to work for a wage

excommunicated: to be officially excluded from church ceremonies and activities

F

factories: trading posts run by the Hudson's Bay Company

Family Compact: an elite class of families that dominated politics and business in Upper Canada in the early nineteenth century

famines: shortages of food so severe and widespread that many people starve

First Nations: groups of people that were the original inhabitants of North America and the descendants of these people

freehold: full ownership of land

free trade: an economic system in which a country or group of countries drop taxes on imported goods

G

garrison: fort

H

habitants: settlers farming small plots of land in New France

hierarchical: a system in which groups or individuals with different status are ranked above or below one another

hinterland: a relatively undeveloped region served by a nearby urban centre

I

imperial preference: an economic system in which Britain gave special economic benefits to its colonies

impressment: when British ships stopped American ships and forced American sailors to serve in the British navy

indentured servants: people under contract to work under specific circumstances, usually a specific period of time

integration: to mix together

Inuit: the original inhabitants of the Arctic and the descendants of these people

J

Jesuit: a group of priests who helped establish the Roman Catholic Church in New France

L

land claims: requests by First Nations for compensation for land improperly used or taken

land grants: sections of land given to individuals or groups by a governing body

land speculators: people who purchase land in the hope of selling it in the future for large profits

Late Loyalists: people who came to Upper Canada up to ten years after the American Revolution and received a grant of land in return for an oath of loyalty to Britain

lay teachers: individuals who teach without formal training in that profession

libel: publishing false statements that damage an individual's or group's reputation

Loyalists: people living in the United States during the American Revolution who wanted to remain loyal to Britain and who left the United States after the end of the revolution

M

mercantilism: an economic theory where countries become wealthy by exporting more goods and services than they import; prompted European countries to establish colonies around the world to help their countries grow wealthy

merchant navy: a naval force used for trade, not war

Métis: a nation of people with European and First Nations ancestry and cultural backgrounds, including a history in the western fur trade

metropolitan centres: port cities that dominate the surrounding region

middlemen: people who trade with both the producers and consumers of a product

militia: a civilian military force (as opposed to a professional force of soldiers)

missionary: a person who travels to another country to spread his or her religion

monopoly: an exclusive right to trade in a region

moral: related to right and wrong

N

nationalists: people with a strong feeling of attachment to a particular country or group of people

negotiation: a discussion in which each side of an issue agrees to give up certain goals in return for others

neutrality: not taking sides in a disagreement or conflict

non-partisan: unbiased or operating outside of the rules of party discipline. *See* party discipline.

O

oath of allegiance: a promise of loyalty

optimism: a positive feeling about the future

P

pardoned: to be officially released from responsibility for breaking a law

party discipline: a political system in which elected officials belong to and follow the policies of political parties

Patriotes: people in Lower Canada joining together to rebel against the British-controlled government

Patriots: people who supported the rebellion against Britain during the American Revolution

pemmican: dried, pounded meat that stores and travels well

petitions: written requests for change that are signed by many people

portage: a place when goods and boats have to be carried between two water routes; also the act of carrying the goods and boats

prejudice: a rigid (usually unfavourable) opinion about a group of people that is applied to all members of that group

primary sources: eyewitness accounts of an event

profit: a financial gain; when the value of goods received in an exchange are more than the value of goods paid

progress: a state in which technology ensures that human society constantly improves

Q

quarantine: a period of isolation for people or animals who may have been in contact with a contagious disease

R

radical: a person who wants to change the government by any means possible

rebellion: violent conflict against the government's authority

reformers: people who want to change the government by legal methods

representation by population: a political system in which territory is divided into electoral districts of roughly the same number of people (as opposed to dividing territory into electoral districts based on the size of territory). The system ensures that areas with larger populations have more representatives.

republic: a government in which the highest power is held by elected officials, not monarchs who inherit power

reserves: land set aside by the government for the exclusive use of First Nations

resolution: a formal statement of a government's intention

responsible government: a government that is accountable to people who can vote in elections

revolutionary committees: groups of people authorized to question and punish anyone who did not support the American Revolution

rhetoric: the art of using words effectively to persuade others to hold a particular point of view or take a particular action

Royal Charter: a formal right to the land and trade of a specific region

Royal Government: a system of government in which a monarch has control

Rupert's Land: the territory draining into Hudson Bay that was named and given to the Hudson's Bay Company by the British monarchy in 1670

S

scurvy: a disease caused by the lack of vitamin C

secondary sources: accounts of an event that includes analysis and interpretation, usually made after the event or by people with no direct experience of the event

segregation: to keep separate

seigneurs: people granted land in New France

siege: an army operation to force a surrender by preventing people and supplies from entering or leaving a fort

slaves: people who are owned by other people

smallpox: a contagious virus

spirituality: a person's sense of his or her place in the universe

T

tenure: right to occupy land

Thirteen Colonies: British colonies along the east coast of North America, south of Nova Scotia. The Thirteen Colonies rebelled from rule by Britain and became the United States of America in 1783.

tithe: a tax used to support the Church

title: officially recognized ownership of a piece of land

tolls: small usage fees for roads; used to help build and repair the roads

Tories: people with conservative political views, who do not want to change the government

treason: a crime against the government

treaty: an agreement between independent nations

trend: a general direction or tendency

U

Underground Railroad: a network of safe houses that helped slaves escape

United Empire Loyalists: *See* Loyalists

V

voyageurs: Europeans licenced by New France to travel and trade with First Nations

W

War Hawks: a group of American politicians from the southern and western states that supported war against Britain in 1812

worldview: the values, beliefs, attitudes, and knowledge that people use to understand and respond to the world around them

Index